This Side
of Heaven

This Side of Heaven

Race, Ethnicity, and Christian Faith

Edited by

ROBERT J. PRIEST
AND ALVARO L. NIEVES

OXFORD
UNIVERSITY PRESS

2007

OXFORD
UNIVERSITY PRESS

Oxford University Press, Inc., publishes works that further
Oxford University's objective of excellence
in research, scholarship, and education.

Oxford   New York
Auckland   Cape Town   Dar es Salaam   Hong Kong   Karachi
Kuala Lumpur   Madrid   Melbourne   Mexico City   Nairobi
New Delhi   Shanghai   Taipei   Toronto

With offices in
Argentina   Austria   Brazil   Chile   Czech Republic   France   Greece
Guatemala   Hungary   Italy   Japan   Poland   Portugal   Singapore
South Korea   Switzerland   Thailand   Turkey   Ukraine   Vietnam

Published by Oxford University Press, Inc.
198 Madison Avenue, New York, New York 10016

www.oup.com

Oxford is a registered trademark of Oxford University Press

Library of Congress Cataloging-in-Publication Data
This side of heaven: race, ethnicity, and Christian faith/edited by Robert J. Priest
and Alvaro L. Nieves.
   p. cm.
Includes bibliographical references and index.
ISBN-13 978-0-19-531056-6; 978-0-19-531057-3 (pbk.)

1. Race relations—Religious aspects—Christianity.   2. Ethnic relations—Religious
aspects—Christianity.   3. Ethnicity—Religious aspects—Christianity.   I. Priest, Robert J.
II. Nieves, Alvaro L.
BT734.2.T45   2006
270.089—dc22   2006004642

Printed in the United States of America
on acid-free paper

Acknowledgments

We wish to express deep appreciation to the many who have helped make this book possible. The authors themselves underwent a long and challenging process of writing and rewriting. Bruce Fields and Henry Allen met with the authors through the process and were invaluable conversation partners, and their partnership in this project is deeply appreciated. Michael Emerson, Gastón Espinosa, Craig Keener, William Larkin, Cheryl Sanders, Timothy Tseng, and Raymond Williams read our work with care, and gave extensive and outstanding feedback and critique. The high standards to which they directed us were a challenge and inspiration. Any remaining shortcomings of this book are not because of failures on their part. Thanks to the many students in race and ethnicity classes at Trinity Evangelical Divinity School, Trinity College, Bethel University, Spring Arbor University, and Taylor University who provided feedback on these chapters. We owe a debt to Douglas Wilson, Carl Brown, and Paul Priest who provided significant help in collating and compiling the feedback from these students. Ethan Christofferson and Paul Priest provided extensive help on editorial matters. Grant Osborne, Steve Roy, and many others—not all of whom can be named—provided feedback on one or more chapters. To each we express our grateful appreciation.

Finally, we wish to thank Dr. Greg Waybright, president of Trinity Evangelical Divinity School; Rev. William Hammell, president of the Evangelical Free Church of America; Dr. Enrique Fernandez, vice president for Interethnic Ministry of the Evangelical Free Church of America; Dr. Lucinda Huffaker of the Wabash Center for Teaching and Learning in Theology and Religion; and Dr. Stanton Jones, provost at Wheaton College for providing strategic support at various stages of our project. Funds that contributed to the activities resulting in this book were received from the Wabash Center for Teaching and Learning in Theology and Religion, the Evangelical Free Church of America, Trinity Evangelical Divinity School, Wheaton College, and the Frederick and Margaret L. Weyerhaueser Foundation.

Contents

Contributors

VINCENT BACOTE is associate professor of theology at Wheaton College in Wheaton, Illinois, and received his Ph.D. from Drew University (2002). He is the author of *The Spirit in Public Theology: Appropriating the Legacy of Abraham Kuyper* (2005) and is a coeditor of *Evangelicals and Scripture* (2004). He has contributed to *Building Unity in the Church of the New Millennium* (2002), *The Gospel in Black and White* (1996), *What Does It Mean to Be Saved?* (2002) and *Best Christian Writing 2000* (2001). He is a columnist for the online magazine *Comment* (wrf.ca/comment) and has published articles in such magazines as *Christianity Today* and *re:generation quarterly*.

PETER CHA is associate professor of pastoral theology at Trinity Evangelical Divinity School, Deerfield, Illinois. He holds a Ph.D. in religion in society and personality from Northwestern University. He is a coauthor of *Following Jesus without Dishonoring Your Parents: Asian American Discipleship* and a coeditor of *Growing Healthy Asian American Churches* (2006).

TRACI GRIFFIN received her Ph.D. in organizational communication in 2002 from Howard University, Washington, D.C. As a former full-time missionary, she has done missionary work in Africa and East Asia. She currently is working as a stay-at-home mom with two young children.

PAUL GORDON HIEBERT is distinguished professor of missions, anthropology, and South Asian studies at Trinity Evangelical Divinity School. He is the author of seven books and many articles in the fields of missions and anthropology. He did ethnographic research on an Indian village, and was a Fulbright Professor at Osmania University in India.

BRIAN M. HOWELL is associate professor of anthropology at Wheaton College, in Wheaton, Illinois. He received his Ph.D. in anthropology from Washington University in St. Louis with a dissertation entitled *At Home in the World: Philippine Baptists and the Creation of Context.* In addition to his work on race and religion, he has published on global Christianity (Philippine Protestantism) and the "Short-Term Missions" phenomenon in various journals.

MICHAEL JESSUP is a professor of sociology at Taylor University in Upland, Indiana. He holds a Ph.D. in sociology from Southern Illinois University. He has published on a variety of topics including pedagogy, marriage and family, postmodernity, social movements, and hate groups. He is currently working on a manuscript on evangelical responses to race and ethnic relations.

MICHAEL JINDRA is an anthropologist and associate professor of sociology and global studies at Spring Arbor University in Michigan. He has published on various topics, including sociology of religion, social theory, cultural change, and African studies, most recently "Christianity and the Proliferation of Ancestors" in the journal *Africa* (2005).

S. STEVE KANG is associate professor of educational ministries at Gordon-Conwell Theological Seminary, South Hamilton, Massachusetts. He holds a Ph.D. in religion in society and personality from Northwestern University. He is the author of *Unveiling the Socioculturally Constructed Multivoiced Self* (2003), coauthor of *A Many-Colored Kingdom* (2004), and coeditor of *Growing Healthy Asian American Churches* (2005). His articles have appeared in *Ex Auditu*, *Christian Education Journal*, and *Religious Education Journal*.

MARLA FREDERICK MCGLATHERY is an anthropologist and assistant professor of African and African American studies and of the study of religion at Harvard University. She is the author of *Between Sundays: Black Women's Everyday Struggles of Faith* (2003), and currently is engaged in research on the influence of religious media on constructions of race and gender in the United States.

J. DEREK MCNEIL is assistant professor of psychology at Wheaton College in Illinois. He received his Ph.D. in counseling psychology from Northwestern University in Evanston, Illinois. He is currently conducting research on training methods for psychology students in the development of cultural competency. He teaches diversity, group therapy, and family therapy at Wheaton College.

ELOISE HIEBERT MENESES is professor of anthropology at Eastern University in St. Davids, Pennsylvania. She teaches in the areas of race and ethnicity, economic systems, and faith and science. Currently, she is completing an ethnography of market women in India that integrates anthropological observation with Christian thinking.

ALVARO L. NIEVES is professor of sociology at Wheaton College, in Wheaton, Illinois. He is the general editor of the *Latino Heritage Bible*. He is presently conducting research on Latino ethnic identity among students in the United States. He teaches research methods, social statistics, and demography at

Wheaton College and serves as an occasional consultant at Argonne National Laboratory.

DAVID W. PAO is associate professor of New Testament at Trinity Evangelical Divinity School. He holds a Ph.D. in the study of religion from Harvard University. He is the author of *Acts and the Isaianic New Exodus* (2000; 2002) and *Thanksgiving: An Investigation of a Pauline Theme* (2002), and coeditor of *Early Christian Voices—In Texts, Traditions, and Symbols* (2003).

JENELL WILLIAMS PARIS is associate professor of anthropology at Bethel University, St. Paul, Minnesota. She holds a Ph.D. in cultural anthropology from American University. She is the author of *Urban Disciples* (2000) and *Birth Control for Christians* (2003).

CARLOS F. POZZI, director of clinical training at Wheaton College, in Wheaton, Illinois, holds an MA in theological studies from Northern Baptist Theological Seminary, as well as a Ph.D. in clinical psychology from the Illinois School of Professional Psychology. Dr. Pozzi has clinical and administrative experience as a clinical therapist for children and adolescents in a day hospital plan, an executive director of Latino Youth Incorporated, a clinical associate for several psychological services, and a supervisor of doctoral-level students in field placement. His research interests have been in the area of utilization rates of health services and prevalence of social and psychological problems among Latinos in the United States. Additionally, Pozzi has published in the area of justice and psychology.

KERSTEN BAYT PRIEST is assistant professor of sociology at Wheaton College. She received an MA (1998) in anthropology from the University of South Carolina, where she researched interracial congregational worship. For two years she conducted research for the Religion, Immigration, and Civil Society Project in Chicago as part of a national study funded by Pew Charitable Trusts. Currently she is working to complete a Ph.D. in sociology at Loyola University.

ROBERT J. PRIEST is professor of mission and intercultural studies and director of the Ph.D. program in intercultural studies at Trinity Evangelical Divinity School. He holds the Ph.D. in anthropology from the University of California, Berkeley. With interests in race and ethnicity, religious conversion, and culture and moral discourse, his work appears in various edited volumes and journals, such as "Missionary Positions: Christian, Modernist, Postmodernist" in *Current Anthropology* 42:29–68. He is currently carrying out research on short-term missionaries.

DOUGLAS A. SWEENEY is associate professor of church history at Trinity Evangelical Divinity School. He holds the Ph.D. in religion from Vanderbilt University. His books include *Nathaniel Taylor, New Haven Theology, and the Legacy of Jonathan Edwards* (Oxford, 2003), *Jonathan Edwards at Home and Abroad: Historical Memories, Cultural Movements, Global Horizons* (2003), and an edition of *Jonathan Edwards's "The Miscellanies," 1153–1360, The Works of Jonathan Edwards*, vol. 23 (2004).

JOSEPH L. THOMAS is assistant professor of church history at Biblical Seminary, Hatfield, Pennsylvania, and is the director of the Christian History Institute. He has taught and written on African American religion and on the Pentecostal movement.

TITE TIÉNOU is senior vice president of education and academic dean at Trinity Evangelical Divinity School, Deerfield, Illinois, where he is also a professor of theology of mission. He holds the Ph.D. (intercultural studies) from Fuller Theological Seminary. He is the author of *Theological Task of the Church in Africa* (also published in French). With interests in Christian systematic theology, mission theology, Christianity in Africa and ethnicity, his work appears in numerous journals, edited books, and dictionaries.

This Side
of Heaven

Introduction

Robert J. Priest and Alvaro L. Nieves

Our Father who art in heaven, hallowed be thy name.
Thy kingdom come, thy will be done on earth as it is in heaven.

The above prayer implicitly recognizes the pervasiveness of sin, injustice, and suffering. But rather than express a longing for withdrawal or escape, this prayer expresses a desire that communities of earth would come to reflect ideals of heaven. "Thy will be done on earth" is not only a prayer, it is a commitment we are expected to embrace and participate in. Christians are to seek peace (Heb 12:14), to hunger and thirst for righteousness/justice (Matt 5:6), to love and actively embrace "others" (Rom 15:7).

Heaven gives us images of perfection, of ideals already achieved: of joy, peace, unity, harmony, and love. People of every ethnic group gather in unity around the throne of God (Rev 7:9–10). In heaven we find no suffering, no sin, no conflict and no struggle. Heaven represents "rest." On occasion, Christians have claimed that their social communities already exemplify such ideals, and that harmonious conformity is all that is now required. The above prayer, however, positions us as living in a world of the "not yet": a world where sin is still present (both in ourselves and others), a world characterized by suffering, injustice, discord, violence, and death. We may claim "citizenship in heaven" (Phil 3:20), but we live "on this side of heaven." On this side of heaven we live in social arenas that call us not to accommodate and conform, but to critique and resist evil (in self and others), to confront powers, and to seek reconciliation. We are called to suffering, to conflict, and to struggle. And yet such suffering and struggle is informed by the hope that we have in Jesus Christ, and in the future he ensures. This book is intended to reflect the authors' own commitment to the above prayer, a commitment inspired by ideals of heaven, but thoroughly grounded in our own earthly social and historical settings.

The Origins of This Book

This book emerged out of a series of activities at two schools in the Chicago area. During the 2000–2001 school year, seven ethnically diverse faculty members teaching at Trinity Evangelical Divinity School (TEDS), with funding from the Wabash Center for Teaching and Learning in Theology and Religion, gathered every two weeks for lunch to discuss seminary education and pastoral training in a racialized and ethnically diverse society and world. In the preceding twenty years, the proportion of European American students at this historically Scandinavian seminary had dropped from 98 percent to 59 percent—a massive shift in the ethnic makeup of the student body. And yet, as in most American seminaries, changes at the level of faculty and curriculum came more slowly. In 2000 nearly half of all accredited seminaries in America lacked even one ethnic minority on the faculty, and half of the rest had but one. This represents a serious weakness in the educational institutions committed to forming and shaping the next generation of religious leadership in America. TEDS had four ethnic minority faculty at this time, each of whom participated in our lunch gatherings, and one of whom, Tite Tiénou, was selected as the new academic dean at TEDS during this year.

During our lunch discussions we asked questions like: In what ways do students from divergent ethnic backgrounds encounter in seminary taken-for-granted practices, assumptions, evaluational criteria, and intellectual questions that privilege cultural patterns, interests, aesthetics, and experiences of white Christian communities? Are minority students socialized away from the competencies and understandings needed for ministry success in their own communities? Are majority students socialized to appreciate and learn from the experiences, questions, concerns, insights, worship aesthetics, and ministry skills of believers from other ethnic or racial groups? To what extent and in what ways do we, in our classes, relate biblical understandings of creation, human identity, ecclesiology, justice, sin, reconciliation, forgiveness, mission, and the kingdom of God to the world of ethnic and racial ideologies, prejudices, struggles with stigma, resentments, aggressions, boundaries and hierarchies of wealth, class, and power? How do we as faculty motivate ourselves, and our students, to redirect long-established reading, teaching, research and writing patterns oriented largely toward a white/Euro-American world in constructive new directions? With what vision and incentives? Our conversations were lengthy.

During this year, two professors from Wheaton College joined us: Alvaro Nieves, a Latino sociologist, and Hank Allen, an African American sociologist. Through them we discovered the Coalition of Christian Colleges and Universities

(CCCU), and found that they also were struggling with how to transform historically white Christian schools into communities responsive to the ethnic and racial diversity that is America and the world. They too were interested in engaging racial and ethnic diversity from within an explicit framework of Christian faith.

Out of these lunch gatherings, we concluded that we needed to foster an interdisciplinary and interethnic intellectual community with sustained patterns of interaction as the base from which to work for understanding and constructive change. Over the next year an expanded group of faculty from Wheaton and Trinity carried out a series of activities focused on race and ethnicity. We read and discussed books together, attended retreats together, taught classes together, read and discussed one another's writings, and convened a conference focused on teaching about race and ethnicity in the context of Christian higher education—a conference attended by many contributors of this book.

We discovered that in the last decade Christian colleges and seminaries had added numerous courses focused on race and ethnicity, but that the faculty of these courses almost universally complained of difficulty in finding appropriate books for their students to read. Books on race and ethnicity written for religious audiences are all too often written at a popular level with moral passion, but fail to exemplify sophisticated historical, anthropological, and sociological understandings of race, culture, ethnic identity, and racial hierarchy. Alternatively, while there are hundreds of books on race and ethnicity written in a more secular voice, many of these exemplify an antireligious bias that makes it difficult for devoutly religious students to trust these authors when they challenge racial and ethnic assumptions that do need to be challenged. Even when an antireligious bias is not present, these books generally fail to explore the particular linkages with which seminarians and other Christians need help. That is, scholars who taught Christian students about race and ethnicity suggested the need for a book that represented cutting-edge biblical, theological, historical, anthropological, psychological, and sociological scholarship and that would constructively explore the linkages that they and their students needed help in exploring: What has been the history of Christian churches and leaders in relation to slavery, segregation, and apartheid? What biblical texts and doctrines have historically been employed on behalf of racial projects? What biblical texts and doctrines are relevant to the racial and ethnic crises of our day? How have, and how might, religious leaders constructively engage such crises? How do congregations shape the values, civic commitments, understandings, and sensitivities of their membership in ways that positively or negatively affect congregants' ways of engaging an ethnically and racially diverse society? In what ways can local congregations be sites for racial reconciliation and justice initiatives? Are there positive models for how churches and other religious institutions have helped to bring healing to racial and ethnic tensions and divides? How might Christians in the professions work to bring justice to business, education, government, and other areas of society? When good intentions fail to accomplish desired ends, how do we analyze what went wrong?

As a result of this feedback, we concluded that an interethnic and interracial team of scholars from diverse disciplines ought to collaborate in such a writing project. Scholars from Bethel University, Eastern University, Gordon-Conwell Theological Seminary, Harvard University, Loyola University, Spring Arbor University, and Taylor University joined scholars from Trinity Evangelical Divinity School and Wheaton College for this writing project. We met annually for three two-day retreats to discuss and plan this joint publication. We were concerned that a book written by authors from diverse disciplines and ethnic backgrounds would require sustained effort to achieve sufficient integration and coherence, and thus committed to a process of writing and rewriting. We solicited feedback from nationally recognized scholars with relevant expertise, received extensive feedback from students in several seminary and college classes, and reworked our chapters in the light of that feedback.

Distinctives of This Book

This book, then, has several distinctives. First, it is interdisciplinary. Anthropologists, biblical scholars, church historians, pastoral, missional, and systematic theologians, psychologists, and sociologists have all contributed. Second, the authors are ethnically diverse. Four contributors are African American (Bacote, Griffin, Frederick McGlathery, McNeil), two are Latino (Nieves, Pozzi), three are Asian American (Cha, Kang, Pao), one is originally from Burkina Faso, though now a U.S. citizen (Tiénou), and others are of European ancestry (Hiebert, Howell, Jessup, Jindra, Meneses, Paris, R. Priest, K. Priest, Sweeney, and Thomas). Third, this book emerged out of a sustained pattern of relationship and interaction on the part of the authors. We know one another and are friends.

Fourth, while this book covers a wide range of topics related to race and ethnicity, it retains a central focus on religious, and more specifically, Christian, institutions and discourses. While earlier scholars believed that government and public education were the primary institutions that could engage social problems related to ethnicity and race, many scholars are increasingly recognizing both the limits of these institutions and that other institutions, especially religious ones, may play a pivotal role either in contributing to a "racialized" society and world, or in promoting reconciliation. For example, the recent influential book *Divided by Faith* (Emerson and Smith 2000) argues that evangelical Christians and their religious institutions have contributed to the "racialization" of our society, but that paradoxically such Christians are also among the most energetic and willing to engage problems associated with race. As authors we are deeply conscious of moral failures vis-à-vis race on the part of Christian communities, but are also deeply convinced that resources, understandings, and motivations inspired by Christian faith can provide significant correctives to ethnic and racial prejudices, animosities, boundaries, and hierarchies of wealth and power.

Fifth, the authors of this book explicitly write out of personal Christian faith. Until recently, normative expectations for scholarly writing insisted that scholarship be written in a secular voice. But recent trends in many disciplines stress "positioned" knowledge, with faith-informed scholarship increasingly seen as having a valued place in public academia (Marsden 1997; Roberts and Turner 2000; Priest 2001; Sterk 2002; Dovre 2002; Frederick 2003; Howell 2005). Especially when the subject involves religion and normative ideals concerning race and ethnicity, there is simply no fully objective or neutral position from which to write. But while many of these chapters explicitly appeal to normative texts within the Christian tradition, each author writes for a public audience in accord with scholarly standards of their discipline.

Finally, while many of our authors have interests abroad, and while Christianity is a global movement (Jenkins 2002) strategically positioned to engage worldwide ethnic and racial problems, this book retains a focus on the authors' own country, the United States of America. With a population that is 1.5 percent Native American, nearly 5 percent Asian American, 13 percent African American, and 14 percent Latino, the United States is steadily growing in the proportion of its population not originally from Europe. The forty million Latinos in the United States (Pew Hispanic Center 2004), for example, outnumber the total populations of Panama, Costa Rica, Nicaragua, Honduras, Uruguay, Paraguay, and Bolivia combined. There are more Latinos in the United States than Canadians in Canada.

The United States is one of the world's most ethnically diverse nations. It has experienced great evils associated with race and ethnicity, but also significant reforms. It is also one of the most religious nations, with Christianity continuing numerically to be the religion of choice, even among recent non-European immigrants (Warner, forthcoming). African Americans overwhelmingly self-identify as Christian (over 90 percent), a majority of these Protestant. Asian Americans self-identify religiously (Tseng et al. 2005) as Protestant (26 percent), Catholic (20 percent), Buddhist (15 percent), Hindu (6 percent), and Muslim (2 percent). Latinos mostly identify religiously (Espinosa et al. 2003) as Catholic (70 percent) or Protestant (23 percent). Native Americans have a religious profile fairly "similar to that of white non-Hispanic Americans" (Kosmin, Mayer, Keysar 2001): with 20 percent Baptist, 17 percent Catholic, and so forth. Only 3 percent identify as adherents of "Indian" or tribal religion.

As a result of 1965 changes in immigration laws ending discrimination against non-Europeans, Christian communities in America now consist of immigrants from Africa, India, Korea, China, and Latin America, as well as Europe. Indeed, several authors of this book are present in America precisely because of 1965 changes in immigration laws. Andrew Walls, Scottish historian of global Christianity, has argued (2002, 69) that "the great issues of twenty-first-century Christianity" will concern relations across such ethnic lines, and that "the principal Christian significance of the United States" now rests in its Christian ethnic diversity and strategic global links. He suggests that "more than in any other nation in the world, the body of Christ could be realized—or fractured—in the United States." With Walls, we are convinced that the ways in which American

Christians engage ethnic and racial diversity is potentially crucial for the larger world. If this book can, in some small way, help American Christians better understand and engage these realities, the results will be felt more broadly.

Organization of the Book

Part 1: Thinking Critically about Culture, Race, and Color

Jenell Williams Paris situates the task of this book within the biblical mandate (Rom 12:1–2) to resist being "conformed" to this "world" and its ideas, but to be "transformed by the renewing of your mind." The biblical assumption here is that even when Christians claim citizenship in heaven (Phil 3:20), they live in earthly societies that quite naturally shape what they assume and take for granted. Thus the Christian is called to a biblically mandated task of deconstructing many taken-for-granted ideas, and reconstructing our thinking, our lives, and our communities on more solid foundations.

Paris's chapter examines the construct of "race" or "races," whereby individuals are assigned to social categories on the basis of physical attributes, in the belief that natural and separate divisions, akin to subspecies, exist within humankind. Historically, the idea of "race" assumed inherent differences in socially relevant abilities and characteristics between biologically based human types, hence that such biologically based differences are a legitimate basis of invidious distinctions between groups defined as races. Alternatively, such biologically based differences are assumed to explain the differential socioeconomic success of people of different "races."

Paris suggests that "race" is one of the most damaging ideas of the modern world, a concept absent from the biblical world, though taken for granted by members of modern societies. She provides an overview of the history of racial ideologies and of social formations based on such ideologies, and suggests that race, as biological construct, is simply invalid and must be deconstructed. The social formations grounded in racial ideologies are human constructions, not biological givens. Eloise Hiebert Meneses' chapter provides a more detailed examination and critique of the biological construct of race, summarizing recent understandings of human genetic relatedness.

But while both Paris and Meneses critique the biological construct of race, this construct has historically been treated as real and instantiated in discourses, laws, census categories, and in ideologies of identity and difference. Race as social construct or social formation is all too real. Thus Paris and Meneses introduce two ideas, maintained throughout this volume, that race as a biological construct is invalid, but that the social formations grounded in this ideology are nonetheless real and must be understood and addressed. Readers must thus understand that when authors of this book deny the validity of the idea of race, it is the biological construct that they deny. When they sometimes proceed to treat race as real, and to use a vocabulary of race ("white," "black," "interracial," "multiracial," etc.), it is race as social construction that is in view.

While "race" roots identity in supposed biologically determined categories, Meneses suggests that criteria for group identity vary empirically, and that anything from phenotype to language, culture, or religion may provide the boundary markers that a group selects to distinguish itself or to distinguish the ethnic other. An analytical category that recognizes the variable and arbitrary nature of these boundary markers is that of "ethnicity," a concept that Meneses suggests is a more adequate analytical category than that of race.

Social groups that regard themselves, and are regarded by others, as constituting a social group based on shared heritage (i.e., having real or putative common ancestry and having memories of a shared past) and on shared markers of identity (which may include any combination of cultural, linguistic, religious, or racial markers) are ethnic groups. Such social group categories are historically and situationally constructed. As Carlos Pozzi's chapter will demonstrate, it is only after they arrive in the United States that many Latin Americans come to see themselves in terms of U.S. ethnic categories like "Latino" or "Hispanic." Chinese, Jew, Serb, Croat, Hutu, Tutsi, Latino, African American, European American, or Asian American are all ethnic categories. The boundaries between such groups are variously constructed through linguistic, religious, cultural, or racial markers. In some cases "race" is not part of an ethnic boundary (think of Serb versus Croat). An ethnic category may not even coincide with a "race" category. The U.S. Census, for example, assumes that Latinos/Hispanics can be of different "races"—with some Latinos "white" and others "black," for example. That is, Latinos may have exclusively European ancestry, or Native American ancestry, or African ancestry, or may have any combination of the above. But if their more immediate ancestors come from Latin America, and their heritage (culturally and linguistically) has links to this region of the world, they become part of a single new ethnic category: Latino. A single individual may be "Latino" within a system of "ethnic categorization," while also being "white" or "black" within a system of "racial categorization." This is why we get such ethnoracial phrases as "non-Hispanic white." The ethnic category "African American," on the other hand, identifies a social group with memories of a shared history (related to the black American experience of slavery, segregation, discrimination, etc.), but a history in which the very idea of race helped to construct the boundaries. Here race and ethnicity overlap, although not completely. Many individuals categorized as "black" within a system of racial categories (recent arrivals from Brazil or Nigeria, for example), would not be "African American" because they lack the shared heritage that this ethnic category implies. In short, "race" and "ethnicity" are divergent, but frequently overlapping, constructs.

In any case, Meneses concludes that the New Testament calls into question even the primacy of ethnic identities and loyalties, and provides a new basis of identity and loyalty that crosscuts partisan ethnic or racial loyalties.

Carlos Pozzi, in his chapter "Race, Ethnicity, and Color among Latinos in the United States," both introduces the reader to America's largest ethnic minority, and illustrates the variable nature of ethnic and racial ideologies and categories. Rather than being immutable because biologically "there," racial categories are elaborated in diverse ways across Latin America and the United States.

The differences between ethnic groups should be understood not as determined by genetic racial codes but in terms of "culture," Michael Jindra suggests in his chapter "Culture Matters." Culture consists of learned patterns of behavior, value, and belief widely shared among members of a given society or social group. People acquire culture through their participation in community, and cultural patterns will vary from one community to another. At one level, all Americans comprise a community with a shared, and continually evolving, culture. And yet, within broad commonalities, there are also cultural differences between (and within) different ethnic communities. Immigrant communities come to America with diverse cultural traditions, and their experience in America has varied enormously depending on how they were racially categorized in the American setting. Such differing experiences, grounded in history and social, economic, and political structures, have markedly affected patterns of social identity, relationship, and cultural change. Jindra explores the relationship of culture to history, social structure, race, socioeconomic success, and educational outcomes.

Culture involves learned ideas and values. When we encounter differences of ideas and values, Jindra suggests, we need to steer between two errors—that of ethnocentric judgment (judgment based on criteria that are simply internal to my own culture) and that of relativism (not exercising any judgment at all). Jindra suggests that all cultures will have elements that need to be corrected by Scripture, but also that within the culture of every community are large swaths of culture that are *adiaphora*—neither commanded nor forbidden by Scripture. The apostle Paul provides a model for Christians. In interactions with cultural others he did not privilege his own culture at their expense, but instead accommodated and affirmed their culture—becoming "all things to all people" (1 Cor 9:22).

If differences between ethnic communities are better understood in terms of culture than in terms of biological race, then it is important in a multicultural society that members of that society understand culture and develop multicultural competence. Americans who work in helping professions (ministry, teaching, counseling, etc.) will often face challenges posed by cultural differences. Psychology has recently developed a whole new wave of thinking and research related to helping others in the context of cultural differences. In the final chapter of this section, psychologists J. Derek McNeil and Carlos Pozzi discuss the need for multicultural competency and outline ways in which multicultural competency can be fostered.

Part 2: Encountering the Other in Ethnic and Racialized Worlds

In the first section of this book, basic concepts related to race, ethnicity, and culture are elaborated. In the second section are several chapters that provide analytic accounts of encounters between people of European ancestry and people of other ancestry, especially African ancestry. Paul Hiebert begins with a very wide-ranging summary of historical ways in which Europeans responded to social "others." He suggests that historical ways of forming oppositional identities and organizing them hierarchically must be countered by biblical teaching focusing on our common humanity, the oneness found in Christ, and the mandate to welcome others, to serve, to seek reconciliation, and to tear down walls that divide.

Joseph L. Thomas and Douglas A. Sweeney focus their historical lens on race relations in American Evangelical Christianity. They explore the history of evangelical ministry across the racial divide, accommodations made to slavery and segregation, the founding of black churches, and the impact of African American Christianity on white evangelicalism. Robert Priest then focuses on a single white evangelical educational institution in the segregationist American South. He explores the way in which key individuals responded to the racialized ideologies and structures of their society while trying to minister within their society, and explores their struggles with the contradictions between their own accommodationist practices and their most fundamental Christian commitments. Finally, Marla Frederick McGlathery and Traci Griffin examine a historically and culturally white parachurch mission organization established during the height of the civil rights era, that currently employs a significant number of African Americans. They explore tensions experienced by African American staff, and especially women, that emerge from the fact that this organization exemplifies conservative social and political attitudes widely shared by theologically conservative suburban whites, but not by theologically conservative black Christians. Given the variability of the term *conservative* in American society, how do we come to understand and appreciate the complexity of evangelical experiences? In their essay, Frederick McGlathery and Griffin consider practical implications and possible solutions for such theologically conservative organizations.

Part 3: Using and Abusing the Bible in Ethnic and Racial Contexts

Michael Jessup begins this section with a chapter on white hate groups, exploring their usage of biblical passages and images in the service of racial hatred. While these groups are heretical in terms of every historic Christian creed, and while responsible biblical scholars will consider the hermeneutic of such groups laughable, it would be a mistake to ignore them and their use of Scripture. Churches must do the hard and careful work of reliably setting forth what Scripture teaches about racial and ethnic realities today.

David Pao, a New Testament scholar, provides a model of just such careful scholarship. He explores the writings of Luke, demonstrating that Luke uses two metaphors (family and table fellowship) to address the issue of the identity of God's people, identities no longer to be defined by ethnicity or blood. That is, Pao demonstrates that the gospel message, as set forth by Luke, relativizes identities grounded in race or ethnicity and brings diverse people together in a new family of God, the church, established by faith in Jesus.

Vincent Bacote, a theologian, argues that key biblical themes (creation and biblical anthropology, Christology, Pentecost, eschatology) and Christian practices (such as hospitality or forgiveness) are directly relevant to present ethnic/racial realities. When the church fulfills its teaching function not only through teaching and preaching Scripture but through practices of worship, baptism, and Eucharist, the church will create a distinctive countercultural community that is ethnically diverse and that provides a foretaste of God's coming kingdom.

Pao and Bacote call for and model a responsible exposition of Scripture, in contrast to the extreme abuses of Scripture discussed by Jessup. But some racial misreadings of Scripture are more subtle and mainstream than those articulated by hate groups. Tite Tiénou suggests that mainstream commentators of Scripture during the heyday of racial ideologies took such racial ideologies for granted, and illegitimately read modern racial constructs back into Scripture, leaving such racial assumptions embedded in the commentaries they produced. This contributed to such racial constructs being seen as natural and God given. Pastors and biblical scholars who continue to rely on such commentaries end up repeating, and thus perpetuating, racial discourses of an earlier era. Tiénou takes as his test discourses on Samaritans as "racial halfbreeds." Other biblical passages and themes can be examined in similar ways (cf. Goldenberg 2003).

Steve Kang argues that it is irresponsible and damaging to the global church when Scripture is read and interpreted only by one segment of the global church that privileges its own interpretations as objective. It must be the whole people of God in partnership, out of diverse contexts, that produces a full and responsible reading of Scripture bearing witness to God's kingdom. Such a reading helps to bring kingdom ideals into existence.

Part 4: Engaging Racial and Ethnic Realities in Congregational Settings

America's 350,000 congregations are both implicated in American racialized patterns and are potentially strategic sites for constructively engaging such racialization. In the final section of this book, we focus on congregations as a base for cultural and racial engagement. First, we examine how recent changes in immigration patterns have created opportunities to rethink and rework the way "church" is done—focusing on two separate cases of Asian immigrants: Filipino Americans (Bayt Priest) and Korean Americans (Cha). Second, we turn to historical racial divides (black/white) that have been engaged in congregational settings—in one case with painfully disappointing results (Bayt Priest and Priest) and in the other with a measure of success, though not without challenges (Howell). In each case, important lessons are there to be learned. Then we end with a chapter (Nieves) designed to help congregational leaders gather information about their communities that enables them to develop ministries responsive to ethnic diversity.

Kersten Bayt Priest begins the section by examining changes that took place when new immigrant Filipinos slowly started to attend a historically European American Roman Catholic church in suburban Chicago. As "outsiders," fellow Filipinos bonded into a subgroup. But genuine interest and respect on the part of parishioners and a new senior priest eventually brought key individuals from the Filipino community into leadership and allowed distinctively Filipino religioethnic celebrations to be permanently included in public worship. The parish now proudly pursues a mission of racial/ethnic "harmony" with several weekends annually set aside for worship to reflect diverse worship traditions of each ethnic group within the parish. Multicultural efforts necessarily require interpersonal negotiation at the local level to achieve Christian community across racial, ethnic, and even intergenerational divides. Different minority groups have distinctive concerns that shape emergent approaches to worship and congregational life. Thus, Peter Cha focuses on the partnership of two Korean Presbyterian congregations in the Chicago area, one a first-generation Korean church, and the other a second-generation (English-language) congregation. He suggests that these ethnic churches are ethnic not because they are responding to or reflecting racism and prejudice, but because their members face culturally specific challenges that such ethnic churches are best prepared to address. He focuses specifically on generational challenges that these two congregations jointly addressed. While Cha stresses the value of multicultural churches, he suggests that the "Christian community needs to recognize the value of diversity as well as of unity, of ethnic congregations as well as of multicultural ones."

The historic divide between African American and European American Christians is taken up in the final chapters of the section. Kersten Bayt Priest and Robert Priest analyze the attempted merger of two South Carolina Baptist congregations, one black and one white. They focus on the ways in which divergent worship practices resulted in (a) conflict over the place and meaning of such practices, (b) interactions that resulted in certain worship practices being favored over others, (c) emergence of varying alternative strategies of accommodation, withdrawal, or resistance, and (d) the reemergence of racial/ethnic identities and boundaries. The chapter ends with practical implications.

In contrast with this unsuccessful merger effort, Brian Howell focuses on a fairly large and growing multiracial Presbyterian church in St. Louis, paying special attention to white and African American relations. The chapter explores ways in which power was addressed through religious practice and discourse, such that power relationships and status became "reversed and redefined in ways that bring traditionally marginalized people to the center."

Alvaro Nieves suggests that congregations need to actively research their communities, the ethnic diversity of their communities, and the sorts of special needs present among diverse ethnic groups, and custom design their congregational ministries to address such community needs. He provides a guided overview of resources available for this task. In doing so, he hopes to equip clergy and lay leaders in gathering information to develop responsive ministries within the context of a new American urban reality. This effort has its potential payoffs in targeting real needs associated with real ethnic (often immigrant) communities. These are efforts that promote good stewardship by increasing ministry effectiveness.

Finally, a conclusion summarizes and reviews key findings of the book, pointing the way forward. Appendix 1 provides a historical timeline on key events in American history related to race and ethnicity, with particular focus on religious events and events referred to in this book. Appendix 2 provides an annotated bibliography of recent publications that may be consulted or read by those who wish to explore these matters further.

As these chapters make clear, human diversity involves tough issues of living in an imperfect "not yet" world. We are called to love our neighbors. It can take tremendous effort and sacrifice on all sides, as in situations of worship, and it may mean reaching out to those unfamiliar to us, or challenging practices or attitudes "of the world." Sometimes, it may be hard to know what to do. Yet we continue to pray "thy kingdom come, thy will be done on earth as it is in heaven."

REFERENCES

Dovre, Paul J., ed. 2002. *The future of religious colleges*. Grand Rapids, MI: Eerdmans.

Emerson, Michael O., and Christian Smith. 2000. *Divided by faith: Evangelical religion and the problem of race in America*. Oxford: Oxford University Press.

Espinosa, Gastón, Virgilio Elizondo, and Jesse Miranda. 2003. *Hispanic churches in American public life: Summary of findings*. Notre Dame, IN: Institute for Latino Studies.

Frederick, Marla. 2003. *Between Sundays: Black women and everyday struggles of faith*. Berkeley and Los Angeles: University of California Press.

Goldenberg, David M. 2003. *The curse of Ham: Race and slavery in early Judaism, Christianity, and Islam*. Princeton, NJ: Princeton University Press.

Howell, Brian. 2005. The anthropology of Christianity: Beyond missions and conversion. *Christian Scholar's Review* 34:353–62.

Jenkins, Philip. 2002. *The next Christendom: The coming of global Christianity*. Oxford: Oxford University Press.

Kosmin, Barry A., Egon Mayer, and Ariela Keysar. 2001. *American religious identification survey*. The Graduate Center of the City University of New York.

Marsden, George. 1997. *The outrageous idea of Christian scholarship*. Oxford: Oxford University Press.

Pew Hispanic Center. 2005. Hispanics: A People in Motion. http://pewresearch.org/assets/files/trends2005-hispanic.pdf. Accessed May 28, 2006.

Priest, Robert J. 2001. Missionary positions: Christian, modernist, postmodernist. *Current Anthropology* 42:29–68.

Roberts, Jon H., and James Turner. 2000. *The sacred and the secular university*. Princeton, NJ: Princeton University Press.

Sterk, Andrea, ed. 2002. *Religion, scholarship, and higher education: Perspectives, models, and future prospects*. Notre Dame, IN: University of Notre Dame Press.

Tseng, Timothy, Antony Alumkal, Peter Cha, Faustino Cruz, Young Hertig, Russell Jeung, Jung Kim, Sharon Kim, Ruth Doyle, Fenggang Yang, David Yoo. 2005. *Asian American religious leadership today: A preliminary inquiry*. Series: Pulpit and Pew Research Reports. Durham, NC: Duke Divinity School.

Walls, Andrew F. 2002. *The cross-cultural process in Christian history: Studies in the trans-mission and appropriation of faith.* Maryknoll, NY: Orbis.

Warner, R. Stephen. Forthcoming. The De-Europeanization of American Christianity, In *A nation of religions: Pluralism in the American public square,* ed. Stephen Prothero. Chapel Hill: University of North Carolina Press.

PART I

Thinking Critically about Culture, Race, and Color

I

Race: Critical Thinking and Transformative Possibilities

Jenell Williams Paris

> Therefore, I urge you, brothers, in view of God's mercy, to offer your bodies as living sacrifices, holy and pleasing to God—this is your spiritual act of worship. Do not conform any longer to the pattern of this world, but be transformed by the renewing of your mind. Then you will be able to test and approve what God's will is—his good, pleasing and perfect will.
>
> —Rom 12:1–2 NIV

Introduction

When Paul wrote his letter to the Romans, the Roman Christians were not living in unity. Though they were all believers in Jesus Christ, they were from different ethnic backgrounds; some were Jews and some were Gentiles. Their cultural backgrounds gave them different understandings of how to live as Christians in the Roman world. Paul's letter is, in part, an encouragement to these Christians to live in unity by putting Christ's ways ahead of their own cultural ways (Keener 1993, 438). In Romans 12, Paul writes that cultural patterns sometimes prevent Christians from discerning what is good, acceptable, and perfect. Christians today, like the early Roman Christians, need to think critically, sorting out what in contemporary culture is Christlike, and what is not. In this, the Holy Spirit must transform our minds, sharpen our discernment, and improve our ability to live wisely in the world.

Just as Jewish and Gentile cultural patterns were a basic part of the Roman world, racial categories are a pattern of our world, and they demand conformity. All members of racialized societies are taught, both explicitly and by custom, to believe in race and live according to racial norms. God made humanity with rich diversity, but people made the categories with which we make sense of that diversity. Racial categories were developed to legitimate European imperialism in the early modern world, and they continue to pattern our world. This essay describes the origin of racial categories, and then analyzes ways in which they shape our minds and behaviors. Then, it encourages Christians to take Paul's admonition to heart, becoming critical thinkers and transformed citizens of the world.

The Origin of Racial Categories

Most scientists today agree that "race," as an idea that people can be scientifically categorized in a taxonomy of distinct biological types or subspecies, lacks scientific merit, as Meneses explains in detail in a later chapter. Despite wide scientific consensus that race is not biologically legitimate, we continue to experience race as very real. We each know our own race, and we assess the race of other persons quickly, often subconsciously. Indeed, race is real, but it is a social construction, not automatically given by biology. Like "higher education" or "dating," race is an idea and a social practice that has a history. It doesn't exist in all cultures, but for those who use it, race helps people make sense of the world around them. It guides people in understanding their own identities, who they are like and unlike, and how to form or avoid relationships with other people. It also contributes to understanding, legitimating, and perpetuating social inequalities of the past and present.

The idea of race developed in piecemeal fashion, emerging first in sixteenth-century Europe, North America, and South America as an informal ideology that legitimated slavery and oppression of Africans and indigenous people. Later, in the seventeenth through twentieth centuries, scientists brought this racialized mindset to bear on their research, further entrenching race as a cultural concept by giving it scientific credibility. Because science is a powerful authority in the modern world, scientific racism helped shape the racialized worldview that is dominant in our world today (Caspari 2003; Smedley 1999).

Europeans began exploring and then dominating much of the rest of the world beginning in the fifteenth century, and they developed ideologies that explained and justified this new global order. Before colonialism began, Europeans had long known people of diverse body features and cultures through trade and conflict with Asians, Africans, and diverse Europeans. These encounters, however, were not racialized. That is, people did not explain human differences and the social order with race categories. Premodern Europeans most frequently used language, custom, region, and religion to define in-groups and out-groups.

Jamestown was the first established American colony, and its seventeenth-century beginnings provide insight into the development of race in the United States (Allen 1997; Nash 1992). British settlers first encountered Native Americans as helpful, but as the British claimed Native land for themselves, group relations became increasingly hostile and violent. In addition, some British set-tlers fled their own colonies to live with Native Americans, increasing hostili-ties toward native people who lived in relative ease compared to European newcomers. The British began categorizing diverse native peoples as "Indi-ans," associating the broadly generalized "Indian" physical type with savagery, violence, and suspicion. Though indigenous body types and cultures ranged widely across the Americas, this new category called "Indian" lumped all native people together and associated them with negative traits.

Along with the motivation for taking indigenous land, the major impetus for race categories was related to labor and profit. Initially, English settlers in Jamestown assumed they would use other Europeans as indentured servants and workers, but this was not successful. In the first decades of the seven-teenth century, the first people to serve as colony laborers were Irish, Scottish, and poor English people. These "surplus" and undesirable populations of the British Isles were shipped to the American colonies to provide labor. As planta-tion labor systems became more oppressive, these workers were sometimes able to run away and assimilate into other colonies. Because their language, culture, and appearance were similar to settlers in other colonies, it was diffi-cult for plantation owners to control them. Plantation owners made a second attempt to develop a stable labor force with Native Americans. They also did not make ideal workers because they were sometimes able to run away, survive in the North American terrain, and rejoin their families. Even more important, Native Americans had not developed immunities to diseases carried by Euro-pean domesticated livestock, and these natives died quickly (Mann 2002; Wil-son 1998).

By the mid-seventeenth century, transport of slaves from Africa to North America became increasingly efficient, and Africans became more available for purchase by plantation owners. Africans made ideal plantation workers be-cause many of them had agricultural skills, but even more important, their language, culture, and appearance made them relatively controllable. They could not run away to their homes, and they could not assimilate into other colonies.

This preference for African labor was institutionalized in custom and law. Within thirty years of Jamestown's founding, color terms began to appear in colony legislation. For example, "negro" servants could be held for life, but not "whites." Later in the century, "white" owners were forbidden from freeing their "negro" slaves. Later, physical punishment for "white" servants was regulated (leaving cruel punishment of "negroes" free from censure).

In Jamestown, color categories for human beings emerged gradually, as the need for the categories became apparent. Fundamentally, color categories allowed plantation owners to stabilize their labor forces, which provided eco-nomic and social stability to the emerging United States. Color, then, became a symbol for social status. A "black" was a lifelong slave, unworthy of political enfranchisement, and denied legal protection from physical abuse. "Black" symbolized savagery, ignorance, lack of intelligence, and an inability to live in a civilized manner. To most Jamestown colonists, this justified slavery. In their view, God made "blacks" with culture and personality characteristics that warranted their enslavement. Indeed, in their minds, slavery might actually be good for certain races of people who would live in savagery if left on their own.

Racial categories emerged piecemeal throughout the Americas, with local nuances and meanings. They shared common characteristics, however. First, they lumped diverse people together with a color label. British Anglicans, Spanish Catholics, and other Europeans of various languages, religions, and cultures came to see themselves as "white." People from Africa, with its hundreds of languages, cultures, and diverse skin colors and body types, were lumped as "black." Second, these color categories were correlated with cultural meaning. "Whites" were viewed as civilized, intelligent, capable of self-government, and self-restraint. "Blacks" were seen as dependent, childlike, and lazy, thus needing slavery to provide order in their lives. "Asians" were viewed as intelligent, similar to whites, but also as crafty and devious. The meanings of racial categories paralleled the political and social realities of the day, as viewed from a European or European American standpoint. Still today, racial categories in the United States best fit people associated with European imperialism in this country— Native Americans, blacks, and whites. Others, such as Latinos and Middle Easterners do not neatly fit into American race categories. Latin Americans developed different forms of racial categorization than did North Americans (see the chapter by Pozzi), and Latinos have a broad range of skin color. Many Middle Easterners, though physically "white," may be considered less than fully white because of their distinctive cultures. Indeed, North American race categories were not designed for these groups, but for those groups most intimately involved in America's earlier history.

Scientific

Racial categories were codified and given greater authority with science. In fact, many people today believe racial categories originated in science, but this is not the case. We have seen that race first emerged as a legitimation for colonialism, and developed informally through vocabulary, cultural norms, and legislation. Later, racially minded scientists formalized these cultural understandings, and race categories gained more credibility and authority. Beginning with the Scientific Revolution of the seventeenth century, scientists developed modern ways of understanding the natural world. These scientific methods and perspectives were applied to humans, as well. Numerous and competing racial schemas were developed; in fact, scientists have never agreed on the number or names of racial categories. For example, Carolus Linnaeus developed a fourfold scheme of Americanus, Africanus, Asiaticus, and Europeaeus. Johann Blumenbach's system had five races: Caucasian, Mongolian, Ethiopian, American, and Malay. J. C. Nott and George Glidden offered ten subgroups of Caucasians, including Indostanic, Nilotic, Teutonic, and Pelasgic (Nott and

Glidden 1969, 450). Others saw three, six, or even ten races of human beings (Gould 1981).

Though idiosyncratic, these scientific categories shared several characteristics. First, they made scientific the scholars' preexisting notions about "race" as a package of physical and cultural traits. Linnaeus's Americanus, for example, was described as "reddish, choleric, and erect; hair—black, straight, thick; wide nostrils, scanty beard; obstinate, merry, free; paints himself with fine red lines; regulated by customs." His Europeaeus was "white, sanguine, muscular; hair—long, flowing; eyes—blue; gentle, acute, inventive; covers himself with close vestments; governed by laws." The Asiaticus race was "sallow, melancholy, stiff; black hair, dark eyes; severe, haughty, avaricious; covered with loose garments; ruled by opinions," and the Africanus was "black, phlegmatic, relaxed; hair—black, frizzled; skin—silky; nose—flat; lips—tumid; women without shame, they lactate profusely; crafty, indolent, negligent; anoints himself with grease; governed by caprice" (Smedley 1999, 161). Scientists believed they could predict a person's personality, appearance, dress, and social structure by knowing that person's race. Scientists today, however, see that seventeenth-century prejudices influenced these supposedly objective findings.

A second shared characteristic of these scientific categories was that they were hierarchically organized. Not surprisingly, the white race, whether called Europeaeus, Caucasian, or white, emerged as superior. The unexamined ethnocentrism of scientists affected their results as they used the assumed superiority of their own way of life as the measure for other peoples and cultures.

Racial science continued through the nineteenth and early twentieth centuries, with anthropologists, biologists, and others seeking to refine racial categories (Baker and Patterson 1994). While some of the categories are still in use today, others have fallen away. Of course, the impact of this scientific tradition is still evident today.

Third, racial science made racial inequalities appear to be natural and permanent. Such inequalities were said to be based on inherent differences between races in socially relevant abilities and characteristics. Scientific categories removed race from its social context, in which Europeans enslaved Africans, Native Americans died en masse, and later, Europeans dominated the political systems of most of the planet. Historic and social explanations for oppression and inequality diminished as "race" provided a nature-based explanation for why some groups of people dominate, and others are dominated. In this view, humans, like plants and animals, adapt to their environments. Those best adapted succeed, and the rest do not. Attributing biological origin to racial categories strengthened the categories by claiming that race and its associated inequalities were natural.

The final implication was the false correlation between race and culture. Skin color was perceived to be like a flag, alerting others to the culture and personality characteristics of a person. In this way, race was correlated with violence, laziness, intellectual abilities, political capacities, and spiritual tendencies. Because race is a false biological concept, however, it cannot predict culture. Scientists now understand cultural variety as being rooted in socialization, geography, cultural elements, and historical particularities.

Race and the American Worldview

"Race" emerged as a folk category, was codified in science, and then became a fundamental part of the American worldview. Some say race became increasingly powerful in response to the antislavery movement of the mid- to late nineteenth century. Smedley writes, "Without the pressures of antislavery, especially by the abolitionists, there might have been less need or incentive to construct the elaborate edifice of race ideology that has been America's legacy. There might also still be some form of slavery" (1999, 201). As abolitionists pressured American government and society, pro-slavery advocates used race to defend the profitable institution of slavery. In this view, God made the "black" race for slavery, and while it may seem cruel, slavery is actually the best way of life for blacks because they are not fit for civilization or self-government.

Many of these rationalizations used the Bible in convoluted ways to explain why blacks have been cursed since the time of Noah, and that Paul supported slavery. The "Curse of Ham" is a racialized interpretation of Genesis 9:18–28. Ham, one of Noah's three sons, sinned against his father (Ham's two brothers were named Japheth and Shem). Noah responded by cursing Canaan (one of Ham's descendants). Racialized biblical interpretation claims that the descendants of Shem are the Semitic people of today, the lineage of Japheth includes today's "white" people, and the descendants of Ham are "black" people. In this view, when Noah said, "Cursed be Canaan; lowest of slaves shall he be to his brothers" (Gen 9:25), this was God's curse on black people forever. This racialized misreading of Scripture legitimized New World slavery and subsequent segregation and racial injustice, despite the clear fact that Noah's curse was on Canaan's descendants, not those of his brothers, and that Scripture identifies Canaan's descendants with the land of Canaan, not Africa. Unfortunately, this racialized view is still taught today and believed by many (Goldenberg 2003; Haynes 2002).

Racial ideologies became more complex and Christianized during the time of pressure against slavery. For example, in *Bible Defence of Slavery*, two nineteenth-century Christians wrote that Northern free blacks were forced to "endure and suffer" freedom, a condition to which they were not suited. One encouraged Southern slave owners, saying that keeping slaves is "a heavy burden—a charge weighty and difficult to manage; but [the slave owner] is bound, by God's authority, to sustain the charge, to endure the labor of caring for them, making them work" (Priest and Brown 1969, 567). In this view, slavery is described as an act of sacrificial love. Though it is difficult to control slaves, it is in their best interest to be enslaved.

While slavery ended with emancipation, race did not. Though freed from slavery, Americans labeled "black" continued to live in a society in which they were viewed in racial terms. Soon after emancipation, new racialized laws developed that kept black people in a subordinate position. For example, in Washington, D.C., "black codes" continued to legalize differential treatment of black people. These laws imposed fines for breaking an established curfew, prohibited religious meetings after 10 P.M., and banned blacks from owning or operating restaurants (Gillette 1995). On a federal level, the *Plessy v. Ferguson* Supreme Court decision (1896) supported the right of railway companies to provide separate cars for blacks and for whites. This, and other legislation, shaped the social position of blacks as separate and inferior for most of the twentieth century.

Blackness first meant slavery, but after emancipation, blackness was reinscribed in American society with new meanings. "Black" was still a symbol for unintelligent, violent, and oversexed, but this category of persons could no longer be restrained with slavery. Post-emancipation legislation carried the essential meaning of blackness into a new century, restraining blacks no longer with slavery, but with segregation. As with categories such as "white" or "Asian," racial categories were both elastic and stable, persisting in their essential meanings and adapting those meanings to changing historical circumstances.

In summary, then, "race" is part of the modern world. It is a product of human inventiveness, not a creation of God. It is an idea that Europeans developed to legitimate and perpetuate global imperialism. Initially a folk category, "race" was given scientific authority, and then became a foundational part of the modern worldview. The historic and social conditions that birthed the notion have passed, but "race" has proved to be remarkably flexible. People adapt, change, and stretch the concept and so it remains a constitutive part of our society.

Race Shapes our Minds

Race is not an occasional problem or an isolated issue in our society. Rather, it is a fundamental concept that constitutes our society, like freedom or individualism. Thus, most aspects of society have racial dimensions, such as health care, criminal justice, education, government, and religion. By considering how both our minds and our behaviors are influenced by racial ideology, we can better understand Paul's advice to live transformed lives.

People come to believe in the reality of race by socialization, the process by which children learn culture. Some people, however, do not believe in race because their cultures do not have this concept. The Ju/'hoansi (also called Bushmen, Ju/wasi, or Kung), a hunter-gatherer group in the Kalahari Desert, refer to themselves as *zhu twa si*, "the harmless people." They refer to all non-Bushmen as *zo si*, "animals without hooves," because, they say, non-Bushmen people are dangerous like lions and hyenas (Thomas 1989). An indigenous group of north Australia refers to themselves as "Tiwi," which means "we, the only people." They use various words for outsiders, but consider no one but themselves to be fully and truly human (Hart, Pilling, and Goodale 1998). The Ju/'hoansi and the Tiwi form in-groups and out-groups on the basis of cultural similarity, and these constructs help make sense of warfare, alliances, and identity. Tiwi, *zo si*, and *zhu twa si* are not, however, race groups. They do not use physical appearance as the fundamental marker of group identity, and they do not use categories such as "white," "Asian," or "Native American."

Categories such as Tiwi, *zo si*, and *zhu twa si* are ethnic categories. Ethnicity has been present throughout history as people mark themselves and others by heritage, language, religion, and other cultural elements. The practice of marking people by biology, using race categories, has a specific history that is historically absent from large portions of the world. Anthropologists argue that ethnicity is better than race as a tool for understanding human ways of life. This is not to say, however, that ethnic categories are without problems. People use ethnicity to develop negative stereotypes and prejudices, and to legitimate violence and even genocide. In America, however, and in most world cultures at present, people are socialized to perceive themselves and others as belonging to a race group. Each member of a racialized society must learn his or her own race and the race of people around him or her, and either adapt to or resist the social meanings of those categories.

Racialized perceptions of self and other are communicated through stereotype and prejudice. A stereotype conveys information about an individual based upon the individual's group. By assessing an individual as "black," "Asian," or some other race, the observer now supposedly knows something about that individual. Stereotypes provide a shorthand way of knowing a person, or a reason for avoiding a person altogether. Similarly, prejudices are beliefs or feelings, usually negative, held toward an individual or a group. Like stereotypes, prejudices are categorical. Individuals are judged on the basis of their group, not their individuality. Prejudices and stereotypes are remarkably inflexible. For example, when an Anglo who is prejudiced against Latinos meets a friendly, intelligent, Latino person, the Anglo typically will not change her prejudice. The individual becomes an exception to the prejudice, but the prejudice persists (Marger 2003).

Race affects our minds deeply. Though we are born without knowledge of race, we are socialized from birth to perceive the world in racial terms. Each of us is assigned a race, and accepts it as part of personal identity. We learn to perceive others as belonging in race categories, and learn the stereotypes associated with the categories. In this way, race affects everyone, not just people who experience discrimination.

Race Shapes our Behaviors

In Romans 12, Paul makes a connection between mind and behavior. A conformed mind leads to conformed behavior, but a renewed mind leads to a transformed life. In a racialized society, people are socialized to perceive themselves and the world around them in racial terms, and this worldview encourages conformity of behavior. Before the Civil Rights era, such conformity was enforced by law. People of different races were legally forbidden from marrying, and the law upheld segregation in education, residences, and other public places. In Washington, D.C., during the 1940s, for example, urban planners tried to relocate African Americans to the Southeast quadrant, an area of the city separated from the rest by the Anacostia River. Throughout the city, realtors and insurers drew lines on maps to demarcate areas where they would not sell properties or insurance to people of color (Gillette 1995). People of color could be legally prosecuted or lynched for crossing legal color boundaries. Race shaped the behaviors of Americans, and it did so explicitly by law and punishment.

The Civil Rights era brought both the end of legal segregation and a new national ideology of integration as the way to build a harmonious multiracial society. Integration has not, however, occurred in many aspects of life. Segregation is not legally required, but it still occurs. Without explicit and legally coercive legitimation, segregation continues by cultural custom and personal choice. Leonard Steinhorn and Barbara Diggs-Brown (1999) describe American integration and segregation as influenced by intimacy (they analyze only African Americans and whites, but still their model is insightful). In their view, integration is strongest in the least intimate spheres of life. Americans are willing to interact with diverse others in public, for example, while driving or shopping. In intermediate spheres of intimacy, such as the workplace, Americans also integrate fairly well. In intimate spheres of life, however, such as marriage, neighborhood, church, and school, Americans choose to segregate. Fewer than 1 percent of U.S. marriages, for instance, are black-white. For other groups, however, intermarriage is somewhat higher. Around 36 percent of Asian American husbands and 45 percent of Asian American wives had white spouses. Around 50 percent of Native American husbands and wives have white spouses (Kennedy 2002).

American churches display patterns similar to other intimate spheres of life, that is, high levels of voluntary segregation. Though Christians often say they desire integration, research shows that like Americans in other spheres of life, American Christians voluntarily segregate. Ninety percent of African American churchgoers belong to historically black denominations such as the African Methodist Episcopal Church and the National Baptist Convention (Steinhorn and Diggs-Brown 1999). For reasons of language, new immigrant populations often develop ethnically distinct churches. Most white Americans choose white churches, though whites are less likely than nonwhites to explain or perceive their choices as being shaped by race.

In both society and church, segregation occurs partly by intentional choices, and partly as an unintended by-product of other choices. When people buy homes, for example, they frequently consider quality of schools, crime rates, proximity to work, and type of home. These preferences frequently put people in communities that are racially homogeneous. A family may then choose to attend a community church because they want their children to be able to walk to church and socialize with neighbors who attend the church. Alternatively, a family may choose to attend a church that feels worshipful, which usually means it is culturally familiar. When people choose a "good home" or a "good church," they may rarely list racial segregation among their guiding principles, but it becomes an unintended consequence of these choices. When a social structure is racialized, individual choices within the structure need not be explicitly racial. Choices that seem natural and nonracial simply comply with the "default setting" of the system. To borrow Paul's language, racial segregation is one of the conforming patterns of this world.

Critical Thinking about Race

Though "race" was absent from the thinking of many people throughout history, race is a fundamental part of our twentieth-first-century worldview. Race is fixed in our minds so we perceive others and ourselves as belonging to racial subgroups of the human species. This creates the impression that our species is too diverse to be unified. In this, racial categories contribute to the lack of unity among all of humanity, and among Christians as well. Race is fixed in our society so that even without intent to segregate, we "naturally" live near, worship with, marry, and socialize with people of our own race. For Christians seeking to transform their world by their presence and actions, a project of deconstruction and reconstruction is in order.

Christians must deconstruct the worldview into which we have been socialized. One way to begin recognizing the contingency of our own way of life is to look at cultures that do not use racial categories. Relatively isolated indigenous cultures, and premodern cultures including those in the Bible, provide insight into worlds without race. For example, the Hebrews were an ethnic group in which the markers of identity involved such things as circumcision, temple worship, religious observances, and heritage. While they stressed ancestry, it was not in the context of an idea of racial purity. Rahab, Ruth, Uriah, and other outsiders were free to join the Hebrew community, and to contribute their genes to the mix. The Jews often articulated purity concerns, but these were religious, not a matter of keeping a biological type genetically pure. The Bible does not indicate that phenotype was a marker of Jewish identity. In addition, Hebrews knew other people in the world as "Philistines," "Caananites," "Egyptians," and others—culture groups, not racial groups.

The New Testament provides similar contexts for study. In Jesus' day, the Judean Jews held strong ethnocentrism against Galilean Jews and Samaritans, but these were subsets of the Jewish ethnic group, not other races. And the oppositions articulated between Jews and Samaritans focused on such things as temple worship, Scripture, ritual, and belief—not phenotype. Jesus didn't have a race, because his culture did not socialize its members to perceive themselves or others in racial terms.

Obviously, like race categories, ethnic groupings offer possibilities for violence, genocide, and hatred. Ethnic categories are not morally superior to race groupings, but they are more accurate to humans' lived experience. Humans live in culture, in ethnic groups that offer members language, religion, socialization, and a distinctive way of life. In the numerous cultures described in the Bible, we see a world without race, which raises creative possibilities for our own world.

This type of Bible study may help us perceive racialization in our own society, as well as envision social orders in which race does not exist. In addition to thinking about society as a whole, we may also identify ways in which our life choices are racialized, conforming to the pattern of this world. We may take hard looks at our lives in the areas of friendships, church membership, neighborhood, schools, club memberships, workplace, financial investments, and many more.

For people of color, it is often relatively easy to perceive racialization because people of color are reminded daily of how race affects their efforts to survive and thrive in society. Perceiving the presence and dynamics of race is frequently more difficult for white people. First, white privilege often allows white people to engage or ignore racial issues as they please. One of my undergraduate students wrote in an essay, "We [whites] don't have to talk about things because race rarely affects us. We don't even see our own whiteness." Second, whiteness is the American norm—the invisible standard against which difference becomes visible. Another student wrote, "I only learned about other cultures in school, and that was from a white American view . . . I always thought that I was 'normal.' I was defining myself as the standard, like other Americans do, without even knowing that I was doing it." White people often say they don't see their race, and sometimes say they don't have culture. White food, white music, white child rearing, white dating, and white education just seem "normal," not racialized at all. This invisibility is one of the primary features of whiteness, and so whites must strive to perceive their place in our racialized world (Frankenburg 1993; Hartigan 2000; Keating 1995; Rodriguez 1999).

Implications for Christians and Churches

Engaging in extended times of critical thinking and analysis of our society and our personal lives is an essential part of living rightly in a racialized society. As a white evangelical Christian, I am part of a social community that has been both praised and critiqued for being quick to act, but slow to think. White evangelicals are eager to solve problems, and to help when people are being harmed. This ready activism is a great blessing, but sometimes Christians act before they deeply understand the dynamics of the problem. Research suggests that good intentions are not enough to solve racism; in fact, well-intentioned efforts combined with a lack of cultural awareness may actually perpetuate racial tensions. White evangelicals, for example, are highly individualistic, relational, and anti-structural. We often "reach out" to nonwhite Christians, but are frequently unable to perceive or value the structural effects of discrimination and inequality in people's lives. Our efforts to be "color-blind," to just see people as people, can be perceived as ignoring the important ways in which race and culture affect people's lives and shape identity (Emerson and Smith 2000).

Christian social justice activists use a circular model including three steps: action, reflection, and prayer. In this model, Christians should continually pray, act, and reflect (reflection includes study, dialogue, and evaluation of action) as they seek to change their world. Any one step done in isolation accomplishes little, and may even do damage. Together, however, these three actions provide a comprehensive way of addressing social and personal change.

For our purposes, this social action model and Paul's words in Romans 12 provide direction for action. In study and reflection, we identify the patterns of this world and analyze ways in which our lives conform to these patterns. In action, we seek to resist these patterns and to live in transformed ways. In prayer, we seek God's help and express gratitude for God's guidance.

Christians today frequently speak of their "comfort zone," which is similar to Paul's "pattern of this world." On a personal level, Christians may go further than "stepping outside our comfort zones," and abolish the comfort zone altogether. With respect to race and ethnicity, the comfort zone is a segregated zone of racial and cultural homogeneity. A Christian may live in society without regard for racial and cultural comfort zones. This may mean developing personal relationships across boundaries of race or culture. It may mean enjoying music, art, or literature created by people of different races or cultures. It may mean living, worshiping, or going to school with diverse groups of people. It may mean joining change-making coalitions in one's city or town. It may mean giving financially to organizations that do justice in our nation or internationally.

On an institutional level, Christians may work to develop churches that do not conform to the racialized patterns of this world. Christians may consider the racial and cultural diversity of church membership and leadership, as well as the commitments to diversity shown by individual leaders of all races. In worship, we may broaden the diversity represented in the worship leadership, instruments, music style, and language. In sermons, we may broaden the range of books and experts cited, and stories or examples used. In church decor, we may broaden the symbols and images used, especially images of Jesus. We may encourage one another to broaden our worship abilities, that is, the ways in which we worship, and with whom.

Though we often long for simplicity, there is no "to do" list that will solve racial and ethnic inequality. As individuals and congregations engage in critical thinking about race and ethnicity, local action steps will emerge that are well suited to various contexts. Mistakes will be made as well, and we will need to be kind to ourselves and to others as well-intentioned efforts backfire or fall flat.

Choosing critical thinking will mean living with some ambiguity and confusion. Dialogue about race as a social construction is new, and Christians are just beginning to explore what this may mean for the ways we understand Scripture, do theology, live in the church, and live in the world (*Christianity Today* 2000; Ham 2002; Sharp 2002; Unander 2000). Minding Paul's advice is tremendously exciting. How might our lives, and the life of the world, be transformed if we seek the renewal of our minds? When we do, we may be surprised by what is good, pleasing, and perfect. Instead of conforming to the pattern of the world, Christians may offer a better way of life and a vision for social change.

REFERENCES

Allen, Theodore. 1997. *The invention of the white race*. Vol. 2. London: Verso.

Baker, Lee D., and Thomas C. Patterson. 1994. Race, racism, and the history of U.S. anthropology. *Transforming Anthropology* 5(1 and 2): 1–7.

Caspari, Rachel. 2003. From types to populations: A century of race, physical anthropology, and the American Anthropological Association. *American Anthropologist* 105(1): 65–76.

Christianity Today. 2000. We can overcome (October) 22:40–49.

Emerson, Michael O., and Christian Smith. 2000. *Divided by faith: Evangelical religion and the problem of race in America*. New York: Oxford University Press.

Frankenberg, Ruth. 1993. *White women, race matters: The social construction of whiteness.* Minneapolis: University of Minnesota Press.

Gilbreath, Edward and Mark Galli. Discussion forum with Elward Ellis, Robert Franklin, Charles Lyons, John Ortberg, J. I. Packer.

Gillette, Howard Jr., 1995. *Between justice and beauty: Race, planning, and the failure of urban policy in Washington, D.C.* Baltimore: Johns Hopkins University Press.

Goldenberg, David. 2003. *The curse of Ham: Race and slavery in early Judaism, Christianity, and Islam.* Princeton, NJ: Princeton University Press.

Gould, Stephen Jay. 1981. *The mismeasure of man.* New York: Norton.

Ham, Ken. 2002. One race. In *Just don't marry one: Interracial dating, marriage and parenting*, ed. G. Yancey and S. Whittum Yancey, 54–69. Valley Forge, PA: Judson.

Hart, C. W. M., Arnold R. Pilling, and Jane C. Goodale. 1988. *The Tiwi of North Australia*, ed. G. Spindler, and L. Spindler. 3rd ed. Chicago: Holt, Rinehart and Winston.

Hartigan, John Jr. 2000. Object lessons in whiteness: Antiracism and the study of white folks. *Identities* 7(3): 373–406.

Haynes, Stephen R. 2002. *Noah's curse: The biblical justification of American slavery.* New York: Oxford University Press.

Keating, AnnLouise. 1995. Interrogating "whiteness," (de)constructing "race." *College English* 57(8): 901–18.

Keener, Craig. 1993. *The IVP Bible background commentary: New Testament.* Downers Grove, IL: InterVarsity.

Kennedy, Randall. 2002. Interracial intimacy. *The Atlantic Monthly* 290(5): 103–10.

Mann, Charles. 2002. 1491. *Atlantic Monthly* 289(3): 41–53.

Marger, Martin N. 2003. *Race and ethnic relations: American and global perspectives.* 6th ed. Belmont, CA: Wadsworth/Thomson Learning.

Nash, Gary B. 1992. *Red, white and black: The peoples of early America.* 3rd ed. Englewood Cliffs, NJ: Prentice Hall.

Nott, J. C., and George R. Glidden. 1969. *Types of mankind.* Repr. Miami: Mnemoyne. (Orig. pub. 1854.)

Priest, Josiah, and W. S. Brown. 1969. *Bible defence of slavery or the origin, history, and fortunes of the negro race.* 6th ed. Detroit: Negro History Press. (Orig. pub. 1853.)

Rodriguez, Roberto. 1999. The study of whiteness. *Black Issues in Higher Education* 16(6): 20–25.

Sharp, Douglas R. 2002. *No partiality: The idolatry of race and the new humanity.* Downers Grove, IL: InterVarsity.

Smedley, Audrey. 1998. *American Anthropological Association statement on "race."* Electronic document, www.aaanet.org/stmts/racepp.htm.

———. 1999. *Race in North America: Origin and evolution of a worldview.* 2nd ed. Boulder, CO: Westview.

Steinhorn, Leonard, and Barbara Diggs-Brown. 1999. *By the color of our skin: The illusion of integration and the reality of race.* New York: Dutton.

Tatum, Beverly Daniel. 1994. Teaching white students about racism: The search for white allies and the restoration of hope. *Teachers College Record* 95(4): 462–76.

Thomas, Elizabeth Marshall. 1989. *The harmless people.* Rev. ed. New York: Vintage.

Unander, Dave. 2000. *Shattering the myth of race: Genetic realities and biblical truths.* Valley Forge, PA: Judson.

Wilson, James. 1998. *The earth shall weep.* New York: Grove.

2

Science and the Myth of Biological Race

Eloise Hiebert Meneses

On April 29, 1992, just one of many race riots in a long line of racial turmoil erupted in Los Angeles when four white police officers were acquitted of all charges in the beating of an unarmed black man. Four thousand National Guard troops were deployed, over fifty people were killed, four thousand were injured, and twelve thousand were arrested. The property damage from three days of rioting was estimated at one billion dollars (*Los Angeles Times* 1992). The violence and suddenness of such riots often surprise people. Yet, they do not happen without cause. Los Angeles was, and continues to be, an arena of tension between racial groups. On ordinary days, the tension can be read in small incidents of discrimination at work, crime in the streets, and segregation in churches. But on extraordinary ones, the pressure from these small tensions builds, producing devastating explosions between communities.

What is race? In the last chapter, Jenell Paris suggested that race is actually a socially constructed phenomenon, a means of categorizing people for social purposes according to physical differences. But, most people do not know that race is only a social reality; they think that it is a biological reality too. They use the term *race* to indicate a group that has similar physical features believed to have come from common ancestry. And, therefore, they think that race is a matter of bloodlines, or common descent—a kind of family relatedness. In fact, I would suggest that people tend to see races as family writ large, as is evident in the use of terms like *sister* or *brother* for members of one's own group. People may even take the descent-based analogy to its farthest extreme and suggest that the various races are like various species of animals, with the accompanying argument that people of different races should not mix, that is, intermarry. The result is that those in-groups different from one's own are viewed as fundamentally strange or "other" (as Paul Hiebert will demonstrate in a later chapter), with a sense of "otherness" that is enhanced by biological differences. People think, then, that human beings come in a definable number of breeds or stocks, and that everyone in the world can be classified into one stock or another.

What is the relationship between race and ethnicity? The term *ethnicity*, is usually used to stress the cultural rather than the physical aspects of group identity. Ethnic groups share language, dress, food, customs, values, and sometimes religion. These are things that can change easily and do historically. Furthermore, these similarities may unite people of different "races" while dividing people of the same "race." Yet, in everyday conversations, people are inclined to use the terms *race* and *ethnicity* as functionally synonymous, with the former emphasizing biological connections within a group, and the latter, cultural connections within the same group. This creates highly oversimplified categories such as "white," which in the United States indicates skin color, common descent from Europe, English language, and even a set of values such as hard work and saving money. The category "Hispanic" may indicate not only the Spanish language but also Catholicism and descent from Spain or Latin America. So, in many people's minds, culture and biology *seem* to be working together to produce distinct physical and cultural groups that can be placed in a larger taxonomy of human beings.

In part, these two terms, *race* and *ethnicity*, along with the idea that people can be classified into types, are a product of about three hundred years of Western science. In the nineteenth century, anthropologists, who study both physical and cultural aspects of human beings, began to measure, identify, and classify the so-called races. They accumulated data from all over the world on variables such as height, weight, skin color, brain size, and head shape, and produced a taxonomy with terms such as *Mongoloid*, *Negroid*, *Caucasoid*, and *Australoid* that are still used and misused popularly today. They debated the number of traits that should be used to make a classification, and the question of whether such different people could possibly have had a common human ancestor. Enormous time and energy went into the project.

Yet now, essentially all anthropologists have given up the attempt to identify races of human beings. This is very simply because the best evidence indicates that there are, physically, *no clear boundary lines* between the various communities of people around the world. Nearly all of the traits that distinguish human beings from one another are found in all communities, though in varying degrees. Skin color, for instance, is composed of degrees of brown, due to varying amounts of a granule called melanin, degrees of yellow from consuming carotenoids, such as carrots, and degrees of pink from variation in capillary depth, making one's blood more or less visible. But all melanin is brown, anyone can eat carrots, and everyone has red blood, so the differences in skin color between groups are only differences in degree, not kind. Furthermore, human beings have very few traits that vary at all. Geneticists have discovered five times as much variation in gorillas as in humans, and ten times as much in chimps. So, humanity as a whole is really a single, relatively homogeneous group. The slight variation that exists is not distributed in such a way as to produce clearly demarcated subgroups.

Yet, despite this fact, most people, especially in racially stratified societies, imagine that they can "see" the different races. Of course, it certainly is possible to see physical differences between individuals such as skin color, color and texture of hair, height and weight, and facial features. But in modern, plural societies, we have all been trained to go a step further, and to identify the individuals we meet as belonging to this or that group. Arguably, the ability to identify group membership within the larger social framework is necessary, particularly in cities where social interaction depends upon being able to make guesses about how strangers will behave toward you (Merry 2002). Yet, the clues to identifying strangers as members of groups do not only come from physical differences. Dress, speech, stance, and context all help in the identification process. So the natural human tendency is to conflate cultural markers with physical ones in an overall evaluation of who someone is. People may imagine that they "see" a physical difference, where a cultural one is the reality. And people may use the physical differences that they do see as social markers for the purpose of inclusion or exclusion. This is in part what is meant by the social construction of race.

In societies where the idea of race has underpinned the development of a racialized social order, there is a sense in which "race" exists and is real. But it is important to remember that the social construction of race does not make the biological existence of race a fact. The myth of biological race needs to be debunked in our own minds and in others'. As long as people believe that humanity is "naturally" divided into biological races, they will give a significance and a finality to ethnic groups that is not warranted. They will, for instance, imagine that cultural characteristics are permanently rooted in people's biological nature, and may think that biological characteristics control behavior. So, in this chapter, I will first describe the nature of human biological relatedness, then trace the history of the science that erroneously convinced us all of the existence of biological races, and finally examine the social reasons why people keep reinventing the concept of race, even after it has been discredited. I believe that Jesus' warnings against idolatry of family are relevant to the matter of race. Christians must not place blood relatedness before "family" relatedness in the church.

Human Biological Relatedness

Let us take a closer look at the actual nature of human biological diversity and relatedness. First, human beings as a whole constitute a very narrow gene pool. One scientist has suggested that, despite the fact that we are dispersed around the globe, we have only the genetic diversity of a small population of chimps in central Africa (MacEachern 2003, 20). Again, other species have far more variation than we do. So, most of the genes we have, 75 percent in fact, we share. For instance, there are genes that control the growth and maintenance of the structure of our bodies, produce the enzymes that assist our bodies' chemical reactions, and direct the processes of reproduction. None of these many genes varies at all among humans, apart from genetically random events (which are generally seriously maladaptive).

Second, most of the physical variation that does exist is spread throughout the entire human population. Physical variations between people are called polymorphisms. Some polymorphisms are external, visible features such as height, weight, body shape, and skin, hair, and eye color. Others are internal, invisible features such as blood types, genetic susceptibilities to disease, and special abilities like oxygen absorption and lactose tolerance. Polymorphisms are caused by variants of genes called alleles that mix and match at every generation producing both resemblances and differences. No two individuals, except for identical twins, are genetic carbon copies of each other. Even full siblings differ from one another enough for us to recognize them. So, there is valuable genetic variation that occurs between us.

But individual variation is not what is at issue in the matter of race. If races existed, such polymorphisms would be *bunched up* to produce genetically distinct groupings. For instance, dark skin might always be associated with black hair and a certain height or weight. Light skin might always be associated with blond hair and a different height or weight. To discover whether such bunching of polymorphisms exists, geneticists take measurements of the alleles found in various "populations" around the globe. (The term *population* simply refers to the people being studied, with boundary lines drawn narrowly or widely, depending on the researcher's purposes.) The results of these measurements, known as gene frequencies, are compared among and between populations.

The primary result of gene frequency studies is that most human polymorphisms are dispersed across the globe. According to the Human Genome Project (HGP), 93 percent of the variation that does exist is found within human populations, and only 7 percent between them. Rosenberg et al. (2002, 2381) explain:

> The average proportion of genetic differences between individuals from different human populations only slightly exceeds that between unrelated individuals from a single population. Remembering that only 25% of human genes vary at all, this means that a mere 1.75% of the human genome varies between populations. The best genetic studies show, then, that the differences between groups of people are only small differences in degree, rather than large differences, or differences in kind.

Blood types are a case in point. As late as World War I, scientists and doctors alike thought that the different "races" must have different types of blood, so they were careful not to give blood transfusions across the race lines. While it is true that there are different blood types, all of the types are found in most human populations, though in different frequencies. The English, for instance, have 25 percent type A, 5 percent type B, and 70 percent type O, while the Chinese have 20 percent A, 24 percent B, and 56 percent O, and the Inuit (Eskimo) have 20 percent A, 7 percent B, and 73 percent O (Zihlman 2000, 6–13). In this manner, most variation is spread throughout humanity, and, conversely, any particular group has within it most human genetic variation. One researcher has suggested:

> If the holocaust comes and a small tribe deep in the New Guinea forests are the only survivors, almost all of the genetic variation now expressed among the innumerable groups of our five billion people will be preserved. (Lewontin quoted in Gould 1996, 353)

Third, even these slight variations between populations do not indicate race lines. If the comparison between populations is along one genetic trait at a time—height for instance—the results will look approximately like a rumpled tablecloth. There will be places in which the frequencies of certain alleles are relatively high, producing tall people, and others in which those frequencies are relatively low, producing shorter people. These peaks in frequency are known as clines. But a cline in one region may be unrelated to a cline in another region. So, for instance, the genes producing tallness can be found at a high frequency among the Nuer of the Sudan and among the Manchu of China. Yet, no one would suggest that Africans and Chinese are one race. Likewise, genes that cause high levels of melanin production can be found in central Africa and south India, producing dark skin among historically disconnected groups. Like a rumpled tablecloth, gene frequencies drift up and down, up and down, across the global map.

Clines do not jump from high to low and back again. They vary gradually across a region. So, for instance,

> if a person could walk from Lagos to Stockholm, or to Bangkok, she would see a progressively shifting spectrum of physical characteristics, reflecting the constant interactions between neighboring communities through many thousands of years. These interactions yield biological relationships among populations that are *clinal*. . . . That is, there is a gradual transition in characteristics between the groups involved, not any sort of sudden boundary between them. (MacEachern 2003, 21)

Hence, perhaps the strongest argument against race is simply the fact that we are all genetically related. There are no pure stocks among us, nor have there ever been in the past. It is this constant genetic interaction with one another, known as "gene flow," that has prevented us from developing races. Unander, himself a geneticist, comments,

> At the level of the [thirty] thousand genes of humanity, there are no racial frontiers. . . . Genetically, we all belong to highly smudged categories within the one human race. (Unander 2000, 7–8)

Still, perhaps we need to compare more than one trait at a time. Attempts have been made to work with multiple traits to identify groups of supposed common ancestry. These studies have demonstrated a lack of covariance. Clines that wax and wane along one trait, wane and wax along another, that is, they do not covary (Templeton 1999, 180). For instance, the clinal map of height does not match the clinal map for skin color, or the clinal map for blood type. If races existed, the clines of various traits would map themselves upon one another to produce distinct groups. Height, skin color, and blood type would vary together. As it is, superimposing clinal maps produces a continuous blur.

The most recent, and statistically most sophisticated, attempt to find covariance has been carried out using the HGP data (Rosenberg et al. 2002). This study, by teasing out microscopic general tendencies, did find a slight "clustering" effect that roughly corresponds with geographical barriers such as oceans, mountains, or deserts. Such genetic clusters are the result of adaptation to local environments and explain the differences that we notice among people of different regions of the earth. They are "transitory configurations of the human body in response to changing selection pressures, which can be environmental and/or cultural" (MacEachern 2003, 20). But *they are not significant enough to constitute "races."* The researchers in the HGP study stated:

> Because most alleles are widespread, genetic differences among human populations derive mainly from gradations in allele frequencies rather than from distinctive "diagnostic" genotypes. Indeed, it was only in the accumulation of small allele-frequency differences across many loci that population structure [i.e., clustering] was identified. (Rosenberg et al. 2002, 2384)

Perhaps the best way to visualize the true genetic situation for human beings is to present a map. In a massive study of human genetic relatedness, Cavalli-Sforza et al. produced the following map.

This map is best understood as a representation of waves of relatedness, much like the isothermal maps that indicate the flow of the wind in a weather report. In the main, genetic relatedness flows across the earth west to east, from Africa to Melanesia and the Americas (ruling out the last four hundred years of migration). It is important to remember that the lines on this map do not reflect sharp boundaries. They merely indicate where degrees of relatedness can be found. Also of note is the fact that people who appear very different externally (phenotype), such as Europeans and sub-Saharan Africans, are actually genetically close (genotype), while those who appear similar, such as central Africans and Melanesians (both with moderately brown skin and tight curly hair), are actually genetically distant. Once again, the best evidence is that human beings do not come in distinct biological types. Templeton (1999, 190) sums up the reason:

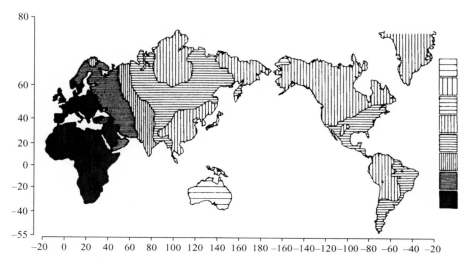

FIGURE 2.1. Human Genetic Relatedness. The map is of the first principle component, a statistical procedure for drawing a line of relatedness, which accounts for 35 percent of the variance. Cavalli-Sforza has maps of the second and third principle components that account for portions of the remaining variance. All of the maps affirm west-to-east relatedness (see above). (Reproduced from Cavalli-Sforza et al. 1994, 135.)

> The major human populations have been interconnected by gene flow . . . during the last one to two hundred thousand years. . . . [Studies] reject the existence of evolutionary sub lineages of humans, . . . and reject the idea of "pure races" in the past. Thus, human "races" have no biological validity under the evolutionary lineage definition of subspecies.

Put simply, there is no such thing, nor has there ever been, in the biological world as race.

The Concept of Race in the History of Science

To say that there is no such *thing* as race is to suggest that we have reified race, that is, made it into a thing (Gould 1996, 27; Goodman 2001, 34). And to the degree that we have constructed such "things" in our minds, we are tempted to believe that they have great explanatory value. So we imagine, for instance, that "an individual's biology *and behavior* are in large part explainable by which race the individual is a member of; and that races are hierarchically arranged" (Goodman 2001, 31, emphasis added). The concept of race seems to explain the biological differences we see, and the behavioral peculiarities we think arise from these differences.

TABLE 2.1. Linnaeus's Typology of People

Home Europeaeus	White	—gentle —governed by laws
Home Americanus	Red	—choleric —governed by customs
Homo Asiaticus	Yellow	—haughty —governed by opinions
Homo Afer	Black	—indolent —governed by caprice

Historically, race as an explanatory concept was first constructed by sixteenth- and seventeenth-century Europeans who were encountering the rest of the world and were eager to understand it and, eventually, to control it. In addition to confusing people with animals, and animals with people (they thought orangutans were people), Europeans tried to account for the differences they discovered by dividing human beings into varying numbers of types. As Paris has described, Linnaeus (1758), who established the scientific taxonomy of the biological world that all scientists use even today, developed a taxonomy of people too. In systematic fashion, he first constructed a set of categories (each with an identifying skin color), then attributed behavioral characteristics to the categories, and finally arranged them in hierarchical order.

Of course, the problem with Linnaeus's taxonomy of people was that it was based thoroughly in what is now called ethnocentrism, that is, interpreting and evaluating other people and their cultures with the worldview and values given to you by your own culture. Linnaeus was Swedish, and "naturally" assumed that his own people and their ways were the most advanced.

Ethnocentrism was not unique to seventeenth-century Europeans. People in most places and times have made similar assumptions about the superiority of their own peoples and cultures. But two things caused European ethnocentrism to have unusually pernicious effects in the ensuing three hundred years. One was that Europeans successfully dominated the globe during this period under colonialism, and the other was that science, which was just blossoming to full fruition, was used to justify this domination.

Perhaps the most clear-cut case of science in the service of the colonial economy was its use to defend slavery. Scientists of the time argued that sub-Saharan Africans (a) were not fully human, (b) had descended from a different ape than whites, (c) had cultures that were primitive, and (d) had a natural bent toward being enslaved. In the early nineteenth century, George Cuvier wrote that Africans were "the most degraded of human races, whose form approaches that of the beast and whose intelligence is nowhere great enough to arrive at regular government," and Charles Lyell, after comparing Africans to apes, remarked, "Each race of Man has its place, like the inferior animals" (Gould 1996, 69). Both men were prominent scientists of their times, and are remembered today as founding fathers of their fields. Yet both held severely ethnocentric views that were touted as scientific objectivity in the defense of slavery. Science was being used to legitimize and justify the emerging global politico-economic order.

The early twentieth century saw the scientific defense of racism reach new heights, as European and American scientists worked together to develop the field of eugenics. Frances Galton (n.d., 17) coined the term, and defined it as "the study of the agencies under social control that may improve or impair the racial qualities of future generations, either physically or mentally." Eugenicists wanted to regulate human breeding in order to better the biological future of humanity. To this end, they developed international scientific organizations, held annual conferences, and reported to government agencies. The central fallacy upon which their project was founded was that the existing social order was a simple reflection of biological differences, and hence social problems were the result of biological deficiencies.

> If ills such as unemployment, feeble-mindedness, or nomadism were genetic in origin, then the rational and efficient way to eliminate these problems would be to prevent people with such hereditary defects from breeding. Eugenicists argued that society paid a high price by allowing the birth of defective individuals who would then have to be cared for by the state. Sterilization of one defective adult could save future generations hundreds or thousands of dollars. (Allen 1989, 886)

Through biological engineering, eugenicists thought they could solve social problems and build the new utopia.

The Nazi experiments of the 1930s and 1940s are the best-known consequence of the science of eugenics. But Americans too were interested in breeding a better race at the time. Eugenicists' reports to the U.S. Congress resulted in legislation against immigration from countries of "poor stock." The Johnson Act of 1924, for instance, restricted immigration from eastern and southern Europe, where criminal genes supposedly abounded, to 2 percent per country. Calvin Coolidge remarked as he signed the bill, "America must be kept American" (Gould 1996, 262). At the state level, eugenicists promoted laws mandating the sterilization of "unfit" people. Between 1911 and 1930, twenty-four states had enacted sterilization laws for "social misfits" and "idiots," identified by their inability to pass intelligence tests. Seventy-five hundred people were forcibly sterilized in Virginia between 1924 and 1972 (Gould 1996, 365). By 1941, sixteen thousand people had been sterilized in California alone, and thirty-six thousand in the nation. The "science" of eugenics was having real social and political impact.

Long after eugenics was thoroughly discredited by the events of World War II, intelligence testing continued to be put to service in defense of race. In fact, many scientists believed, and ordinary people assumed, that the most significant difference between the races was in the area of intelligence. Intelligence testing had actually been invented as a means of assessing school achievement in France. It was later used to measure levels of "retardation" in institutions for the developmentally disabled in the United States. These are legitimate uses of such tests. But, based on notions of race-based intelligence difference, the United States government next took to measuring immigrants for their relative "fitness" to enter the country, and then to the testing of candidates for the army and for college (Lieberman 2003, 46ff.). Eventually, all school children were administered intelligence tests, and the results were used to defend the notions that the poor were less intelligent than the rich, women were less intelligent than men, and blacks were less intelligent than whites. Once again, science was being used to confirm and legitimize the existent social order.

It has been nearly a century since Alfred Binet designed the first IQ tests, and there have been many tests of the tests to check for their validity. By now, most scholars agree that intelligence tests, even in their currently refined forms, measure not just innate mental ability but also educational achievement, economic opportunity, and cultural background. They are, for instance, correlated with scholastic achievement at .80 (1.0 would be a perfect correlation), making it difficult to distinguish whether the test is actually measuring intelligence or hard work in school. The correlation of test scores with occupational status is .50–.70; with income, .35; and with job performance, .20–.25 (Flynn 1980, 26). It is extremely likely that environmental circumstances are heavily influencing people's test scores.

This is not to say that there is no effect from inherited mental ability at the individual level. Studies do show a correlation in IQ scores for identical twins reared apart (.72) and for parents and biological, rather than adopted, children (.30) (Scarr and Weinberg 1978, 32). But score differences (or similarities) among individuals who are members of the same group do not explain differences in averages between groups (Gould 1996, 186). When comparing individuals, factors such as environment, education, nutrition, and so forth can be controlled, and therefore ruled out, as causes of the different scores. When comparing group averages, such factors cannot be controlled. Evidence that inheritance does *not* contribute to group average differences in IQ scores can be found in the results of studies of "mixed" black-white children. These studies have repeatedly demonstrated that having white ancestry gives no advantage on IQ test scores to children who are classified as "blacks" because of their skin color (Flynn 1980, 73–84). In one such study, the authors concluded that

> the results were unequivocal. Blacks who had a large number of European ancestors did no better or worse on the tests than blacks of almost total African ancestry. These studies dispute the hypothesis that IQ differences between blacks and whites are in large part the result of genetic differences. (Scarr and Weinberg 1978, 32)

Ironically, group average differences in IQ scores most likely measure the impact of *racism*, rather than race. That is, the deprivation caused by racism accounts for the lower scores of minority and inner-city children as against other more advantaged children (Hudson, quoted in Lieberman 2003, 51).

The lesson from history is that the dominant people of a time nearly always evaluate those they have dominated as being inferior. Under the Roman Empire, the orator Cicero wrote to his friend, Atticus, "Do not obtain your slaves from Britain because they are so stupid and so utterly incapable of being taught that they are not fit to form a part of the household of Athens" (Parrillo 2002, 17). Later, in the seventh century, a Moor, one of the conquerors of Spain, wrote of northern Europeans, "They are of cold temperament and never reach maturity. They are of great stature and of a white colour. But they lack all sharpness of wit and penetration of intellect" (Flynn 1980, 217). These same "stupid" Europeans, much later, dominated a large part of the globe and made similar evaluations of others. Power, in the form of colonialism, backed up by a legitimizing rationale, in the form of science, turned ordinary ethnocentrism into truly pernicious racism.

How did the matter get turned around? In the United States, the anthropologist Franz Boas did much to reverse scientific opinion on race. Boas demonstrated that immigrant children were significantly taller than their own parents, indicating a strong influence on stature from nutrition. In 1940, he published *Race, Language, and Culture*, arguing that biology does not determine culture, and that the various cultures of the world are to be equally valued. In addition, over time, the hard facts from studies of anatomy, brain size, intelligence, and genetics just kept contradicting the idea of race. So, in the end, the attempt to classify the races failed, not only due to lack of evidence but also due to the existence of ample counterevidence.

There are occasional attempts to resurrect the concept of biological race in science (e.g., Herrnstein and Murray 1994). Gould (1996, 60) warns that biological determinism is always popular in times of political retrenchment. That is, an argument that people "naturally" belong in their circumstances can be useful to elite or powerful groups in times when competition is high and resources are tight. But for scientists, as for Christians, the intrinsic value of the truth must be paramount. In a 1994 statement, the American Anthropological Association declared "differentiating species into biologically defined "races" has proven meaningless and unscientific as a way of explaining variation (whether in intelligence or other traits)" (www.aaanet.org/stmts/race.htm).

And MacEachern reminds us: "Science is not an exercise in nostalgia: when a term progresses from being burnished by long use to being made obsolete by increasing knowledge, it needs to be discarded" (2003, 33).

Race, Ethnicity, and Christian Implications

In a classic article, Fredrik Barth (1969) has argued that people use both physical and cultural differences as "markers" of ethnic identity in order to create social boundaries. Although ethnicity is at least partly socially constructed for contemporary purposes, most people believe that it is simply the natural product of common cultural history and biological ancestry. The result of this artificial conflation of the physical with the cultural is a very powerful group solidarity and identity. Barth (13) called ethnic identity the most "basic, most general, identity, presumptively determined by [a person's] origin and background," and Clifford Geertz (1973, 259) suggests that ethnic identity is experienced as "primordial" or "given." Ethnic identity is deeply felt as *who you are*, and hence it draws together "people like us," and separates them out from "others" (Fenton 1999, 105).

Yet, in reality, ethnicity does not just spring naturally from common background, either physical or cultural. Ethnic groups must be *mobilized* by the creation of boundaries between them, and by the selection of identifying markers to distinguish them from one another. Ethnicity is about social classifications emerging within *relationships* . . . for ethnicity to spring to life it is necessary that *real or perceived differences of ancestry, culture, and language are mobilized in social transactions* (Fenton 1999, 6 emphasis in the original).

So, in the ethnic group formation process, boundaries are established first by restrictions on social contact, especially intermarriage, and markers are selected next to identify and distinguish the groups. In this process, physical markers are especially welcome because of the symbolic power of suggesting common descent. The kinship principle is the strongest bond in human society. By using the language and symbols of family (i.e., biological) relatedness, a group can create a good deal more internal solidarity than would be possible with just a common culture. The result is that ethnic groups may perpetuate the concept of race as part of their own internal formation process.

Ethnicity gives people a sense of belonging and identity, as well as a culture and a social group. More than this, Barth argued that the formation of ethnic groups is a means of political protection and economic support in large and complex societies. In many parts of the world, ethnic groups are politically organized to lobby for such tangible resources as representation in government, land redistribution, and access to jobs. Internally, they may construct networks of resource sharing that allocate everything from money to information. In that sense, ethnic groups do in fact function as "families" in the larger society.

But ethnic boundaries divide as well as unite. The twentieth century was the most violent century in human history, due largely to postcolonial ethnic wars and conflicts. The family principle writ large can, in fact, be dangerous. The commitments made, the loyalties given, and the passions aroused by people who see themselves as "brothers" and "sisters" to one another, and oppose themselves to identified "others," can cause hurtfulness as mild as snubs and as severe as riots. Hence, this is surely an arena in which Christians should beware of being overly conformed to the world's ways, failing to be fully "transformed by the renewing of [our] minds" (Rom 12:1–2).

Jesus indicated clearly that family loyalties can potentially subvert our allegiance to him. He said, for instance, "Whoever comes to me and does not hate father and mother, wife and children, brothers and sisters, yes, and even life itself, cannot be my disciple" (Luke 14:26). He told a would-be follower who was concerned about his obligations to his parents to "let the dead bury the dead" (Matt 8:21–22). And, when he illustrated the love we should have for one another, Jesus chose not the love that results from blood ties, but the care of a good neighbor for a stranger (Luke 10:25–37).

In announcing the advent of the kingdom of God, Jesus established a new kind of family loyalty, one based on adherence not to biological inheritance, but to the will of God (Mark 3:33–35) and the infilling of the Holy Spirit (John 3:1–8). This new family, the Church, transcends the boundaries of biological family and ethnicity. Membership in the Church, therefore, is to be based on only one criterion: the willingness to follow Jesus as Lord, thereby subordinating all other loyalties that might divide the community of his followers.

Christians are members of the societies in which we live. We are born into ethnic groups, identify with them, and relate to one another across their boundaries. But Christians are also members of the Church, the multicultural, multiethnic, body of Christ. The Church, the new family composed of disciples of Christ, must not only teach but also demonstrate the practical love of Jesus for people of varying ethnic backgrounds. It must do this, in both ordinary and extraordinary times, by structuring itself to accommodate ethnic diversity internally, and by advocating social justice in society externally. Loving one another across any social divide is difficult. But it is made possible by Jesus' sacrificial death on our behalf. Paul reminds us: For [Jesus] is our peace, in his flesh he has made both groups into one and has broken down the dividing wall, that is, the hostility between us (Eph 2:14).

Acknowledgements: Special thanks go to David Unander and Robert Priest for exceptionally careful reading of this chapter. Though not responsible for the particular argument I have presented here, they have assisted me significantly in correcting errors, both in fact and in line of reasoning.

REFERENCES

Allen, Garland E. 1989. Eugenics and American social history, 1880–1950. *Genome* 31:885–89.
Barth, Fredrik. 1969. Introduction. In *Ethnic groups and boundaries*, ed. F. Barth, 9–38. Boston: Little, Brown.
Boas, Franz. 1940. *Race, language, and culture.* New York: Macmillan.
Cavalli-Sforza, L. Luca, Paolo Menozzi, and Alberto Piazza. 1994. *The history and geography of human genes.* Princeton, NJ: Princeton University Press.
Fenton, Steve. 1999. *Ethnicity: Racism, class and culture.* New York: Rowman & Littlefield.
Flynn, James R. 1980. *Race, IQ and Jensen.* London: Routledge & Kegan Paul.
Galton, Francis. n.d. *Inquiries into human faculty and its development.* 2nd ed. New York: Dutton.
Geertz, Clifford. 1973. The integrative revolution: primordial sentiments and civil politics in the new states. Chapter 10 in *The interpretation of cultures*, ed. , 255–310. New York: Basic.
Goodman, Alan H. 2001. Biological diversity and cultural diversity: From race to radical bioculturalism. In *Cultural diversity in the United States*, ed. Ida Susser and Thomas C. Patterson, 29–45. Malden, Mass.: Blackwell.
Gould, Stephen Jay. 1996. *The mismeasure of man.* New York: Norton.
Herrnstein, Richard J., and Charles Murray. 1994. *The bell curve.* New York: The Free Press.

Lieberman, Leonard. 2003. A history of "scientific" racialism. In *Race and ethnicity: An anthropological focus on the United States and the world*, ed. Raymond Scupin, 36–66. Englewood Cliffs, NJ: Prentice Hall.

Linnaeus, Carolus. 1758. *Systema naturae*. 10th ed. Stockholm: *Laurentii Salvii Holminiae*.

Los Angeles Times. 1992. Understanding the riots: Los Angeles before and after the Rodney King case. May 11.

MacEachern, Scott. 2003. The concept of race in anthropology. In *Race and ethnicity: An anthropological focus on the United States and the world*, ed. Raymond Scupin, 10–35. Englewood Cliffs, NJ: Prentice Hall.

Merry, Sally Engle. 2002. Urban danger; life in a neighborhood of strangers. In *Urban life*, ed. George Gmelch and Walter P. Zenner, 115–26. Prospect Heights, IL: Waveland.

Parrillo, Vincent N. 2002. *Understanding race and ethnic relations*. Boston: Allyn and Bacon.

Rosenberg, Noah A., Jonathan Pritchard, James Weber, Howard Cann, Kenneth Kidd, Lev Zhivotovsky, Marcus Feldman. 2002. Genetic structure of human populations. *Science* 298:2381–85.

Scarr, Sandra, and Richard A. Weinberg. 1978. Attitudes, interests, and IQ. *Human Nature* 1:29–36.

Templeton, Alan R. 1999. Human races: A genetic and evolutionary perspective. In *The biological basis of human behavior: A critical review*, ed. Robert W. Sussman, 180–92. Upper Saddle River, NJ: Prentice Hall.

Unander, David. 2000. *Shattering the myth of race*. Valley Forge, PA: Judson.

Zihlman, Adrienne L. 2000. *Human evolution coloring book*. 2nd ed. New York: HarperResource.

3

Race, Ethnicity, and Color among Latinos in the United States

Carlos Pozzi

Several weeks ago I was visiting a Brazilian friend in Chicago. As we walked down the street, we began talking about the increasing crime rate in the city. The conversation led to the issue of race and his apparent fear of "black people." "I am scared of them, both here and in Brazil," he said. "When I see them in the street I get nervous and I try to avoid them." I was somewhat surprised. You see, my friend is dark complexioned and has most of the physical features one would associate with a person of African descent. In the United States he would probably be considered black. However, he did not consider himself black and believes that others in his native country would not consider him black. Similar struggles are part of the lives of most Latin Americans in the United States. The definitions of race and ethnicity in the United States are often different from those encountered in Latin America. Many Latin Americans experience diverse categorizations and different identities that shift depending on settings, social context, and peer groups. Needless to say, this phenomenon often leads to confusion and increases adjustment difficulty.

Issues of race and skin color are a prominent part of Latin American society and have been since the colonial period. Latin American culture was strongly influenced by the introduction of African slaves and the intermingling among Spaniards, African slaves, and Native Americans. In later years this culture was affected by the arrival of European immigrants and the migration of Latin Americans into the United States. What resulted was a complex web of socially constructed rules to identify and classify race. Latin Americans in the United States are often faced with the need to know how to negotiate complex social rules related to race, ethnicity, and skin color. They also need to find ways of adapting their native rules to suit their new interactions with the culture in the United States, which defines race very differently. The process of adjustment is made increasingly difficult as a result. About fifteen years ago a good friend of mine had an experience that serves to illustrate this point. Pito, as we knew him, was a graduate student in theology and a coworker of mine in a cleaning company in suburban Chicago. One morning the manager of the company called us to his office and gave us specific instructions about the several jobs scheduled for that day. He asked me to leave Pito at one job and move on to the others. I was then instructed to pick up Pito after the two other jobs were completed. This was a deviation from the way we had worked in the past. When we questioned our supervisor about the new rules, he stated that several of the customers had complained about having a black man in their house. Until that time neither Pito nor I had realized that Pito was considered to be black in the United States. In Puerto Rico, Pito was defined as "trigueño" or of wheat color; this is a very desirable skin color among those from the Caribbean.

As prominent and complex as these issues are, they have not been given the focus they deserve in sociological and anthropological literature. One possible explanation for this lack of attention among researchers is the belief that Latinos are a homogeneous group. Popular North American culture views the Latino culture as a single ethnic minority group, not as a people formed by different groups from different counties with different heritages and relationships to the United States.

A closer look at Latin American society suggests that race and skin color are considerable issues among Latinos in Latin America and in the United States. To fully understand these issues one must understand the social rules that govern their behavior, the developmental history of those rules, and the changes and challenges encountered as a result of their interaction with the host culture. What are the social rules that govern race relations in Latin America? How do Latin Americans negotiate those rules in their native countries and in the United States? This chapter hopes to answer some of these questions. I intend to explore the ways in which Latinos negotiate their race-based categories and some of the historical and social factors that have influenced the definition of those categories. I will review the history of race and race relationships in Latin America and among Latinos in the United States and discuss some of the unique ways in which Latinos manage their ethnic and racial differences. Through this discussion we will see Latinos as a prime example of a community with a variety of socially constructed ideas of race that are not based only on physical or familial characteristics but are influenced by social and environmental variables. This chapter will explore the common themes and the current issues faced by Latinos of different nationalities, skin tones, and levels of acculturation related to the issue of skin color and is intended to increase understanding of the Latino population in the United States and to stimulate a discussion of the issues previously mentioned.

There are several reasons to explore these issues. First, the Latino population is growing. According to the U.S. Census Bureau, in 2000 there were 35 million

Latinos in the United States, making up 12.6 percent of the U.S. population. More recent numbers suggest that Latinos are the largest minority group in the United States. According to the U.S. Census Bureau (2004b), the nation's Hispanic population reached 41.3 million as of July 2004, and Hispanics accounted for about half of the nation's population growth between July 1, 2003, and July 1, 2004. The projected growth suggests that by 2010 Latinos will make up 15.5 percent of the U.S. population compared with 13.1 percent for African Americans (U.S. Census Bureau 2004a).

Second, Latinos are diverse both in their ethnicity and in their relationship with the United States. For example, there is great variation in the percentage of the population identifying itself as indigenous in Latin America. Some countries such as Bolivia and Guatemala have indigenous populations of approximately 60 percent, while other countries like Costa Rica have an indigenous population of less that 6 percent (Arora 1995). Also, people of African descent have been in Latin America since they accompanied the early conquistadores into Mexico. Moore-Stevenson (2002) argued that in the period between the mid-sixteenth century and the mid-seventeenth century the number of Africans in many American countries exceeded the number of natives. As with indigenous people, the current percentage of individuals of African descent in Latin America varies by region. In some regions, such as the Caribbean, it is believed that the majority of the population is of African heritage.

In addition to the ethnic diversity, Latinos are also diverse in their experiences in North American society. For example, for many Puerto Ricans, the connection to U.S. society was the result of direct military aggression on the part of the United States. Many Cubans came to the United States as political refugees. There are other Latino groups that have been in what is now U.S. territory since the beginning of the sixteenth century. Within these heterogeneous Latino groups there are both individuals who have been in this territory for centuries and those who arrived only yesterday. The initial reason for contact with the United States often influences the group's attitudes toward the host country. The diversity in racial composition, history, and relationship to the United States make Latinos a desirable group for inquiry.

Latinos in the United States

Four major groups make up the Hispanic population of the United States: Mexican Americans, Puerto Ricans, Cubans, and Central and South Americans. Mexican Americans are the largest Hispanic group in the United States. They have inhabited the area that is now the Southwest of the United States since the beginning of the sixteenth century and before the first Pilgrims landed in Plymouth. Mexican Americans trace their ancestry back to the Aztec civilization, which attained its height about AD 1500. Like other Latino groups, Mexican Americans were affected by the importation of slaves around AD 1516, the colonization by Spain and France, and the beginning of the migration of other European groups.

The concept of "Mexican American" emerged as a result of the settlement of the Mexican American war in 1848. The Treaty of Guadalupe Hidalgo, which ended the war between the United States and Mexico, permitted the annexation of Texas (previously Mexican territory) by the United States. As part of the treaty, the United States granted citizenship to Mexicans who remained in the annexed land. Mexicans continue to migrate to the United States by the thousands. Among this group there are individuals whose families have lived in the United States for centuries and others who arrived from Mexico this morning.

Puerto Ricans are the second largest Hispanic group in the United States. Their involvement with the United States intensified following the U.S. invasion of the island in 1898 during the Spanish American War. Through legislation passed in Congress in 1917 and 1919, Puerto Ricans became U.S. citizens, which led to mass migrations to the United States during most of the twentieth century.

The island held its first election in 1948, when they elected Luis Muñoz Marin governor. During his administration, the island entered the current political arrangement with the United States. This Commonwealth status of the island is a unique arrangement that places the island under U.S. control with very limited freedom. Puerto Ricans can travel freely from the island without the use of a passport. This made it easy for migrant farm workers to move to Hawaii, Florida, and Long Island as farm help in the first half the century. Through a program sponsored by the U.S. Department of Labor and the U.S. Department of Agriculture, young Puerto Rican males came to the United States as seasonal agricultural workers. A large number of these workers remained in the United States and settled in or around metropolitan areas in the Northeast.

Cubans are the third-largest Hispanic group in the United States. Their involvement in the States dates back to 1830 when the first Cuban immigrants settled in Florida. Until 1960, the number of Cubans in the United States was modest. Three distinct waves of immigrants followed the Cuban Revolution of 1959. The first wave of people left Cuba right after the revolution, between 1959 and 1962. During this initial exodus, two hundred thousand Cubans migrated to the United States. The second wave was clandestine, with approximately thirty thousand Cubans arriving by private plane and boat between 1962 and 1965. In 1965, the Cuban government allowed twice-daily flights to the United States and approximately three hundred thousand Cubans had migrated by 1975 when the operation was halted. Finally, in 1980, 124,000 Cubans migrated to the United States as part of the Mariel Boat Lift. Cuban immigrants are clearly divided by economic, class, and color lines. Early immigrants are the richest and best educated of all Hispanic groups. They are also mostly white. The immigrants of the 1980 migration, on the other hand, have a higher unemployment rate, are less educated, and experience more poverty. Not surprising to researchers, they also have darker skin.

Although immigrants from Central and South Americans have been in the United States since 1820, they have not been closely observed because their numbers are still not significant. The largest immigration of Central and South Americans has come in the last thirty years, following the unrest in Guatemala,

El Salvador, and Nicaragua. The immigrants from these countries are diverse, ranging from Guatemalan Indians to wealthy Nicaraguan exiles. This population is also often underemployed and overworked, the dynamics of which official statistical records do not address.

In recent years a large number of people from the Dominican Republic have immigrated to the United States. Currently over half a million Dominicans live in Florida and the Northeast. A majority of Dominicans migrated to the United States via Puerto Rico and were forced to undertake very dangerous journeys to arrive here. They come to the United States typically in search of employment.

While the Latino population continues to grow, their adjustment to the "American culture" has not become easier. In general, Latino families continue to be less educated and live within a lower socioeconomic status than their Anglo counterparts. For example, for the population age twenty-five and over, only 57 percent of Mexicans have a high school education compared with 88.4 percent of non-Hispanic whites (Robles 2004). Other Latino groups fare better. For Cubans in the same age group, 73 percent of them complete high school. Hispanics are more likely to live in larger households, to be unemployed, to have lower occupational status, earn less, and to live in poverty than non-Hispanic whites. Latinos are also more likely to be younger than Anglos with 35.7 percent of the Latino population being under the age of eighteen compared with 23.5 percent of the non-Hispanic white population (Robles 2004). According to the National Council of La Raza (2002), Latino males are the group of American workers most likely to be working or looking for work, but even so, 11.2 percent of all Latino workers live in poverty.

Race and Skin Color among Latinos

The social, economic, and political realities of Latinos in Latin America and in the United States differ significantly. The history of race relations and attitudes toward people with various phenotypes also differ significantly. Though commonalties exist, they may often be overshadowed by differences, making generalizations difficult. Consequently, the common themes discussed later in this chapter are not intended to be generalizations, but rather attitudes and practices, which the available literature suggests are shared by a large percentage of the Latino population.

Latinos' struggle with issues of race is clearly not a new phenomenon. On the contrary, Latin American has been forced to deal with these issues since the time of colonization. The specific ways of dealing with race and skin color have been different in different countries. Cuba, for example, where about one-third of the population is black, was the only Spanish-speaking country to grant blacks universal suffrage. However, following contact with the United States, racial categories became more clearly defined and exclusive. In the 1930s, the Harlem Renaissance writer, Langston Hughes, described the racial situation that he observed. He noticed that hotels and beaches in Cuba, owned by North Americans, excluded blacks. He himself was excluded from many places frequented by other tourist because of his skin color. Safa (1998) argues that such racial distinctions continue in spite of the Communist Party's attempt to remove racial inequalities in education and occupation.

In the Southwest, after the occupation by the United States in the mid-nineteenth century, there was a move to differentiate the European (Spanish) residents from others who had been "mixed" with "native blood." Spanish Europeans adapted the name "Hispanos" rather than "Mexican" to distinguish themselves from the rest of the Latino population. Every Latin American country and region developed different ways of addressing the issues of race and skin color. However, available research suggests commonalities that can be discussed.

Latinos Tend to Deny Racist Attitudes

Race-based preferences among Latinos are strongly denied. Most Latinos will strongly argue that they do not have racial preference. According to Cruz-Janzen (2002) the denial of racism is a significant manifestation of racism in the Latino community. Issues of race are not discussed and are rarely the subject of arguments. Speaking of Cuban racism, De la Torre (1999) argues that "Cuban racism is rooted in the belief that we are not racist, even though the primary criterion of social classification is color." In the case of Cuba, De la Torre discusses several ways in which this denial of racism is justified. First is the writings of Jose Marti, a Cuban poet and freedom fighter who advocated for the rights of blacks in the island. According to De la Torre, Marti's claims that race was socially constructed led to the Cuban belief that if there was no race, then there was no racism. De la Torre also argues that Cubans justify their racial oppression by comparing it with the racism in the United States. Claiming things like the lack of segregation on the island and the integration of the Cuban armed forces, Cubans attempt to claim that racism does not exist like it does in the United States. A look at the social and political history of the island in the twentieth century suggests the contrary.

Even though racism is denied in most of Latin America, racially based attitudes permeate Latino culture and are preserved through covert racist mechanisms. Color is often associated with behavior; negative behavior is associated with blackness while positive and desirable behavior is associated with whiteness. Therefore, whiteness is more desirable and valuable. In this hierarchy of color among Hispanics, the Native American characteristics are more desirable than the darker, African-looking ones. Oboler (1995) observed that implicit in the statements collected through her research is the understanding of the attributed value to "being white." White is clearly good and desirable, while black is bad and to be rejected.

Cruz-Janzen (2002) argues, "Latino racism entails subliminal acceptance of the fictitious superiority of whites coupled with the fictitious inferiority of all others, with blacks and Indians at the bottom." The word "subliminal" is essential in this definition. Racism in Latin America is rarely overt, and when it is, it is rarely defined as racism. For example, several months ago I received a call from several members of my family to discuss their dislike of my daughter's boyfriend, an African American young man. My family members are good evangelical Christians who will never admit to being racist. However, they put a great deal of effort into trying to convince me that there was something wrong with my daughter dating a dark-skinned man. Their arguments included traditional racist arguments like the appeal to nature, and more ethnic arguments such as "*cada oveja con su pareja*" (each sheep with its partner or equal). These types of attitudes toward people of African or native heritage are common but often not defined as racist.

These types of attitudes are also often expressed through common music and proverbs. For example, I was driving with my brother-in-law several years ago. An African American child crossed the street in front of my car. I immediately stepped on the brakes. My brother-in-law said, "*Si le das lo tienes que pagar como blanco*" ("If you hit him you will need to pay him as if he was white"). Another commonly used proverb is "*negro pero lindo*" ("black but cute"). This expresses the idea that blackness and beauty are mutually exclusive and, although they may appear together, the combination is rare. Blackness is only acceptable in the rare cases in which it conforms to the socially created perception of beauty. The list of "*dichos*" goes on and on. Dundes (1975) argues that jokes and proverbs are responsible for attitudes held by one group about another. Arora (1995) argues that proverbs about Indians in Latin America significantly influence attitudes toward those groups. She further argues that proverbial sayings and other kinds of folk stereotypes are not passive reflections of attitudes toward ethnic groups, but play an active role in the creation and propagation of those attitudes. The Spanish language as it is used in Latin America has no shortage of such proverbs.

Latin American music is also filled with racial references. This is usually not considered offensive because of the defused racial lines. Afro-Caribbean music is filled with images of blackness and references to other groups in ways that would be considered severely offensive in North American society today. Ismael Rivera, a Puerto Rican singer, sings about *El Negro Bembon*, "The black man with big lips." El Gran Combo ridicules Oriental facial features and speech patterns in a song called *La China*, "The Chinese Woman." Cuban singers have for decades expressed the perceived sexuality of black women in songs like *El Vaile de Encarnacion*, "The Dance of Incarnation." However, racial attitudes in music are not limited to Afro-Caribbean music. A recent hit by Colombian singer Carlos Vive questions the ability of an Indian to be "cultured" suggesting that social sophistication and native heritage are mutually exclusive.

The expression of racial attitudes in Latino music is not limited to the content of the songs. Racial attitudes are also expressed to the value attributed to specific music. In most Latin American countries black music is clearly distinguished from white music. Black music, such as Punta in Honduras or

Bomba y Plena in Puerto Rico, is considered inferior in its musical quality, primitive and barbaric, associated with sexual depravity, and therefore sinful or unholy.

There are several other examples of how racially based prejudices are negotiated in Latin America. In the Dominican Republic, individuals of black descent are usually referred to as "Indios" or "Indians" alluding to the natives who inhabited the island prior to the Spanish invasion. According to Safa (1998), blackness in the Dominican Republic is attributed to Haiti and, consequently, individuals with similar phenotypes can be classified differently based on nation of origin. A black person from the Dominican Republic can be seen as "Indian" while a person with similar physical characteristic and skin color from Haiti can be classified as black.

For most Latinos, the above example would not be interpreted as racist. On the contrary, many Latinos would see themselves as the victims of racism and would be blind to the fact that they may contribute to such racism against other Latinos.

Racial Attitudes Influence the Lives of Latinos

Even though racism is often denied, it exerts significant influence in the lives of Latinos. In a study of race and life circumstances in Brazil, Lovell and Wood (1998) found that there is a significant difference between whites and non-whites in education, jobs, life expectancy, infant mortality, and other life variables. They found that children born to white mothers outlived those born to Afro-Brazilian mothers by 6.65 years. White children have a higher school enrollment rate (73.6 percent) than nonwhite children (64.7 percent). In a study of race and skin color in Nicaragua, Lancaster (1991) found that European-looking Nicaraguans are considered more attractive when compared with the more native or African-looking individual.

Hall (1994) studied the marital and economic patterns of Latinos in the United States in the context of the variation of skin tone. He found that Puerto Ricans, who tended to be the darkest Hispanic group assimilating into U.S. society, had the lowest intermarriage rate with members of the mainstream population. Also, in a study of skin color among Mexicans in the United States, Murguia and Telles (1996) found that skin color affected education and employment rates. Seven percent of light Mexican Americans were in the lowest educational category compared with 19.2 percent of medium and 18 percent of dark Mexican Americans.

Fletcher (2002) argues that although Latinos span the racial spectrum, the majority of those in the United States are of mixed race. This reality, however, is not reflected in the offerings of the two Spanish television networks. The faces seen in the programming of these networks tend to be white and European looking. Fletcher continues to argue that the lack of diversity on Spanish-language television is, in part, a result of the racial attitudes that prevail in Latin America.

Issues of Race and Skin Color Are Different among Latinos than among the Rest of U.S. Society

Safa (1998), like many other authors, argues that race and social class are not defined by biology but by a fluid history and therefore are "negotiated phenomenon." The social construction of race in Latin America is different from that in the United States in several ways. First, Safa argues that race in the United States is based on ancestry. According to the "one drop" rule, any person having African ancestry is black. In Latin America, national identity and social class may supersede racial identity allowing the racial lines to be much more fluid and to be mediated by other social markers such as education, social class, employment, and other "negotiated" categories. As described by Fitzpatrick (1987), "In the United States a man's color determines what class he belongs to; in Puerto Rico, a man's class determines what his color is" (106). This does not negate the importance of phenotype. Skin color and physical characteristics still influence race categories. These categories are mediated by other social factors as well such as socioeconomic status and family of origin. They are fluid constructs that vary across social and national contexts. This is why my Brazilian friend does not have to see himself or be defined by his native community as black even though his biological characteristics lead to that classification in the United States.

Another way in which the socially constructed racial categories are different from Latin Americans involves the recognition of shades of color. In the United States the categories tend to be clear: black or white. Most Latin American cultures recognize the existence of shades of blackness and whiteness. Categories such as "trigueño" or "mulatto" account for different levels of blackness and provide a more socially acceptable category for blacks with lighter skin.

This concept of shades of darkness has a long history. Hernandez (1994) argued that throughout the colonization process Spanish structure created a caste system with four segregated levels: Pure Spaniards from Spain, pure Spaniards born in the New World, mulattos/mestizos, and enslaved Africans and natives. Throughout the history of Latin America there has been a number of recognized categories or shades of blackness or whiteness. Many of them continue to be used today to identify individuals by the color of their skin.

Racial Categories among Latinos Are Fluid

Among Latin Americans, race is fluid and can be negotiated or changed. Race is defined by social status and other social mediators. When one of these mediators can be changed, then the perceived race or skin color is changed. For example, if one changes socioeconomic status, educational level, or family, one influences the cultural definition of their skin color and that of their offspring. According to Fitzpatrick (1971), during the colonization period it was common for Spaniards to recognize their children born to slave women and to award them freedom at baptism. This practice allowed the child to move up from the bottom of the race hierarchy.

In the Latino culture the selection of marriage partners determines the color of the skin of your children and their social status. Marriage is often seen as an opportunity to erase blackness. It is common to hear Latino families say that when one marries white they are "bettering the race" *"mejorando la raza."* Hall (1994) proposes what he called "the bleaching syndrome," which is the move toward a more desired "white" identity. He argues that for Hispanic Americans who exhibit the "bleaching syndrome," marriage becomes a vehicle for the exchange of status. In other words, marry white to better the race and your position in society.

Using the concept of different shades of whiteness, Latino culture developed a social hierarchy based on perceived color with blacks being at the bottom and pure whites on top. In this multilevel color-based hierarchy, one moves up the hierarchy through the elimination of the physical characteristics of black or native heritage. Cruz-Jansen (2002) argues that this phenomenon creates the category of "social whites" or individuals who attempt to be defined as white based on their social status. She argues that social whites can move up the racial hierarchy but would never get to the top. One can never completely eliminate the stigma associated with black or Indian racial characteristics. As my grandmother used to say, *"aunque te vistas de ceda, mona te quedas"* ("you may dress in silk but you are still a monkey").

While to marry white is to better the race, to marry black (or darker than you) is to worsen the race. It is not unusual to hear parents refer to their darker children as *"grifos"* who have "kinky" hair. Based on this principal, my family can argue that if my daughter dates a dark-skinned man she is damaging her heritage, taking a step back in the process of bettering the race, and that their children would be black and ugly.

Latinos, Race, and Their Interaction with U.S. Culture

The available research on race issues among Latinos in the United States suggests at least two patterns. Latinos who immigrate to the United States often find themselves being categorized with other Latinos who are different from them in social class, nation of origin, and economic status in their nation of origin. This classification puts them in the same level of second-class citizenship with African Americans. They find themselves being classified as minorities with African Americans and often find themselves in contact with African Americans in their neighborhoods and employment. It is common for many of them to resent the categorization as Hispanics and what they may consider to be a demotion in social class. Many of their issues of race, which are often denied in Latin America, move to the forefront as they now find themselves living in proximity to and relating to people they often see as inferior. Their need for affiliation forces them to associate with other Latinos whom they would have not associated with in their country of origin because of the differences in social class.

Oboler (1995) conducted a study to explore the experience of immigration among Latinos from different Latin American countries. She interviewed a number of recent immigrants registered in an English program. She found that many of the individuals interviewed resented the term *Hispanic* in part because it classified them as something other than white. The term *Hispanics* often negates their racial identification in their countries of origin and their positions of power.

Oboler suggested that self-identification for the immigrant group is also influenced by perceived position in the country of origin. Those who have less power may see the classification as Hispanics as a step up in the social hierarchy while those who are in a powerful position in their countries of origin may find themselves being classified as less than others in the United States.

Supporting Oboler's argument, Etzioni (2003) argues that the vast majority of Latinos prefer to classify themselves as a variety of ethnic groups rather than as one. Etzioni points out that in the 1990 census, when people were allowed to check "other" as a racial category, the vast majority of the ten million people who choose to do so were Latinos. Logan (2003) analyzed the 2000 census data for Latinos and found that about half of Latinos identified themselves by using their own terminology such as "Latino," "Hispanic," or other similar words.

The grouping with other Latinos from different countries is not the only difficulty Oboler identified among her interviewees. She noticed that many were clearly disturbed by being called black even when they possess the physical characteristics normally coded as "black" in the United States. To illustrate this she presented a portion from an interview with a Garifuna man (Garifuna are a group of African descendants who live in northern Honduras): "Now, I don't get offended when they call me Hispanic, even though I am not Hispanic. What bothers me is when they call me black, because I don't offend anyone, and I don't like it when they offend me" (1995, 130). Although racial classifications are part of Latin American lives, the clear distinction in race-based categories found in the United States appears to be a novelty for recent immigrants.

On the other hand, individuals who have lived in the United States for a longer period and those who are born in the United States from Latino parents tend to accept the label of minority and to ally themselves with others in that same situation. Safa (1998) argues that this is the case with "Neuyoricans" (Puerto Ricans from New York) who have created a minority identity apart from that on the island. This identity tends to borrow from African American popular culture to the extent that many of the practices are indistinguishable. In doing so they not only affirm their position as a distinct group with distinct experiences from Puerto Ricans on the island but also they embrace their African heritage to an extent that those on the island would not.

Latinos, Race, and Religious Life

Religious expression is essential in the lives of Latinos in the United States. According to Deck and Tirres (1999), Latinos have a rich religious history that has also been affected by cultural perceptions of race. As with the racial origins of Latino culture, Latino religious history is strongly influenced by at least three distinct traditions: Catholicism, native religions, and African religions. Eventually, the mixture of these influences created unique religious expressions that include African and native expressions of religious life. Along with Catholicism and Protestantism, Latino religious lives involve the influences of Santerismo, Curanderos, Spiritualism, Candomble, and other alternative religious expressions.

Latinos in the United States continue to identify as Catholics. Espinosa, Elizondo, and Miranda (2003), in a national survey, found that 70 percent of American Latinos reported being Catholics. They argue that this number is similar to those found in other surveys done in the 1970s. They did find, however, that participation in the Catholic Church tends to drop in subsequent generations so that second- and third-generation Latinos report lesser percentages of membership in the Catholic Church. They found that 23 percent of American Latinos are Protestant. They also point out that of those identifying themselves as Catholics, 26 percent reported having a born-again experience, usually associated with the Charismatic Movement within the Catholic Church or with Evangelical/Pentecostal Protestantism. In fact, they found that 28 percent of Latinos report being Pentecostal or Charismatic. These findings support the conclusions of Levitt (2002), who argues that by 2025 half of all Latinos will be Protestant.

Latino religious expressions have significantly influenced the ideas of race and ethnic identity. Since the colonization period, religious practices were used as ways to negotiate race and influence racial perception. Fitzpatrick (1987) argues that the religious practice of baptism among early black or native Catholics was often a step out of slavery for their children (particularly to those born from relationships between slave masters and black mistresses). The practice of selecting godparents and the social relationships that emerge out of that practice (compadres) also served to negotiate and change racial identification. A black person or a slave choosing a white godparent for their child allowed the child the opportunity to move higher in the color hierarchy.

The religious practices that emerge from the interaction of Catholicism and African or native beliefs are influential in the lives of Latinos. Many Caribbean Latinos are strongly influenced by Afro-Caribbean practices such as Santerismo. Santerismo is a religious system developed by slaves in the Caribbean after being forced to convert to Catholicism. It involves traditional African religious practices hidden behind Catholic practices. For example, in Santerismo many Catholic saints actually represent African gods. Often these alternative religious beliefs are held alongside other religious identities. It is not uncommon for most believers of Santerismo to also be devoted Catholics.

The use of Curanderos (female construction: Curanderas) or other forms of native healers is also a common experience among Latinos. Curanderos are natural healers similar to medicine doctors in some native traditions who assist with the healing of the body and the soul. The religious meaning of the Curandero differs among Latino groups. The Curandero is often used by Latinos as a substitute for or as an addition to traditional medicine.

Both African and native religious traditions are extremely influential in traditional religious practices among Latinos. For example, the Latino church, particularly those attended by Latinos from the Caribbean, often struggles with the format of the worship between traditional "High Church" services and more lively forms of worship influenced by Afro-Caribbean music. Goizueta (2003) argues that the Virgin of Guadalupe often referred to as "*La Morenita*" or "the dark-skinned woman" serves as an icon of Mexican identity. The African and native influence in Latino church life is also evident with the canonization of San Martin de Porres, a black Latino saint, and the recent canonization of Juan Diego, the native man who first reported the apparition of La Virgen de Guadalupe.

Racial Reconciliation and the Latino Church

Latin American society has barely begun to address issues of color. This lack of attention is in part attributed to the denial of racism in our culture. If we do not admit to racism we have nothing to address. While reading a recent article by De la Torre (1999), I was reminded of the words of a close friend. She often cites the old Cuban saying "*Aqui todos somos café con leche; Unos mas café, otros mas leche*" ("Here we are all coffee and milk; some more coffee, others more milk"). De La Torre points out that " '*leche*' " has access to employment, state services, power, wealth, and privilege, while '*café*' is disenfranchised. '*Leche*' is rich, civilized, intelligent, and modern, while '*café*' is poor, savage, ignorant and primitive." As long as Latinos deny their intergroup racism, "*leche*" will continue to have advantages that "*café*" does not.

The Latino church, as part of our community, participates in the sins of this community. The Latino denial of intergroup racism leaves the church with at least two significant problems. First, the Latino church falls into the trap of imitating the culture's attitude toward racism. In the church, racial attitudes are present, influence intergroup relations, and are denied as in the general Latino culture. Second, the church fails to take a stand against a significant social problem often perpetuating color-based stereotypes rather than challenging them.

What are we as church to do in response to intergroup racism? Needless to say, an elaborate answer to this question is beyond the scope of this paper. However, it would be irresponsible of me not to try at least a superficial outline of possible action steps.

First, as a church and as a culture we need to accept our responsibility regarding intergroup racism among Latinos. It is not enough for us to compare ourselves with other societies where racism is explicit in order to justify our own racial attitudes. A lesser sin is still a sin. Our expression of racism is different from expressions of racism in the United States, for example, but it is still racism and it is still evil. Throughout the centuries the church has assisted in perpetuating beliefs about racial superiority. From its involvement in the colonization process to the traditional association of white with good and black with evil, the church has played a crucial role in establishing and maintaining the structures that allowed for intergroup racism. It is necessary for the church to examine itself and challenge those ecclesiastical structures and teachings that promote race-based biases.

Second, it is crucial for the church to develop a theology of race that seeks to understand our own racial/ethnic realities. One possible starting point for Latinos involves a focus on our "mixed" heritage—mixed both culturally and racially. We are a *mestizo* culture—struggling with issues of identity, and with exclusion and marginalization. De la Torre (2002) argues that when we turn our attention to the biblical text we participate in a dialogue between the written word and the meaning of our identity. In reading the biblical text, our *mestizaje* should inform our interpretation. We discover that Jesus was from Galilee—a marginal region with ethnic mixture—and that Jesus himself had mixed ancestry. Jesus of Galilee is understandable to *mestizo* men and women because he himself experienced *mestizo* reality as his own. We believe in a Christ with mixed ethnic background. We also believe in a Christ who lived as an immigrant. Identification with that Christ requires us to accept both his multiethnic heritage and our own. De La Torre advocates for the reconciliation of different parts of our identity. Recognizing the multiethnic heritage of Latinos, he argues that it is from this existential space that we must construct the philosophical and theological bases upon which to reconcile our multiple parts. Rather than racial and cultural mixture being destructive, through Jesus of Galilee the living Mestizo Messiah (Elizondo 2004), there is unity, meaning, hope, and liberation. Indeed, the very future of humanity will increasingly be *mestizo* (Elizondo 2000), which means that as Latino Christians work to reconcile different elements of their multiethnic heritage, they are simply modeling a process increasingly relevant to a wider humanity.

Final Comments

As I close this discussion, I hope at a minimum the reader understands several things. First, as clearly explained by Dr. Meneses in a previous chapter, the physical and cultural markers of ethnic identity are socially determined rather than biologically given. The Latino community with its fluid ethnic and racial lines provides a rich example of the social construction of race and ethnicity.

Second, the classification of Latinos as one ethnic or racial group in the United States is a cultural, social, and political classification. Latino groups are extremely diverse not only in terms of cultural background or nation of origin but also in their own social construction of race and ethnicity.

Third, there is great need for further research that would stimulate a deeper understanding of issues related to diversity among Latinos and the Latino church. Until now, most psychological and sociological research has preferred either to conceptualize Latinos as one group or ignore intergroup differences in sampling, or to use one specific Latino group such as Mexicans or Puerto Ricans as representative of the whole Latino community. Both of these approaches ignore the immense differences among Latino groups. Regarding the theological literature, the issue of racism among Latinos has barely been addressed. We hope that upcoming books and chapters, like this one, will shed light on the issue. However, there continues to be a great need for further research.

Fourth, with the knowledge of the diversity among Latinos there is the need to develop a balance among individuals, groups, and the social understanding of the context in which these groups operate. As with many others, Latinos are individuals who are a part of multiple groups with multiple identities, operating within multiple social contexts. As with most other groups, the social construction of race among Latinos may vary across different contexts.

And finally, I hope the readers will critically analyze their own categories of race and be willing to suspend those categories in order to better understand the classifications others may use and the social utility of those classifications.

REFERENCES

Arora, Shirley L. 1995. Proverbs and prejudice: El Indio in Hispanic proverbial speech. *De Proverbio* 1(2), http//www.Hartford-hwp.com/archives/41/083.html. Accessed May 19, 2003.

Cruz-Janzen, M. 2002. Ethnic identity and racial formation: Race and racism American style and "a lo Latino." In *Transnational Latina/o communities: Politics, processes, and cultures*, ed. C. G. Vélez-Ibáñez, A. Sampalio, M. González-Estay, 147–66. Lanham, MD: Rowman & Littlefield.

Deck, A. F., and C. Tirres. 1999. Latino popular religion and the struggle for justice. In *Religion, race, and justice in a changing America*, ed. G. Orfield and H. J. Lebowitz, 137–52. New York: The Century Foundation Press.

De La Torre, M. A. 1999. Masking Hispanic Racism: A Cuban case study. *Journal of Hispanic/Latino Theology* 6:57–73.

———2002. *The quest for the Cuban Christ: A historical search*. Gainesville: University Press of Florida.

Dundes, Alan. 1975. Slur international: Folk Comparisons of ethnicity and national character. *Southern Folklore Quarterly* 39:15–38.

Elizondo, Virgil. 2000. *The future is mestizo: Life where cultures meet*. Boulder: University Press of Colorado.

———. 2004. *A God of incredible surprises: Jesus of Galilee*. Rowman & Littlefield.

Espinosa G., Elizondo, V., and Miranda, J. 2003. Hispanic churches in American public life: Summary of findings. Notre Dame, IN: Institute for Latino Studies.

Etzioni, A. 2003. Inventing Hispanics: A diverse minority resists being labeled. In *Race and ethnic relations* (13th ed.), ed. J. A. Kromkowski, 99–101. Guilford, CT: McGraw-Hill/Dushkin.

Fitzpatrick, J. P. 1971. *Puerto Rican Americans: The meaning of migration to the mainland.* Englewood Cliff, NJ: Prentice Hall.

Fletcher, M. A. 2002. The blond, blue-eyed face of Spanish TV. In *Race and ethnic relations,* 12th ed., ed. J. A. Kromkowski, 117–19. Guilford, CT: McGraw-Hill/Dushkin.

Goizueta, R. 2003. Our Lady of Guadalupe: The heart of Mexican identity. In *Religion and the Creation of Race and Ethnicity,* ed. C. Prentiss, 140–51. New York: New York University Press.

Hall, R. E. 1994. The "bleaching syndrome": Implications of light skin for Hispanic American assimilation. *Hispanic Journal of Behavioral Sciences* 16(3): 307–14.

Hernandez, J. 1994. Hispanics blend diversity. In *Handbook of Hispanic cultures in the United States: Sociology,* ed. F. Padilla, 17–34. Houston: Arte Público Press.

Lancaster, R. N. 1991. Skin color, race and racism in Nicaragua. *Ethnology* 30:339–53.

Levitt, Peggy. 2002. Two nations under God? Latino religious life in the United States. In *Latinos Remaking America.* Ed. Marcelo M. Suárez-Orozco and Mariela M. Paez. Berkeley and Los Angeles: University of California Press, 150–64.

Logan. John R. 2003. "How race counts for Hispanic Americans." Report of the Lewis Mumford Center, the University of Albany. Online: http://eric.ed.gov/ERICDocs/data/ericdocs2/content_storage_ 01/0000000b/80/23/25/15.pdf. Accessed May 28, 2006.

Lovell, P. A., and C. H. Wood. 1998. Skin color, racial identity, and life chances in Brazil. *Latin American Perspective* 25(3): 90–109.

Moore-Stevenson, A. 2002. Afro-Mexicans in Mexico and California, http//www .mundoafrolatino.com (accessed May 15, 2003).

Murguia, E., and E. Telles. 1996. Phenotype and schooling among Mexican Americans. *Sociology of Education* 69:276–89.

National Council of La Raza. 2002 (September). Worrisome income, poverty data for Latinos signal need for measures to spark economic opportunity, http://www .nclr.org/content/news/detail/2296. Accessed May 29, 2006.

Oboler, S. 1995. *Ethnic labels, Latino lives: Identity and the politics of (re)presentation in the United States.* Minneapolis: University of Minnesota Press.

Robles, Bárbara. 2004. An asset approach to education diversity policies: exporting democracy. *Aztlan: International Journal of Chicano Studies Research* 29: 195–97.

Safa, H. 1998. Race and national identity in the Americas. *Latin American Perspective* 25(3): 3–20.

Scarano, F. A. 1996. The Jibaro masquerade and the subaltern politics of creole identity formation in Puerto Rico, 1745–1823. *American Historical Review* 10:1398–1431.

U.S. Census Bureau. 2004a. U.S. Interim Projections by Age, Sex, Race, and Hispanic Origin, http//www.census.gov/ipc/www/usinterimproj. Accessed May 29, 2006.

Hispanic population passes 40 million; http//www.census.gov/popest/topics/methodology/v2004_nat_char_meth.html. Accessed November 14, 2005.

4

Culture Matters: Diversity in the United States and Its Implications

Michael Jindra

Discussion of multiculturalism more often involves injunctions about tolerance and mutual niceness than any serious exploration of what different cultures consist of or how they have created variations in basic behaviors.
—social historian Peter Stearns, *Chronicle of Higher Education*, May 2, 2003

Are there significant cultural differences among American ethnic groups? In 1986, when Nigerian novelist Wole Soyinka delivered his Nobel Prize lecture, he made blanket statements about the tendencies of the "black race" (Todorov 1995, 55–56). Most of us have heard generalizations about "races." As seen in previous chapters, the confusion of race and culture has a long history and is still common. A student of mine once expressed surprise that a Korean adopted by Americans acted more like an American than a Korean, assuming it was genetics that determined behavior rather than socialization. "Race" or biology does not account for group differences. What does? Culture, in fact, can explain much human diversity (Cohen 1998; Smith 2003, 150). Individuals can be socialized into different cultures with no regard to their phenotype, as in the case of adoptees. "Color" says little about culture.

    In this chapter, I will focus on the concept of culture and cultural differences. In God's eyes, we are the same, equally valued and appreciated. Culturally, we share similarities, such as a concern for marriage and the socialization of children. We all like good health and peace. Yet here, and in many other areas of culture, we also see significant differences. People throughout the world marry and rear children in quite different ways. Different cultures often focus on different ideals. Some are more hierarchical; others more egalitarian. Some stress social solidarity; others are more competitive. Styles of communication differ, and people have different senses of time, self, and space (Hall 1973). It is the key and complex role of culture that helps us understand differences among ethnic groups.

What Is Culture?

Culture is a complex topic, but simply put, culture is a social group's distinctive way of life, the beliefs and practices that members find "normal" and correct (Shweder 2003). Something as simple as a proper greeting turns out to reveal key features of a culture. Formal bowing in Japan tells us about the differing statuses of the individuals. Many cultures use different words when greeting someone, depending on whether one is meeting someone younger or older, a man or a woman, a friend or a stranger. Even languages such as Spanish, French, and German distinguish between formal and informal relationships, while Americans don't make such distinctions. This matches the American refusal to distinguish between "friends" and "acquaintances" in linguistic practice. When calling someone a "friend" in most other countries, it means we have a close, ongoing relationship with that person, while in the United States we use the term rather loosely, when we really mean "acquaintance" rather than "friend." This has caused confusion for international visitors who may assume something different from most Americans, and the topic is usually part of any "introduction to American culture" orientation for newcomers.

Likewise, many people from non-Western countries are shocked at the way many Americans pamper and even humanize pets, especially dogs and cats. Dogs in many cultures are not thought of as pets or companions, but instead may be used for hunting, protection, or as roving garbage collectors. In some cultures, dogs are what one eats. This is shocking to most Americans, who arbitrarily include dogs, cats, and horses in the category of "animals that are almost human," and thus should not be eaten (Sahlins 1976, 171). Most people in the world consider pet cemeteries, grooming salons, pet clothing, pet therapists, and even special food for pets as quite strange, and may critically note at the same time how senior citizens live in nursing homes instead of with family. Many are equally shocked to find that some senior citizens prefer this to living with family because they value their privacy and want to avoid being dependent on family. When we live abroad, we quickly learn that notions and practices of privacy and dependency can vary radically.

Cultures have developed in different locales, as geography and other factors facilitate the development of distinctive languages whose unique and key concepts and practices intimately tie back into and reinforce notions of cosmology and ethical practice. Differing key ideas and narratives (life is a circle, an eternal return; life is a linear path toward some better end; humans are intimately tied up with creation; humans are stewards or masters of creation) have crucial implications for practice and material culture (Smith 2003, 48ff.). Everything from art to the economy is affected. People who have close interactions will tend to learn and share similar patterns of discourse, behavior, and thought.

Different cultures and subcultures may value different emotional styles (Middleton 2003, 37–38). People in cultures differ over when to express emotions, and with what intensity. Many Asian cultures, for instance, value social grace and cohesion over personal expressiveness and independence (Hsu 1963). Recent studies also show that East Asians are more aware of social context than most Americans, who tend to focus on individual action. When describing scenes they have observed, East Asians describe the surroundings, whereas Americans focus on the movement (Nisbett 2003). Again, this is not due to any genetic difference, but to processes of socialization into one's culture. In Africa, social interdependence is stressed, while Americans stress independence and self-reliance. This has enormous implications for behavior, and can lead to many misunderstandings when individuals from the two cultures interact, especially over money matters (Maranz 2001).

Cultural values also help us understand how societies are organized and develop. The dominant American values of individualism and self-reliance (Holmes and Holmes 2002; see Kusserow 2004 for a more complex view of individualism) have helped produce a vibrant economy, but also family instability, a bureaucratic state that needs to provide a safety net, and a focus on rights over responsibilities; orientations toward progress, science, and exploration has led to many accomplishments and improvements, but also to occasional aggression, as in the case of Native Americans; and a focus on youth, mobility, and productivity that serves the economy but can lead to the devaluation of the elderly and their segregation from the rest of society (Kottak and Kozaitis 2003, 11–12). In sum, when we understand the role of culture, we take seriously how people's values and beliefs are connected with their practices and ways of life.

Culture is not a simple or uniform thing, however, because one may have competing definitions and practices of what is correct. Even more generally agreed upon values may be in tension with one another. In the United States, notions of "freedom" and "family" are strong, but they are in competition, since many Americans use their freedom to move away from their families and pursue careers. Also, most cultures today are not systems in the strict sense of the word, but composites or fragments of diverse origins. In the United States, different traditions (mostly from Europe) contributed to create the dominant culture (Huntington 2004). Most white Americans take these cultural values and practices for granted, and don't think of them as anything but "normal."

Cultures also change over time. While this has always happened, the process has been speeded up as technology has allowed more mobility, social groups come more in contact with other cultures, and the process of culture change becomes more intense. Borrowings of cultural elements occur, and the boundaries between cultures become more blurred (Bashkow 2004). Though intensified in recent times, this process has been occurring for a long time, especially in the Americas, with its fusion of European, Native American, and African histories (Walker 2001). Technology, social forces such as the media and advertising, and social movements also influence how cultures change. Over the last decades, white youth culture has continually appropriated portions of minority cultures, particularly inner-city black culture, in the belief that they are partaking of "black authenticity." Through media, we can consume other cultures or, more accurately, select portions of other cultures (Samuels 1991).

Focal Institutions

One way to understand the culture of a distinct social group is to examine specific cultural activities or symbols that offer a "window" into the culture. A classic example from anthropology is the Balinese (Indonesia) cockfight, which reveals key notions about gender, status, and worldview (Geertz 1973, 412ff.). Observing how people from different cultures deal with death always reveals fundamental notions about relationships and worldview (Corr, Nabe, and Corr 2000).

One can't always identify a "cultural focus" (Herskovits 1964, 182) in every culture, but important events, such as the life cycle rituals of weddings or funerals, reveal central concerns of specific cultures. In the United States, the court system could be a focal institution (Vansina 1994, 297n; Hammond 1998, 108). It embodies the long-standing customs and history of English common law, and is rooted in a central document, the Constitution, to define the rules by which Americans operate and to which new Americans swear allegiance. The court's contemporary importance signifies a move away from local authorities to centralized, bureaucratic rule, and it is relied upon to settle key moral issues, definitions of life and death, and redress of injustice. It prioritizes the individual and focuses on rights, rather than responsibilities. It certainly doesn't tell us everything about American culture, but it does give us an insight into central themes. For someone seeking to understand the United States, the court system is certainly one of the places to examine.

Likewise, for Americans involved with an unfamiliar culture, it pays to look for focal institutions or central events. Among Latinos (especially Mexicans), an institution that reveals key themes is the *Quinceañera* (fifteenth birthday) celebration of Latina womanhood. The event serves to introduce the girl to society as a young woman. The *Quinceañera* is hosted by the family, incorporates the relatives and friends of the family, and usually involves a Catholic mass. Preparations for the mass and following reception begin well in advance of the event, and the expense can be tremendous. The event tells us about gender ideals and relations, family status and connections, religious values and, more recently, the influence of popular culture. Like most rituals, the *Quinceañera* is not a tradition-bound event that has never changed. Though it may have roots in a combination of indigenous Indian and Spanish custom (Deiter 2002, 36), it actually became popular only in the twentieth century. Thus, it also reveals how culture changes. American popular culture, for instance, has become increasingly important among Latino youth, and the *Quinceañera* shows the tension between popular culture and Latino Catholicism. The secular focus of the event as a "debut" and show of ostentatious consumption sometimes overwhelms the religious meaning of the event as a demonstration of fidelity, and some Catholic churches are reacting by attempting to put a stronger Christian focus on the event (Deiter 2002).

When looking at focal institutions, one must always be aware of the partial, perspectival view they give us. The *Quinceañera* focuses more on female ideals. One would need to look elsewhere to find out more about male life, such as the bullfight, which contains ideas of hierarchy, honor, valor, style, and machismo (Graña 1987). It is, however, popular only in certain Latino countries and among certain groups of people, so, like the *Quinceañera*, it only gives a partial view.

Possible focal points among other ethnic groups are certainly debatable. Among Chinese and Koreans, the Confucian influence has maintained key notions of filial piety that have kept families strong, but also promoted family tensions. For African Americans, the black church has certainly been a source and outlet for much expressive culture, and has had a strong influence on other cultures nationally and internationally through its musical forms. The spirituality found in the black church has played a major role in the lives of African Americans, and in the way they "interpret, inform and reshape their social conditions" (Frederick 2003, ix). The movement came largely out of the black church, most black political leaders have been nurtured in the church, and social and community topics and issues of personal transformation are also discussed chiefly through the church.

Communication Styles

When entering another culture, differences in communication styles are likely to be some of the first things to be encountered (Hall 2002). One may be surprised or even shocked by how vocal the locals are, or how reticent they are, depending on what one is used to. East Asians, for instance, tend to be less outspoken and talkative than most Americans, a practice tied into a different worldview and understanding of self and other (Kim and Markus 2002). White Americans tend to be more comfortable with impersonal work relationships and mere acquaintances, while Latinos value developing closer friendships among people who work together. People in cultures that stress family loyalty will, in general, be less likely to sacrifice family relationships in order to further careers (Samovar, Porter, and Stefani 1998, 108f.). Along with this, many white Americans focus on efficiency and economy, sometimes to the neglect of social relationships.

Misunderstandings can easily occur unless one is aware of different communication styles. For instance, whites may regard blacks as less respectful when they are more vocal, while whites might seem to be insincere to blacks because they tend to hide their true feelings or ideas to maintain social peace (Kochman 1981; Hecht, Jackson, and Ribeau 2003). Another writer discussed how black and white women sometimes have "difficult" dialogues because of mutual stereotypes, but also how it is possible to develop good relationships (Houston 2000). Still another looked at other everyday interactions among people from different cultures that can cause hurt feelings or create misunderstandings (Williams 2000; cf. Martin 2000). Interactions between African Americans and Koreans, for example, can be tense, because African Americans want Korean grocers to be friendly and hire locals, while Koreans say it is not their culture to smile frequently with strangers. Koreans' strong family orientation means relatives are preferred over local people for jobs, which creates resentment (Kottak and Kozaitis 2003, 80). Competition for economic resources such as jobs and housing, and over political power, can cause tensions. Perceived discrimination and mutual stereotypes can create problems, for instance, between Latinos and African Americans (Niemann 1999).

Latino expressivity can be understood by comparing Latino notions of public space with Anglo-American ones, for example. Anglos generally construct invisible boundaries around their bodies, and apologies must be issued for even near bumping. Latinos would let this pass without comment, seeing it as normal. For Anglos, this space cannot be violated even verbally, since publicly flattering women is likely to be viewed as harassment, whereas it is a more ambiguous practice among Latinos.

Styles of public expressiveness vary among cultures. Misunderstandings and hurt feelings can easily result, especially in pluralistic work or social situations. Stereotypes about "rude" behavior can be reinforced, unless one has a deeper understanding of stylistic differences. As a first step, it is important to know the unique communication patterns and values of our own culture, and realize that not everyone shares them.

Family

Differences in family dynamics are other things one may notice among cultures (Lynch and Hanson 2004). If you are a white American, you may be surprised at how much family members of many minority ethnic groups rely on one another. People from other cultures may be surprised at how individualistic some white American family members are, as each person busily attends to his or her own activities. One article I have my students read, written from a Latino perspective, portrays white families as disconnected and disrespectful (Gangotena 2003), and while my white students tend to view the portrayal as exaggerated or even offensive, it has at least a ring of truth to it. (Films such as *Mississippi Masala* or *My Big Fat Greek Wedding* also portray ethnic family differences, a little over-the-top in the latter case.)

Family issues are central to all cultures. Compared with more individualistic white Americans, Latinos generally have a stronger focus on the extended family as a source of social and material support (Gangotena 2003;

Marín and Marín 1991). Issues of *machismo* and *marianismo* (male dominance, and female submission and domesticity, respectively) can create tensions and distance among Latino males and females (Abalos 2002). Generational tensions among Latinos growing up in the United States and their foreign-born parents have also created problems in families. Latino children have found American popular culture attractive, but its glorification of sexuality and delinquency is at odds with their parents' more conservative family and work-oriented values (Suro 1999, 3–26). As Carlos Pozzi points out in this text, children of immigrants may take on a different identity than that of their parents.

Family issues among African Americans are framed by a different history. The tragic nature of the forced relocation of slaves meant that most African social institutions, such as marriage customs, were severely broken by slavery in the New World. Under slavery, family life suffered, as spouses and children were often kept apart, and men were essentially emasculated, denied normal roles of husband and provider. According to sociologist Orlando Patterson (1998), problems that beset the African American family—such as low marriage and high single-parenthood rates, and tension between the sexes—can largely be traced back to the time of slavery.

Asian Americans generally carry the "model minority" stereotype of high academic and economic achievement, but also pay a price with high levels of family pressure to succeed, which creates its own family tensions, and sometimes alienation and loneliness (Nam 2001; Ng 1998). Not all Asian groups fit this stereotype, however. Some of those from rural parts of Southeast Asia, such as the Hmong, struggle economically in the United States, partially because their cultures were small-scale, relatively egalitarian cultures that did not have a tradition of literacy.

In most Asian cultures, the individual is not an entirely independent entity, but is seen as being bound in relationships. There is strong social pressure to conform, while respecting and honoring parents and elders are held in higher regard. The focus on hierarchy contrasts and sometimes clashes with the American emphasis on egalitarianism (such as the common American practice of using first names with strangers rather than surnames). Understandings of ethics can differ. Americans tend to see relational issues (e.g., caring for relatives) as a personal choice, while an Indian's decisions are influenced more by culturally determined obligations (Miller 1991). Shame, dependent on social context, is a stronger motivator among Asians (and in other areas such as the Mediterranean), whereas guilt, more individualistic and rooted in Christian theology, is stronger among Americans.

Asian families also have their battles with the influence of American popular culture. American dating practices, for instance, are not acceptable to many Asian families, especially more recent immigrants. American teens are given much more independence than in Asian families, especially in meeting members of the opposite sex. Some Indian parents, for instance, see this influence as "cultural contamination of the worst sort" (Hegde 1998, 49) when their children begin to act more like autonomous Americans (Nam 2001).

Many Asian Americans, especially Chinese and Koreans, are now Christians. Many Chinese have found aspects of Christianity compatible with Confucian moral values, with its focus on attachment to family, and this helps reinforce some of the traditional values in the face of American popular culture pressures on their children. The result is that tensions, especially on family and gender issues, are played out among three identities: American, Christian, and Chinese (Yang 1999). Though Asians now face less prejudice than other minority groups, they still have to deal with unique family and identity questions, as Peter Cha points out in his chapter.

Diversity within and between Cultures

Virtually all minorities in the United States display tremendous diversity of class, religion, ideology, and other factors. Not all members of an ethnic group share the central values of their own culture. Some Latinos ignore the *Quinceañera*. Some blacks are alienated from historic African American churches, are Muslim, or find liturgical or other traditions such as the Jehovah's Witnesses more attractive. Women and men may have different perspectives on practices or ideals.

Class is an important factor when considering cultural differences (Hall, Neitz, and Battani 2003, 43ff.). People in different ethnic groups but in the same social class may have commonalities. The upper classes of different ethnicities may share tastes in music, food, or religious or political beliefs. Lower-class whites may reject aspects of middle- or upper-class whites. But social classes within an ethnic group also share many ethnic traits (Landrine and Klonoff 1996, 88; Pattillo-McCoy 1999, 12; Abrahams 1970, 22ff.), so ethnicity is clearly important. And while the similar classes of different ethnic groups have commonalities, there are significant differences among them, which can only be related to ethnicity.

The level of "acculturation" to dominant Euro-American values and practices varies widely among minority individuals. Acculturation can be understood through surveys and ethnographic research that examines the strength of beliefs and practices unique to ethnic group members (Landrine and Klonoff 1996, 62ff.). When compared with practices of the dominant culture, minorities can range from "traditional" to "acculturated" with "bicultural" in between (Landrine and Klonoff 1996; Padilla 1980). Most often, traditional cultural practices are maintained through family and religion, while acculturation to the dominant culture occurs through schools and popular culture. The speed of this process, however, has many variables, from family structure to societal reception (Portes and Rumbaut 2001, chap. 3).

Socially constructed notions of racial difference have made it harder for some groups, such as blacks, to enter the dominant culture (Yancey 2003, 156ff.). Other groups, such as some Asians, have found it easier. Some resist acculturation, and prefer oppositional identities, sometimes in response to discrimination or rejection from dominant cultures (Pattillo-McCoy 1999, 120ff.).

If we try to treat all people just "as individuals" and ignore the different histories and cultures of peoples, and how they may be subtly stereotyped by others, we do not realize the obstacles that minorities often face (Plaut 2002). As mentioned above, cultures are not entirely unified or well defined, but are often sites of conflict. Dominant groups have used socially constructed notions about minority groups (such as "racial" tendencies) to control people and create divisions and social hierarchies among cultures in a bid to maintain positions of dominance (Landrine and Klonoff 1996, 8ff.). Minority groups of all kinds (not only ethnic but also religious) must deal with pressures to either assimilate to dominant group ideals, and thus give up part of their identity, or to reject some of those dominant ideals and thus risk continued stigmatization and marginalization (Young 2001; Shannon 2001).

Culture is something we all have whether we know it or not, while "ethnicity" is consciously adopted identity that can be changed (Waters 1990). It can also be imposed by others. African Americans, for instance, are sometimes considered "white" in Africa, and "black" in the United States, no matter what their skin color. Former tennis champion Yannick Noah, whose father and mother were from Cameroon and France, respectively, has mentioned that he is considered white in Africa, and black in France (Landrine and Klonoff 1996, 13). Out of the contact of different cultures may come an enormous amount of creativity, along with the destabilization of traditional identities as people combine cultural symbols/practices in unique ways to create new expressive forms, a process that postcolonial scholars refer to as "hybridity" (Bhabha 1990).

What Do We Want? Cultural Influences on Motivation

In the United States, it is common for us to want to see people as individuals, "deep down," and not as members of groups. This dominant "sameness" model argues that we are essentially "all the same" or that "we all want the same thing" (Plaut 2002, 373, 376). Euro-Americans especially give priority to the individual and thus tend to ignore the social and cultural context of individuals. Thus, Euro-American views of diversity are rather superficial, regarded simply as something visible (Wood 2003). In other words, cultural differences "are superficial and mostly irrelevant" (Plaut 2002, 365, 372). Contributing to this, many scholars have a view of human nature that tends to view humans as rational "instrumentalists" or utilitarians whose goal is to acquire more resources and power or "maximize their utility," to use the economics language from where this often originates (Douglas and Ney 1998).

Scholars who take religion and culture seriously, however, do not assume, ethnocentrically, that all people want the same things, or are like "us." Instead, humans are regarded as "moral, believing" creatures whose basic orientation is toward finding meaning in often contrasting narratives, whether ideological (e.g., nationalist or progressive), religious, or otherwise (Smith 2003, 63ff.). We want different things and have different priorities (Selznick 1992, 527). For instance, students from different ethnic groups "often bring dramatically different sets of values to day-to-day classes in high school," such as differing study habits or social activity (Light 2001, 140). Many college students are motivated by the "success" narrative popular in our culture, and believe that college is primarily a way to a better job and life. Others are motivated by an "expressive" narrative (think of the writers Thoreau and Emerson, or many artists), and look to college as a way to understand beauty or sharpen their talents of self-expression. Both "success" and "expressive" narratives are found in American culture, though the former may be the dominant one, and has often been used to define American culture.

In other cultures, the dominant narratives often concern the importance of social bonding (such as kin loyalty), with less value put on the entrepreneurial individualists that the United States produces in abundance. In the United States, commerce requires long work hours and mobility in people and jobs, which hurts social bonds. This is one reason why economic productivity has tended to be high in the United States. But the Amish, for instance, explicitly reject modes of life that would earn them higher incomes if it means neglecting faith and family. Different cultural (and subcultural) emphases on living in the present or for the future influence economic indicators (Day, Papataxiarchis, and Stewart 1999).

In order to understand contrasting cultural orientations, one must reach back into history and examine the interaction of geography, history, social organization, and worldview (e.g., Forde 1954). These factors all influence the practices and patterns of ethnic groups, such as their predominance in certain occupations. Literacy rates, locations on trading routes, and beliefs about personal or family success all play a role (Sowell 1996). Cultural norms are also influenced tremendously by different environments and social structures. When Germany was split into east and west after World War II, the ensuing forty-five years of life under radically different political economies created two "mutually unintelligible ways of thinking about the world" (Bellah 1998, 614). Cultural beliefs and practices may have been formulated under situations of oppression, such as slavery (Patterson 1998), or in environments where opportunities were severely limited (Ogbu 2000, 194). In other words, cultures change when they adapt to circumstances not all of their own making. Limited job opportunities may help slot ethnic groups toward certain enterprises or occupations, such as when labor discrimination forced Chinese immigrants into operating laundries and restaurants where they weren't a threat to others (Sowell 1996, 224).

The topic of cultural differences is a sensitive one. In order to unify cultures, to lessen conflict, or for fear of offending someone, many scholars, educators, and others tend to emphasize human similarities and downplay the differences (Plaut 2002, 375f.; Shweder 2003, 4). Many textbooks prefer noncontroversial statements of tolerance, and refuse to deal with the complex realities of cultural difference. Many social scientists deny "the existence of cultural boundaries just when so many peoples are being called upon to mark them" by promoting ethnic identities and diversity (Sahlins 1999, 414). Not only does this distort cultures but it also exacerbates the tendency in the dominant culture to ignore the differences, and thus disadvantages minorities who see and live these differences all the time, and often feel excluded or de-valued because of them (Kim and Markus 2002; Markus, Steele, and Steele 2002, 454).

Social Issues, Structure, and Culture

The above discussion should give us a sense of how culture is related to eco-nomic indicators such as income or social indicators such as suicide rates (which is related to the level of social bonding), health, crime, or education. Culture certainly plays a role, but there are clearly other important factors also, such as the "structure" of the economy, or systemic discrimination that can in-fluence these social factors. When looking at the social problems of other groups, it may be tempting to blame these people directly for their own prob-lems by arguing, "We don't have these problems. Why do they? Something must be wrong with them." On the other end, the desire not to "blame" a cul-ture for problems makes it easy to look only to external, structural factors of so-ciety (such as racism) to explain issues such as poverty and education, when culture is clearly an important factor (Patterson 1998, viii; Thernstrom and Thernstrom 2003, 83).

Understanding the role of culture helps us avoid both extremes. Culture is the mediating element between the structural and the personal; it is a struc-ture, in a sense, since it has a power that is hard to resist, but yet cultural values and behaviors involve some choice. In some circumstances, individuals can join or opt out of specific cultural behaviors. The Bible, in fact, tells us to look for sin in structures, cultures, and, of course, in persons (Myers 2003).

Cultural and structural factors often work together in complex ways. Cul-tural factors, such as the high rates of single parenthood among African Amer-icans mentioned above, have kept many African Americans from rising into the middle class. But the structural force of persistent residential segregation has also held back black attempts to rise into the middle class (and is one rea-son why one can find commonalities across ethnic lines). While residential segregation among whites and many minority groups has declined signifi-cantly, it remains stubbornly high between blacks and whites (Massey and Denton 1993). The causes are complex, but it certainly involves images and fears of blacks that are reinforced by distorted media coverage, which can be used by real estate agents to create selling pressures in areas that are changing. Ideas about "racial" difference, a reflexive antagonism toward people who look different, and cultural differences on all sides combine to reinforce segrega-tion. Different expressive styles and priorities create feelings of estrangement and resentment, while competition over jobs and resources also plays a role.

Segregation "created the structural conditions for the emergence of an op-positional culture that devalues work, schooling, and marriage and that stresses attitudes and behaviors that are antithetical and often hostile to success in the larger economy" (Massey and Denton 1993, 8). Segregation also has a significant impact on black middle-class neighborhoods, many of which suffer from the same problems, though to a lesser extent, as lower-class black neighborhoods. "Gangsta styles" of consumption are often just as attractive to middle-class youth, a few of whom turn to crime to maintain status, while others success-fully resist these styles, and are less popular as a result (Pattillo-McCoy 1999, 120ff.).

The history of white oppression of blacks has understandably prompted suspicious attitudes toward dominant white practices. This unfortunately has contributed to attitudes that have kept some African Americans from doing bet-ter in school. High-achieving black high school students are sometimes accused of "acting white" by other blacks, hurting both their performance and others who have higher aspirations (Ogbu 2003). There are also other explanations for "academic disengagement" among black students, some of which relate to specif-ically black peer pressure, and others to pressures that are common across all American cultures (Ogbu 2003, 188–217). The powerful role of the media (through television, film, music, and advertising), for instance, can dramatically influence cultural styles and attitudes of mass society, and targeted subgroups such as teens (Hall, Neitz, and Battani 2003).

Implications: Ourselves and Others

Keep in mind that while we may have described some key elements of some ethnic cultures, we have only brushed the surface. The richness of these cul-tures is something that can be brought out only with a much fuller portrayal, as will be found in many of the sources cited in this chapter. Also, it is important to remember that while culture is a consensus, there are always dissenting ele-ments. Other factors, such as class, age, and religious diversity within ethnic cultures, mean that any cultural patterns can always be questioned, and one will always find contrasting subcultures in each ethnic culture. People can ad-here to or reject their ostensible ethnic identities, and they can even do this sev-eral times over their lives. Or, more commonly, they can adapt different elements of ethnic identities over time. They can have ambivalent feelings toward their ethnicity. They could be "third-culture" individuals, at home in no particular ethnicity or country (especially if having had an international upbringing in missions or foreign service).

How do we relate to people from cultures other than our own? How do we understand cultural practices different from our own? We are more comfortable with "our own kind," but our Christian faith contains a strong orientation to reach out to others unlike ourselves (Deut 10:19). It also teaches us to be wary about putting our own ethnic identity above our unity in the faith. Christianity, from early in its history, has regarded cultural difference not primarily as an ob-stacle, but as a potential strength. The notion of communion (e.g., of the Trinity, of saints, expressed in the Eucharist) found in Christianity assumes a "certain theological understanding of human life," that humanity is fully realized in a community, where different voices come together (Taylor 2002, 191).

Despite its problems—such as confusing American culture with Christianity—Christianity has been better at adapting to other cultural contexts than other religions (Sanneh 1989). Christianity does not make one particular language into "God's language," as Islam does with Arabic (though it came close with Latin). The Christian notion of *imago dei* emphasizes that all people are created in God's image and are worthy of respect. The modern notion of human rights has a strong Christian heritage (Tierney 1997). The notion of original sin helps us recall that all peoples are prone to the temptations of ethnocentrism, while also remembering that there are universal truths that God has called us to, and to which we can compare all cultures.

Cultures embody traditions. Among other things, a tradition is an argument about character and virtue, about the good (MacIntyre 1984, 221ff.; Griffin and Walker 2004). Unless one is a total relativist, evaluating the worth of different cultural practices is unavoidable. This, of course, can be problematic when it leads to ethnocentrism, but its opposite, which is perhaps more common among academics, winds up in an implausible relativism (Moody-Adams 1997, 15, 210ff.). But we can only do this once we have made an attempt to understand the culture (Taylor 1994, 70; Mouw 1987). There are no "perfect" cultures, and our imperfect understanding of other cultures means that we should be careful when we are tempted to criticize other cultures.

It is important to find a balance between the twin errors of ethnocentrism and relativism. The temptation to venerate our way of life is matched by the temptation to say that one cannot judge them at all. Both are mistakes. The Bible has clear statements of morals and laws such as humility and hospitality, and opposition to idolatry and selfishness, but it also allows for variability in practice. Christians have recognized *adiaphora*, a Greek term that was adopted by Christian theologians to allow for practices that are "neither commanded nor forbidden in the Word of God." The New Testament Church emerged out of the particularistic Jewish culture, and had to learn to adapt to a situation where many of the Jewish laws did not apply. Even apostles such as Peter had problems with this, as described in Acts 10–11. In 1 Corinthians 9–10, Paul discusses becoming all things to all people, which, of course, is not an argument for relativism, but an expression of the Christian virtues of self-sacrifice and of love for neighbor to serve the higher purpose of loving God.

Differing ideas and practices also exist for our own benefit, as alternative practices with which we can evaluate our own cultures, and avoid falling into an unthinking defense of our own way of life. Christians such as Eloise Meneses and John Stapleford (2000) have examined different cultural forms in order to enable us to find "balanced Christian living in different cultural systems." For example, one Japanese American Christian reflected on the different strengths and weaknesses of the various influences on her: her Japanese family upbringing, and the American popular and school cultures. She has learned to gain strength from hard work and sacrifice, but to try to be more open about family problems, and not be silenced by shame (Nagasawa 2000). In other words, from a Christian perspective she has tried to get "the best of both (cultural) worlds."

Along the same lines, a recent book highlights some of the things the "church can learn from ethnic immigrant cultures" (Griffin and Walker 2004). According to the authors, ethnic immigrant cultures present an alternative to the consumer-oriented assimilationist culture that dominates the United States. Their focus on tradition, community, and responsible authority goes against the grain of a fast-changing individualistic society. The church, they argue, can learn how to "not be conformed to this world" by the examples of ethnic cultures, which retain a distinctive tradition that includes strong bonds and commitments. At the same time, we should also remember not to value our ethnic identity above our identity as Christians.

The valuing of difference has been a part of Christian theology since the beginning, though Christians haven't always followed through on the practice, as we see in other chapters of this book. Living, working, and worshiping in multicultural environments may make us uncomfortable at first, if we are not used to doing this. Just as Christ reached out to diverse peoples, we should do the same. Seek out multicultural neighborhoods and churches. Spend time just hanging out, getting to know the people, places, and history. Find out what the most important events are, the "focal institutions" or the key symbols. (Ethnic festivals usually offer a superficial portrayal of cultures.) You may not know the cultural rules or language, and it may be initially awkward. You may not like everything you see, but you will learn new ideas and practices, and you may begin to get a sense of the internal dynamics of cultures, and the challenges members of these cultures face as minorities. Communication and reconciliation among peoples from different backgrounds will not take place without an understanding of the complexity of their unique cultures.

REFERENCES

Abalos, David T. 2002. *The Latino male: A radical redefinition.* Boulder, CO: Lynne Rienner.

Abrahams, Roger. 1970. *Positively black.* New York: Prentice Hall.

Bashkow, Ira. 2004. A Neo-Boasian conception of cultural boundaries. *American Anthropologist* 106(3):443–58.

Bellah, Robert. 1998. Is there a common American culture? *Journal of the American Academy of Religion* 66(3):613–25.

Bhabha, Homi. 1990. *Nation and narration.* London: Routledge.

Cohen, Mark Nathan. 1998. Culture, not race, explains human diversity. *Chronicle of Higher Education* (April 17):B4–B5.

Corr, Charles, Clyde Nabe, and Donna M. Corr. 2000. *Death and dying, life and living.* 3rd ed. Belmont, CA: Wadsworth.

Day, Sophie. Evthymios Papataxiarchis, and Michael Stewart. 1999. *Consider the lilies of the field.* Boulder, CO: Westview.

Deiter, Kristen. 2002. From church blessing to Quinceañera Barbie: America as "spiritual benefactor" in La Quinceañera. *Christian Scholar's Review* 32(1):31–48.

Douglas, Mary, and Steven Ney. 1998. *Missing persons.* Berkeley and Los Angeles: University of California Press.

Forde, Daryll, ed. 1954. *African worlds.* London: Oxford University Press.

Frederick, Marla. 2003. *Between Sundays: Black women and everyday struggles of faith.* Berkeley and Los Angeles: University of California Press.

Gangotena, Margarita. 2003. The rhetoric of *La Familia* among Mexican Americans. In *Our voices: Essays in culture, ethnicity and communication,* ed. A. Gonzalez, M. Houston, and V. Chen, 72–73. Los Angeles: Roxbury.

Geertz, Clifford. 1973. *The interpretation of cultures.* New York: Basic.

Graña, César. 1987. The bullfight and Spanish national decadence. *Society* 24(5):33–37.

Griffin, Mark, and Theron Walker. 2004. *Living on the borders.* Grand Rapids, MI: Brazos.

Hall, Bradford J. 2002. *Among cultures: Challenges of communication.* Fort Worth: Harcourt College.

Hall, Edward T. 1973. *The silent language.* Garden City, NY: Anchor Press/Doubleday.

Hall, John R., Mary Jo Neitz, and Marshall Battani. 2003. *Sociology on culture.* New York: Routledge.

Hammond, Phillip. 1998. *With liberty for all.* Louisville: Westminster John Knox.

Hecht, Michael L., Ronald L. Jackson II, and Sidney A. Ribeau. 2003. *African American communication.* 2nd ed. Mahwah, NJ: Lawrence Erlbaum Associates.

Hegde, Radha S. 1997. Swinging the trapeze: The negotiation of identity among Asian Indian immigrant women in the United States. In *Communication and identity across cultures,* ed. A. Gonzalez and D. V. Tanno, 34–35. Thousand Oaks, CA: Sage.

Herskovits, Melville. 1964. *Cultural dynamics.* New York: Knopf.

Holmes, Lowell D., and Ellen Rhoads Holmes. 2002. The American cultural configuration. In *Distant mirrors: American as a foreign culture.* 3rd ed. ed. P. DeVita and J. Armstrong. Belmont, CA: Wadsworth.

Houston, Marsha. 2000. When black women talk with white women. In *Our voices: Essays in culture, ethnicity and communication,* ed. A. Gonzalez, M. Houston, and V. Chen. Los Angeles: Roxbury.

Hsu, Francis L. K. 1963. *Clan, caste and club.* Princeton, NJ: D. Van Nostrand.

Huntington, Samuel. 2004. *Who are we? The challenges to America's national identity.* New York: Simon & Schuster.

Kim, Heejung S., and Hazel Rose Markus. 2002. Freedom of speech and freedom of silence: An analysis of talking as a cultural practice. In *Engaging cultural differences,* ed. R Shweder, M. Minow, and H. R. Markus. New York: Russell Sage Foundation.

Kochman, Thomas. 1981. *Black and white styles in conflict.* Chicago: University of Chicago.

Kottak, Conrad Phillip, and Kathryn A. Kozaitis. 2003. *On being different.* 2nd ed. Boston: McGraw Hill.

Kusserow, Adrie. 2004. American individualisms: Child rearing and social class in three neighborhoods. New York: Palgrave Macmillan.

Landrine, Hope, and Elizabeth A. Klonoff. 1996. *African American acculturation.* Thousand Oaks, CA: Sage.

Light, Richard J. 2001. *Making the most of college.* Cambridge, MA: Harvard University Press.

Lynch, Eleanor W., and Marci J. Hanson. 2004. *Developing cross-cultural competence.* 3rd ed. Baltimore: Brookes Publishing.

MacIntyre, Alasdair. 1984. *After virtue.* South Bend, IN: Notre Dame University Press.

Maranz, David. 2001. *African friends and money matters.* Dallas: SIL International.

Marín, G., and B. V. Marín. 1991. *Research with Hispanic populations.* Newbury Park, CA: Sage.

Markus, Hazel R., Claude M. Steele, and Dorothy M. Steele. 2002. Color blindness as a barrier to inclusion: Assimilation and nonimmigrant minorities. In *Engaging Cultural Differences*, ed. R. Shweder, M. Minow, and H. R. Markus, 453–72. New York: Russell Sage Foundation.

Martin, Judith. 2000. Everyone behaving badly. *New York Times Book Review.* October 15.

Massey, Douglas, and Nancy Denton. 1993. *American apartheid.* Cambridge, MA: Harvard University Press.

Meneses, Eloise Hiebert, and John Stapleford. 2000. Defeating the Baals: Balanced Christian living in different cultural systems. *Christian Scholar's Review* 30(1):83–106.

Middleton, Dwight R. 2003. *The challenge of human diversity.* 2nd ed. Prospect Heights, IL: Waveland.

Miller, Joan G. 1991. A cultural perspective on the morality of beneficence and interpersonal responsibility. In S. Ting-Toomey and F. Korzenny (eds.). *International and Intercultural Communication Annual* 15: 11–27.

Moody-Adams, Michelle. 1997. *Fieldwork in familiar places.* Cambridge, MA: Harvard University Press.

Mouw, Richard J. 1987. Christian philosophy and cultural diversity. *Christian Scholar's Review* 17(2):109–21.

Myers, Bryant. 2003. *Walking with the poor.* Maryknoll, NY: Orbis.

Nagasawa, Mako. 2000. The best of both worlds. *Regeneration Quarterly* 6(3):26–28.

Nam, Vickie, ed. 2001. *Yell-oh girls!: Emerging voices explore culture, identity and growing up Asian American.* New York: HarperCollins.

Ng, Franklin. 1998. *Asian American family life and community.* New York: Garland.

Niemann, Yolanda Flores. 1999. Social ecological contexts of prejudice between Hispanics and blacks. In *Race, ethnicity and nationality in the United States*, ed. P. Wong, 170–90. Boulder, CO: Westview.

Nisbett, Richard. 2003. *The geography of thought: How Asians and Westerners think differently . . . and why.* New York: Free Press.

Ogbu, John. 2000. Understanding cultural diversity and learning. In *Schooling the symbolic animal*, ed. B. Levinson, 190–206. Lanham, MD: Rowman & Littlefield.

———. 2003. *Black American students in an affluent suburb.* Mahwah, NJ: Lawrence Erlbaum.

Padilla, A. 1980. *Acculturation.* Boulder, CO: Westview.

Patterson, Orlando. 1998. *Rituals of blood: Consequences of slavery in two American centuries.* New York: Basic Civitas.

Pattillo-McCoy, Mary. 1999. *Black picket fences.* Chicago: University of Chicago Press.

Plaut, Victoria C. 2002. Cultural models of diversity in America: The psychology of difference and inclusion. In *Engaging cultural differences*, ed. R Shweder, M. Minow, and H. R. Markus, 365–95. New York: Russell Sage Foundation.

Portes, Alejandro, and Rubén G. Rumbaut. 2001. *Legacies: The story of the immigrant second generation.* Berkeley and Los Angeles: University of California Press.

Sahlins, Marshall. 1976. *Culture and practical reason.* Chicago: University of Chicago Press.

———. Two or three things that I know about culture. *Journal of the Royal Anthropological Institute* 5:399–422.

Samovar, Larry A., Richard Porter, and Lisa A. Stefani. 1998. *Communication between cultures.* 3rd ed. Belmont, CA: Wadsworth.

Samuels, David. 1991. The rap on rap. *The New Republic* 205(20):24–29.

Sanneh, Lamin. 1989. *Translating the message: The missionary impact on culture*. Mary-knoll, NY: Orbis.

Selznick, Philip. 1992. *The moral commonwealth: Social theory and the promise of community*. Berkeley and Los Angeles: University of California Press.

Shannon, Christopher. 2001. *A world made safe for differences*. Lanham, MD: Rowman and Littlefield.

Shweder, Richard. 2003. *Why do men barbecue?* Cambridge, MA: Harvard University Press.

Smith, Christian. 2003. *Moral, believing animals: An essay on human personhood and culture*. Oxford: Oxford University Press.

Sowell, Thomas. 1996. *Migrations and cultures: A world view*. New York: Basic.

Suro, Roberto. 1999. *Strangers among us: Latino lives in a changing America*. New York: Vintage.

Taylor, Charles. 1994. *Multiculturalism: Examining the politics of recognition*. Ed. A. Gutman. Princeton, NJ: Princeton University Press.

———. 2002. Democracy, inclusive and exclusive. In *Meaning and modernity: Religion polity and self*, ed. R. Madsen, William Sullivan, Ann Swidler, Steven Tipton. Berkeley and Los Angeles: University of California Press.

Thernstrom, Abigail, and Stephan Thernstrom. 2003. *No excuses: Closing the racial gap in learning*. New York: Simon & Schuster.

Tierney, Brian. 1997. *The idea of natural rights*. Atlanta: Scholars Press.

Todorov, Tzvetan. 1995. *The morals of history*. Minneapolis: University of Minnesota Press.

Vansina, Jan. 1994. *Living with Africa*. Madison: University of Wisconsin Press.

Walker, Sheila S., ed. 2001. *African roots/American cultures*. Lanham, MD: Rowman and Littlefield.

Waters, Mary C. 1990. *Ethnic options: Choosing identities in America*. Berkeley and Los Angeles: University of California Press.

Williams, Lena. 2000. *It's the little things: The everyday interactions that get under the skin of blacks and whites*. New York: Harcourt.

Wood, Peter. 2003. *Diversity: The invention of a concept*. San Francisco: Encounter.

Yancey, George. 2003. *Who is white?: Latinos, Asians, and the new black/nonblack divide*. Boulder, CO: Lynne Rienner.

Yang, Fenggang. 1999. *Chinese Christians in America*. Pittsburgh: Pennsylvania State University Press.

Young, Iris Marion. 2001. Justice and the politics of difference. In *The new social theory reader*, ed. S. Seidman, and J. Alexander. London: Routledge.

5

Developing Multicultural Competency

J. Derek McNeil and Carlos Pozzi

A few years ago I (McNeil) had a European American student in my diversity (psychology) class who was just plain tired of all this multicultural stuff, and she felt irritated enough to say so during a lecture. As an African American instructor teaching a course on diversity, I recognize the tense nature of the material and I anticipate strong reactions to the class. Moreover, the course is required, so there may be a number of students who enter the experience already feeling uncomfortable with the subject matter, and some may even be a bit hostile. I have to expect that there may be students who finish the course unconvinced about the importance of developing multicultural skills, although I hope that they leave more informed. However, I seldom have students in the class that are willing to reveal this degree of annoyance. In this particular case I had a difficult time simply dismissing this student as just another unenlightened neophyte because, quite frankly, I liked her. I was her instructor in another course where she showed real intellectual talent and clinical aptitude. Yet, in the diversity course she seemed emotionally overwhelmed with the content and the process. Learning how "ethnic minorities" were institutionally disadvantaged and, conversely, how European Americans had a systemic advantage, seemed disturbing to her understanding of the world. While acknowledging the historical impacts of racism, she said she didn't feel particularly advantaged, and she stated that she resented being made to feel that there was "nothing good about being white." I was convinced that she misunderstood what I was trying to accomplish in the class, but her resistance forced me to think more about the difficulties she and other students might be having with these issues. It became clear that any success I was going to have at getting her to reevaluate her perspective would depend on my ability to provide experiences in the course that would respect her disorientation and respond to her real sense of cultural vulnerability.

This example is one of a number of experiences that have challenged our thinking about what it means to teach multicultural competencies. Consequently, this chapter has grown out of the authors' work and experience training graduate students in clinical psychology at Wheaton College—a school that intentionally fosters the integration of scholarship with Christian faith. Together we have over sixteen years of experience teaching and training students about ethnic and racial diversity, and we've drawn on this background for both research and anecdotal support. In this chapter we will offer not only knowledge that has been gained over the years but also ideas that we are still exploring. Our job as trainers has been to help students develop greater "competency" when working with individuals or families from different ethnic or racial backgrounds. There is still some discussion in the field about the use of the terms *multicultural* and *competency*, which we will address later. But generally we believe our task has been to increase the knowledge level and enhance the skills of our students in intercultural situations. For this chapter we are employing the term *multicultural* more narrowly as it relates to ethnic and racial diversity, but it is important to note that within psychology the term is also used to describe gender, ability, sexual orientation, and religious differences (Atkinson 2004). We recognize that helping students in psychology develop cultural competency is a specialization, but there are lessons that we have gleaned that can serve a broader conversation. More important, as members of Christ's body we are concerned with how the church may be more effective in dealing with the racial divide in this country and ethnic (and ethnoreligious) tensions globally. We believe that psychology can be a useful tool toward this end.

The materials presented here are most relevant for those interested in understanding the psychological processes involved in developing greater competency in intercultural situations and for those exploring the methods that would be most effective in training. Consistent with the other chapters in this book (see especially the chapter by Nieves), we are concerned with providing resources and skills for the readers so that they may be able to "act locally." The example of the resistant student reveals some of the interesting complexities that we have to face as we attempt to motivate students to turn social and ethical values into interpersonal skills. But essentially, this is the challenge of developing multicultural competencies. We are asking for more than knowledge acquisition; many of our students must reorientate their self-perceptions and understand the implication of their behaviors as cultural beings. We are also asking them to engage in a lifelong process of relearning that, at some point, will force them to reevaluate the meaning of their ethnic identities and cultural heritages. With the changing demographic situation in the United States and the increasing global community, we must develop a more sophisticated understanding of ethnic, racial, and cultural diversity.

It is important to note that our students are required to have this additional training to increase their overall competency as therapists. In the late 1960s and early 1970s, professional psychology in the United States recognized the need to train practitioners for an increasingly diverse national population. The field provided guidelines but not strategies, so most trainers developed their own strategies and techniques drawing on experience and available resources. Our initial strategy was to inform students and advocate multicultural openness using moral persuasion with a bit of theological leverage. While this strategy was effective in raising their consciousness, and in some cases inducing guilt, it seldom answered the question of "why" these competencies were important, and "what" were the particular skills that lead to greater cultural sensitivity in intercultural situations. These earlier strategies were heavily focused on persuading dominant-culture members to become more tolerant of ethnic minority members. This meant a great deal of focus was on the historical dilemmas of black/white relations, with less consideration given for the growing ethnic pluralism and interethnic relations.

Moreover, for those students who had little positive contact with diverse groups of people, the challenges to their worldview and identities were not always effective in persuading them to reevaluate their values and beliefs. Without additional support and engagement, these students were likely to avoid future discussions and withdraw from the broader conversation. Subsequently, we've found that our students were less inclined to incorporate multicultural strategies if they did not believe living or working in a multiethnic social community was personally meaningful. Moral and ethical arguments could be dismissed as "political correctness" if students did not feel that it served their professional, personal, or spiritual interests. Clearly, opposition to engaging in a multicultural community is both a "sociogenic" (having to do with social groups) and "psychogenic" (having to do with cognitive and affective characteristics of individuals) process (Avruch 1998, 18), and we must begin to understand and respect both sociological and psychological factors.

In serving our task, we'll offer a brief view of psychology and multiculturalism as a way to provide a context for our exercise. We'll look at a few of the assumptions within the multicultural movement in psychology that have helped the growth of cultural awareness, but have also hindered in the actualization of its goals. We have structured the last parts of the chapter around the "why" and the "what" questions as a way to consider alternative strategies. The first section will address the "why" question and focus on the need for a new vision and rationale in developing multicultural competency. We not only believe that we must encourage a response to the demographic or structural realities but we're also suggesting that people need a narrative, vision, or meaning system, if you will, to assist their movement into a new multicultural paradigm. The "what" question focuses on the effectiveness of our methods in helping people develop greater competency in varied intercultural situations. Once a rationale is engaged, we need to have the personal technology to help us be effective and efficient. Moreover, the "what" question forces us to consider the images and language of the current national metaphors (or narratives) of interethnic relations ("melting pot," "salad bowl," "mosaic," etc.) and to ask ourselves what kind of society we want (Prentice and Miller 1999) and how we get there. An examination of the "what" would include such issues as defining the competencies, skills, and action steps. We'll end the chapter looking at a few implications for the racial reconciliation movement in the evangelical church.

Psychology and the Multicultural Movement

The relationship between Western psychology and culture is complex and more entangled than needs to be unraveled for this chapter, but its approach could be generically characterized as pragmatic and focused on tolerance. Over the last twenty years, the multicultural movement has had a significant influence on professional psychology, through the extension of services, training of students, and its ethics codes (Atkinson 2004). However, the ideology of the field of psychology is still largely a by-product of the western European scientific tradition, valuing universalism and individualism and remaining resistant to the particularities of a deeper examination of culture (Gergen et al. 1996). Hence, as a movement within psychology in the United States, multiculturalism retained an emphasis on equal (individual) rights in obtaining "more universally shared interests in civil and political liberties" (Gutman 1994, 4). In the clinical setting, we have emphasized the importance of avoiding "ethnic/racial insensitivity." Consequently, there has been, and still is, a tendency to view race and ethnicity as ancillary and therefore supplemental to the core theoretical and conceptual ideas in the field.

Only in the last decade has "mainstream psychology" come to recognize the relevance of culture and ethnicity to its theories, research, and practices (Matsumoto 2000). This has been primarily in response to the shifting demographic trends in the United States (Atkinson 2004), and an emerging awareness of the limitations of a Western psychology in a multicultural world. But even so, culture has still to emerge as a central force in the broader field of psychology (Pedersen et al. 1996). We would suggest two factors that play into the inadequate treatment of culture and still affect the way we think about being trained as multiculturally competent. The first is the influence of the civil rights movement on the multicultural movement (in the United States), which has emphasized the political equality of group identity (Fredrickson 1999) rather than the maintenance of ethnic identity and cultural heritage. The second is the dominance of the subfields of clinical and counseling psychology in the application of culture to psychology. Both movements have been essentially important in psychology and in the shaping of our thinking, but they have also had limitations.

As an extension of the Civil Rights era, the multicultural movement has been most attentive to prejudice, discrimination, and unequal treatment (opportunities) of disadvantaged groups, with the assumption that the goal is to minimize the impact and presence of these phenomena. Cultural and ethnic identity are most often treated as a personal marker of group membership. Therefore culture is seen as a unique demographic characteristic of the individual (ethnic) client, and less as a meaning system that influences all human behavior. Hence, the goal becomes increased tolerance for ethnic and racial "otherness," with a focus on eliminating racism and, more recently, other forms of discrimination. However, this has been done with little questioning of cultural ideals and meaning systems in shaping our views of "otherness." This legacy has also encouraged us to frame the issues in political categories: black versus white, the dominant group versus minority groups, or left versus right. This sort of "binary" thinking (Dozier 2002, 40) is instinctual, not just political, but this basic reasoning is exaggerated when groups are struggling for social power. However, we would argue that the demographic shifts will increase the need for us to broaden our understanding of the complexity of life in a more culturally pluralistic society if we are to avoid social fragmentation. Moreover, the "globalization" of psychology will require the recalibration of many of its concepts and frameworks, and the reconstruction of others.

The second factor, the dominance of the subfields of clinical and counseling psychology, has lead to the assumption that managing culture is about the adaptive application of (Western) psychology in different contexts. It is clear, within the subfields of clinical and counseling psychology, that the practitioner must be prepared to consider context, culture, and the salience of ethnic identity in their work with an increasingly diverse client population. The American Psychological Association (APA) and other governing bodies have issued ethical guidelines that endorse greater cultural awareness and sensitivities. This has been an excellent push in the practice of psychology, but less is done to reevaluate the latent cultural assumption within psychology itself. Moreover, the guidelines have been criticized because they are limited to work-related activities, while ignoring the psychologists' overall social attitudes and behaviors (Atkinson 2004). They call for a change of behavior in one particular context, the vocation setting, but not a change in the systemic worldview of the psychologist. The challenge for the subfields (clinical and counseling) continues to be how we operationalize these values into real-world competencies, and move beyond counseling through stereotypical profiles. Our argument is that the field of psychology must reexamine its approach to culture and recognize its own embeddedness. When training practitioners, the task is to expand their worldviews (meaning systems) and provide a variety of personal cultural experiences that might encourage the practice of a more culturally sensitive psychology. We are coming to understand that this is a more complex task than might initially be assumed.

Why It Is Important to Ask "Why?"

It is not unusual for people to presuppose that negative attitudes about interracial contact come from the lack of social enlightenment or limited exposure. In other words, there is a tacit assumption that racism is an "antiprogressive" attitude that could be eliminated with education and resocialization. It is assumed that those who are more progressive have learned to be more "tolerant" of racial differences. However, this is social reform at a more elementary level; it focuses more on the elimination of social hostility and inequity than social engagement. While ignorance or the lack of exposure may be factors, they are not always the essential reasons that people remain resistant to interacting with other ethnic groups. This has served as a popular notion to explain interpersonal racism and discrimination between people groups (whites and blacks), but it neglects the primacy of cultural and ethnic identity, the salience of structural competition between these groups, and a history of extended mutual hostility.

It also does not reflect what we are learning from neuroscience, about how these meaning systems imprint on the brain through our limbic system (Dozier 2002). The limbic system is a primitive area of the brain that influences our emotions and motivation, and coupled with our meaning systems, provides us with strong "physiological reactions" around the meanings (values, beliefs, religious, political, etc.) we construct (Dozier 2002), and are embedded in our memories. These meanings are often constructed in a "thick" cultural context, and entrenched in the mores of our social group. Consequently, we need to acknowledge that simply transmitting information about other cultures and ethnic groups does not always promote social understanding and cultural acceptance (Prentice and Miller 1999). Our meaning systems must be reexamined and, in some cases, decoupled from a more primitive sense of threat to our social-group identity. Otherwise the sense of threat and risk will increase, making it almost impossible for us to resist a fight-or-flight reaction. This has been most evident as we consider the nature of entrenched conflicts around the world.

We believe students, or practitioners who are trying to develop greater intercultural openness, must come to question their sociohistorical models/ myths of racial and ethnic relations (Fredrickson 1999; Meneses, this volume) and the more personally owned (constructed) aspects of the self, their ethnic identity, and worldview.

These models or myths are those central ideas (core beliefs) we hold about race and ethnic relations that have emerged out of multiple levels of social phenomena—individual, groups, social networks, communities, institutions, and systems—and their historical legacy. Hence, our menu of ideological choices is shaped by an exchange of these multiple levels of social experience and their historical interaction. Our social groups matter a great deal more than we suspect in the shaping of our choices and behaviors. But what allows us to be unconscious of their influence when we are making decisions in social relations? More specifically, why are some students open to new models about race and ethnicity while others are quite resistant?

The socialization and enculturation within our familial and communal contexts orients us and provides us with a cultural "schema" or map that tells us what landmarks are important to us in adopting a view of ourselves in the world. Hence, we are consciously and unconsciously provided the makings of an "internal compass" that assists us, in the midst of all the possible choices, to choose. In addition, our social group provides us with a perspective of other groups and a set of cultural styles or "tools" (Emerson and Smith 2000) that shape our interactions and relations. Beginning the process of intercultural openness means that we are willing (motivated) to hear alternative narratives (myths) and hear other perspectives, which can be quite disorientating if they differ dramatically from our own. It suggests that the students we are training look at themselves first to understand the complexity of their identity (personal and group) before they begin to examine "the other." This has been the shift in the field from earlier assumptions that diversity was all about understanding the other's "otherness." Hiebert (this volume) suggests we must begin to understand "our view" of Others, and the (affect-laden) categories we create in our minds for them. Without examining the operational narratives and meaning systems that support our categories, we are likely to choose an inadequate perspective from which to judge our own behavior and that of others.

In truth, learning about culture means more than the examination of another group's customs or language; it involves a fundamentally different way of defining oneself and one's relationship to others (Dalton, Elias, and Wandersman 2000). It is also more than the advocacy of adequate representation of racial groups in different environments and social positions; ultimately, diversity must incorporate building structures and spaces where people feel they belong (Takeuchi 2002). Consequently, we are faced with finding new ways of "viewing, understanding, studying and thinking about psychology" (Matsumoto 2000) in a multicultural context. This would suggest that as people are interested in becoming more multiculturally competent students of psychology, we must examine our own cultural identity, beliefs, and attitudes as well as the treatment of these issues within the field and larger social context. Hence, taking multiculturalism seriously will certainly involve a shift in perspective, but it may also require the more dramatic changes that occur when one shifts one's worldview and meaning systems. It is not enough to simply increase one's consciousness; we must also make an impression upon our memories.

A New Narrative

In a number of ways we have tried to suggest that our beliefs and meaning systems are quite complex and not easily changed. Moreover, developing new relationships may create a number of tensions in old relationships and force significant changes in our relational network. We have found that learning to be culturally sensitive, because it often entails a shift in our worldview and in our relationships, requires motivation (why) as well as a new skills set. Hence, "why" questions are relevant because they signal a reassessment of old attitudes (memories), but they also challenge social relations, sometimes to the degree that a person may feel a sense of disloyalty to her social or ethnic group. People with superficial or linear interest may feel more burdened with the experience, and possibly overwhelmed with the personal challenge. At one point during a class a student said, "Don't you understand that you are asking me to change the way I feel about my relatives and the whole way I was brought up?" Asking ourselves "why" we feel the way we do about the ideas we hold, and asking "why" we should consider a new paradigm can lower our sense of threat and allows us to consider the possibility of a new perspective. Talking about and distinguishing between feelings of loyalty and feelings of resentment and hostility can help lessen negative emotional reactivity (Dozier 2002).

On another level, the "why" questions push the development and emergence of a new narrative (myth) that can compete with our old narratives. When we speak here of narrative, we are referring to a set of explanations that assumes a coherent framework from which we construct meaning. Our socialization and enculturation provides us with a set of explanations that are in some form naive and unchallenged, but are intertwined with our core beliefs. When core ideas are challenged or overwhelmed, we react viscerally to the immediate threat. Consequently, our naive ideas are initially bolstered, not discarded. However, it is in a context of "optimal stress" that alternative explanations can be further explored and considered. Optimal stress is the notion that we can absorb a moderate level of stress that serves to stimulate our need for new, more adaptive explanations or strategies. Some people will remain resistant if the threat is too extensive to their meaning system or functional narrative. Others will move into a moratorium or a liminal (between) space as they sort out the consequences to their beliefs and social relations. Clearly, if any changes are to be sustained, the motivation and commitment to a new "paradigm" is likely to be complex and multilayered. Hence, a more comprehensive narrative is needed, a paradigm that holds a more complex set of explanations. Narrative, in this sense, has a mythic quality, a story that integrates elements that we have assumed would be incompatible.

It is at this point that we would argue that Christians need a biblical theology of ethnic relations, or a functional narrative that can help us recontextualize and reconstitute the old tensions and offer new relational alternatives. While we believe that we must first find ways to appeal to students and help them see how intercultural skills can serve them, we eventually must also provide them with deeper (more complex) reasons (why) to incorporate change into their life practices. An unsophisticated theology of tolerance is adequate for superficial contact, but not for sustained interaction. We are in need of a theology of identification, one that allows individuals to see the interconnectedness of their identity, clan, and nation with the identity, clan, and tribe of the other. We must be able to see and accept a vision of the world that does not devalue an individual's cultural identity but, in contrast, places it in context with others. Hence, our students must begin to see themselves as coparticipants in a larger multicultural society or community. Inevitably, these are religious and spiritual beliefs (narratives) because they require a degree of transcendence, in contrast to those sets of explanations that reaffirm one clan's identity and dominance over the identity of other groups. It is this sense of transcendence and identification that allows some space for reconciling the tensions that arise from mutually conflictual histories and the tension of social loyalties, thereby allowing people to address structural constraints that have inhibited more collaborative social relations.

Practically, through the process of storytelling, we have learned a great deal from our students about the impact that ethnically diverse students have on one another. Students already have some degree of identification with one another because of their shared status, but hearing the stories of the "other" seems to forge a deeper identification. We can't overstate the importance of their identifying with peers who are ethnically, racially, or culturally different from themselves. We realize that the potency of these classes is in the relationships that develop over time. However, we are also aware of the need for additional new competencies and metaskills—mental (reflective) strategies that help an individual process and use his skills more effectively in different settings.

The "What" and "How" of Multicultural Competency

Now that we have offered a rationale for pursuing multicultural competencies, we will shift our focus to provide a more functional definition of those competencies, and a strategy for developing them. Our first challenge is to offer a workable definition and then a reasonable set of strategies.

The attempts made to achieve standard methods of education and training, with respect to multicultural competency, are depressed by various pragmatic points. First, although researchers have identified essential variables to the development of a culturally competent individual, there is no consensus in the field on a definition of multicultural competency (Ridley, Mendoza, and Kanitz 1994). The question "What does a culturally competent person believe, know, or do?" remains conspicuously unanswered (Cheatham 1994). Consequently, in our experience, training institutions do not have a firm grasp of what distinguishes a multiculturally competent graduate from one who is not. Moreover, these institutions struggle to determine what particular competencies they should seek to achieve in their programs. One reason that the concept of "competency" remains questionable is because it doesn't quite capture the dynamic and complex nature of an intercultural interaction. Each intercultural interaction is to some degree a unique and multilayered situation. One cannot be multiculturally successful simply because you have digested the appropriate knowledge set. For example, conceptually understanding the way a bicycle works and riding it competently are two different sets of skills. Moreover, riding that same bicycle down a steep mountainous dirt trail in Colorado or riding on a crowded street in Beijing require a varied set of skills, or metaskills. It is difficult for one to have the same degree of competency in all of these different terrains, just as it is difficult for one to be competent in different cultural terrains.

In spite of this lack of agreement about the concept of competency, there appears to be a set of skills that can increase one's success in intercultural situations. There have been significant advances made with respect to achieving a more concrete, operational understanding of multicultural competency and its aspects. Sue et al. (1982) identified three broad areas in which different levels of competencies could be evaluated and developed: "Awareness" stresses one's understanding of one's own beliefs and attitudes and how they are the product of prior cultural learning; "knowledge" reflects the understanding of the culture and worldviews of others; and "skills" (metaskills) involves the process of actively developing and practicing appropriate behavior in relationship to individuals of different cultures. We believe that metaskills, or reflective-skills, such as the ability to recognize the benefits and limitations of one's own worldview, the ability to manage conflict, adaptively problem solve, and the ability to understand the use of language and its meaning in different contexts, are critically important.

Another possible, and maybe more complete definition is offered by Hansen, Pepitone-Arreola-Rockwell, and Greene (2000). They argue that multicultural competence involves (1) awareness and knowledge of how age, gender, race, ethnicity, national origin, religion, sexual orientation, disability, language, and socioeconomic status are crucial dimensions to an informed professional understanding of human behavior, and (2) skills necessary for work effectively and ethically with culturally diverse individuals, groups, and communities. This definition assumes a dialectical relationship between understanding people as individuals and understanding them as representative of the groups with whom they identify. Multicultural competence is finding some reasonable, responsible, and ethical balance among these factors; a balance that is likely to be challenging for each professional situation (Hansen, Pepitone-Arreola-Rockwell, and Greene 2000).

For this chapter we would suggest that becoming more culturally competent begins with the ability to describe and analyze one's ethnic identity, and develops into an awareness of how culture influences the attitudes, beliefs, and behaviors of self and others. It includes the ability to understand how differences help or hinder social interactions and social relations. Finally, cultural competence requires the skills and metaskills necessary to resolve conflicts, make decisions, and function in novel cultural and interpersonal situations. Hence, developing multicultural competencies is a multilayered learning process that moves beyond acquiring basic knowledge (pedagogy). Furthermore, we believe it is best to use a "scaffolding" or building method, where skills are assembled through a number of different conceptual and contextual experiences. However, before we offer more methods, we will turn to the literature and review the methods that have been found to be more effective.

The lack of consensus in the psychology literature regarding multicultural competencies has consequently left a number of training programs uncertain as to what teaching and training methods are most useful in the development of a culturally competent individual (Carey, Reinat, and Fontes 1990). In other words, how do we become competent if we don't agree on what competency is? What are the steps to take in our professional and personal lives to put us in the route toward competency? In examining the methodology of integration, we turn to "Strategies and Techniques for Counselor Training Based on the Multicultural Counseling Competencies" (Arrendondo and Arciniega 2001). In this commentary on the "Multicultural Counseling Competencies" (Arrendondo et al. 1996; Sue, Arrendondo, and McDavis 1992), the authors draw upon recent studies in order to outline potentially effective recommendations. First, they state that providing students with only one course in multicultural counseling is clearly ineffective in producing competent clinicians or multicultural competence. Instead, focusing on systemic change, instilling a value for diversity training, and emphasizing students' cultural attitude/beliefs, knowledge, and skill across one's classes and training experiences is encouraged. Second, the authors support a competency-based approach, where guidelines for long-term development are outlined and embraced.

Although no clear training guidelines exist, some studies have examined factors that may enhance a student's ability to work with particular populations. Most of these recommendations can be classified into three groups: (1) development of knowledge and understanding; (2) self-awareness; and (3) increasing level of comfort in "other" settings. Knowledge and understanding have been reasonable goals for the classroom. Course work can be used to transmit knowledge and conceptual material relevant to cultural competency. In one study, even a one-credit-hour course was associated with a more positive, nonracist racial identity on the part of white students (Neville et al. 1996). But as we have stated, coursework alone is insufficient in increasing knowledge about other populations. Some have noted that exposure to pedagogical models that incorporate diverse learning styles may better prepare students for their work with diverse populations (Ponterotto, Alexander, and Grieger 1995). Other ideas involve attending professional meetings regarding the topic, reading material regarding the population(s) in question, watching movies that portray the culture or practices of the population, and learning about the history and culture of the population (Arrendondo et al. 1996).

Not surprisingly, practical experience has also been examined for its value in fostering cultural competency. Allison et al. (1996) found that for counselors, the number of therapy cases handled during training was a significant predictor of competence in work with ten of thirteen client groups. Repeated or extended exposure to a culture can increase one's level of comfort with that culture. While we all do not have this type of opportunity, it does suggest that interactive exposure is a significant factor. Other experiences of value may include exposure to ethnically diverse faculty and supervisors and to diversity within the research enterprise (Allison et al. 1996). A diverse faculty is more likely to offer students alternative means of thinking and conducting research. In addition, students would benefit from exposure to community-based research, and collaborative, empowering models of inquiry and problem-solving strategies.

Finally, the literature suggests that students need to be able to identify goals and assess their progress. Either the inconsistencies or lack of substantive program outcome assessment or both (Ridley, Mendoza, and Kanitz 1994) exacerbates the uncertainty students may hold about the usefulness and relevance of the course's materials and training experiences. With respect to the question "Can we systematically measure the outcomes in such a way as to assure us of the development of competent students?" the answer is yes. But more important for this exercise, the literature suggests that we must be intentional and systematic about developing our skills and increasing our exposure. In an article by Coleman, "Portfolio Assessment of Multicultural Counseling Competency" (1996), Coleman proposes a series of factors that can be measured in a more in-depth manner with the use of portfolios. Coleman refers to Tierney, Carter, and Desai (1991) in proposing the development of the portfolio that would necessitate the collaboration of the student and supervisor in deciding the goals of the portfolio, developing measurement guidelines for demonstrating specific competencies, including the material used in the portfolio and criteria used in evaluation, the actual creation of the portfolio, and the chance for assessment and feedback from the supervisor. The reliability and validity of portfolios have not yet been established and there are methodologically practical questions that need to be addressed, but the portfolios offer new possibilities for the evaluation of the multicultural competency development of students in training programs (Coleman 1996).

This review of the psychology training literature allows us to offer some principles for training students but, more broadly, allows us to offer strategies for developing multicultural skills. We can draw from the literature seven strategies that we believe would serve a methodology for developing competencies.

1. Identify and engage in creative approaches to emphasize the value of diversity, and provide extended opportunities for the examination of attitudes and beliefs.
2. Encourage individuals to increase their knowledge of their cultural group as well as their knowledge about other groups.
3. Increase the individual's "cultural toolkit" by exposing them to alternative learning styles, in multiple contexts.
4. Provide multiple opportunities for exposure to diverse people and diverse settings with immersion or extended experiences.
5. Encourage people to become lifelong learners who can enter diverse contexts as students of the history of a people and their contexts.
6. Increase contact with people from diverse backgrounds, and develop supportive partnerships.
7. Encourage individuals to develop ways to assess their skills, knowledge, and beliefs as it relates to their multicultural goals.

Conclusion

Helping psychology students become more culturally competent in clinical situations to some degree is a specialized process, but there are a number of lessons that we have learned that can serve the church. We would urge that the church (and its members) realizes that there will be little ethnic or racial reconciliation without a comprehensive approach to increasing the motivation and the skills of its members. First, there must be a strong biblical and theological thrust that places the importance of diverse Christian communities at the center of the work of God. While we would suggest a model that focuses both on increasing knowledge and nurturing skills, we would argue that the model must first have a spiritual and moral center. People must know "why" developing these skills is important and how they apply to their lives. Second, we should be careful to avoid superficial or personal remedies that lack a social and systemic critique. This certainly suggests that a more sophisticated conversation about ethnicity and race must take place in our churches and communities.

Finally, we would argue that developing multicultural skills and competencies would be critical to the success of any movement within the church for multiracial or multiethnic Christianity. While we recognize that enhancing personal multicultural skills does not guarantee a successful movement or ministry, we believe these skills are indispensable for any long-term success. Consequently, the church must be more intentional in developing methods and models to increase skills and competencies within their congregations. We believe that developing multicultural competencies and intercultural skills must be approached as a lifelong learning process—a process that creates new boundaries for our communities and new relationships for the kingdom of God.

REFERENCES

Allison, Kevin W., Ruben J. Echemendia, Isaiah Crawford, and W. LaVome Robinson. 1996. Predicting cultural competence: Implications for practice and training. *Professional Psychology—Research and Practice* 27 (August): 386–93.

Arrendondo, P., and G. M. Arciniega. 2001. Strategies and techniques for counselor training based on multicultural counseling competencies. *Journal of Multicultural Counseling and Development* 29:263–73.

Arrendondo, P., R. Toporek, S. P. Brown, J. Jones, D. C. Locke, J. Sanchez, and H. Stadler. 1996. Operationalization of multicultural counseling competencies. *Journal of Multicultural Counseling and Development* 24:42–78.

Atkinson, D. R. 2004. *Counseling American minorities.* 6th ed. New York: McGraw-Hill.

Avruch, Kevin. 1998. *Culture and conflict resolution.* Washington, DC: U.S. Institute of Peace.

Carey, J. C., M. Reinat, and L. Fontes. 1990. School counselors' perceptions of training needs in multicultural counseling. *Counselor Education and Supervision* 29:155–69.

Cheatham, H. E. 1994. A response. *The Counseling Psychologist* 22:290–95.

Coleman, H. L. K. 1996. Portfolio assessment of multicultural counseling competency. *The Counseling Psychologist* 24:216–29.

Dalton, James, Maurice Elias, and Abraham Wandersman. 2000. *Community psychology: Linking individuals and communities.* Belmont, CA: Wadsworth.

Dozier, Rush Jr. 2002. *Why we hate: Understanding, curbing, and eliminating hate in ourselves and our world.* Chicago: McGraw-Hill.

Emerson, Michael, and Christian Smith. 2000. *Divided by faith: Evangelical religion and the problem of race in America.* Oxford: Oxford University Press.

Fredrickson, George. 1999. Models of American ethnic relations. In *Cultural divides: Understanding and overcoming group conflict,* ed. Deborah A. Prentice and Dale T. Miller. New York: Russell Sage Foundation.

Gergen, Kenneth J., Aydan Gulerce, Andrew Lock, and Girishwar Misra. 1996. Psychological science in cultural context. *American Pyschologist* 51:496–503.

Gutman, Amy, ed. 1994. *Multiculturalism: Charles Taylor.* Princeton, NJ: Princeton University Press.

Hansen, N. D., F. Pepitone-Arreola-Rockwell, and A. F. Greene. 2000. Multicultural competence: Criteria and case examples. *Professional Psychology: Research and Practice* 31:652–60.

Matsumoto, D. 2000. *Culture and psychology.* Belmont, Calif.: Wadsworth/Thomson Learning.

Neville, H. A., M. J. Heppner, C. E. Louie, C. E. Thompson, L. Brooks, and C. E. Baker. 1996. The impact of multicultural training on white racial identity attitudes and counseling competencies. *Professional Psychology* 27:83–89.

Pedersen, P. B., J. G. Draguns, W. J. Lonner, andand J. E. Trimble, ed. 1996. *Counseling across cultures.* 4th ed. Thousand Oaks, CA: Sage.

Ponterotto, J. G., C. M. Alexander, and I. Grieger. 1995. A multicultural competency checklist for counseling training programs. *Journal of Multicultural Counseling and Development* 23:11–20.

Prentice, D. A., and D. T. Miller, ed. 1999. *Cultural divides: Understanding and overcoming group conflict.* New York: Russell Sage Foundation.

Ridley, C. E., D. W. Mendoza, and B. E. Kanitz. 1994. Multicultural training: Reexamination, operationalization, and integration. *The Counseling Psychologist* 22:227–89.

Sue, D. W., P. Arrendondo, and R. J. McDavis. 1992. Multicultural counseling competencies and standards: A call to the profession. *Journal of Counseling and Development* 70:477–83.

Sue, D. W., J. E. Bernier, A. Durran, L. Feinberg, P. B. Pedersen, E. J. Smith, and E. Vasquez-Nuttall. 1982. Position paper: Cross-cultural counseling competencies. *The Counseling Psychologist* 10:45–52.

Takeuchi, David. 2002. Race, place, and diversity. *Family Therapy Magazine* (March/April): 10–13.

Tierney, R. J., M. A. Carter, and L. E. Desai. 1991. Portfolio assessment in the reading-writing classroom. Norward, MA: Christopher-Gordon.

PART II

Encountering the Other in Ethnic and Racialized Worlds

6

Western Images of Others and Otherness

Paul G. Hiebert

Mending Wall
Before I built a wall I'd ask to know
What was I walling in or walling out,
And to whom I was like to give offence.
Something there is that doesn't love a wall,
That wants it down.
                              —Robert Frost

"We would rather have our daughter marry a non-Christian white than a Christian non-white." These were the words of white American evangelical parents who had grown up in the church. How can such sinful attitudes persist after generations of Christian teaching? Or are they sinful? And why does "race" matter when it comes to marriage, if two persons love each other? Our everyday relationships with other people are deeply shaped by how we see them—by who we think they are, and who we think we are. But who are we?

Constructing Identities

In large measure we are who our society says we are. We all live in communities made up of different kinds of people: women and men, tall and short, young and old, dark- and light-skinned, long- and short-nosed, poor and rich. Some of these differences are innate, others acquired. Most we ignore, or note only in passing. Others we highlight to organize our society. It is these that our society uses as markers to give us our identities as persons in social contexts. They define who we are and how we should behave. They set us apart from "others," and shape how we see and relate to them. In other words, our identities as persons and as groups of people and the expected relationships between us are social constructs.

Societies generally take note of social variables, such as wealth, religion, and political views in creating identities and social categories. They also take note of biological variables, such as gender, physical features such as color, and age as markers. In the case of ethnic or racial identities, it is not the biological realities that determine the social categories we use to think and live with, but the biological markers our society takes note of, and the categories it creates on the basis of these, that give people their identities.

Social categories are built by establishing oppositions—by showing the differences between "us" and "others." Each society and each age recreates its "others" in order to define itself. Edward Said notes that "far from a static thing then, identity of self or of 'other' is a much worked-over historical, social, intellectual, and political process that takes place as a contest involving individuals and institutions in all societies" (1995, 332).

Many social identities are hierarchically ordered. For example, class, caste, gender, and ethnicity are generally ranked, with the powerful at the top. For the most part, it is those who have the power to define the categories and impose these on a society as a whole who define themselves as more "human," "advanced," and "superior." Over time, people come to see these categories as innately real because these shape and explain their collective experiences. The excluded and oppressed have their own views of who they are, but these views are generally ignored by the dominant community.

One of a person's primary sociopsychological identities is ethnicity—the feeling that she or he is part of a group because the members are the "same kind" of people. This "consciousness of kind" is based on the belief that the group shares the same inherited characteristics. Often these are thought to be "based on a myth of collective ancestry, which usually carries with it traits believed to be innate" (Horowitz 1985, 52). In other words, members may be said to share the same "blood." Often ethnicity is associated with language, religion, and particular cultural practices that form a common heritage. One or more of these markers may serve as sources of ethnic divisiveness that lead to disdain, discrimination, accusations of inferior ancestry, and violence among ethnic groups.

Racism is an extreme form of ethnocentrism, which is particularly oppressive. Fredrickson writes:

> It originates from a mindset that regards "them" as different from "us" in ways that are permanent and unbridgeable. This sense of difference provides a motive or rationale for using our power advantage to treat the ethno-racial Other in ways that we would regard as cruel or unjust if applied to members of our own group. (2002, 9)

In other words, racism is what happens when ethnicity is seen as biologically inherent and hierarchically organized.

Both ethnic hostility and racism shape and are shaped by how people see and relate to Others they encounter in everyday life, but there is much more to them than this. They are institutionalized in social and cultural structures of domination that divide peoples into different categories on the basis of what are thought to be unalterable characteristics. An analysis of how Euro-Americans have viewed Others, however, can help us study the complex structures that make up ethnocentrism and racism. In this chapter we will draw on McGrane (1989), and look at some of the historical forces that have shaped how Europeans and North Americans have viewed Others over the past few centuries and how these perceptions have led to the racism that now plagues our societies. We will then examine ways to change our perceptions of Others to build bridges of understanding and love between us.

European Encounters with Others and Otherness

People have always had stereotypes of their Others. In the sixteenth century, Sebastian Münster described the Scotch as faithful and vengeful; the Jews, prudent but envious; the Persians, steadfast but disloyal; the Egyptians, stable and crafty; the Greeks, wise but deceitful; and the Spaniards, drunken, violent, and sophisticated. In 1527 Henry Agrippa declared, "In singing also the Italians bleat, the Spaniards Whine, the Germans Howl, and the French Quaver" (Harris 1968, 399–400).

During the High Middle Ages educated Europeans often imagined foreigners in two ways. One was as "monsters." North Europeans had many stories of humanoids who lived in the forests and prairies, and were embodiments of evil forces (Jeffrey 1980). They spoke of *satyr* (half human–half goat), *pyrs* (hairy woodmen), water-sprites, the Old Norse *îviôr*, the Scandinavian *bergrisar*, trolls living under bridges, giants in mountain castles, ogres, and werewolves. After the coming of Christianity, these monsters were sometimes said to be "descendants of Cain." The second category was as "infidels." Muslim armies had taken Palestine, and were in Spain and attacking Vienna. They were clearly humans, but they had heard the gospel and rejected it. Therefore, they had to be driven back and killed. The result was, in part, the Crusades.

The Age of Exploration (1500–1700)

European perceptions of the world changed radically at the end of the fifteenth century. Explorers, seeking new routes to the spices of India, discovered unknown lands and strange people not found on their maps. The age was one of exploration, and of redrawing physical and mental maps to include hitherto unknown lands and peoples.

Europe's encounter with Others during the Age of Exploration raised profound questions. Who were these Others? Were they humans? Did they have souls that needed to be saved? Could they be enslaved and killed, or was this murder? The encounter with new peoples raised questions not only of geography but also of sociology, economics, politics, and theology.

The Western commercial world saw the newly discovered Others as a source of goods and labor—of gold and slaves. European exploration was not random. The explorers were looking *for* something: namely spices, gold, and labor. But what right did the Europeans have to enslave other peoples? Many argued that these Others were like children. Therefore the Europeans were justified in their colonial expansion in which they acted as parents, educating and managing the natives' wealth for the natives' own good (McGrane 1989).

The Christian response was that these beings were truly humans. If so, how should Christians relate to them? Were they children of Adam and Eve? If so, they needed salvation. If not, they might be humans untouched by the Fall. The church concluded that these people were sinners in need of salvation, and the descendants of Adam and Eve. They were not Christian heretics who distorted the gospel, nor Muslim infidels who rejected it. They had not heard the gospel. They were "pagans" and "heathens" who were potential Christians. The result was the birth of the modern mission movement, first by the Catholics and later by the Protestants.

Scientists took a different view of these Others. Science was becoming increasingly secular. The earth of the fifteenth century was seen as an island (*Orbis Terrarum*) made up of Europe, Asia, and Africa, with the Holy City of Jerusalem in the center and God in control. This sacred space was surrounded by the dark, inhuman, evil void of the deep waters. Crossing the seas and discovering new lands radically changed how Europeans viewed the earth. Now, for the first time, the world was seen as a uniform, continuous, secular space covered by continents and oceans. In this new world, Others were no longer "fallen" and in need of redemption. They were secular humans who could be compared with other humans. In these comparisons they were seen as "barbarians" and "savages." It was Western explorers who named and studied others and their lands.

The Age of Enlightenment: (1700–)

The definition of the "Others" changed with the coming of the Enlightenment. The shift is epitomized in the experiences of Robinson Crusoe, the leading character in Daniel Defoe's novel, *Robinson Crusoe* (1719). Crusoe was the quintessential Enlightenment man—solitary individual, Cartesian rationalist, and technological inventor (McGrane 1989, 44). After almost eighteen years alone on an island, he came across charred human bones on a beach. "Cannibals!" he thought. From the depth of his European body and soul he vomits. His initial reaction was that these were "beasts," "savages," and "evil"—a response that fit the Age of Exploration. By contrast, he was "human" and "good."

Crusoe decides to slaughter all the savages he can, but, on further reflection, he undergoes a worldview shift. He writes:

> What authority or call had I to pretend to be judge and executioner
> upon these men as criminals, whom Heaven had thought fit for so
> many ages to suffer unpunished to go on; . . . It is certain these peo-
> ple do not commit this as a crime; it is not against their own con-
> sciences reproving or their light reproaching them. (Defoe 1961, 168)

Crusoe decides that it is wrong for him to judge other people by *his* standards.
They must be judged in the light of *their own* morality and culture. But it is
clear that his culture is more advanced, and these people need to be taught true
morality.

When Crusoe rescues one of the cannibals, the cannibal places his own
neck under Crusoe's foot, voluntarily subordinating himself to Crusoe. Rather
than ask his name, Crusoe exercises the sovereign right of the explorer and
names him—he is "Friday," and he will address Crusoe as "Master." Thereby
Crusoe transforms the stranger from a nameless *savage* who exists beyond the
boundaries of humanity and civilization, into Friday, a *primitive human being*,
who is a subordinate member in Crusoe's world. Crusoe teaches Friday English, and gives him a place to live halfway between Crusoe's house and the for-
est inhabited by beasts and cannibals. Friday is awestruck by Crusoe's gun and
wants to worship it. Crusoe teaches him that it is not miraculous, and can be
explained in natural terms.

In their daily encounters, Crusoe is increasingly forced to recognize Friday's full humanity. How, then, can Crusoe account for the differences between
them? His answer is that Friday is unenlightened, therefore naked, primitive,
and non-Christian, while he is Enlightened, clothed, and Christian. But Friday
can be taught, and saved through Crusoe's efforts. Typical of the Enlightenment understanding, there is no mention of what Friday thought of Crusoe, or
of Crusoe's attempts to "civilize" him. In the Enlightenment imagination, as
seen in Daniel Defoe's novel, Others will naturally wish to subordinate themselves to Europeans.

Crusoe illustrates the transition to the world of the Enlightenment. Three
fundamental shifts marked this change in the popular and scientific worlds.
First, Others were no longer "savages," but "unenlightened"; and evil was no
longer "sin," it was ignorance. The earlier distinction between refined-Christian
versus idolatrous-savage was replaced by the *civilized*-European versus the
superstitious-ignorant-*primitive*.

Second, in time the others became "aboriginals." They represented humans
who had not evolved as those who lived in the West. These Others still lived in the
"Stone Age." They were living fossils. But if these others are now like European
ancestors once were, they help modern people understand their own story.
Joseph Conrad captures this view in his description of Africa.

> We penetrated deeper and deeper into the heart of darkness. . . . But
> suddenly as we struggled around a bend, there would be a glimpse of
> peaked grass roofs, a burst of yells, a whirl of black limbs, a mass of

hands, clapping, of feet stomping, of bodies swaying. . . . It was
unearthly, and the men were—No, they were not inhuman. . . . They
howled and leaped . . . but what thrilled you was just the thought of
their humanity—like yours—the thought of your remote kinship.
(1950, 105)

Euro-Americans of the time saw the world as a great museum (McGrane
1989). In the Amazon they saw their remotest ancestors; in New Guinea, they
saw stage two, and so on. The people of the world revealed *their* history, and the
only audience that could understand the play was, of course, "them." They had
the benefit of hindsight: they knew how the story ended, they *were* how the
story ended. It was clear to scientists that Western civilization was the most
evolved of all cultures. In this light, the colonial venture was not oppressive. It
was the benevolent efforts of enlightened people to help the Others join them
in their full humanity.

But there remained in the minds of some a gnawing doubt. Was it possible
that savages were Noble Savages who were happier than modern humans?
Herman Melville captured this doubt in his description of the encounter of a
French admiral and a native king.

The admiral came forward with uncovered head and extended one
hand, while the old king saluted him by a stately flourish of his
weapon. The next moment they stood side by side, these two extremes of the social scale—the polished Frenchman, and the poor tat-
tooed savage. . . . At what an immeasurable distance, thought I, are
these two beings removed from each other! In the one is shown the
result of long centuries of progressive refinement, which have gradually converted the mere creature into the semblance of all that is elevated and grand; while the other, after the lapse of the same period,
has not advanced one step in the career of improvement. "Yet after
all," quoth I to myself, "insensible as he is to a thousand wants, and
removed from harassing cares, may not the savage be the happier
man of the two?" (1974, 33)

The third shift was that the Others became Children. They could be enlightened through education by Western parents and teachers. This justified
the subordination of social others, the colonization of the world to bring light to
those trapped in darkness and ignorance.

At the heart of the Enlightenment was science, which was assumed by
most modern people to provide objective and true knowledge. They believed it
discovered differences that exist in nature itself. Its definitions of things had an
aura of reality and truthfulness about them that traditional taxonomies did not.
It told people how things "really were."

As Eloise Meneses and Jenell Williams Paris show in preceding chapters,
the triumph of science in the natural fields opened the door for the scientific
study of humans. In 1735 Carl Linnaeus included humans as a species in the
primate genus, and tried to divide them into varieties. This opened the way for

scientific racism, which saw humans as part of the animal kingdom rather than as children of God endowed with spiritual capacities other creatures did not have (Fredrickson 2002, 57). In 1863 The Ethnological Society in England split over the question of whether human beings were "of one blood," or different species descended from different primates. The Anthropological Society of London held that Negroes were a different species from Europeans (Reining 1970, 5). By the end of the century, however, anthropologists affirmed the biological unity of human beings. Christians argued, on the basis of Genesis, that all humans were of one kind.

Eloise Meneses, in chapter 2, traces how the study of humans emerged as a science, and how this took the form of racial determinism. The study of race became a central object of scientific study. People were not humans to be known personally. They were objects to be counted, analyzed, and reduced to general categories, laws, and theories. They were lumped into anonymous collectives in which particularities were eliminated by definition, and broad generalizations formulated. The result was the theory of racial determinism and modern racism.

Science organized races, like it did all animal species, in terms of a hierarchy. Rudyard Kipling captures this view of life. "Mule, horse, elephant, or bullock, he obeys his driver, and the driver his sergeant, and the sergeant his lieutenant, and the lieutenant his captain, and the captain his major, and the major his colonel, and the colonel his brigadier commanding three regiments, and the brigadier his general, who obeys the Viceroy, who is the servant of the Empress" (quoted in Said 1995, 45). With regard to race, the categories were ranked along a hierarchy from inferior to superior, from dark to light skin, from curly to straight hair, from little to much body hair. This was used to justify conquest, colonialism, and slavery. The inferiors must be treated as inferiors. In colonialism this led to standard rationalizations:

> The natives are lazy; they do not respond like civilized men to the offer of wages; they need to be taught the virtues of civilized forms of labor by means other than those appropriate to civilized man. . . . Being more childlike than Europeans, it is dangerous for natives to have free access to alcoholic drinks. . . . Such people, if given a chance, prefer to walk rather than to ride, they like to sleep on the cold ground rather than on warm beds; they work in the rain without feeling wet, work in the sun without feeling hot, and carry loads on their heads without getting tired. Life is not so dear in these people as to Europeans; when their children die, they are not so deeply disturbed and when they themselves suffer injury, it does not hurt as much as it does in the civilized man. (Harris 1968, 135)

The dominant community created the racial categories, and imposed it on the powerless. Moreover, the powerful use defining characteristics that favor themselves over the others. It was whites who defined and named themselves, and named others "nonwhites" and "colored." Whites studied nonwhites; not the other way around. Because whites were doing the studying, they assigned what they saw as their characteristics to the highest rank. Euro-Americans were the normal humans, the standard against which the others were measured. They were Occidental, civilized, law-abiding. The opposite characteristics were assigned to their Others. Others were Oriental, uncivilized, primitive, and ruled by passions, not reason. In doing so, whites defined themselves over against their Others. Their classifications reinforced the sense of the otherness of the Others, particularly since that otherness was defined in terms of what were seen as innate, unchangeable characteristics, and overlooked similarities and commonalities among peoples.

Some scientists argued that even though some races are inferior, they could be perfected and made potentially equal to the higher races. Given enough time and teaching, the inferior races could be civilized and come to resemble their European conquerors. This led to notions of the "White Man's burden." Many who argued against slavery in the United States did so not on the basis of the equality of all humans, but on the humanitarian argument that the inferior should be helped, not enslaved, by the superior. Christians like Count J. A. De Gobineau argued that people from other races could be converted because Christianity appeals to the lowly and simple, and could be understood and accepted by the lowest types of humans. But, he argued, this does not mean that in other matters they are equal to Europeans.

But racial identities were also contested. The powerless had their own classifications and definitions of themselves, even though in public life they had to live with the definitions of themselves given them by the dominant community. The powerless lived with a tension of who they really were. The dominant community had no such crisis. Its members were secure and comfortable in their identity. In fact, they often saw no problem with racism, and assumed that because there was no problem with this racism that it simply was the way of things, and they were doing well by showing kindness to Others.

Scholarly classification helped create a particularly virulent type of racism. What counts in racism is not so much about what people are or think, but what they are shaped to be and to think. Social identities are not only mental images of self and other, they are social constructs based on contests involving concrete political issues such as immigration laws, legislation of personal conduct, legitimization of violence, the content of education, and the direction of foreign policy. In Europe the result was colonialism in which Others were ruled in order to improve their lot in life by making them more like white Euro-Americans. The West defined all Others, reconstructed their histories, and determined how they should progress. In the end, two-thirds of the world was ruled by a few European countries. The inequality of races and the necessary domination of the many by the few were assumed by the end of the nineteenth century.

In the end, such classifications and hierarchy dehumanize Others; they are objects to be studied and controlled, not humans to relate to. George Orwell writes:

When you walk through a town like this—two hundred thousand inhabitants, of whom at least twenty thousand own literally nothing except the rags they stand up in—when you see how the people live, and still more, how easily they die, it is difficult to believe that you're walking among human beings. All colonial empires are in reality founded upon that fact. The people have brown faces—besides they have so many of them! Are they really the same flesh as yourself? Do they even have names? Or are they merely a kind of undifferentiated brown stuff, about as individual as bees or coral insects? They arise out of the earth, they sweat and starve for a few years, and then they sink back into the nameless mounds of the graveyard and nobody notices that they are gone. And even the graves themselves soon fade back into the soil. (1956, 251)

The Enlightenment deeply influenced Western Christian whites. Christians led the fight against slavery and human exploitation. They were also shaped by the world around them. Enlightenment attitudes were used to justify segregated churches, and even slavery. They supported the mission movement, and saw whites as uniquely called to propagate Christianity and civilization around the world (Taber 1991). Missionaries sacrificed their lives to bring the gospel to people around the world, but many took for granted the racial superiority of whites, and opposed intermarriage with the "natives." Henry Venn, a leading missionary to India, wrote that the white missionary was "another and superior race than his converts" (Taber 1991, 62). All this must be said, but as Sanneh (1993) points out, many of the missionaries were concerned with communicating the gospel to other peoples. They lived with the people and often defended them against oppression by business and government. Moreover, by translating the Bible into native languages, communicating to them a universal gospel, and baptizing the converts into the global church, the missionaries dignified the people, and helped them more than other westerners to preserve their cultural identities.

The Age of Post-Enlightenment (1930–)

The Enlightenment reached its peak at the end of the nineteenth century. Two world wars and the rise of anticolonial and nativistic movements began to call the Enlightenment project into question. Moreover, prolonged encounters with people in other cultures led westerners, in their encounters with Others, to increasingly see them as fully human, and their cultures as having much worth. Even Crusoe came to see Friday increasingly as human.

To acknowledge the full humanity of other peoples raised new questions. "How could the Others be equal to us and yet remain Other?" Enlightenment scholars studied people from their scientific point of view. Now they tried to see the world through the eyes of the people they were studying. The Others now became *natives*. Others were no longer primitive. They were fully rational beings having their own autonomous cultures. The word *civilization* associated with a hierarchical view of peoples was rejected in favor of *culture* in which all are different but equal. Cultures are now seen as unique and autonomous.

Each is seen as discrete, bounded and self-contained, and functions to maintain a harmonious society. Cultures are also seen as morally neutral. People in one culture should not judge other cultures. To do so is ethnocentric and imperialistic.

This post-Enlightenment view of Others is an important corrective to the arrogance and oppressions of the past, but it leaves Others as simply *others*. There is an insurmountable wall between Us and Them. In a world of diversity, the question is how can people of different communities build a world of harmony, justice, and love. The underlying notion that race is natural, stable, and inherent is false. Identities are not natural and stable, but constructed and contested. But to say that human realities are constantly being made and unmade is unsettling and leads to fear. Reactions to this fear lead to patriotism, xenophobia, and chauvinism. Said asks:

> Can one divide human reality, as human reality seems to be genuinely divided, into clearly different cultures, histories, traditions, societies, even races, and survive the consequences humanly? By surviving the consequences humanly, I mean to ask whether there is any way of avoiding the hostility expressed by the division, say, of men into "us" . . . and "they." (1995, 45)

A Christian View of Others

Christians must address the issues of racism, injustice, and hostility, and show how humans of different kinds can live together in peace and justice, or the gospel becomes good news only for a few: the powerful. We must address the sin of racism in the church. Too often we have been influenced more by the world in which we live than by the Word of God. We must not see others as savages, primitives, or irreconcilably other. How then should we view Others?

The Oneness of Humanity

First, Christians must constantly reaffirm the biblical teaching that at the deepest level of identity all humans are one. On the surface they are males and females, blacks, browns, and whites, rich and poor, old and young, but underneath these differences they are all fully human. This oneness of humanity is declared in the creation account (Gen 1:26), and affirmed by the universalism implicit in the Old Testament (Gen 12; Ps 67; 72:17; 148:11–13; Isa 11:10; 19:23–25; 45:22; 56:7; 60:3; 66:18; Jer 4:2; 33:9; Mic 4:1–2; Hag 2:7). In Christ and in the New Testament the implications of this common humanity are worked out more fully.

In affirming the oneness of humanity, Christians must not deny the great difficulty in understanding people in other cultures. It is easy to say that we love them when we have few deep relationships with other people. Far too often we claim to know what others are thinking and feeling, when, in fact, we may

be totally wrong. The more people study cultural differences, the more they realize how difficult it is to see others as humans like themselves, and to build
deep interethnic relationships of mutuality and love, but the more they see the
necessity to do so.

The Oneness of Christians

Scripture leads to a second conclusion: in the church believers are members of
one new people (*ethnos*). In Christ, God's kingdom has come to earth (Matt
4:17–25). A new age is at hand. The church is the sign and manifestation of that
kingdom, and all who follow Jesus as their Lord become members of a new
people. Stott writes, "For the sake of the glory of God and the evangelization of
the world, nothing is more important than that the church should be, and
should be seen to be, God's new society (1979, 10).

Peter, when he went to the house of Cornelius, learned that the church is a
new community not based on the old identities of this world. His amazement
at what was taking place can be detected in his words in the house of Cornelius,
"Truly I perceive that God shows no partiality" (Acts 10:34).

For Paul, unity and living as fellow citizens in the new kingdom are the
way the church demonstrates that it is indeed the church. In Ephesians Paul
describes the hostilities that divide humans (2:11–12), shows how Christ brought
those hostilities to an end (2:13–18), and argues that Christians united in Christ
are God's object lesson to the world (2:19–22). Paul writes, "[Christ] tore down
the wall we used to keep each other at a distance. . . . Then he started over. Instead of continuing with two groups of people separated by centuries of ani-
mosity and suspicion, he created a new kind of human being, a fresh start for
everyone" (Eph 2:14–15 [Peterson 1993, 404]). It should come as no surprise
that in the churches Paul planted, Jews, Greeks, barbarians, Thracians, Egyptians, and Romans were able to feel at home. This mutual acceptance of Jews
and Gentiles in the church was itself a testimony to the world of the transforming power of the gospel. Paul says that in Christ, Christians *are* one body (Eph
4:4). If they are not part of the body, they are not a part of Christ. This unity of
a shared new life in Christ bridges the human distinctions of ethnicity (Gal
2:11–21), class (1 Cor 10:11), and gender (Gal 3:28; Acts 2:44f.; 4:32). Rader
writes, "Ephesians sees the church as the community in which the deepest hostility between men was healed. . . . When the church views herself in the light
of Ephesians 2:11–22 then it is impossible for her to be conformed to the divisions which exist in society. It is her nature to be the place where divisions are
healed" (1978, 253, 255).

The importance of the unity of and fellowship within the church is seen in
Christ's high priestly prayer. On the eve of his death he is not concerned for
himself, but for his followers. He prayed, "I have given them the glory that you
gave me, that they may be one as we are one: I in them and you in me. May they
be brought to complete unity to let the world know that you sent me and have
loved them; even as you have loved me" (John 17:22–23). The unity of the
church is not a by-product of the good news; it is an essential part of the gospel.

During this time when the kingdom of God has come but is not in its full-ness, Christians continue to live in two worlds, in the kingdoms of this world and in the kingdom of God. The former is the temporary, the latter eternal. The identities of Christians in this world (the old *aeon*) are relativized because they are passing away. The Christian's new identity as a member in the family of Christ is eternal, and takes precedence over all earthly identities.

Tearing Down Race Walls

If races and racism are socially constructed, they can be deconstructed. To do so, however, is not easy. Christians must deal with both our personal perceptions of ourselves and others, and the social systems in which we live that divide people into hostile groups. To start with, we must examine our own attitudes toward race and racism. We then must work to transform the sociocultural systems that perpetuate racism—to bring reconciliation, love, and peace among the people of the world.

To deal with perceptions of ourselves and others, Christians must begin ex-amining our understanding of our social identities. We are daughters and sons, husbands and wives, mothers and fathers, teachers and students, pastors and parishioners, merchants and customers, Chinese, Nigerians, Native Ameri-cans, African Americans, Hispanics, and Anglo Americans. We activate each identity in appropriate social contexts. We do not act as husband or wife to stu-dents in class, or as teachers to presidents of the United States.

We must also examine how we prioritize these social identities. Some are primary, some are more surface identities. One person may be a male-motorcyclist-American-Democrat, in that order. Another may be a Baptist-mother-teacher-gardener. When identities come into conflict, people choose one identity at the expense of the other. For example, when the Christian parents said they would rather have their child marry a non-Christian white than a Christian nonwhite, they were saying that their ethnic identity was deeper than their Chris-tian identity.

Christians must learn to see our primary identity as human beings. When we meet Others, we must see them first as fellow humans, and only secondarily as males or females, Americans or Arabs, rich or poor. In reaching out to the lost, Christians must meet them at the deepest level of their common humanity.

Christians must also learn to see our primary identity as Christians. When we meet other Christians, we must see them as brothers and sisters in the same family. This belonging to a new community is our eternal identity. Our oneness with other Christians is deeper than the identities that divide us on earth, such as ethnicity (Jew or Gentile), class (slave or free), and gender (male or female), which are not eternal. In the church, at least, Christians should manifest this eternal reality, and not be captive to the world around them.

How can Christians learn to see their world this way? We cannot expect new believers to immediately put their new identity in Christ at the deepest level of their hierarchy of identities. Learning to see others as truly humans, and as members of the same family must be an intentional part of all discipling processes. Christians must begin by seeking relationships with people outside our circles. We must learn how to build relationships with Others by asking others about themselves, and seeking to learn to know them, rather than talking about ourselves. We need to build multiethnic fellowships, and work to break down the walls that divide us. Our churches must model the oneness of the body of Christ. New Christians must be led to deal with their racism, for it is sin. It divides the body of Christ, and it closes the door to effective witness to nonbelievers. And all this must be modeled by those who are mature in faith.

But Christians must do more than tear down the walls that divide people so deeply. We need to celebrate our oneness and build relationships of unity and love. If our primary identities are ethnic, cultural, and national, we may gather for worship and fellowship, but we know that when tensions arise, these underlying differences will divide us, and we will be ready to war against one another. If, on the other hand, "human" and "Christian" are our primary identities, we can celebrate ethnic, gender, and cultural differences knowing that when problems arise we will remain united.

Unity in the body of Christ does not rest in uniformity, but in the common "blood" that Christians have in Christ. We may disagree and quarrel, but neither can take away that identity from the other. Unity in the church that breaks down walls of ethnicity, gender, and class takes place wherever Christ is Lord of our lives. Yancey writes, "A society that welcomes people of all races and social classes, that is characterized by love and not polarization, that cares most for its weakest members, that stands for justice and righteousness in a world enamored with selfishness and decadence, a society in which members compete for the privilege of serving one another—this is what Jesus meant by the kingdom of God" (1995, 253).

REFERENCES

Conrad, Joseph. 1950. *Heart of darkness*. New York: Signet. (Orig. pub. 1890.)

Defoe, Daniel. 1961. *Robinson Crusoe*. New York: Doubleday. (Orig. pub. 1719.)

Fredrickson, George M. 2002. *Racism: A short history*. Princeton, NJ: Princeton University Press.

Harris, Marvin. 1968. *The rise of anthropological theory*. New York: Thomas Y. Crowell Co.

Horowitz, Donald L. 1985. *Ethnic groups in conflict*. Berkeley and Los Angeles: University of California Press.

Jeffrey, David L. 1980. Medieval monsters. In *Manlike monsters on trial*, ed. Marjorie Halpin and Michael Ames. Vancouver: University of British Columbia Press.

McGrane, Bernard. 1989. *Beyond anthropology: Society and the other*. New York: Columbia University Press.

Melville, Herman. 1974. *Typee*. New York: Airmont. (Orig. pub. 1846.)

Orwell, George. 1956. *The Orwell reader*. San Francisco: Harcourt, Brace, Jovanovich.

Peterson, Eugene. 1993. *The message: New Testament with Psalms and Proverbs*. Colorado Springs, CO: NavPress.

Rader, William. 1978. *The Church and racial hostility: A history of interpretation of Ephesians 2:11–12*. Tübingen: J. C. B. Mohr.

Reining, Conrad. 1970. A lost period of applied anthropology. In *Applied anthropology: Readings in the uses of the science of man*, ed. James A. Clifton. Boston: Houghton Mifflin.

Said, Edward W. 1995. *Orientalism: Western conceptions of the Orient*. London: Penguin. (Orig. pub. 1978.)

Sanneh, Lamin. 1993. *Encountering the West: Christianity and the global cultural process*. Maryknoll, NY: Orbis.

Stott, John R. W. 1979. *The message of Ephesians*. Downers Grove, IL: InterVarsity.

Taber, Charles R. 1991. *The world is too much with us: "Culture" in modern Protestant missions*. Macon, GA: Mercer University Press.

Yancey, Philip. 1995. *The Jesus I never knew*. Grand Rapids, MI: Zondervan.

7

Crossing the Color Line:
A Brief Historical Survey of
Race Relations in American
Evangelical Christianity

Joseph L. Thomas and Douglas A. Sweeney

My brothers, as believers in our glorious Lord Jesus Christ, don't show favoritism. Suppose a man comes into your meeting wearing a gold ring and fine clothes, and a poor man in shabby clothes also comes in. If you show special attention to the man wearing fine clothes and say, "Here's a good seat for you," but say to the poor man, "You stand there" or "Sit on the floor by my feet," have you not discriminated among yourselves and become judges with evil thoughts? Listen, my dear brothers: Has not God chosen those who are poor in the eyes of the world to be rich in faith and to inherit the kingdom he promised those who love him? . . . If you really keep the royal law found in Scripture, "Love your neighbor as yourself," you are doing right. But if you show favoritism, you sin and are convicted by the law as lawbreakers. . . . Speak and act as those who are going to be judged by the law that gives freedom, because judgment without mercy will be shown to anyone who has not been merciful. Mercy triumphs over judgment!
—James 2:1–13

Evangelicals always have been earnest about sharing the gospel with their neighbors.[1] Indeed, the very name of the movement, *evangelical,* literally means "gospel." It is no surprise then to learn that evangelicals, past and present, have taken the preaching of the good news of Jesus Christ as their first priority. While early gospel pioneers usually put some effort into ameliorating the often impoverished and marginalized circumstances of their black, white, and Native American audiences, it is fair to say that for most evangelists it was enough to secure their souls for heaven.

Even as evangelicals placed most of their emphasis on gospel preaching, and their commitment to "the whole counsel of God," daily Bible reading and weekly biblical exposition at church kept evangelicals searching the Scriptures for the will of God. As a result, evangelicalism has never lacked a prophetic witness to address its own shortcomings and that of the larger American society. Certainly evangelical Christians have often supported and participated in the social sins of American culture. And yet a great number of evangelical individuals, organizations, and churches, both black and white, have dedicated their lives to improving the lot of the disenfranchised and correcting social injustice.

The maltreatment and enslavement of people of different ethnicities has a history spanning several millennia. Historically, slavery and injustice were a common part of human existence. A meaningful response to the status quo of human bondage required evangelicals to reexamine the role of the gospel in society. To a measurable extent this is what took place within evangelical churches between the eighteenth and twentieth centuries. It did not occur in all parts of the evangelical movement, or at all times, and some wings had a reactionary response and worked to preserve the unjust social order as it existed. Yet in the main, the more that evangelicals continued to reflect theologically on the Scriptures, the more they became convinced of the basic equality of all people, socially as well as spiritually, in the eyes of God.

This chapter offers an introductory and reflective history of the American evangelical movement as it wrestled with the issues of race and ethnicity. It is hoped that readers will better understand and appreciate its manifest shortcomings as well as the positive strivings that evangelicalism has made in creating a less prejudiced and more inclusive church. The evangelical movement did not enter on the world stage as a tabula rasa. As a part of the church, it inherited a long history deeply entrenched in the sins of slavery and ethnic oppression. The reader will find, however, that the biblical themes of spiritual liberation and human equality have worked together in the history of evangelicalism to make the Christian church a more biblical one, if not yet a perfect one.

Gospel Outreach to the Africans

Christian outreach to the African slaves brought to the New World began at a snail's pace. In fact, before the 1720s virtually nothing took place worthy of mention in a brief survey such as this one. In 1724 a well-known clergyman, Thomas Bray (1658–1730), did establish an organization that made an effort among the slaves. Best known as a founder and fundraiser for Anglican missions to North America—*The Society for Promoting Christian Knowledge* (1699) and *The Society for the Propagation of the Gospel in Foreign Parts* (1701)—Bray also started a mission to American Indians and slaves. Named *The Associates of Dr. Bray*, this mission sponsored teachers and schools for the dispossessed in England's colonies. The *Associates* achieved modest success in preaching the Bible to the slaves, and greater success in spreading their culture among non-English in America. But it was not until the revivals of the colonial Great Awakening that large numbers of African slaves underwent conversion.

A major reason for the delay in Christian outreach to the slaves was that slave masters viewed such ministry through thick lenses of suspicion. They shared a poorly grounded belief that, in the tradition of English law, Christian baptism freed slaves not only from bondage to their sins but also from bondage to their masters as well. Consequently, slave masters resisted encroachments from evangelists. Many evangelists, for their part, insisted that baptism did not necessitate physical liberation, but rather made the slaves more obedient and submissive.

By the early eighteenth century several colonies had passed legislation clearly stating that Christian baptism did not grant slaves their freedom. But even after this legislation, many masters viewed slave ministries as economically detrimental. The evangelists, they argued, took the slaves away from their work and made them "uppity," independent, and ungovernable. In one of the tragedies of church history, many evangelists gained access to the slaves of such fearful masters with assurances that the gospel had few social effects at all—at least of the sort the masters feared. They emphasized such Scripture texts as Ephesians 6:5–9 ("Slaves, obey your earthly masters with respect and fear. . . .") and Colossians 3:22–25 ("Slaves, obey your earthly masters in everything; and do it, not only when their eye is on you and to win their favor, but with sincerity of heart and reverence for the Lord. . . ."). Some of them promised never to preach on God's deliverance of the Israelites from their bondage to the Egyptians. In short, the pact they made with these masters led to distortions in their preaching, and wound up helping the masters more than it did the slaves. White evangelists wanted to reach the slaves with the gospel of Christ. But in the words of the Reverend Peter Randolph, a former slave in rural Virginia, "the[ir] gospel was so mixed with slavery, that people could see no beauty in it, and feel no reverence for it" (Randolph 1999, 64).

Beginning in roughly the 1740s, America's evangelical preachers experienced unparalleled success in sharing the gospel with the slaves. Many leading revivalists, from the Church of England's George Whitefield (1715–70) to the Presbyterian Samuel Davies (1723–61)—not to mention countless Baptists and Methodists near the century's end—preached to audiences white and black, male and female, slave and free. Before long, black Christians themselves provided leadership in the revivals, offering exhortation and public prayer in racially mixed crowds. By 1800, tens of thousands of slaves believed the gospel message.

Relatively few evangelicals championed slave emancipation. Jonathan Edwards (1703–58) owned several slaves (we know the names of six of them). George Whitefield fought for the legalization of slavery in Georgia and petitioned Parliament for the right to employ slave labor at his orphanage. He claimed that "Georgia never . . . will be a flourishing province without Negroes." Moreover, he purchased more than twenty slaves himself throughout his life. He even acquired a slave plantation in the middle of the 1740s, "through the bounty of my good friends . . . in South Carolina," as he said (Gallay 1988, 33). Samuel Davies baptized hundreds of slaves in his brief, fifteen-year ministry (he died of pneumonia shortly after assuming the presidency of Princeton). But he excluded many others for viewing baptism as a promotion to "Equality with their Masters." One notable exception was the Puritan jurist Samuel Sewall, author of the antislavery tract *The Selling of Joseph: A Memoir* (1700). In this remarkable book Sewall countered many proslavery theological arguments, especially the contention that Africans were relegated to a life of slavery based on the curse placed on Ham by his father Noah. Taking to heart the biblical message of equality, such as James 2:1–13, Sewall declared slavery a "barbarous Usage of our Friends and Kinsfolk in Africa" (Haynes 2002, 181).

Clearly, then, evangelical outreach had its limits. Indeed, for most of these evangelicals, the gospel offered forgiveness of sin and eternal life in Christ, not deliverance here and now. In their mind, the benefits of salvation so far outshone mere temporal freedom that a compromise with slavery proved a small price to pay.

But this accommodation to slavery on the part of evangelicals established a pattern of prejudice that would plague them for years to come. Before the middle of the twentieth century, most of the leading white revivalists would condone discrimination. During the Second Great Awakening of the early nineteenth century, for example, many revivals were racialized, black people being quarantined in segregated seating. This took place at Cane Ridge (1801), known as "America's Pentecost," by far the largest camp meeting in American history. It even took place at many services held by Charles Grandison Finney, who spoke out frequently against the system of slavery. Perhaps the most celebrated of all the nineteenth-century revival preachers, Finney allowed for segregation despite his progressive racial views, which included the establishment of Oberlin College, the nation's first integrated school. He deemed it inexpedient to allow black people to serve as church trustees, and he opposed more radical abolitionists for politicizing the gospel. Such was the nature of the color line that it caused normally judicious individuals to pursue contradictory practices.

Both Dwight L. Moody (1837–99) and Billy Sunday (1862–1935) allowed for segregated seating at their meetings in the South, alienating many African Americans. In the words of one black Christian, Moody's "conduct toward the Negroes during his Southern tour has been shameless, and I would not have him preach in a barroom, let alone a church." Another black pastor complained that Moody "placed caste above Christianity" (Blum 2001, 290). And the black abolitionist, Frederick Douglass (1817?–95), compared Moody's meetings rather unfavorably with those of the noted agnostic lecturer, Robert Ingersoll: "Infidel though Mr. Ingersoll may be called, he never turned his back upon his colored brothers, as did the evangelical Christians of [Philadelphia] on the occasion of the late visit of Mr. Moody. Of all the forms of Negro hate in this world, save me from that one which clothes itself with the name of the loving Jesus. . . . The Negro can go into the circus, the theatre, and can be admitted to the lectures of Mr. Ingersoll, but he cannot go into an evangelical Christian meeting" (Blum 2001, 290).

Even Billy Graham (1918–) opposed discrimination gradually. Graham was never happy with race relations in his native South. While he angered many erstwhile friends in the summer of 1957 by inviting Martin Luther King Jr. (1929–68) to pray at his highly publicized crusade in New York City, he had only recently (1954) desegregated his crusades for good, after the U.S. Supreme Court declared the "separate but equal" doctrine unconstitutional in *Brown v. Board of Education*. And he seemed to symbolize to promoters of African American civil rights the "white moderate" approach to racial discrimination—an approach that King himself condemned in April of 1963 in his famous "Letter from Birmingham Jail":

> I must confess that over the past few years I have been gravely disappointed with the white moderate. I have almost reached the regrettable conclusion that the Negro's great stumbling block in his stride toward freedom is not the White Citizen's Counciler or the Ku Klux Klanner, but the white moderate, who is more devoted to "order" than to justice; who prefers a negative peace which is the absence of tension to a positive peace which is the presence of justice; who constantly says: "I agree with you in the goal you seek, but I cannot agree with your methods of direct action"; who paternalistically believes he can set the timetable for another man's freedom; who lives by a mythical concept of time and who constantly advises the Negro to wait for a "more convenient season." Shallow understanding from people of good will is more frustrating than absolute misunderstanding from people of ill will. (King 1999, 526)

All too many white evangelicals probably exemplified the "white moderate" approach that King critiqued, an approach that served to reinforce the color line.

But again, paradoxically, and despite undeniable moral failure, ever since the Great Awakening white evangelicals promoted the gospel among millions of African Americans—a gospel that helped motivate, underpin, and justify quests for freedom and justice. Some early slaveholders led the way. In a little-known letter draft (whose final copy has since been lost), Jonathan Edwards denounced the abuses of the transatlantic slave trade. In a better-known public letter, George Whitefield criticized cruelty to slaves. "God has a quarrel with you," he wrote to his slaveholding colleagues in the South. For you have treated your slaves "as bad or worse than brutes" (Whitefield 1771, 4:37–41). Whitefield persuaded some wealthy converts, the Bryan family of South Carolina, to become courageous leaders in ministry to the slaves. They never liberated their slaves. But in 1743 the Bryans left the Anglican Church in order to form the Stony Creek Independent (Presbyterian) Church—a congregation that would receive their slaves as regular church members. They denounced all cruelty to the slaves and became such vocal racial reformers that their neighbors feared they would lead a slave insurrection.

Some other evangelicals opposed slaveholding altogether, and engaged in dangerous and often subversive abolitionist activity. White and black Moravian

Christians, for example, shared the holy kiss of peace, sponsored each other in Christian baptism, laid hands on each other's heads, sat and communed together in church, even washed each other's feet. John Wesley (1703–91) and his American Methodist followers opposed the system of slavery strenuously in the early years of their movement (though later on, most Methodists backed away from such radical opposition and their denomination split over slavery in 1843–44). So did several Baptist groups, as well as numerous other sects, such as the Quakers, who are marginally connected to evangelicalism. Some New England Congregationalists (spiritual descendants of Jonathan Edwards) became important early spokesmen for the cause of abolition. Edwards's own son, Jonathan Edwards Jr. (1745–1801), along with colleagues like Samuel Hopkins (1721–1803), published tracts and preached against the slave trade.

Out of the Second Great Awakening—the massive series of revivals that filled the first third of the nineteenth century—came a coordinated effort to evangelize, liberate, and educate America's slaves. Hundreds of thousands of black men and women responded by placing their faith in Jesus Christ. And dozens of charitable societies emerged to minister to their needs. Of course, in American social history this is the age of important leaders like David Walker, Denmark Vesey, Nat Turner, and Frederick Douglass—outspoken black prophets who preached powerfully against the sins of slavery and racism. But there were white evangelicals, too, who made a difference among the slaves. Though often much less bold in prophetic witness—and at times neglecting to witness altogether—they devoted countless hours and millions of dollars to help those living in bondage.

To take just one (rather conservative) example, the most important white evangelical educator of the slaves was a Georgia man, the Reverend Charles Colcock Jones (1804–63). Jones, an ordained minister, spent decades as a missionary to slaves. During the 1830s and 1840s he wrote a catechism and teaching aid for slaves and slave missionaries, spending a great deal of time in the trenches teaching and preaching to slaves as well. He came from a prominent slaveholding family, defended slavery as being set forth from the Bible, and always argued that his work would not inhibit the southern economy. He believed that the slaves had to be "civilized" before they would merit their freedom. But some have said that he did more to improve the lives of plantation slaves than any other individual in antebellum America.

Most significant of all, the evangelical awakenings yielded a harvest of black antislavery reformers and black gospel ministers. Inspired by a scriptural commitment to the demands of divine justice, many black Christians began to raise their voices against the system of slavery—and the Christians who so often condoned it. Perhaps the most powerful testimony came from the former slave, Frederick Douglass, who excoriated Christians for their complicity in this evil. "The church and the slave prison stand next to each other," he fumed. "The church-going bell and the auctioneer's bell chime in with each other; the pulpit and the auctioneer's block stand in the same neighbourhood." What is more, Christian ministries are profiting from the arrangement. "We have men sold to build churches, women sold to support missionaries, and babies sold to buy Bibles and communion services." Douglass summarized his concern in words that have haunted Christians since: "Between the Christianity of this land and the Christianity of Christ I recognize the widest possible difference" (Douglass 1999, 106–7).

There were scores of black gospel ministers who emerged from the awakenings. Some served as pastors of predominantly white, northern congregations— the Reverend Lemuel Haynes (1753–1833), for example, a black Edwardsian in Vermont. But an even greater number served among the slaves and in black churches. This scandalized most nonevangelicals, who used it to denigrate the revivals and worked to outlaw all black preaching in several states. But many black preachers and churches survived and, by the end of the nineteenth century, millions of African Americans worshiped on their own.

Slave Religion and the Rise of Independent Black Churches

By the time of the first U.S. census in 1790, approximately 20 percent of this country's nearly four million inhabitants were black. Most black residents were slaves working on large southern plantations, though some lived on small farms or in the homes of urban professionals. Most slaves worshiped, when they could, in the so-called invisible institution, the secret churches that met after hours for (often) illegal prayer and praise.

Slave religion is one of the miracles of American religious history. Usually unbeknownst to their masters, and often in violation of orders and even laws against such activity, countless antebellum slaves "stole away" for secret worship in brush arbors, swamps, and forests throughout the land. They preached, prayed, sang, and danced into the wee hours of the night, more often than not after a long and grueling day's work. As recounted in the Reverend Peter Randolph's autobiography:

> The slaves assembled in the swamps, out of reach of the patrols. They have an understanding among themselves as to the time and place of getting together. This is often done by the first one arriving breaking boughs from the trees, and bending them in the direction of the selected spot. Arrangements are then made for conducting the exercises. They first ask each other how they feel, the state of their minds, etc. The male members then select a certain space, in separate groups, for their division of the meeting. Preaching in order, by the brethren; then praying and singing all round, until they generally feel quite happy. The speaker usually commences by calling himself unworthy, and talks very slowly, until, feeling the spirit, he grows excited, and in a short time, there fall to the ground twenty or thirty men and women under its influence. (Randolph 1999, 67)

Despite the great risks involved, the slaves continued to gather together, often stressing Scripture texts and songs opposed by their white oppressors.

They recalled Old Testament history, the Israelites' exodus from Egypt, as well as their crossing of the Jordan River into the promised land (often a symbol to them of the passage across the Mason-Dixon line). They spoke of God's justice in the biblical words of the ancient Hebrew prophets. And they sang many poignant Negro spirituals that expressed their longing for freedom—here on earth as well as in heaven. Coincidentally, the more deeply slaves embraced the biblical message the more they identified with Israel's time of slavery under Pharaoh. If for whites the "virgin" soil of America became a new promised land, blacks always had a more ambivalent reaction, viewing it simultaneously as the land of Egypt.

While most black people in 1790 worshiped secretly after dark, others worshiped publicly in more traditional church facilities. And while most of these were meeting either in mainly white congregations (usually in back pews or galleries) or in segregated black churches ruled by white denominations, there were some who had by then begun to worship independently. These founded what became the historic Afro-American churches, the preeminent institutions in the development of black culture.

It appears that the first independent African church in North America was the African Baptist or Bluestone Baptist Church near Mecklenburg, Virginia (founded in 1758). But the first African church for which we have ample documentation was the Silver Bluff Baptist Church near Aiken, South Carolina. Founded in 1773 directly across the Savannah River and twelve miles east from Augusta, Georgia, its first regular pastor was a young slave named David George (ca. 1742–1810). George belonged to a planter and Indian trader named George Galphin. When the Connecticut Baptist preacher, Wait Palmer, visited Aiken and led a revival near Galphin's plantation, George converted to Christianity. Then after Palmer left the region, George took over his work with the slaves. No sooner had he done so than the American Revolution broke out, British troops invaded Savannah, and George's master deserted the farm. George eventually led his new church to freedom in Halifax, Nova Scotia. He planted and pastored several black churches in Canada's Maritime Provinces. And in 1792 he moved with 1,196 North American blacks to Sierra Leone, a new British colony of freed slaves. He settled in Freetown and founded an alehouse and the First African Baptist Church, which he served until his death in 1810.

The black revival near Savannah produced other ministers as well. The Reverend George Liele (ca. 1750–1820), for example, converted in about 1773 and two years later became the first licensed black clergyman in America. Liele's master, Henry Sharp, who was himself a Baptist deacon, manumitted him to serve as a regional missionary. After the Revolutionary War, Liele left for Jamaica, covering his family's travel expenses by laboring as an indentured servant—eventually for the Scottish General Archibald Campbell, the new governor of Jamaica whose British troops had earlier invaded Savannah! Liele earned his freedom and founded the "Native Baptist" church of the West Indies. But before he left the United States he had baptized a slave named Andrew Bryan (1737–1812), who quickly became the most important black church leader in Savannah. Bryan founded in 1788 the First African Baptist Church in

Savannah. He suffered a whipping from local whites for this unauthorized activity. But he won the sympathy of his master, received ordination to the ministry, acquired his freedom, and went on to found two other local African churches. By 1802 Bryan's First Church boasted 850 members.

As a result of this gospel labor, no fewer than ten independent black churches existed in the United States by the end of the eighteenth century. By the end of the Civil War, there were no fewer than 205—and many more, no doubt, for which no records survive. Baptists are fiercely independent, and frequently nondenominational, although some black Baptists formed associations throughout the nineteenth century. The first major black Baptist denomination arose in 1895 from a merger of three smaller African American ministry groups: the Foreign Mission Baptist Convention of 1880, the American National Baptist Convention of 1886, and the Baptist National Education Convention of 1893. Their merger yielded the National Baptist Convention, U.S.A., Inc., to this day the largest black denomination in the world.

Today there are many other independent black denominations, but seven that are usually categorized by scholars as "historic" black churches.[2] All seven denominations have ties to the broader evangelical movement. But for reasons that should be clear at this point in our survey of their histories, few of their members feel very comfortable aligning with white evangelicals. For reasons much harder to fathom, most white Christian leaders (not to mention the rank-and-file within their churches) remain largely ignorant of these historic, African American denominations—despite the fact that they comprise well over twenty million members. Even though there is room in this chapter only to sketch the origins and development of the largest of the denominational churches, both white and black Christians need to hear the whole story of the independent black churches. Though the Baptists founded the first independent black churches in America, the Methodists founded the first independent black denominations. And though the Reverend Peter Spencer (1782–1843) founded the first such denomination—in Dover, Delaware, in 1813, eventually named the Union American Methodist Episcopal Church—it was the Reverend Richard Allen (1760–1831) who, in 1816, founded the first permanent, and still the largest, black denomination in the country: the historic African Methodist Episcopal Church.

Born into slavery in Philadelphia, Allen was born again in Delaware at the age of seventeen (he had been sold to another master). He soon began preaching on his plantation as well as in local Methodist churches, persuading many, including his master, to convert to Christianity. He purchased his freedom, received a license to preach in 1783, and traveled the Mid-Atlantic states as an itinerant Methodist minister, performing odd jobs to pay the bills. He soon garnered quite a reputation, gained the support of leading Methodists such as the Reverend Francis Asbury (1745–1816), and even attended the storied Christmas Conference of 1784 that gave birth to the predominantly white Methodist Episcopal Church.

In 1786, Allen returned to Philadelphia and joined St. George's Methodist Church. He led prayer and study services there for the city's African Methodists, attracting dozens of new black members to the church. This raised the church's racial tensions. St. George's leadership responded by enforcing racial segregation at its Sunday worship services. And in November of 1787 this racist policy came to a boil. Allen himself described what happened in his autobiography:

> A number of us usually attended St. George's church in Fourth
> street; and when the colored people began to get numerous in attend-
> ing the church, they moved us from the seats we usually sat on, and
> placed us around the wall, and on Sabbath morning we went to
> church and the sexton stood at the door, and told us to go in the
> gallery. He told us to go, and we would see where to sit. We expected
> to take the seats over the ones we formerly occupied below, not know-
> ing any better. We took those seats. Meeting had begun, and they
> were nearly done singing, and just as we got to the seats, the elder
> said, "Let us pray." We had not been long upon our knees before I
> heard considerable scuffling and low talking. I raised my head up
> and saw one of the trustees . . . having hold of the Rev. Absalom
> Jones [another black leader at St. George's], pulling him up off of his
> knees, and saying, "You must get up—you must not kneel here."
> Mr. Jones replied, "Wait until prayer is over." [The trustee] said, "No,
> you must get up now, or I will call for aid and force you away." Mr.
> Jones said, "Wait until prayer is over, and I will get up and trouble
> you no more." With that he beckoned to one of the other trustees . . .
> to come to his assistance. He came, and went to William White to
> pull him up. By this time prayer was over, and we all went out of the
> church in a body, and they were no more plagued with us in the
> church. (Allen 1999, 146)

The offended group of black Methodists soon began to meet on their own. Some formed a black Episcopal church. But Allen and most of the others, being Methodists by conviction, grew dissatisfied with this option and in 1794 founded another Methodist church—named the Bethel African Methodist Episcopal Church, or "Mother Bethel." Bishop Asbury, by now the leading Methodist in America, presided at the church's dedication.

For the next twenty-two years, Allen worked toward the legal independence of Mother Bethel from the white Methodist church. Local white Methodist leaders resisted his calls for black autonomy. But in 1799 Bishop Asbury ordained him into the Methodist ministry. And then in 1816, after a protracted legal battle, the African Methodist Episcopal Church became independent. Several other black Methodist groups joined the new denomination. And Allen himself was consecrated—again, by a sympathetic Asbury—to serve as the Church's founding bishop.

The last quarter of the nineteenth century witnessed the nadir of white and black relations. The combination of a record number of lynchings, Supreme

Court decisions disenfranchising blacks, and the respectability of "scientific racism" in academia all served to undermine the advances made during the Reconstruction era. Yet even during this seemingly hopeless period, many African Americans foresaw a day when racial prejudice would end and they would be accepted as equals. The official motto of the A.M.E. church as spoken by Bishop Daniel Payne was "God our Father; Christ our Redeemer; Man our Brother" (Paris 1985, 13). For mainline Baptist and Methodist churches at the dawn of the twentieth century, this hope coalesced around the unifying phrase, the "Fatherhood of God and the Brotherhood of Man" (Wheeler 1986, 46). R. H. Cain, U.S. congressman and A.M.E. bishop, expressed this same sentiment to the U.S. Congress: "I hope that the time is not far distant when . . . there shall be no white, no black, no East, no West, no North, no South, but one common brotherhood and one united people, going forward in the progress of nations" (Meier 1969, 2). The hopes and dreams of mainline African Americans unfortunately came to no avail as America struggled under the throes of Jim Crowism. There was, however, one exception to this national segregationist pattern. Small, multiethnic communities developed on the margins of American society in the nascent Holiness-Pentecostal movement.

The Holiness-Pentecostal Movement

The Holiness-Pentecostal wing of the evangelical movement set about crossing the color line in the late nineteenth and early twentieth centuries. Committed to absolute notions of holiness and church unity, "the saints" regarded racial prejudice as sinful. Jim Crow legislation and attitudes, however, made the prospect of integrated revivals and churches a dangerous endeavor. While preaching a sermon on tearing down the "middle wall of partition" between Jews and Gentiles (Eph 2:14) at a camp meeting in Alabama, Church of God (Anderson, Indiana) female evangelist, Lena Shoffner, in a moment of eschatological passion, unhooked the rope segregating the crowd. Blacks and whites rushed to the altar together to pray and seek God. When word spread of this social transgression, local citizens quickly dispersed the revival. To escape injury, most of the evangelists fled to nearby houses friendly to their cause. One man was forced to make his escape into the night dressed as a woman.

Even in the face of open opposition, small interracial communities of Holiness-Pentecostal believers began to spring up all across Jim Crow America. A few examples will demonstrate how truly countercultural they were. One Native American evangelist from the Southern California and Arizona Holiness Association, W. A. Caleb, reported that people were shocked to hear him preach, "God is no respecter of persons" (Washburn 1985, 244). And when readers of the Indiana Holiness paper *Gospel Trumpet* became concerned with the publication of Charles Carroll's *The Negro Is a Beast*, they sought advice from the publication's editor, William G. Schell. Schell replied, "No, the Negro is not a beast . . . and we can not hold in our hearts any hatred or prejudice against our brother because he is black" (Schell 1901). Schell later rebutted the scientific racism of Carroll with his own book, *Is the Negro a Beast?* Finally, J. O. McClurkan, founder of the Pentecostal Alliance in Nashville, Tennessee, expressed the sentiments of the Holiness folk well when he wrote:

> Thank God that holiness is the great resolvent of this problem. The sanctified heart is absolutely cleansed of all war or race prejudice. Holiness deepens and sweetens and broadens the nature until every man of all and every section and nationality and color and condition is loved as a brother. There is no North, no South, no Jew, no Greek, no Barbarian to the sanctified. (McClurkan 1901, 8)

The height of interracial fellowship within Holiness-Pentecostalism occurred at the Azusa Street revival during the first decade of the twentieth century. Led by the African American Holiness preacher, William J. Seymour, a radically egalitarian atmosphere quickly developed. Combining elements from Holiness and Pentecostal theology, Seymour helped the participants to rethink and reexperience the meaning of Jesus' high-priestly prayer for unity found in John 17. Enthralled by God's doings at the Apostolic Faith mission, Seymour exclaimed that the revival "has been a melting time. The people are all melted together by the power of the blood and the Holy Spirit. They are made one lump, one bread, all one body in Christ Jesus. There is no Jew or Gentile, bond or free, in the Azusa Street Mission" (Seymour 1906, 1). The impact on the Pentecostal movement would be immense, as people came from all across the nation and around the world in pursuit of the coveted Spirit baptism. But for many the experience also meant dying to old prejudices. This led one participant, the prolific traveler, writer, and evangelist, Frank Bartleman, to observe that "the 'color line' was washed away in the blood" (Bartleman 1980, 54).

The Church of God in Christ is the first and largest African American Pentecostal denomination to result from the Azusa Street revival. In 1895, two years after Charles H. Mason (1866–1961) experienced entire sanctification along the lines of the Holiness movement, he left his local Baptist church and founded a new church in a cotton gin shed in Lexington, Mississippi. He hoped to attract a congregation that respected the importance of entire sanctification and empowerment by the Spirit for supernatural Christian ministry. Soon he was joined in nearby Jackson, Mississippi, by Charles Price Jones (1865–1949), a Baptist pastor who shared his passion for radical holiness. Jones started the Holiness magazine *Truth* and, together with Mason, called a conference of like-minded African Americans. These Christians decided at the conference to found a new denomination called (eventually) the Church of God in Christ.

Over the course of the next several years, Mason and Jones made spiritual progress. Where they could they teamed with white Holiness evangelists to preach the "full salvation" of entire sanctification. For example, Jones worked with J. O. McClurkan and the Pentecostal Alliance in Nashville. In time Mason grew frustrated that the group remained unable to heal the sick or cast out demons. In fact, he began to fear that the group had not been completely filled with the Spirit. So in 1906, when he learned of the great Azusa Street revival, he traveled to Los Angeles with two fellow ministers to check it out. He came back claiming that he, too, had received the baptism in the Spirit, along with the gift of speaking in tongues. He said that the Church of God in Christ should join the Pentecostal movement (which distinguished itself from the Holiness movement by insisting upon the necessity of the special gifts of the Spirit, most importantly, glossolalia). Jones resisted Mason's new teaching and the denomination split, Jones leaving to form the smaller Church of Christ (Holiness). Mason now became the most powerful leader of the Church of God in Christ. He made it a Pentecostal body. And he served as its General Overseer for half a century, until his death in the fall of 1961.

The practice of interracial fellowship endured for about a generation within the Holiness-Pentecostal movement. As segregationist policies tightened their grip throughout the country, racial integration among "the saints" became one of their casualties. Intense persecution caused many whites, and some blacks, to call for separate fellowships so as not to hamper evangelism. For example, a group of white ministers in 1914 ended their relationship with the mostly black Church of God in Christ to form the Assemblies of God. Furthermore, the lack of a fully developed interracial theology failed to supplant the segregationist beliefs—often based on spurious interpretations of Scripture—that still lingered among some Holiness-Pentecostals. Altogether, these served to bring to a close an era of relative ethnic unity. Two more generations would pass before Holiness-Pentecostal churches began to reflect upon their racially inclusive pasts and reach their hands back across the color line.

Several generations of evangelistic interaction between blacks and whites suggests that Afro-American Protestantism, whether expressed in Baptist, Methodist, or Pentecostal forms, evolved as a special hybrid of black culture and international evangelicalism. Rooted deeply in the Bible and empowered by the Spirit, black faith was facilitated initially by evangelical witness. For better and for worse, then, black and white evangelical Christians have been knit together with yarns from a common spiritual ancestry. White evangelicals first announced the gospel to those they had enslaved, providing the means of grace for Africans in exile. In turn, black Christians developed their own ecclesiastical traditions, improving upon the message they heard and returning significant contributions to the evangelical movement. The Africans' full-bodied, improvisational, communal worship and praise; their dynamic preaching methods; their commitment to biblical justice; even dozens of their spirituals have leavened the evangelical movement here and abroad.

In recent years, moreover, a small but significant group of black leaders has embraced the term *evangelical*, forging ties with the broader evangelical movement. Through African American ministry groups like the National Black Evangelical Association (founded in 1963), and the ministries of black clergy such as John Perkins (1930–), E. V. Hill (1933–2003), Tom Skinner (1942–94) and T. D. Jakes (1957–), a growing number of black Christians are making connections to evangelicalism while retaining their allegiances to African American culture.

Conclusion

It is never pleasant to consider the sins of our evangelical past, especially those involving our multiethnic heritage. When we do, one common reaction is to try to disassociate ourselves from our spiritual forebears, perhaps even to wonder if they were Christians at all. Thereby, it is thought, we free ourselves to begin again, to create a church unsullied with the sinful baggage of the past, now able to preach an inclusive gospel message. Another frequent response is to walk away from the church altogether. "If this is the history of the people of God then I want nothing to do with it," many are tempted to say. A final reaction typical of many current evangelicals is to attribute such behavior to the past and believe that all is well with the church today. We believe that all of these reactions, while understandable, are shortsighted and miss the point for studying the experiences and events of our evangelical ancestors.

All of us are born into a web of sociality. This means no one is able to escape completely from the hold that culture has on us. And culture is always the momentary embodiment of our accumulative past, our shared history. The linear nature of history means that while it is possible—as a society and as a church—to improve upon past wrongdoings, we must always recognize our entanglement with it. We carry the past with us, personally and corporately, even as we work to make the future a more biblical one. It is our hope that this chapter has illustrated the struggles each generation of evangelicals has faced in regard to racial prejudice and ethnic fellowship. Yet it is also our hope that the progress we evangelicals have made toward loving our neighbors and not showing favoritism has not been overwhelmed by our own sordid past. There is no place of innocence from which any of us begin. Therefore, a careful study into the ethnic insensitivities of our own religious tradition should provide a realistic framework for us to evaluate our present circumstances.

By most historical accounts, the origins of the evangelical movement predate by half a century the founding of the United States. In America evangelicals have found fertile soil for their gospel message. It is no surprise then to learn that the history of evangelicalism is very much wrapped up with the history of the United States. American society and evangelical churches have influenced each other on many issues, including the problem of race. W. E. B. Du Bois prophesied at the beginning of the twentieth century that the problem of the color line would be the most important issue facing the nation (Du Bois 1989, xxxi). What he predicted for the last century could be said for all of American history. As a result, evangelicals have had to wrestle with the same problem, in various social contexts, over the last three centuries. The evangelical movement has never been monolithic. While some evangelicals have been implicated in the nation's sins of slavery and segregation, others have fought vigorously to end the mistreatment of minority groups and sought to heal the nation. Thanks in part to socially active and prophetic evangelicals in the nineteenth and twentieth centuries, African Americans and other minorities, not to mention whites, no longer endure the curse of slavery and legal segregation.

Nevertheless, only 5.5 percent of churches in the United States presently comprise an interracial membership (DeYoung et al. 2003, 74). So for this generation of black, brown, and white evangelicals there is more work to do. Our evangelical history suggests that we have the spiritual resources to find a solution to the present miasma. But as the case has been in the past, we must start with our own church communities and confess our sins to one another so that we may be healed.

NOTES

1. The following chapter has been adapted from Douglas A. Sweeney, *America's Evangelicals: The story of a people who have changed the face of the world* (Grand Rapids, MI: Baker, 2005). Used by permission of the publisher.

2. Accurate denominational membership statistics are notoriously difficult to maintain. But at the beginning of the twenty-first century, the historic black denominations reported the following membership totals: National Baptist Convention, U.S.A., Inc., 8 million (a controverted figure); National Baptist Convention of America, 3.5 million; Progressive National Baptist Convention, Inc., 2.5 million; African Methodist Episcopal Church, 2 million; African Methodist Episcopal Zion Church, 1.2 million; Christian Methodist Episcopal Church, 886,000; and Church of God in Christ, 5.49 million. At press time, the African Methodist Episcopal Zion Church and the Christian Methodist Episcopal Church were working toward but had not yet completed a formal merger.

REFERENCES

Allen, Richard. 1999. Life experience and gospel labors. In *African American religious history: A documentary witness*, ed. Milton C. Sernett. 2nd ed. Durham, NC: Duke University Press.

Bartleman, Frank. 1980. *Azusa street: The roots of modern-day Pentecost.* South Plainfield, NJ: Bridge.

Blum, Edward J. 2001. Gilded crosses: Postbellum revivalism and the reforging of American nationalism. *Journal of Presbyterian History* 79(4): 277–92.

DeYoung, Curtiss Paul, Michael O. Emerson, George Yancey, and Karen Chai Kim. 2003. *United by faith: The multiracial congregation as an answer to the problem of race.* New York: Oxford University Press.

Douglass, Frederick. 1999. Slaveholding religion and the Christianity of Christ. In *African American religious history: A documentary witness*, ed. Milton C. Sernett. 2nd ed. Durham, NC: Duke University Press.

Du Bois, W. E. B. 1989. *The souls of black folk.* New York: Bantam.

Gallay, Alan. 1988. Planters and slaves in the Great Awakening. In *Masters and slaves in the house of the Lord: Race and religion in the American South 1740–1870*, ed. John B. Boles. Lexington: University Press of Kentucky.

Haynes, Stephen R. 2002. *Noah's curse: The biblical justification of American slavery.* New York: Oxford University Press.

King, Martin Luther. 1999. Letter from Birmingham jail—April 16, 1963. In *African*

American religious history: A documentary witness, ed. Milton C. Sernett, 2nd ed. Durham, NC: Duke University Press.

McClurkan, James O. 1901. That they may be one. *Zion's Outlook* 7:8.

Meier, August. 1969. *Negro thought in America 1880–1915: Racial ideologies in the age of Booker T. Washington*. Ann Arbor: University of Michigan Press.

Paris, Peter J. 1985. *The social teaching of the black churches*. Philadelphia: Fortress.

Randolph, Peter. 1999. Plantation churches: Visible and invisible. In *African American religious history: A documentary witness*, ed. Milton C. Sernett. 2nd ed. Durham, NC: Duke University Press.

Seymour, William J. 1906. *The Apostolic Faith* (Los Angeles) December: 1.

Washburn, Josephine. 1985. *History and reminiscences of the Holiness church work in Southern California and Arizona*. New York: Garland.

Wheeler, Edward L. 1986. *Uplifting the race: The black minister in the new South 1865–1902*. Lanham, MA: University Press of America.

Whitefield, George. 1771. A letter to the inhabitants of Maryland, Virginia, North and South-Carolina. In *The works of the Reverend George Whitefield*. 4 vols. London: E. and C. Dilly Publisher.

8

Sharing the Gospel in a Racially Segregated Society: The Case of Columbia Bible College, 1923–1963

Robert J. Priest

Evangelical Christians insist that the gospel is for everyone, irrespective of skin color, and live with the hope of a future in which people from "every tribe and nation" will be fully united "around the throne" (Rev 5).[1] But "on this side of heaven," Christians live and act as members of fully human societies—sinfully human societies. Such societies create powerful social structures, undergirded by strong political, legal, and cultural supports. These structures provide marked constraints on the kinds of action and interaction that are tolerated. In America, and especially the American South, such structures organized society around a color line, a line that both separated blacks and whites and subordinated blacks while privileging whites. In the previous chapter Joe Thomas and Douglas Sweeney provided a sweeping historical overview of ways in which white evangelicals in the United States ministered across this "color line." This chapter, by contrast, focuses on the middle decades of the twentieth century and provides a microanalysis of a single evangelical institution in the heart of the American South, Columbia Bible College, the first school of higher education in the state of South Carolina to voluntarily desegregate, in 1963. This chapter explores ways in which Columbia Bible College presidents, faculty, and students responded to racialized ideologies and structures of their society while trying to minister within their society, and struggled with the contradictions between their own accommodationist practices and their most fundamental Christian commitments. The chapter will end with a review of lessons that contemporary Christians should learn from this past.

Columbia Bible College was founded in 1923 under the leadership of Dr. Robert C. McQuilkin to train missionaries who would cross all boundaries with the gospel. But it existed in a context that insisted that one boundary, that of race, should be maintained. No document declared CBC segregated. No board meeting addressed the issue. But CBC was white.

In the late 1940s a trickle of letters began to arrive asking if CBC accepted "Negro" students. McQuilkin replied that due "to state laws and local regulations," it was not possible to accept them. The matter was first raised in a board meeting when McQuilkin read his response to an inquiry from an African American.

Feb. 23, 1952

Dear Brother Gardner:

Your letter asks if it were possible for a Colored person to secure admission [at CBC]. . . . Bible schools in the North admit Colored students. . . . Schools in the South have a problem because of state laws. It would not have been possible to establish CBC here in South Carolina had Negro students been admitted. However, the problem never arose because we did not have applicants from our Colored brethren and it would be a poor situation for them apart from the effect on the school. We do seek earnestly the guidance of the Lord with regard to this question. In your case . . . I think you should apply to one of the splendid schools in your section of the country. Praying the Lord's guidance in all your Christian life and service and especially in your training for Him.

This letter implies CBC was segregationist, not by conviction, but as an adjustment to legal context.

The Segregationist Context

What was the context? After the Civil War, South Carolina refused to extend citizenship to blacks and to ratify the Fourteenth Amendment. So in 1867 Congress pushed through a Reconstruction program designed to guarantee rights to blacks. South Carolina's constitution stipulated that "all educational institutions supported by public funds should be 'free and open' to all youth of the State 'without regard to race and color,'" and the University of South Carolina became racially integrated (Hollis 1982, 16–17).

But in 1877, newly elected governor Wade Hampton closed the university. Three years later it reopened for whites only. In 1895, with state government again under white control, a new constitution was drafted. It stated: "Separate schools shall be provided for children of the white and colored races, and no child of either race shall ever be permitted to attend a school provided for children of the other race" (art. 11, sec. 7). It provided for a system of higher education with separate schools for "men and women of the Negro race" (art. 11, sec. 8).

A year later, in *Plessy v. Ferguson* (1896), the U.S. Supreme Court ratified the rights of states to segregate races in public conveyances and schools. But another Supreme Court decision, *Berea College v. Kentucky* (1908), even more radically gave license to segregation. Berea was a Christian college in Kentucky that "prided itself on its racially mixed student body" (Kluger 1976, 87). Kentucky passed a law aimed at Berea, saying "any institution could teach members of both races only if they were taught separately in classes conducted at least twenty-five miles apart" (Kluger 1976, 87). Berea sued. Kentucky's Supreme Court supported the Commonwealth of Kentucky. Berea appealed to the U.S. Supreme Court. The Commonwealth of Kentucky brief argued: "If the progress, advancement and civilization of the twentieth century is to go forward, then it must be left, not only to the unadulterated blood of the Anglo-Saxon-Caucasian race, but to the highest types and geniuses of that race" (Kluger 1976, 87). Berea answered that it had been formed "to promote the cause of Christ" and deemed racial differences irrelevant to its purpose. Its purpose, it said, was protected by the Constitution (Kluger 1976, 87). The Supreme Court sided with Kentucky, saying mandatory segregation did not violate Berea's religious rights.

In *Plessy*, the Court had said states could segregate races in public state-controlled settings. But in *Berea*, the court endorsed the idea that all interracial contact could be outlawed. This decision "flashed the green light, and . . . Jim Crow laws went on the books throughout the South and ended biracial attendance at barber shops and baseball parks, in auditoriums and pool halls, at circuses and domino matches" (Kluger 1976, 88). This decision chilled efforts by private institutions to resist segregation. Not only might state governments take action against private violation of segregationist norms, but the federal courts would support them. And so segregation became deeply entrenched in the South—undergirded by a powerful mix of laws and cultural norms, prejudices and fears.

Among segregationist laws that entered South Carolina law code was one governing education—repeated every decade from 1896 through 1962: "It shall be unlawful for pupils of one race to attend the schools provided by boards of trustees for persons of another race" (1896 [22] 170; 1902 Code, 1231; 1912 Code, 1780; 1922 Code, 2648; 1932 Code, 5406; 1942 Code, 5377; 1952 Code, 21–751; and 1962 Code, 21–751). McQuilkin probably had this law and the state constitution in view when he spoke of laws that would prohibit integration. In other states, similar laws had been applied to religious schools, and *Berea* had established that states could enforce segregation of religious institutions.

McQuilkin's Views on Race

In letters written in 1944 McQuilkin spelled out his views on race. To a white woman in Mississippi he wrote:

> It seems to me a large number of people in the South who love Negroes love them as servants. But many Negroes as they are educated

and press on towards higher things will not want to be regarded as servants. . . . One thing science is contradicting today is the idea of the "inferior races." Inherently there is no reason for the Negro being considered an inferior race. I have always been surprised by the tradition that God's curse is upon the Negro. I do not see anything in the Bible to support this. No doubt Negroes are descendants of Ham. But I see no evidence they are descendants of Canaan. The Bible does not say Ham was cursed. It was Canaan, the son of Ham, who was cursed. These were the Canaanites [who] became servants to the Israelites. There is no connection between the curse pronounced on Canaan and the Negro race.

When asked about racial intermarriage he quoted Acts 17:26, "And hath made of one blood all nations . . . ," and stressed that all people "are of one blood. There is no biological reason why there should not be intermarriage." The Old Testament ban on intermarriage with Canaanites "was because of their idolatry." That is, the motivation was religious purity, not racial. He concludes, "There is no prohibition in the Bible against a person of one race marrying a person of another." After dismissing scientific and religious arguments against intermarriage, he turned to practical considerations. He suggested an interracial marriage may work "in Egypt or Brazil" where there is no "color bar," but that in a society with the "color bar," such marriage may be "unwise," putting stress on the marriage and creating problems for children. But he insists "no one should say [such marriage] is sinful." It is worth noting that he was writing when South Carolina code prescribed either a minimum of a $500 fine, or a year in jail, or both for the partners of an interracial marriage and for the minister conducting such a marriage (1942 Code, 1438).

Accommodation

Clearly McQuilkin's sentiments were not segregationist. Yet he accommodated segregation. Why? First was a respect for law and government. Second, he feared consequences for CBC were it to desegregate. Such fears were not groundless. In 1944, a few blocks away, the South Carolina State House of Representatives

adopted a resolution which "indignantly and vehemently" denounced all organizations seeking "the amalgamation of the white and Negro races by co-mingling of the races on any basis of equality." . . . Legislators reaffirmed their . . . allegiance to "established white supremacy," and pledged "our lives and sacred honor to maintaining it, whatever the cost." (Quint 1958, 2)

This same legislature had granted approval for CBC to confer accredited degrees (1935 [130]99). What the state can give, it can take away.

In many respects McQuilkin's stance was typical of American evangelicalism during this period. From the mid-1800s to 1920 evangelicals had led crusades for prohibition, abolitionism, women's suffrage, and prison reform. Many held an eschatology in which the church would help bring the kingdom of God on earth. But in the 1920s evangelicals suffered a "great reversal" (Moberg 1977) and were increasingly marginalized from institutions of society and from leadership in mainline churches. They retrenched, embraced premillennealism, and concluded they had been wrong to focus efforts on changing society. One should preach the gospel, not try to change society.

Theological modernists, in this period, came to define the gospel in terms of its social thrust. For most evangelicals, therefore, the social gospel and modernism (or theological liberalism) were synonymous. Evangelicals felt that placing one's energies and hopes in political and societal change was misguided and heterodox. Only in the 1960s would there be a resurgence of evangelical social concern.

Coinciding with evangelical disengagement from society was a Southern religious emphasis on "the spirituality of the church," a doctrine stressed by Southern Presbyterians (Maddex 1976) that churches should not engage politics. McQuilkin himself was an ordained Presbyterian minister, with extensive Presbyterian ties. That is, convergent ideas about political disengagement came from both a national evangelical network, and a Southern regional one.

McQuilkin was not publicly involved in pushing for social and political change on any matter. He saw his calling as that of furthering the gospel—which he felt alone had the power to change the situation, as his letters repeatedly stressed. In personal life he was not segregationist. Black church leaders were occasionally guests in his home. One daughter described her desperate wish as a teenager that she could rise from the dining room table and pull the blinds so neighbors would not see her family dining with blacks.

McQuilkin privately expressed support for justice efforts. For example, in 1943 (Nov. 8) he wrote a Mr. R. Beverly Herbert:

> I just learned . . . you are to appear before the Pardon Board on behalf of a Negro condemned to the electric chair for killing his employer. I want to write a word of appreciation for your interest in seeing justice done. . . . The first aggressor was the white man, and it was not premeditated murder. If it had been a white man involved and not a Negro they never would have given him the death sentence . . . I hope you will be successful in getting a commutation of this sentence to . . . whatever seems fair.

Many white evangelicals with ministries to black Americans corresponded with McQuilkin. Their letters indicate they thought segregation wrong. But their focus was "gospel," not social change. As they repeated, "the gospel has the answer." Clearly such ideological commitments affected the ways in which they acted and failed to act on the issue of segregation.

Separate Ministry to Blacks

In the 1930s, Mrs. McQuilkin began teaching Bible in both white and black public schools. The highest prize for memorizing Scripture was a trip to summer camp. But when African American students earned their week at camp, Mrs. McQuilkin could find no camps that would accept black children. So in 1941 she founded Bethel Camp. While never formally related to the Bible College, Bethel was run by Mrs. McQuilkin and Bible College students.

In 1949 Dr. McQuilkin wrote in a private letter about the idea of a Bible Institute for blacks, since "it would not be in accord with South Carolina law" for CBC "to have Negro students." Such a Bible Institute would be a natural extension of Mrs. McQuilkin's Bible Camp and conferences. He notes, "Columbia Bible College students and faculty take part in these conferences and have real fellowship with Negro Christians." In 1951 a CBC alumni newsletter told of a committee formed to try to bring into existence a Negro Bible Institute.

The Changing Cultural and Legal Climate

But times were changing. By 1950 the cultural and legal climate of America was changing with reference to fundamental moral assumptions. The strategy of the NAACP had been to follow the "Margold strategy": not to directly challenge segregation, but to show that the "equal" clause of *Plessy v. Ferguson* had never been achieved. Beyond doubt segregated schools were not equal. In 1930 South Carolina was spending ten times as much on the education of every white child as on every black child (Kluger 1976, 134). In the late 1940s, black residents of Clarendon County, South Carolina, went to court to obtain better schools. But in December of 1950, Thurgood Marshall refiled the case arguing (in *Briggs v. Elliot*) that segregation laws were inherently unconstitutional. Until this time, the NAACP had stressed a quest for equality. But now segregation itself was directly attacked as unconstitutional. This case, combined with others, eventually was decided by the Supreme Court in *Brown v. Board of Education* (1954). December of 1950, then, was a turning point. Now that segregation was directly attacked, South Carolina began a major campaign to create equal education facilities—and thus safeguard the principle of "separation" (Kluger 1976, 334).

Controversy over the Proposed Bible Institute for Blacks

It was in this context that many heard of plans for a Bible Institute for Negroes. Paul Keppel, a Presbyterian minister, shot off a letter expressing concern that this indicated support for segregation: "I am writing out of disappointment and confusion. . . . Perhaps my ideals of the Bible College are too high. But somehow I always expected my *alma mater* to be guided [only] by . . . the will of God as revealed in the Scriptures." McQuilkin replied:

I appreciate your writing frankly. . . . It is certainly true that we want CBC "to be guided [only] by . . . the will of God as revealed in the Scriptures." As we prayed for the work among the Negroes through the years, I think it is true that we never even thought of . . . segregation in connection with the . . . Bible Institute for Negro young people. [Recently] a former faculty member mentioned he did not favor this Bible Institute because he did not favor segregation. This was the first intimation I had that people would connect this Bible Institute with . . . segregation. Your letter was the next and so it is certainly true that it may give that impression.

He then stressed that the history of Bethel went way back, that there was a need for further training of those "led to the Lord" at Bethel—young people needing further training at an "elementary" level. He pointed to practical difficulties of ministering to blacks and whites in a segregated society without ministering to each separately. But he insisted such segregation was not personally motivated: "In this Bethel Camp our Bible College students and Mrs. McQuilkin and other leaders sit at the table with the Negroes." He concluded that "this whole burning issue of non-segregation may indeed have an important influence on the development of a Negro Bible Institute." In another letter (July of 1951) he stressed, "There are great problems with organizing a Bible school for Negroes at this time. There are many both among white and Negro leaders that consider it a backward step for them to have a school of their own instead of having them come into a white school." That same month McQuilkin had a stroke, and withdrew from most commitments.

Two months later Mr. Isaac Leevy, an African American funeral home director, donated thirty acres for Bethel and the Negro Bible Institute. This gift seems to have resolved doubts about the proposed institute. A board of directors was formed, with Mrs. McQuilkin serving as president of the board and CBC professor Charles Wenzel as director. Plans moved ahead. On July 15, 1952, Dr. McQuilkin died, and Presbyterian minister Dr. G. Allen Fleece became the new president of CBC.

On May 17, 1954, the Supreme Court, in *Brown v. Board of Education*, declared segregated public education unconstitutional. Its implementation decree on May 31, 1955, however, provided no fixed deadlines, and segregation would not end for nearly a decade.

On July 24, 1955, Rev. James M. Hinton, president of the South Carolina chapter of the NAACP, wrote to Mr. Wenzel:

Columbia Bible College should not only preach a GOSPEL OF NON-SEGREGATION, BUT SHOULD OPEN ITS DOORS TO ALL QUALIFIED RACES AND PEOPLE. . . . Closing the doors to Negroes . . . , stamps it, as one condoning segregation. Hence it is not competent to preach and teach THE VERY INCLUSIVE GOSPEL OF JESUS CHRIST, "WHOSOEVER WILL, LET HIM COME." It is regrettable, that in this late day, Columbia Bible College would open a segregated

Bible School, rather than admit Negroes to Columbia Bible College . . . Christians should be able to STUDY TOGETHER, WOR-
SHIP TOGETHER, AND LIVE TOGETHER. Anything less than that,
is not acceptable to CHRIST. The joy you will find in operating the
Segregated School, will diminish greatly, because of the segregated
approach.

I was unable to discover a reply. In the October 1955 (page 20) issue of *HIS*
Magazine (an InterVarsity Christian Fellowship publication), a news item
stated:

Columbia Bible College recently initiated a separate Negro Bible
School. Tennessee Temple College has taken similar action. So far
no interdenominational college in the Southern U.S. has followed
the lead of some state and denominational schools in planning to admit Negroes.

CBC alumni expressed dismay. In letters to them, and to Joseph Bayly (editor
of *HIS*), Fleece said CBC "had not opened a separate Negro Bible Institute."
He said Mrs. McQuilkin had founded her ministry long before recent Supreme
Court decisions, and the proposed Institute was not a response to recent
events. While a CBC professor, Mr. Wenzel, led this ministry, it was at his own
initiative. Fleece stressed that although CBC was supportive of this ministry,
there was no official connection between the two.

Joseph Bayly apologized for carrying "misinformation" about CBC and
promised to print Fleece's "full description of the background of this new
school." Then he exhorted Fleece, in a lengthy letter, to integrate CBC as a positive example to others.

I was unable to find Fleece's reply. But in other letters he stressed that CBC
could best minister the gospel "by working within the cultural framework of
the area," and also that this was a matter for the board of trustees with "no one
of us in a position to say what will be done."

Interestingly, CBC board minutes show Fleece had already brought this
matter to the board. Board minutes say, simply: "May 9, 1955. Dr. Fleece requested that the board individually give careful thought to its policy on integration anticipating definite action at a later meeting. It was voted to concur with
this request." Yet this matter is not taken up in board minutes until 1962 and
1963 when Fleece again brought it up for action. Why not?

Factors Inhibiting Integration

Several factors are probably relevant. First, there were at least two board members who opposed desegregation, and doubtless this became quickly known.
One professor, George Dollar—who would later move to Bob Jones University—
advocated segregation in class. Dollar, however, was only briefly at CBC in the
late 1950s. On the other hand, two long-time faculty members frequently cited

by alumni as their most popular professors, addressed race differently. They were poles apart, except on "race."

Frank Sells was a fiery fundamentalist who preached against everything from lipstick to psychology, but also against racism. When newly married, Sells's wife responded to a racial joke he told, by telling him with deadly seriousness that she never wanted to hear such a joke again (personal interview with Sells). Apparently Sells acquired from his wife a deep empathy for the plight of black Americans. Board minutes repeatedly note his ministry activities to the black community. Alumni described how Sells debunked the idea that the Bible teaches anything about blacks being cursed or inferior—and assigned students to write three letters to three different people explaining why the "curse" in Genesis 9 had nothing to do with the "Negro" race. In the mid-1990s, three decades after retiring, Sells, an independently wealthy widower, was known to many African Americans in Columbia as an eccentric old man who frequently stopped black families in restaurants asking if they minded him giving a small gift to their "wonderful child" ($5, $10, or even $20 seemed typical). Having heard of this, and subsequently observing it, I inquired as to the motive. Sells replied that he was using his money as his wife would have wanted. He added that those children may have terrible things said or done to them by white men. He wanted another memory to help them deal with such an experience, the memory of another white man giving them a gift and telling them they were beautiful.

On the other hand, "Buck" Hatch had done graduate work in social science at the University of Chicago, and taught psychology and anthropology. Alumni recall that in an indirect but subversive fashion he profoundly called into question racist assumptions and sentiments of his students. He would whisper to his anthropology class, "If the people of South Carolina knew what I was teaching you they would burn this place to the ground." Church historian David Calhoun, for example, born and reared in the South, credited Sells and Hatch with profoundly challenging his own racism (personal conversation). But while Sells and Hatch opposed racism, even they did not believe in actively challenging the social order. Fleece, then, faced a small but vigorous block resistant to integration, and few to actively support it.

A second fact ties in with this. In his early presidency, Fleece complained of lack of support from alumni, faced internal problems with faculty, and struggled frequently with health. Once Fleece realized board members opposed integration, his initially weak position may have led him to avoid a conflict he felt unsure of winning.

A third factor involves the financial base. As a small unendowed Bible College, CBC was more directly dependent on the goodwill of its immediate community for survival than were, for example, larger, well-endowed, and established mainline schools—a few of which actively led the fight for civil rights, such as Vanderbilt Divinity School (Johnson et al. 2001). Such dependence makes prophetic speaking for a just but unpopular cause particularly difficult. Furthermore, between 1955 and 1962 CBC was moving its campus—raising money, purchasing land, building a new campus, trying to sell the old campus. Board minutes focused exclusively on problems related to this move. Both enrollment and finances were constantly a problem. This was not an ideal time to initiate a controversial policy change.

After the 1954 *Brown v. Board of Education* decision, CBC's segregation is no longer explained with reference to state laws, but with reference to "working within the cultural framework of the area." Those who publicly questioned this framework faced consequences. When Dr. Travelstead, a University of South Carolina dean, called for integration, his dismissal was immediate (Edgar 1998, 527; Lesesne 2001, 125). Segregationist sentiment took increasingly virulent forms. The state legislature, in defiance of the U.S. Supreme Court, passed a series of segregationist laws in 1956. One law (no. 813, sec. 3) mandated that if federal courts required any public institution of higher learning to admit a pupil of another race, the board of that institution must close the school until the student withdrew or the court revoked its order. And if such an institution closed, then the South Carolina State College (a black school) "shall likewise be closed until such time as the other institution is opened." This law was indicative of a volatile political climate in which barricades were manned against integration. Belknap (1987) documents a rash of bombings and violence in the late 1950s directed against integration efforts. He writes, "Those [institutions] which suffered the greatest damage were white institutions attempting to desegregate" (53).

While Christians from other branches of Christianity or other periods of history might have deliberately challenged the sociocultural order, CBC was part of an evangelicalism emphasizing "the gospel" and missions, and deemphasizing efforts to directly address sociocultural change. Quite apart from other factors mentioned above, it was ill suited and uninclined to directly challenge the sociocultural order in the volatile situation of the late 1950s.

Internal Struggle

CBC was caught between its accommodation of segregation and its goal of crossing cultural boundaries with the gospel. That is, students were trained as missionaries to cross cultural and "racial" boundaries. They ate and had fellowship with African Americans off campus. But in accommodation to fears of segregationist reprisals, those they ministered to were not allowed to cross back with them. In September of 1962, two CBC students asked permission to have a wedding on campus to which they could invite "Negro friends" with whom they had ministered in their assigned "Christian service." The board responded that "as a college we should not engage in social activities which could be divisive and not customary in the community. Therefore this request is rejected."

The following illustrates how CBC's own commitment to missions fed back into an ongoing critique of its accommodation to segregation. John (a pseudonym) was a child of missionary parents. At CBC his ministry assignment was at Fort Jackson. In November of 1961 he asked a CBC administrator for permission to bring Puerto Rican soldiers to the cafeteria for Sunday lunch.

Permission was given, but without an awareness that many Puerto Ricans were black. Upon his arrival with a bus of black Puerto Ricans, the administrator informed him they could not eat in the cafeteria. Back they went to Fort Jackson without lunch. John "covered" the situation, but felt betrayed. As a student officer, he was scheduled to preach in chapel the following week. John changed his sermon to focus on "the Good Samaritan, who looked at people's need, not their station or color." John described what happened:

> I remember summarizing what had happened to me without naming names, [and then] pointing to the great slogan on the chapel wall, "To know Him and to make Him known!" and declaring rhetorically, "Yes, to know Him and make Him known, if you are the right color; Yes, to know Him and make Him known, as long as they live across the seas where they cannot be seen; Yes, to know Him and make Him known as long as we don't have to eat with them. Yes, to know Him and make Him known, as long as they don't marry our children. Then for the final punch I told the story of Zulueta, the black man in Cuba who saved my life by giving me a blood transfusion. I said that a black man's blood runs through my veins, and maybe I, too, should be excluded from the dining hall. I simply spoke, then closed in prayer.
>
> I recall after the message, complete silence. No one spoke; they just filed out of chapel. I felt stupid and alone. One fellow said, "Boy, are you in trouble." Shortly after, while in my room, I got a message to see Dr. Fleece.
>
> What did he say? First he rebuked me for speaking publicly against the school when I should have spoken first with him. He said that was a cowardly act. If I had known all the facts, I would have spoken differently. I remember admitting I was so angry I did not want arbitration. I felt betrayed, humiliated when in the very act of evangelizing. I recall Dr. Fleece being cautious and carefully weighing his words. I remember feeling that he wanted to hug me and tell me I had done great. He never said that. But he communicated it.
>
> There was no doubt that although he did not accept my speaking out publicly, he was in accord with my position on race. I'll never forget how he shared with me his own battle with race, the struggles he had at his church in Chattanooga and with the board at CBC. He spoke cautiously, but at times very emotionally and on one occasion broke into tears. Ever since, I have held Dr. Fleece in the highest of regards.
>
> But because of school policy, board politics, etc. Dr. Fleece felt it would be better for me to quietly leave. This was not an expulsion as such. . . . Since I had finished all my course work I did get my diploma in the mail. But I was asked privately by Dr. Fleece not to attend graduation. Ever since then I have felt funny stepping onto the CBC campus.

The Final Decision

Days after John's sermon, South Carolinians learned that Harvey Gantt, a black Charlestonian, was seeking admission to Clemson College. Weeks later, the South Carolina General Assembly voted to fly the Confederate flag atop the State House. It came down only in 2000.

On May 11, 1962, Dr. Fleece reintroduced the subject to CBC's board. The minutes read: "Dr. Fleece read a letter from Dr. Clyde Taylor, of EFMA, advising that African republics are threatening to forbid entrance to graduates of institutions which are not integrated. Dr. Fleece was asked to advise Dr. Taylor that no Negro has yet been admitted to any of the schools or colleges of this state."

In July 1962 the South Carolina Methodist Conference rejected a resolution to desegregate Wofford and Columbia colleges. And Harvey Gantt, who would later become mayor of Charlotte, and whose application to Clemson had been rejected because of his race, began his legal fight for acceptance at Clemson.

By the early 1960's the federal government began to force the issue. Governors in Mississippi and Alabama fought desegregation until federal courts mandated school integration and enforced it with federal troops. On September 30 and October 1, 1962, a riot in opposition to the court-ordered admission of James Meredith to the University of Mississippi left two dead and hundreds injured. Thousands of troops patrolled the streets of Oxford and guarded James Meredith as he attended classes. Governor Wallace stood in "the schoolhouse door" at the University of Alabama, to prevent the court-mandated entrance of black students, and stepped aside only when President Kennedy federalized and called on the Alabama National Guard. This left South Carolina the only southern state in which not a single white institution of higher learning had accepted a black student.

In January 1963 a federal court ordered Gantt admitted to Clemson. Although Clemson said it would appeal, Gantt commenced classes without incident.

On March 29, 1963, Fleece again brought this matter to the CBC board. The minutes state:

> Dr. Fleece reported that Miss Janet Wingard, a graduate student who is a missionary on furlough, came to discuss the problem of refusing to accept students because of race. . . .
>
> Dr. Fleece reminded the Board of a letter previously received from Dr. Clyde Taylor stating that in the not-too-distant future our graduates will be refused entrance into African republics. Dr. Fleece also stated that students are now being advised by some mission boards not to enter CBC because of this. He was convinced we should follow the course the Lord has for the Bible College and not enter into segregation or integration as such. Our one approach should be "What is God's plan for CBC?"

Dr. Fleece recommended that we, without public announcement, instruct our Admissions Committee to admit a few mature, exceptionally qualified Negro students. . . .

On motion, duly seconded, it was voted that in the future no one be refused admission to the Bible College on the basis of race solely. After a detailed discussion, including a session of prayer, the vote was as follows: Affirmative – 8; Negative – 2.

On September 5, 1963, Peter Spencer, a black Jamaican, began classes at CBC several days before Gantt returned to Clemson with a second black student, both there by court order, and several days before three black students began classes at the University of South Carolina, again by court order. On October 10, Furman University dropped its racial bars voluntarily—according to *The New York Times* the first white institution of higher education in South Carolina to do so. Yet CBC's board made this decision months earlier, and already had one black student. Furman would not have its first black student until 1965—a year after CBC accepted its first African American. On October 23, 1963, Clemson declared it would accept black students. Until then, both it and the University of South Carolina accepted black students only under court order. Lewis Jones, an expert on South Carolina religious history, identified Wofford "as the first white college [in South Carolina] to desegregate voluntarily" (1983, 286). But Wofford's decision did not come until the spring of 1964, with its first student matriculating that fall. CBC, then, seems to be the first white institution of higher education in South Carolina to voluntarily desegregate.

On September 20, 1963, CBC's board minutes indicate that Fleece announced the resignation of three board members (one of whom had been absent for the crucial vote). Dr. Fleece reported that "our first Negro student, Peter Spencer, from Jamaica, had the highest recommendation and has proven to be everything we could desire." While board members resigned, I found no evidence that either faculty or students protested or left. George Dollar had left several years earlier.

In 1966 the Citadel accepted its first black student, and another South Carolina institution, Anderson College, became the first college to lose federal aid for not complying with the 1964 Civil Rights Act desegregation rules. In 1971 the federal government finally addressed itself to private religious education, threatening to revoke Bob Jones University's tax-exempt status unless they ceased to discriminate against blacks. Bob Jones began accepting black students "married within their race," but refused to accept single blacks, and maintained rigorous interracial dating rules. In 1983, when Bob Jones failed to back down, the Supreme Court upheld the right of the federal government to revoke Bob Jones's tax-exempt status. In contrast, CBC was never to adopt rules banning interracial dating or marriage. In 2000 Bob Jones University finally removed its ban on interracial dating and marriage.

What were factors contributing to CBC's decision to integrate? Several can be mentioned. By 1963 CBC had a strong president able and willing to take initiative, enrollment and finances were strong, the social and political climate had changed making integration an inevitable eventuality, and an act less likely to bring dire consequences.

Two further factors seem to have been pivotal. First, CBC stressed that only the Bible had authority, and stuck to a hermeneutic focused on the clear teaching of Scripture. The Bible does not teach racism, or that race is to function as the basis of segregation or social hierarchy. And the dominant teaching at CBC reflected that, despite failures of practice. While some schools in the Bible College tradition employed a hermeneutic overly dependent on the extrabiblical apparatus of Scofield Reference Bible notes, which codified racist (mis)readings of Scripture (Adeyemo 1977, 14–19), CBC actively discouraged use of the Scofield Bible and stressed a hermeneutic unmediated by extrabiblical authorities.

Second, CBC focused on people's need for the gospel. Evil was understood as personal sin. The gospel was for persons, not structures. Paradoxically, the gospel focus brought CBC into tension with social structures. Students and staff ministered to and with American blacks in various contexts and developed personal relationships with them, which in turn led to difficulties and embarrassments when returning to a segregated campus. Student expressions of concern kept pressure on the administration to recognize that policies conflicted with deeper spiritual commitments. The single strongest source of pressure came from missionary alumni who threw themselves into ministry and communion with dark-skinned "brothers and sisters in Christ." When such brothers and sisters expressed a desire to study God's Word at the missionaries' alma mater, missionaries found themselves thrown into an inarticulate state of confusion, embarrassment, and fear that if people knew CBC would deny them entry based on race this would discredit the gospel being preached. A steady stream of concern came from missionaries wishing CBC would accept Haitian or African pastors. Did Dr. Fleece realize, for example, what a disadvantage CBC missionary graduates to dark-skinned people had when Communists offered such people genuine community and pointed to U.S. Christian segregation by race to undercut the validity of the Christian message? How could missionaries respond, if they had to admit their own Christian alma mater segregated by race? As is evident even in that key board meeting, it was this feedback from the mission field that helped tip the balance toward a nonsegregationist policy.

It is easy to criticize those of another era, and to imagine that *we* would never have been like *them*. In this chapter, I have attempted to avoid easy judgmentalism about specific individuals and their actions. And yet, both in this chapter and in the preceding chapter by Thomas and Sweeney, one finds white evangelical communities with blind spots. While affirming the authority of Scripture alone, the Scripture itself was selectively read and preached. Biblical and theological themes directly relevant to Christian community in a segregationist society (themes such as those covered in this volume by Bacote, Pao or Tienou) were absent or undeveloped. Despite extensive New Testament treatment of Christian commensality (see Pao) and stinging critique of Peter for selectively choosing not to share a table with Gentiles, I found no evidence that CBC leaders generated systematic reflection on such passages in the light of their own selective accommodation to segregationist norms. Quite apart from how we judge this denial of commensality on the CBC campus, it is the apparent failure to agonize over the implications of this for African American brothers and sisters, and the failure to systematically bring Scripture to bear on it, that must be critiqued. As Thomas and Sweeney's chapter makes clear, CBC was not unique in emphasizing evangelism, personal piety, and Scripture in a combination that failed to adequately apprehend and engage the moral evil being inflicted on African Americans (even through the denial of commensality). It is possible to be biblically orthodox, personally pious, and warmly evangelical and yet to have major blind spots about the appropriate way to live out one's faith in a racialized world. What blind spots will future generations accuse us of having?

Implications for Christians, Churches, and Related Institutions

(1) *The importance of Scripture.* The Bible is pivotal to the Christian faith. When twisted and misused for racial ends, the results can be terrible (see the chapter by Jessup). But in McQuilkin's letters, Sells's classroom lectures, or John's chapel message we glimpse another side. When the Bible is handled with a responsible hermeneutic, grounded in the core truths of the Christian faith, related to the great moral crises of the day, and taught or preached effectively, there is no greater force for personal change in belief and behavior (2 Tim 3:16–17). That is, any effort by Christians to jointly address problems of racism in our world must lay the right foundations through careful and relevant treatments of Scripture.

(2) *The importance of a credible gospel.* John could not bring himself to tell black Puerto Ricans the truth, that his Bible College would not let them eat in the cafeteria because they were black. Those individuals at CBC with the deepest relations with black Americans, intuitively and viscerally recognized that Christian accommodation to sinful patterns denying the common humanity of others would create a fundamental crisis of credibility for their Christian gospel. That is, any Christian effort to focus only on the gospel, and not also on appropriate forms of social engagement, will lose even the ability to credibly commend the gospel to others.

(3) *The importance of understanding social and cultural structures.* Leaders at CBC, and most evangelical Christians today (Emerson and Smith 2000), have a tendency to read the world in individualistic and antistructural terms, focusing on the moral virtues and sanctification of individuals, but failing to develop the intellectual and theological tool kit needed for understanding and appropriately engaging larger social structures. That is, we need forms of engagement grounded in historical and structural analyses of social inequalities associated with race. For this, we need the help of sociology, anthropology, history, and related disciplines.

(4) *The importance of intentional human agency.* While the individual alone, even a college president, may be unable to unilaterally change structures or

patterns, the actions of individuals, when fitted together with the actions of others, cumulatively have great potential to bring about change. When a young preacher's bride rebuked her husband for a racial joke, she helped redirect his sensibilities and concerns in ways that were still evident sixty years later. When Joseph Bayly or Janet Wingard exhorted Fleece to integrate CBC, or when John preached his chapel sermon, such exhortations cumulatively were heard, and helped turn the tide. Agency requires the courage to take risks, as John did in his chapel message. Fleece's own convictions deepened through time. After leaving CBC, Fleece became pastor of a Presbyterian church in Chattanooga, Tennessee. When the church refused to accept blacks as members, despite his advocacy on their behalf, Fleece tendered his resignation as an ultimatum. His resignation was accepted. But a strong message was sent. This very church (now *New City Fellowship*) has subsequently become known as a successful model of a large multiracial church, indeed the very inspiration for the multiracial church in St. Louis described in Brian Howell's chapter. When Christians, with appropriate understandings of Scripture and society, and concern for the credibility of the gospel, act lovingly, wisely, and courageously in faith, such actions often have positive consequences that stretch into the future, consequences sometimes known only to God.

NOTE

1. I want to thank Johnny Miller, former president of Columbia International University, for granting me access to Columbia Bible College board minutes and presidential correspondence. Thanks also to those who lived through this history and who either granted interviews, or provided feedback on this paper, or both: Sara Petty, Buck Hatch, Jack Layman, Frank Sells, Robertson McQuilkin, Virginia Bowers, Marguerite Cartee, Peter Spencer, and David Calhoun. Thanks to the "faculty reading group" at Trinity Evangelical Divinity School, which read and provided feedback on this chapter, and to the many students who similarly gave constructive feedback. I want to express special thanks to the following scholars for their helpful critique of earlier versions of this paper: Michael Emerson, Timothy Tseng, Raymond Williams, and Douglas Sweeney.

REFERENCES

Adeyemo, Tokunboh. 1977. *Is Africa cursed?* Nairobi: CLMC.
Belknap, Michael R. 1987. *Federal law and Southern order.* Athens: University of Georgia Press.
Edgar, Walter. 1998. *South Carolina: A history.* Columbia: University of South Carolina Press.
Emerson, Michael, and Christian Smith. 2000. *Divided by faith: Evangelical religion and the problem of race in America.* Oxford: Oxford University Press.
Hollis, Daniel W. 1982. *A brief history of the University of South Carolina.* Columbia, SC: Institute for Southern Studies.
Johnson, Dale A. With the assistance of James Lawson, Gene Davenport, Langdon Gilkey, Les Silverman, John Compton, and Charles Rees. 2001. The Lawson affair, 1960: A conversation. In *Vanderbilt Divinity School: Education, contest, and change,* ed. Dale Johnson, 131–77. Nashville, TN: Vanderbilt University Press.

Jones, Lewis P. 1983. South Carolina. In *Religion in the Southern states*, ed. Samuel S. Hill, 263–87. Macon, GA: Mercer University Press.

Kluger, Richard. 1976. *Simple justice: The history of* Brown v. Board of Education *and black America's struggle for equality*. New York: Vintage.

Lesesne, Henry H. 2001. *A history of the University of South Carolina*. Columbia: University of South Carolina Press.

Maddex, Jack P. 1776. From theocracy to spirituality: The Southern Presbyterian reversal on church and state. *Journal of Presbyterian History* 54:438–57.

Moberg, David. 1977. *The great reversal: Evangelism and social concern*. Philadelphia: Lippincott.

Quint, Howard H. 1958. *Profile in black and white: A frank portrait of South Carolina*. Westport, CT: Greenwood.

9

"Becoming Conservative, Becoming *White?*": Black Evangelicals and the Para-Church Movement

Marla Frederick McGlathery and Traci Griffin

The sounds of urban hip-hop filled the Atlanta auditorium as six of the most melodious young voices blended with electric keyboard and drums to give praises to God. Some dressed in FUBU attire, probably as a sign of contemporary fashion or possibly as a public indicator of their individual consciousness. FUBU, a label whose meaning, "For Us By Us," reflects the designers' advocacy for black political and economic empowerment had triumphed as the designer gear of choice among young people at the turn of the new millennium. Others, wearing braided hair, locks, perms, and freestyle naturals with corresponding accessories, seemed to embody the essence of black cultural style as they worked to transcend the material world and enter into a spiritual world void of labels, politics, and color. With one's eyes closed, one would insist that Erykah Badu, Jill Scott, and Lauryn Hill, premier vocalists among the neosoul movement, had taken control of the stage. "Your kingdom shall reign over all the earth. Sing unto the ancient of days. For none can compare to your matchless worth, Sing unto the ancient of days!" Ron Kenoly's song, first released on Integrity Music's Hosanna label, had been remade to include a more "urban" contemporary beat appealing to an entirely new generation of evangelical youth. The lyrics spilled forth as hundreds of bobbing heads and raised hands carried on in worship.

We stood in the center of the crowd amazed at the changing of the guard. Having attended earlier conferences sponsored by IMANI, a division of Discipleship Ministries, a U.S.-based international evangelical missions organization, we knew firsthand the changes that had taken place.[1] When IMANI first organized, the music for the meeting reflected the primarily white cultural milieu of its umbrella organization. At those early meetings, participants sang from scripted pages words that few knew before attending the conference. It was not *their* music. So, at midnight, after seminars, dinner, and evening prayer meetings, conferees would gather around the piano in the downtown hotel and sing worship songs more familiar to the gospel with which they had grown up. These late-night sessions lasted early into the morning.

Looking at the sea of worshipers gathered just ten years later, we pondered whether John McAllister, in founding Discipleship Ministries in the mid 1900s amid ongoing desegregation upheavals, had envisioned the dramatic cultural shifts that would now become a part of the ministry. The culture of the organization had emerged out of what was most familiar and accessible to McAllister, white, middle-class, suburban America. Historically, the songs, the format, the structure, and the tone of the movement have reflected this environment. However, with the increasing number of African American employees and other participants, a seemingly irreversible change emerged. Yet, merging the style of worship has proved to be the least of Discipleship Ministries' challenges as African Americans embrace the theological mission of the organization, while largely holding at bay the varied social and political assumptions that emerge—both internally and externally—with the development of an interracial organization in post–civil rights America. African American presence within this ministry raises fundamental questions about the complexities of race and culture and the problems with conflating the two concepts. While culture relates to "learned ways of knowing," race refers more immediately to the ways in which difference undergirds practice and the historic distribution of power. Race, as anthropologists remind us, is a fluid and unstable category, pregnant with meaning, created through a history of European colonialism (Baker 1998; Harrison 1995; Smedley 1993).

In this paper we examine the development of Discipleship Ministries primarily as it relates to the presence and growth of African American leadership within this biblically conservative, evangelical missions organization. We argue that the conflation of *biblical conservatism* with forms of American *cultural and political conservatism* creates barriers for African American participation in evangelical religious communities. In the first section of the paper we examine the development of Discipleship Ministries as a biblically conservative organization established during the height of the civil rights movement, and the subsequent growth of black membership within the organization. Next, we examine the forms of conservatism, both cultural and political, that create internal and external tensions for African American participation. We then ask the question, "What color is a conservative?" as a means of exploring the sorted racialized meanings that accompany various forms of conservatism. In the final section we consider the practical implications of our thesis and possible solutions. In particular, we look at the creation of a contextualized ministry like IMANI in light of DeYoung, et al.'s argument for multiracial church communities.

Biblical Conservatism and the History of Discipleship Ministries

Discipleship Ministries was established in the mid-1900s as a mission organization, a vehicle to aid the local church in reaching people with the gospel. Today,
Discipleship Ministries is an international organization that administers outreach to a broad range of people from various nations and backgrounds. This
broadening perspective reflects Discipleship Ministries' desire to help fulfill the
Great Commission in anticipation of the Second Coming of Jesus Christ (Matt
28:19). According to Discipleship Ministries' statement of belief, they understand God to exist in three persons: the Father, the Son, and the Holy Spirit. Convictions about the authenticity, authority, and inerrancy of the Bible as a book
divinely inspired by God stand as the premier thesis upon which all of Discipleship Ministry doctrines are developed. Belief in man as created in God's image,
Jesus' death and resurrection as provision for salvation, the Holy Spirit as regen-
erator of individual hearts, and the inevitable return of Christ for the reward of
saints and the punishment of sinners are beliefs generally expressed as the driving motivation behind the formation and function of Discipleship Ministries.

Discipleship Ministries is only one of several evangelical organizations—
including seminaries, colleges, religious broadcasting networks, magazines,
journals, and a host of other mission organizations—formed in the mid-1900s
as a critique of both fundamentalism and the social gospel (Smith 1998; Weber
1991). In response to fundamentalism's rejection of the world and the social
gospel's seeming rejection of the tenets of individual salvation by grace, Christian reformists who defined themselves as "neoevangelicals" began to resurrect
a movement that would advocate an "engaged orthodoxy." "In keeping with their
nineteenth-century Protestant heritage, they [evangelicals] were fully committed
to maintaining and promoting confidently traditional, orthodox Protestant theology and belief, *while at the same time* becoming confidently and proactively engaged in the intellectual, cultural, social, and political life of the nation" (Smith
1998, 10). Unlike their fundamentalist cousins, these reformers wanted their
faith to become relevant to life's everyday experiences without completely de-
taching themselves from the world.

As the evangelical movement has grown, it has incorporated individuals
from all walks of life. However, while becoming "a mosaic socially, politically,
economically and regionally," there is one tenet that holds them together (Emerson and Smith 2000, 3). Evangelicals believe in the authority of the biblical text
as a means of understanding the world and the human condition within it
(Smith 1998; Weber 1991). As biblical conservatives, evangelicals desire to conserve what they consider the integrity of the Scripture and the authority of its
message. Such believers often hold to doctrines that are generally debatable
within more liberal circles: the Virgin Birth, Jesus' physical death and bodily
resurrection, the inevitability of his return, and the need for people to individually receive Jesus as their Savior. Individuals who hold to such a view of the
Bible desire to apply the principles taught within it as faithfully as possible to
their personal lives.

The development of the neoevangelical movement in mid-century American society, however, took place within the social context of a nation ravaged by racial confrontations. Evangelicalism reemerged from its nineteenth-century heritage as a religious movement in conjunction with growing American conservatism regarding civil rights and social justice concerns.

In light of this history, the founding of John McAllister's Discipleship Ministries reflected not only his own white, middle-class upbringing but also the social legacy of a racially polarized America. Those who helped to lay the foundation of the organization reached out to those who were most like them and again most immediately accessible. Yet, from the nascent stages of the organization, there was a desire to reach out to all people and to incorporate all ethnic groups in the spreading of the gospel. This desire, however, was hampered by the social context in which the organization emerged: segregated American society.

As Discipleship Ministries maintained a desire to reach out to all people, societal stressors played a major role in the formation and development of its mission as it pertained to African Americans. Such challenges hindered the growth of African American staff during the early years of the organization. While the ministry began in the early 1950s, the first black staff members did not join the organization until around 1966–67.

During the 1960s and 1970s, given the drawbacks of a racially polarized society, the founders and leaders of Discipleship Ministries wrestled with developing the most effective means of reaching bitter, turned-off, black people at a time when tensions were still high regarding civil rights issues. Even as black people joined Discipleship Ministries around the late 1960s and 1970s, the continued efforts to recruit and retain more African Americans were met with a degree of difficulty. Yet, African American commitment to joining Discipleship Ministries was based upon its commitment to biblical authority and its desire to serve as a standard-bearer for missions. Despite the challenges and, even in some cases, because of the biblical call for Christians to live in community, many blacks chose to take on the challenges of remaining with Discipleship Ministries as a part of their biblical call to reconciliation. They believe, as Discipleship Ministries advocates, in the need to conserve the biblical text and live lifestyles that reflect that call.

Cultural Conservatism

Much of the conflict for African Americans within Discipleship Ministries arises over the fluidity of the term *conservative*. While all within the organization embrace a type of biblical conservatism that rests upon the ultimate authority of Scripture, this belief manifests itself differently given the social context from which individuals emerge. The challenges that develop within Discipleship Ministries, as in other mission-type organizations, relate inescapably to the history of African Americans within the United States. Interpretations of *how* the Bible is sifted through one's heritage and experience to affect one's view of society and politics inevitably vary. Those who join staff not only join a missions organization but they also presumably adopt a particular way of viewing the world and their experience in it. In areas as complex as finances and family structure, missionaries with Discipleship Ministries create alternative cultural patterns that often conflict with the cultural knowledge of their home communities.

Financially, men and women who see the vision of Discipleship Ministries and accept the challenge to become a part of the organization often relinquish the possibilities of cushy, well-paid jobs in the secular world in order to assume the challenges of full-time ministry. Instead of anticipating the bimonthly or monthly checks from a well-established employer, as their college degrees promised, all of those who enlist with Discipleship Ministries agree to rely upon contributions from donors as their primary source of income. This funding structure at Discipleship Ministries requires that its members solicit and receive their salary through the gifts of family members, friends, churches, and others who understand their ministry and desire to see the Great Commission fulfilled. In this way Discipleship Ministries is unique and countercultural in its approach to monetary gain and the establishment of societal prestige. Its philosophy on compensation resonates with the process by which many missionaries secure their livelihood.

African Americans who answer the call to "leave everything and follow Him" in order to "catch men for Christ"—through the vehicle of Discipleship Ministries—relinquish the quest for upward mobility that inspires the vast majority of college-educated Americans. While serving with such an organization may create struggles for individuals regardless of race, for African American employees, the issue is exacerbated because of the history of racial uplift and the anticipated success that comes with a college education. For many whose families come from a history of slavery and sharecropping, or migration and urbanization, their family members often see becoming a missionary with Discipleship as a waste of a college education. Employment without the benefit of absolute financial security and upward mobility is not the mark of success that families immediately identify.

While African American ministers with Discipleship experience resistance from their families, often some of the greatest resistance has come from the leadership of historically black churches. By working with a white mission organization without consistently identifying with and seeing their mission work as a continuation of historically black mission efforts, many Discipleship employees weaken their connection with African American communities. Their means of acquiring their salaries can highlight and exaggerate this tension. As one male contributor in the southern region acknowledged in a personal interview: "Black churches look at you and say, 'We don't understand how come you're involved with this predominantly white organization!' and they have a hard time understanding how [Discipleship Ministries] works, certain ministries. And you constantly have to explain why are you with [Discipleship Ministries] and why you do this. I remember my wife and I went out [to garner funds] . . . and this black pastor laughed at us. He said, 'You mean you both have degrees and you're working for this organization raising money.' And, he laughed at us."

This approach to earning is further complicated for many onlookers by the presumed structure of absolute male and female roles within the family. In other words, not only are these college graduates not earning their full potential in the secular marketplace, but women college graduates often choose to stay home in order to raise small children. This approach to home management may appear strange to family and friends, but within the social milieu of Discipleship Ministries, this standard of home governance is not only a cultural model that works, but it is also a model understood to be supported by conservative evangelical interpretations of Scripture.

Among many evangelicals, the feminist movement of the 1970s ushered in a new understanding of family and gender that served to disrupt biblical models of family. Thus, preservation of traditional male/female roles in the home is of primary importance. The moral collapse of the nation for many is assumed to be the result of the feminist movement and the disruption of male and female responsibilities within the home and in the workplace. Women are to be caretakers at home while men provide financial support for the family based upon their work outside the home. Men within the ministry often adopt their model for headship in the home as that of a "servant leader," one who carries responsibilities outside the home and then comes home to assist his wife with domestic duties. While they relate that role to the verse in Ephesians 5:25, "Husbands, love your wives, just as Christ loved the Church and gave himself up for her," and provide domestic assistance, the primary categories remain fixed.

For those in Discipleship Ministries, this approach regarding the family is a significant aspect of the culture of the organization. Traditionally, women have left the field and returned home to attend to children when couples make decisions to start families. As models and methods are changing within the organization, however, increasing numbers of couples are trading off, in that women are so needed in the ministry field that they must coordinate with their husbands in order to reach their target audiences.

The expectation at Discipleship Ministries that mothers not work outside of the home immediately disconnected the experiences of African American female Discipleship workers from the experiences of African Americans with whom they minister. While many women missionaries embrace this model of family life and see it as an expression of their biblical ministry, their decision to stay at home is often criticized by working women in their families. One woman explained that her mother calls her "Suzie homemaker," sarcastically disapproving of her daughter's decision to spend her days home-schooling her children and preparing meals for her family. In contrast to many white evangelical women from middle-class backgrounds who receive support from their mothers who also made similar decisions, black women often have to *explain* why they have made such a decision.

Given the history of black women's involvement in the U.S. labor market, such decisions stand outside the norm. Having worked throughout the period of American slavery and then continuing their work through the periods of industrialization and urbanization, black women have maintained a consistent presence in the American labor force (Davis 1981; Hunter 1997; Landry 2000). While there are historical examples of women who have chosen to become homemakers along with a growing number of contemporary "Mocha Moms,"[2] the vast majority of these women have historically worked outside of the home, serving as domestics, farm laborers, factory workers, and teachers. When possible, they have earned advanced degrees in an attempt to educate their children, stabilize their family income, and move up the social ladder. Black Discipleship Ministry families must thus make the adjustment not only to societal pressure to convert but also family pressure that often does not value the choices they have made. In some regards, black missionaries' transition into a white mission organization can be viewed as a transition out of African American religious, social, and economic traditions.

Further complicating this problem is that upon becoming a part of contemporary interracial evangelical mission organizations, many workers do not know the history of African American evangelical missions or the struggle of the black church in America. Without this knowledge, the appeal of white-conversion Christianity can appear unproblematic. Those who want to share the gospel with the world and be held accountable for living lives of moral integrity would "naturally" become a part of such an organization. Their presence, however, immediately places them in a position that requires them to work against the stigma within African American communities regarding the racist history of white missionary organizations in places like the United States, Africa, and South America. African American employees with Discipleship give it legitimacy in the face of social critique. As one missionary explained:

> I could help [Discipleship Ministries] not be seen as a white organization in the black community because back then there was still this— black churches had a real problem with white [missionaries] comin' in and telling them this is how—these are some things you need to do. But as I would come in and share my testimony and share some of the things that I was doing in the community, it made [Discipleship] much more acceptable.

Discipleship Ministries' attempts to enlist more African American workers illustrate the desire on their part to recruit and maintain an African American presence. Their presence, however, does not come without significant financial and social compromise. While salary raising and home governance are two cultural shifts discussed here, numerous others from worship style to leadership styles also exist. Historically, the idea of joining with a large, white, missionary organization has been viewed negatively. As one long-term employee explained, "even though [Discipleship Ministries] was now trying to open up and make sure that more Blacks were involved, back [home] people were being discouraged from even working for [Discipleship]." Their communities found their involvement disturbing. Yet, their communities were not the only places of contention. Discipleship Ministry workers themselves wrestled with the ongoing cultural tensions. They felt as though they were expected to change, essentially giving up many aspects of African American religious and social traditions in order to embrace the social milieu of a more white and middle-class Christian culture. As one senior missionary explained: "Their concept of—and all of this is not intentional but just happens—their definition of discipleship is to become less of whatever culture you're [a part of and] asked to become more [a part of theirs]. And that was very subtle. I don't think it was intentional—to become more and more white."

Political Conservatism

In addition to the elements of white cultural conservatism that have been intertwined with evangelical missions, another form of conservatism obscures the participation of African Americans within Discipleship Ministries—political conservatism. Some white biblical conservatives have frequently allowed their history of privilege and power in the United States to influence their interpretations of Scripture and subsequently their interpretations of politics. These interpretations combine to provide for a political conservatism that resonates with that history. While it is important to note that everyone who subscribes to biblical conservatism does not hold simultaneously to a type of political conservatism, the pattern of practice is common.

The challenge for Christian conservatives, however, becomes apparent in knowing the history of American political conservatism. Historically, political conservatism has been used as a means of preserving the benefits of the union for white men—whether related to voting, jobs, or social institutions. Following emancipation, laws were written and maintained to garner social, political, and economic privilege for whites, as recently freed blacks worked to become a part of the mainstream of American society. Segregation laws, labor laws, and redistricting laws all worked to secure the narrow and elite participation of white men in the upper strata of American society. These same laws guaranteed the disproportionate displacement of African Americans in menial-labor jobs, second-rate classrooms, and economically disadvantaged communities. This stratification of people along the lines of perceived genetic and biological differences worked to reinforce racialized hierarchies.

The drive to maintain white privilege became the hallmark of white political conservatism during the civil rights era. These conservatives labored to ensure the ongoing stratification of whites and blacks in government, private sector, and social relations. During the Civil Rights era, conservatives worked against legislation such as the Voting Rights Act of 1965, the Civil Rights Amendment, and the Equal Rights Amendment, which were introduced as a means of securing greater representation of minorities and women in labor, education, and government. In order to advance their objectives, political conservatives advocated for states' rights and minimal influence of the federal government in state and local concerns (Omi and Winant 1994; Edsall and Edsall 1992; Lubiano 1997). This history leaves contemporary biblical conservatives in a quandary when they align with political conservatism.

According to sociologists Christian Smith and Michael Emerson, it is precisely the conservative theological tenets of evangelical Christianity that bolster the political conservatism of many of its adherents. In contemporary society many political conservatives want to retain traditional values, but such values carry with them a myriad of meanings over the years. In addition, evangelical Christians tend not to advocate for structural change when considering social problems. In discussing evangelicals' lack of participation in the civil rights movement, Emerson and Smith explain, "Because evangelicals view their primary task as evangelism and discipleship, they tend to avoid issues that hinder these activities. Thus, they are generally not countercultural. With some significant exceptions, they avoid 'rocking the boat,' and live within the confines of the larger culture." "Evangelicals," the authors contend, "usually fail to challenge the system not just out of concern for evangelism, but also because they support the American system and enjoy its fruits. They share the Protestant work ethic, support *laissez-faire* economics, and sometimes fail to evaluate whether the social system is consistent with their Christianity" (Emerson and Smith 2000, 21–22).

This relationship between evangelicals' political conservatism and their religious beliefs becomes evident in a simple discussion of success. The emphasis upon *individual* salvation as a means for transformation translates into a Horatio Alger understanding of success. Those who are successful become so by ingenuity, discipline, and persistence. The individualism latent in American society and the emphasis upon the individual in evangelical Christianity validate the political imperative to focus upon the individual—instead of the structures of society—as bearer of change. African Americans within this community must sift through the taken-for-granted claims of the organization in order to relate to both the white members of their working groups who have traditionally advocated for individual transformation as well as larger African American communities that have, of necessity, focused on structural change.

According to one senior African American worker, upon joining the ministry, he noticed that the view of Christian service was dramatically different between black missionaries and their white counterparts.

> [In the] African-American community—we're involved in social justice. Social justice is part of being a Christian and ministering to the needs of the poor or having an opportunity to help people get jobs. Discipleship is more than memorizing some scriptures. . . . Discipleship from an African-American point of view . . . is holistic so you can't separate justice. You can't separate poverty. You cannot separate other issues. To say it another way, white upper-middle class [people] would deal with issues that they saw that they were most familiar

with, most aware of. And African Americans deal with the issues that we're most aware of, the issues that we see every day that in order for us to live the Christian life we have to deal with racism, we have to deal with injustice, we have to deal with prejudice . . . so there were some issues they were not familiar with.

As a result, the ways in which many white evangelicals have responded has historically manifested itself as a lack of concern regarding issues of social justice. They have maintained an almost complete rejection of various cultural theologies, such as Latin American liberation theology or black liberation theology, which focus on biblical mandates to correct unjust systems of power. They have adopted a biblical conservatism that undergirds and supports their political conservatism. David Washington, one senior African American staff member, who has served with Discipleship Ministries for more than two decades, explains.

> Unfortunately, the history of the white evangelical movement of the post–World War II period has been generally characterized by a glowing ignorance, if not exclusion of Blacks. The rise and profusion of black liberation theology of the 60s and 70s was somewhat reactionary to the stereotyped, "white-oriented" religion and overall social attitude of that period. Many black Americans of the younger generation turned their backs on the Christian Church as a result.

Lawrence Jackson, a Discipleship Ministries employee for nine years adds to this discussion noting that, "Jesus was about social justice!" He continues, referencing the Old Testament passage, Leviticus 25, which includes the discussion of the "Year of Jubilee."

> Consecrate the fiftieth year and sound the trumpet throughout your land to all its inhabitants. It shall be a jubilee for you; each one of you is to return to his family property and each to his own clan. . . . In this Year of Jubilee everyone is to return to his own property.

Jackson also mentions that Easton's *Bible Dictionary*—more than likely used among biblical conservatives—delineates some of the objectives of the Year of Jubilee. (1) It would prevent the accumulation of land on the part of a few to the detriment of the community at large. (2) It would render it impossible for anyone to be born to absolute poverty, since everyone had his hereditary land. (3) It would preclude those inequalities that are produced by extremes of riches and poverty, and that make one man domineering over another. (4) It would utterly do away with slavery (of any kind socially).

Jackson summarizes, stating that, "not only is the Bible for social justice, it gives a solution to social injustice!" Christian scholars Craig Keener and Glenn Usry agree in concluding that, "although selfish people have twisted the Bible, like everything else, for perverse ends, the fact that the abolitionists used the Bible as a moral authority to combat prejudice suggests that it may be put to similar use for justice today. The Bible actually has more to say about justice than one might guess from many contemporary churches' selective use of it" (Keener and Usry 1996, 111).

The polarization of the greater society into black and white camps extended into the religious communities in which people served. Conservative evangelicals' complete rejection of black liberation theology seemed to bolster concerns that the religion practiced by many white evangelicals served to further oppress blacks. Debra Somers, an African American employee of Discipleship Ministries for more than twenty-five years, suggests that "across the country—that was a period of time—late '60s, '70s—when white evangelicalism had a very bad reputation in the black community because of what had happened earlier during that time. White flight had taken place and there was a lot of bitterness towards white organizations."

The adaptation of biblical conservatism to certain forms of cultural and political conservatism, such as a belief in strict individualism without a critique of social systems and a belief in preestablished domestic responsibilities, creates a brand of conservatism that is of a particular American (i.e., white American) construct. This hodgepodge of conservative values emerges from a history of white and middle-class privilege. This history has had its influence within Discipleship Ministries' history because, as John Jones, an employee of the organization with almost thirty years of experience, notes, "It was a predominantly white organization with predominantly white ideas and philosophies. It's not an organization that many African Americans will feel comfortable in . . . everything from its music to its structure, to its audience to its materials to its culture were middle-class, upper-middle-class conservative white people."

Today, large numbers of biblical conservatives tend to be more concerned about the absence of prayer in public schools, fighting against escalating abortion rates, and reversing America's decline as a Christian nation. As a result, they wage war against those they believe endorse values antithetical to Christianity. Able to enjoy the fruits of their American middle-class lifestyle, these Christians often comfortably affirm their conservatism without paying attention to the complexities of race that political conservatism has raised. As mentioned by John Jones, they deal with those issues with which they are most familiar. As educated, middle-class, and charitable citizens (i.e., givers of charity and not recipients), large numbers of evangelical conservatives have solidified their political conservatism within the parameters of a meticulous and narrowly crafted interpretation of biblical Christianity.

"What Color Is a Conservative?"

The very title of Representative J. C. Watts's 2002 autobiography, *What Color Is a Conservative?* raises complex and compelling questions about the relationship between race and political ideologies (Watts 2002). As the lone black Republican in the U.S. House of Representatives, Watts found early in his career that his political conservatism, born from his biblical conservatism, made him a rival of not only Democrats but also many other black leaders in Congress. Given the history of racial formation in the United States, there exists an established, though tedious and tenuous relationship between race, politics, and culture. Racial categories, both black and white, are socially constructed, grounded in the political and economic histories of America and not in biology or religion (Smedley 1993; Baker 1998; Mukhopadhyay and Moses 1997).

As civil rights measures took shape in the 1980s, discussions of whiteness and explicit discussions of racial privilege gave way to notions of a color-blind society. *American* became the pseudonym for *white*, as political conservatives shifted their language to adjust to changing social norms and expectations. It was no longer politically expedient to publicly advocate for separate white and black neighborhoods, jobs, and facilities. This transition left the category of *white* as a neutral though a no less powerful explication of privilege. Americans, according to conservatives, were middle class, independent, patriotic, and noncritical of American history or contemporary engagement with the world. Moreover, not only were conservatives American, they were not anti-American. They were not unpatriotic. Strikingly, those who were often identified as anti-Americans by political conservatives were often civil rights leaders, Pan-Africanists, or those challenging American policy at home and abroad, advocating for equitable labor markets and government restrictions on the growth and development of free-market capitalism. They championed the rights of women and minorities as concerns to be addressed not only by private charities but also through government intervention.

This reading of Americans versus anti-Americans by political conservatives has worked to solidify racial categories by drawing attention away from race toward a color-blind society while simultaneously supporting legislation and other policies that hold the possibility of reifying racialized disparity. While this move toward discarding race is theoretically sound and probably biblically justified, it often serves as a means of evading serious conversations about race and the need to account for racialized inequality. According to anthropologist Lee Baker, "Although disregarding race is logically accurate and theoretically sound in terms of biological categories, it is historically, socially, and politically problematic. It disregards the complex processes of racial formation and evades racism" (1998, 227). Whiteness under this new paradigm becomes a neutral and normative category. Commentators no longer speak of white versus black, but rather American versus non-American, patriots versus antipatriots, English-speakers versus non–English speakers, supporters of states' rights versus Big Government.

In this political climate, J. C. Watts's question, "What color is a conservative?" is both profound and naive. Watts, like many conservative African Americans, insists on being identified as "American," without qualification. Labels only serve to obscure African Americans' equal investment in the history and development of this country. In peculiar form, his question harkens back to W. E. B. Du Bois's caustic reminder that for people of color in the United States, "one ever feels his twoness,—an American, a Negro; two souls, two thoughts, two unreconciled strivings; two warring ideals in one dark body, whose dogged strength alone keeps it from being torn asunder" (Du Bois 1995, 45). Written nearly a century ago, Du Bois's notion of "two warring ideals" illuminates the immense tension that still exists for those striving to be simply American.

Watts is unable to affirm his conservatism without his racial identity being challenged. The impetus for Watts's question is based upon the presumption, in public discourse at least, that conservatives are whites. If we advocate for political conservatism, as Watts suggests, then we must look at the reasons for moving away from discussions of race when historically political conservatives have based their campaigns upon race-based separation. Have the times changed, or have the politics merely changed?

Furthermore, before we answer Representative Watts's question, "What color is a conservative?" we must ask what kind of conservative he is talking about. A biblical conservative? Cultural conservative? Or a political conservative? As biblical conservatives become trapped within this quagmire of political and cultural conservatism, the challenges of working within an interracial missions organization at this historic juncture are both illuminated and obscured. Does biblical conservatism really have a color? Should there even be discussions of race in an organization committed to spiritual revival and wholeness? When these discussions come up, what form should they assume? And, what happens when an organization like Discipleship Ministries commits to establishing "an African American expression of Christianity" through a ministry like IMANI?

Conservatism in Shades of Brown: Embracing an African American Evangelical Identity

IMANI was created as a means of attracting larger numbers of African Americans to Discipleship ministries. Before it began, African Americans who participated in this evangelical subculture felt as though they had to "cross over." They had to abandon their home churches and adjust to the political and cultural conservatism of many white coworkers in order to fit into this presumed race-neutral organization where all are merely American Christians. According to DeYoung et al.:

> Even today African Americans often have more traditional theological beliefs than mainline Protestant white Christians, yet they possess more progressive social and political ideas than Evangelical white Christians. This distinction has led to the development of an African-American form of Christianity qualitatively different from either mainline Protestantism or white Evangelicalism. . . . This qualitative difference is an argument for religious segregation in the black community since it means that African Americans in white churches will be either a theological or political mismatch for the rest of the congregation. (2003, 109–10)

While black religion fits into the category of "evangelical" based upon its orientation toward "salvation, revival, holiness, and biblical literalism," the majority of African Americans do not identify themselves as evangelicals. Citing James Hunter's assessment of contemporary conservative evangelicalism, Milton Sernett concludes that "although the vast majority of black Bible-believers in the traditionally black denominations can be considered evangelical in a very broad sense, they are not participants in the contemporary evangelical subculture" (Sernett 1991, 143). Their lack of participation in evangelical institutions like Discipleship Ministries stems from a number of reasons including conservative evangelicalism's earlier inefficient handling of race concerns. The creation of IMANI is not a new phenomenon in the history of evangelicalism. In 1963 black evangelicals in predominantly white evangelical organizations formed the National Black Evangelical Association (NBEA) as a means of pushing black causes within the larger structures of American evangelicalism. Included in the list of concerns to be addressed at their 1975 convention in New York City were "evangelical pan-Africanism, assisting black youth, especially college students; and increased involvement in social action projects like Operation LIVE, a street-level counseling ministry" (Sernett 1991, 144). As black evangelicals, their mission was to articulate the gospel message as that which is both individually and socially relevant.

To the extent that blacks embrace evangelical conservatism as developed in organizations like Discipleship Ministries without a simultaneous critique of these organizations, they are judged to be white. This judgment highlights the need to create a black cultural expression of this entity called an evangelical conservative. Witnessing the low numbers of African American involvement and the ongoing critiques from African American church leaders, IMANI staff members initiated a missiological method called contextualization. Contextualized ministry brings the gospel to African Americans in a form that is both meaningful and practical. It reaches out to those who have felt ostracized by the atmosphere of predominately white fellowship group meetings. IMANI simultaneously helps to build better community relations with the churches from which their participants emerge. However, the bottom line behind white resistance to contextualized ministry, according to one worker, is control.

> For a white staff person to engage in contextualization . . . creating a contextualization for African-American [participants]—it implies that they have to relinquish control and white people just don't want to do that. It's very difficult for them to do that. And that's the bottom core issue, relinquishing control.

For this missionary, contextualization is not only about creating a worship environment that is culturally relevant for African Americans but it is also about the power dynamics latent in such an attempt. To formulate an atmosphere that reaches those traditionally excluded from the mainline worship service and the ministry as a whole requires white employees to abandon complete control of the format and how they had consistently thought about doing things. This, the worker argues, is the problem. In this instance it is easier to see how culture interacts with race in such a way as to demand that attention be given not only to the variations that exist in cultural styles but also to the power dynamics involved in creating the spaces in which to express these styles. By giving voice to black cultural expressions of evangelical Christianity within a conservative organization like Discipleship Ministries, IMANI participants not only gain the support of African American communities but they also expand the involvement of black youth in the ministry.

Implications for Christians, Congregations, and Related Institutions

While it is certainly easier and possibly desirable for many religious organizations to evade conversations about race in an attempt to form a multiracial spiritual community, problems created by unspoken tensions can prove more damaging than direct confrontation. The willingness of members of Discipleship Ministries and IMANI to engage in serious and often confrontational dialogue on the topic of race demonstrates their ability to soberly explore reconciliation and true Christian community building. The establishment of IMANI has certainly drawn greater numbers of African Americans to the mission field through Discipleship Ministries. Their work in the organization, however, will continue as people struggle to understand the ways in which the conflation of biblical conservatism, cultural conservatism, and political conservatism hinder full African American participation.

The challenge of evangelical communities will be to embark upon the very tedious process of figuring out which practices, histories, and ways of knowing are indeed biblical and which are either cultural, political, or both. Which must exist and which can be discarded? Which inspire Christian character and which merely aid in promoting certain American middle-class attitudes and perspectives? Which are Christian and which are merely manifestations of rhetoric from either Republicans, Democrats, or both?

This process is crucial not only because it affects how historically white evangelical communities interact with African Americans but it also informs how these same communities interact with the larger global community. The dramatic increase in missions work around the globe mandates that missionaries understand the extent to which their proclamations are biblical and the extent to which they are laced with American cultural and political ideals. Confronting these distinctions is the long story of missions and it forms the contemporary urgency of mission organizations.

In seeing the future of missions, and Discipleship Ministries in particular, one pioneering African American missionary had this to say:

> Until we see more laborers go to the harvest from the ethnic minority communities then it's going to be an issue. Not just with [Discipleship Ministries] but I mean all over. Until we see churches have [as a] goal—ownership, until we see partnerships among different black and white churches, ethnic churches praying and reaching our cities

then we have not arrived. We arrive when there's revival, significant momentum towards fulfilling the Great Commission. And . . . remember, that's the goal. The goal is not having faces of color, the goal is the awakening . . . the Great Commission . . . will not happen until Third-World people are equipped and mobilized to share the gospel of Jesus Christ. That is the key. It's not the white people going and doing all this stuff. . . . It's Third-World people that's going to be the key to revival and the key to the fulfillment of the Great Commission because then you have everybody involved in sharing this thing. So, once people realize that, I think there will be more interested because whites in this country are becoming fewer and fewer. And there are more Muslims coming here, there are more Hindus coming here, there are more Third-World people coming here. If we don't make changes now all those [Discipleship Ministries] and [names other missionary organizations] all of them will be out of business, they will not exist.

According to this lifetime employee, the creation of organizations like IMANI is thus, ironically, not only about the cultivation of African American evangelical leadership but it is also and primarily about sustaining the mission and goal of Discipleship Ministries—reaching the world with the gospel of Jesus Christ.

NOTES

1. References to "Discipleship Ministries," "IMANI," and personal names used in conjunction with these organizations are all pseudonyms, employed to preserve the confidentiality of those involved.

2. Mocha Moms have experienced tremendous growth over the last decade as a support organization for primarily college-educated women of color who have chosen to leave professional careers in order to downscale their lifestyles and become stay-at-home moms.

REFERENCES

Baker, Lee D. 1998. *From savage to negro: Anthropology and the construction of race, 1896–1954.* Berkeley and Los Angeles: University of California Press.

Davis, Angela. 1981. *Women, race and class.* New York: Random House.

DeYoung, Curtis Paul, Michael O. Emerson, Karen Chai Kim, and George Yancey. 2003. *United by faith: The multiracial congregation as an answer to the problem of race.* Oxford: Oxford University Press.

Du Bois, W. E. B. 1995. *The souls of black folk.* New York: Penguin.

Edsall, Thomas and Mary Edsall. 1992. *Chain reaction: The impact of race, rights, and taxes on American politics.* New York: W. W. Norton.

Emerson, Michael O., and Christian Smith. 2000. *Divided by faith: Evangelical religion and the problem of race in America.* Oxford: Oxford University Press.

Harrison, Faye V. 1995. The persistent power of "race" in the cultural and political economy of racism. *Annual Review of Anthropology* 24:47–74.

Hunter, Tara W. 1997. *To 'joy my freedom: Southern black women's lives and labors after the Civil War.* Cambridge, MA: Harvard University Press.

Keener, Craig, and Glenn Usry. 1996. *Black man's religion: Can Christianity be afrocentric?* Downers Grove, IL: InterVarsity.

Landry, Bart. 2000. *Black working wives: Pioneers of the American family revolution.* Berkeley and Los Angeles: University of California Press.

Lubiano, Wahneema, ed. 1997. *The house that race built: Black Americans, U.S. terrain.* New York: Pantheon.

Mukhopadhyay, Carol C., and Yolanda T. Moses. 1997. Reestablishing "race" in anthropological discourse. *American Anthropologist* 99:517–33.

Omi, Michael and Howard Winant. 1994. *Racial formation in the United States.* New York: Routledge.

Sernett, Milton G. 1991. Black religion and the question of evangelical identity. In *The variety of American evangelicalism,* ed. Donald W. Dayton, and Robert K. Johnston. Downers Grove, IL: InterVarsity.

Smedley, Audrey. 1993. *Race in North America: Origin and evolution of a worldview.* Boulder, CO: Westview.

Smith, Christian. 1998. *American evangelicalism: Embattled and thriving.* Chicago: University of Chicago.

Watts, J. C. Jr. With Chriss Winston. 2002. *What color is a conservative? My life and my politics.* New York: HarperCollins.

Weber, Timothy P. 1991. Premillennialism and the Branches of Evangelicalism. In *The variety of American evangelicalism,* ed. Donald W. Dayton, and Robert K. Johnston. Downers Grove, IL: InterVarsity.

PART III

Using and Abusing the Bible in Ethnic and Racial Contexts

10

The Sword of Truth in a Sea of Lies: The Theology of Hate

Michael Jessup

> The question is not whether we will be extremists, but what kind of
> extremists we will be. Will we be extremists for hate or for love?
> —Martin Luther King Jr., *Letter from
> Birmingham Jail*

College campuses throughout the United States can be hotbeds of
hate activity. The FBI and the U.S. Department of Education estimate five hundred thousand college students are targets of racially
based slurs and physical attacks (Southern Policy Law Center 2004).
These range from racist cartoons in campus publications or racist
graffiti to Affirmative Action bake sales—with prices tied to race,
ethnicity, and religion. The Southern Poverty Law Center, the Anti-
Defamation League, and the FBI routinely track more than seven
hundred hate organizations, two hundred patriot/militia groups, and
more than eight thousand cases of hate crimes each year. Although
actual numbers are elusive, they estimate between thirty thousand
and fifty thousand people are involved in hate organizations. The af-
termath of September 11, 2001, has also fueled a rise in ethnic nationalism and the growth of hate organizations and hate group
activities. Since 2002, the number of active hate organizations rose
6 percent, and the number of hate Web sites was up 12 percent (Potok 2004). *Stormfront* (Stormfront.org), the largest and most powerful hate site on the Internet, recently celebrated its tenth birthday,
boasting 52,566 registered users. In fact, *Stormfront* is the 338th
largest electronic forum, and ranks in the top one percent, in terms
of use, of Internet sites (Kim 2005). Recently, 150 to 200 anti-
immigration vigilantes called Minutemen now patrol the U.S.-Mexico
border. These "undocumented border patrol agents," claiming fifteen

thousand strong, are attempting to "protect America from the tens of millions of invading illegal aliens who are devouring and plundering our nation" (Holthouse 2005).

Organizations like the Aryan Nations, Kingdom Identity Ministries, the Knights of the Ku Klux Klan, Kinsman Redeemer Ministries, as well as various skinhead and neo-Nazi organizations, all invoke the name of God and vociferously proclaim, "God is on our side." For most of these radical groups, God is at the center, offering a virulent racist theology and a vigilante form of Christianity. This paper focuses on how hate organizations theologically frame race and ethnicity, and provides a biblical response to hate theology.

Who Joins?

Although scholarship regarding hate organizations and their participants is inconclusive and sometimes contradictory, a general profile emerges. Aho (1990), for example, found that compared with the general population, hate believers: (1) had slightly higher levels of formal education; (2) were most likely middle-aged white males; (3) had higher rates of marital stability and fertility; (4) worked in occupations more socially isolated from their immediate communities (e.g., mining, lumbering, and maritime trades); (5) lived in rural communities; and (6) were raised in Protestant churches (80.5%). Moreover, theologically, many declared a strong allegiance to Calvinism and dispensationalism. Additionally, new research indicates that contemporary hate organizations are targeting more college students, suburbanites, and women, and are aggressively recruiting younger, upwardly mobile members with computer skills (Apple and Messner 2001; Cannon and Cohen 1999; Cloud, Grace, Roche, and Shannon 1999).

Framing the Theology of Hate

Building on the works of Erving Goffman, frames are patterns of interpretation that a social movement organization uses to structure experiences and render events meaningful (Goffman 1974; Snow, Rochford, Worden, and Benford 1986; Snow and Benford 1992; Hunt and Benford 1994). A majority of white supremacist organizations (e.g., Aryan Nations, American Front, White Knights of the Ku Klux Klan) cluster around an active, process-derived theology-of-hate frame. A theology-of-hate frame punctuates and encodes objects, situations, events, and experiences, and sequences actions making past, present, and future behaviors meaningful. Moreover, this theology-of-hate frame is vital for attracting and keeping movement believers, and also shapes how organizations respond to counter-frames of opponents (Johnson et al. 1995; White 2001). In essence, this theology of hate is the glue that provides group identity and meaning, and serves as the basis for claiming ethnic, racial, and national superiority. The theology-of-hate frame is divided into three overlapping ideologies: (1) the biblical/theological origins of white racial superiority; (2) the diagnostic theology—the determination of some aspect of social life as problematic and in need of change; and (3) the prognostic theology—the search for a solution to diagnosed problems, specifying strategies, tactics, and targets.

Biblical/Theological Origins of White Racial Superiority

This analysis of the theology of hate, often referred to as Identity Christianity, must begin with a caveat: there is no center of orthodoxy, few universally accepted dogmas, and no respected theologians (Barkun 1997). Moreover, the ideas argued by these groups are heretical as measured by every historic Christian creed and by the standards of all historic Christian communions. This theology of hate is heretical, is in a constant state of flux, and is full of contradictions and idiosyncratic biblical hermeneutics. Despite its theological and philosophical flaws, it would be unwise to discredit its presence, power, and peril. The theological origins of hate are polygenist, arguing that there are several distinct genetic origins for humans. This theology of hate begins with the assumption that Aryans and people of color were separate creations of God. It is commonly believed that nonwhites were part of God's first creation, and are referred to as "mud people," or "the beasts of the field" (Aho 1990; Goodrick-Clarke 2002; Walters 2000; Zeskind 1986). God's first creation produced people of color, and these people were created in God's shadow. These people ultimately were inferior to whites, less intellectually endowed, and descended from animals not God. It is generally believed that God is white, and hears only the prayers of whites (Kaplan 1997; Barkun 1997). Moreover, people of color are without souls, and do not share in redemption. All nonwhites are excluded from the redemptive work of Christ because "the seed of the Serpent cannot be saved" (Gayman 1994, 9; Walters 2000).

Adam and Eve, however, were the first white people created by God on the eighth day. This new white race was specially chosen by God, and endowed with exceptional spiritual and intellectual capacities. As stated in the doctrinal beliefs of the Kingdom Identity Ministries, "We believe God chose unto himself a special race of people that are above all people upon the face of the Earth. . . . We believe the White, Anglo-Saxon, Germanic, and the kindred people to be God's true, literal Children of Israel" (Kingdom Identity Ministries 2003, 5). Hate theologians argue the Hebrew word for Adam meant "ruddy"— to show blood in the face, to be fair-skinned. Likewise, the Bible is written only for whites. As Mark Downy, pastor of Kinsman Redeemer Ministries, states:

> In Genesis, God created Adam, the first man. The Holy Bible is a history book of Adam's people. The Hebrew word for man is *Adam* itself and actually means to show blood in the face; to be fair; rosy cheeked; to be ruddy; and to be able to blush or flush. One must admit that the other races do not fit this description and therefore, cannot descend

through Adam. God declared, "Everything after its own kind." From Adam, there proceeded a chosen line who followed God after righteousness. From Adam's son Seth, to Noah the chosen line remained racially pure and faithful to God. Noah and his family were preserved during the Great Flood while God destroyed the disobedient. Noah's son, Shem, continued the chosen line and these people became known as Shemites or Semites. (Kinsman Redeemer Ministries)

Hate theology, furthermore, claims that race mixing (i.e., interracial dating, marriage, and even worship) was the original sin in the garden. When bestiality is prohibited and punishable by death (Lev 20:15–16), this is perceived as evidence declaring that God forbids race mixing (Daniels 1997; Walters 2000). Hate theology claims race mixing is an abomination to God—a satanic attempt to destroy the chosen seedline. Race mixing undermines God's original design and creation (Deut 21), and leads to the inevitable pollution of the white race (Aho 1990; Dobratz and Shanks-Meile 1997; Swain and Nieli 2003). Accordingly, Richard Butler, founder of the Aryan Nations and the self-proclaimed head of the Church of Jesus Christ-Christian, decrees that white persons consorting with blacks are guilty of race treason, and should be punished by death (Aryan Nations n.d.). These theological beliefs obviously justify white racial supremacy and terrorism against Jews and nonwhites.

Jews are said to represent a second creation or seedline—the result of a seduction of Eve by Satan, producing Cain (Kaplan 1997; Walters 2000; Dobratz and Shanks-Meile 1997). Cain was the product of the union between Eve and the serpent, and is literally presented as "the son of Satan, and father of the Jews." Satan planned to perpetuate his own seedline through Cain. Satan took the form of a serpent, "a highly intelligent two-legged beast of the field" and, presumably, a purebred Negro. Hence, the Jews and people of color are the literal children of Satan—the embodiment of evil (Aho 1990; Sharpe 2000; Young 1990). As stated in the doctrinal statement of the Kingdom Identity Ministries, "We believe in an existing being known as the Devil or Satan . . . who has the literal seed or posterity in the earth commonly called Jews today. These children of Satan through Cain . . . are contrary to all men, though they often pose as ministers of righteousness" (Kingdom Identity Ministries, 1999). It is also assumed that Adam was only the father of Abel, and later Seth. Cain and Abel had different fathers, and were only related by their mother (Goodrick-Clarke 2002).

This "two-seeds" doctrine flows from a twisted hermeneutical approach from three central texts.

1. Revelation 2:9: "I know your afflictions and your poverty—yet you are rich! I know the slander of those who say they are Jews and are not, but are a synagogue of Satan" (NIV).
2. Revelation 3:9: "I will make those who are the synagogue of Satan, who claim to be Jews though they are not, but are liars—I will make them come and fall down at your feet and acknowledge that I have loved you" (NIV).

3. John 8:44: "You [Cain] belong to your father, the devil, and you want to carry out your father's desire. He was a murderer from the beginning, not holding to the truth, for there is not truth in him. When he lies, he speaks his native language, for he is a liar and the father of lies" (NIV).

In the New Testament, the teachings of Jesus also are used to reinforce this dual-seedline analogy. Jesus' condemnation, for example, of the Pharisees and Sadducees as a "brood of vipers" (Matt 3:7–9) is said to expose the Jews as the literal race of snakes (Satan). Later, Jesus' warning concerning false prophets who come as wolves in sheep's clothing is reinterpreted as a warning of Satan's offspring trying to pass themselves off as God's true white offspring. In Jesus' parable of the wheat and the weeds (Matt 13:24–30), hate theologians argue that Jesus is describing the Jews as the "seeds of the serpent," whose purpose is to destroy God's white Israel. Finally, when Jesus was on the Mount of Transfiguration (Matt 17:2), his clothing was "as white as snow." Similarly, when the angels appear at the resurrection, Jesus is described as wearing "clothing white as snow" (Matt 28:3). For hate theology, this proves God's preference for the color white (Walters 2000).

Hate adherents also presuppose Jesus' life and ministry were to bring salvation only to "God's chosen" (Swain and Nieli 2003, 214). For example, Jesus said, "I am not sent but unto the lost sheep of the House of Israel" (Matt 15:24). In the conversion of Zacchaeus in Luke 19:9–10, Jesus said, "Today salvation has come to this house, because he also is a son of Abraham; for the Son of Man has come to seek and save that which was lost." Therefore, Zacchaeus found salvation only because he was already an Israelite. Finally, Jesus commanded his disciples, "Do not go into the way of the Gentiles, and do not enter a city of the Samaritans. But go rather to the lost sheep of the house of Israel" (Matt 10:5–6). These examples elucidate that Jesus' message is directed specifically to the house of Israel—God's chosen.

Hate theology also uses the word *Jew* in its own unique ways. The word *Jew* in the Bible must be understood, it is asserted, in three different senses. First, *Jew* can be a geographical reference—someone who is from the country of Judea. Jesus was given the title "King of the Jews" by Roman authorities merely because of his birth in Bethlehem of Judea. Obviously, Christ could not come from a child of Satan (Swift, 2003) http://www.nidlink.com/~aryanvic/jcjew.html). Second, *Jew* also designates a distinct race of people—biological descendants of Satan. Third, *Jew* can also mean an ungodly religion, where satanic beliefs were corrupted by pagan Babylonian beliefs and morals to form Judaism (Walters 2000). Hence, hate adherents believe, "Modern Jews . . . have no relationship to Abraham, to Isaac, to Jacob, or to any of the Hebrew characters of the Old Testament. These Jews could be lumped . . . with those spoken of in Revelation 2:9 and 3:9. We believe that all of those people who claim to be the true descendants of Abraham, Isaac, and Jacob and call themselves Jews but are not" (Gayman in Swain and Nieli 2003, 220–21).

Likewise, the word *Gentile* is also twisted. Gentiles were the great multitude of lost Israelites dispersed from the northern kingdom—heathen peoples estranged from the covenants God made to Israel. If Jesus was sent only to white Israel, then Paul was sent out to preach to the Gentiles—white Israelites living in dispersion among other races. Hence, when Paul (Eph 2:16) refers to God reconciling believers into one body through the cross of Jesus, he is actually referring to the unification of the Jews from both the northern and southern kingdoms (Gayman in Swain and Nieli 2003, 219).

Finally, Aryans are the true children of God. If Adam and Eve were the first white people, then Anglo-Saxons are the real biblical chosen people—the true Israelites. This theological frame borrows extensively from British-Israelism doctrine (Barkun 1997; Kaplan 1997; Zeskind 1986). Briefly, British-Israelism begins with the idea that the Caucasian nations of Europe are actually the ten lost tribes of Israel. Through a series of migrations, the people of Israel migrated and established themselves in northern Europe. According to British-Israelism, ancient Israel divided itself into two kingdoms following Solomon's reign. Descending from Jacob, the northern kingdom consisted of ten of twelve tribes. The northern kingdom borrowed extensively from religious and cultural customs of the surrounding non-Hebrew tribes. When the victorious Assyrians conquered these tribes and recolonized the area, the ten tribes were thought to be lost. British-Israelism, however, argues that when the people of the northern kingdom went into Assyrian captivity, they did not remain there, but escaped in successive, independent waves. Using different names (Scutai, Sak-Geloths, Massegetae, Khumri, Cimmerians, Goths, Ostrogoths, Visigoths, etc.), they moved westward, across Asia Minor, then into Europe, and eventually into the Scandinavian countries and the British Isles. Later, the United States was identified as the thirteenth tribe of Manasseh (The Anglo-Saxon-Celtic Belief 1941). For many hate believers, the United States is the true promised land—the birthright nation, the Zion of God (Walters 2000; Goff 1955). As Mark Downey states, "The United States of America and Canada uniquely fulfill the prophesied place of the regathering of all the tribes of Israel" (Kinsman Redeemer Ministries 2003).

TABLE 10.1. Tribal Migrations of Israel

Tribe of Israel	Western Nation
Dan	Denmark
Gad	Italy
Asher	Sweden
Issachar	Finland
Simeon	Spain
Zebulen	France
Naphatali	Norway
Benjamin	Iceland
Reuben	Netherlands
Judah	Germany
Ephraim	Great Britain
Manasseh	United States

The theology of hate adherents contend that because the tribes were disobedient, God took away the title of Israel, and punished them for a period of seven times for each tribe. (A time consists of 360 years, so each punishment lasted 2,520 years.) Coincidently, western European nations formed exactly 2,520 years after punishment. For example, 2,520 years from the captivity of Dan, the first royal monarch of Denmark ascended to the throne; and 2,520 years from the day the tribe of Manasseh was taken into captivity by the Assyrians is the 4th of July 1776.

Diagnostic Theology

Though the hour is late, and the process of degeneracy well-advanced, it is NOT TOO LATE for the remaining Aryan men and women to form a community, an ethnic state, and eventually, a NEW NATION.

—Gentry n.d., 2

A diagnostic theology identifies some aspect of social life as problematic and in need of change. Problem identification and attribution of blame are inherently part of this diagnostic framing process (Snow and Benford 1988; Kinder and Sanders 1996). When hate believers describe race in America, they frame the issue in theological ideas and language. Identity adherents claim that Jews are the root of most, if not all, of the social ills in American society (Aho 1990). America's social problems are caused by an advancing and consuming proliferation of a Jewish and a nonwhite culture of degeneracy. For example, the National Alliance (n.d.) claims:

> Jewish control of the American mass media is the sole most important fact of life, not just in America, but in the whole world today. There is nothing—plague, famine, economic collapse, even nuclear war—more dangerous to the future of our people. . . . The Jew-controlled entertainment media have taken the lead in persuading a whole generation that homosexuality is a normal and acceptable way of life; that there is nothing at all wrong with White women dating or marrying Black men, or with White men marrying Asian women; that all races are inherently equal in ability and character—except that the character of the White race is suspect because of a history of oppressing other races; and that any effort by Whites at racial self-preservation is reprehensible.

Jews are responsible for abortion, drugs, liquor, gambling, humanism, sexual perversions, AIDS, and race mixing. "The Jew is like a destroying virus that attacks our racial body to destroy our White culture and purity of our race" (Ridgeway 1990, 169). Jews are also portrayed as sexual deviants, claiming that the Talmud legitimates child molestation, necrophilia, and bestiality (Herrell 1996). Recently, some hate organizations (e.g., National Alliance) believe that the Jews had knowledge of the September 11, 2001, attacks, and engineered the U.S. war on terror to eliminate Israel's enemies.

In addition to hatred toward nonwhites—particularly African Americans, Hispanics, and nonwhite immigrants—homosexuality is the new target of many hate organizations. Homosexuals are considered traitors to the white race. Hate organizations, based on Deuteronomy 22:5 and Leviticus 20:13, decree that homosexuality is a crime against God and nature. The Alabama Knights of the Ku Klan Klan states, "My fellow Christians do not let your children be enticed by these perverted satanists! [sic] Stand against the immorality! These defoulers of Gods [sic] law want only to convert your children into there [sic] lifestyle. Do what ever [sic] is necessary to protect your children!!!!!" (Alabama Ku Klux Klan 2003).

In a battle of good and evil, the white forces of good will be pitted against the armies of Satan, represented by the Jewish-controlled federal government known as ZOG (Zionist Occupied Government). Identity followers will be required to wage a war against the illegitimate ZOG. Among hate believers there is a fear that the federal government, aided by blacks, liberals, gays, Catholics, and Hispanics, will work to control, eliminate, or restrict the role of whites (Aho 1990; Young 1990; Sharpe 2000). Consequently, "Washington D.C. is the seat of . . . Satan" ($100 Billion Freemen Lien, reprinted in Walters 2000, 63). There is also a growing fear of a New World Order—the establishment of a one-world government controlled by Jews. Since the federal government supports this New World Order, and is unashamedly pro-Israel, the government is considered an illegal, foreign-occupying force (Aho 1990; Sharpe 2000; Dobratz and Shanks-Meile 1997; Southern Poverty Law Center 1996). The call to reclaim white sovereignty requires organized aggression against the federal government. The National Alliance (2003) states:

> With the growth of mass democracy, the rise in the influence of the mass media on public opinion, and the insinuation of the Jews into a position of control over the media, the U.S. Government was gradually transformed into the malignant monster it is today: the single most dangerous and destructive enemy our race has ever known.

Moreover, there is a mounting fear of an organized world conspiracy against whites and a paranoid fear of the extermination of the white race.

Prognostic Theology

We must secure the existence of our people and a future for White children.
—David Lane (quote used by many skinhead organizations)

The prognostic ideology illustrates how the problems in the diagnostic frame are to be addressed. Solutions are suggested, and strategies, tactics, and targets are identified (Snow and Benford 1988). The prognostic frame begins with a postmillennial interpretation of the Bible, envisioning a racial apocalypse and the extermination of the enemies of God. Essentially, the second coming of Christ and the destruction of the world are near, yet in order for the second coming of Christ to occur, God's law on earth must be first established through a great battle (Armageddon). America is entering a period of tribulation, and whites have a special role to play as "elect": driving out the forces of evil. The reestablishment of white sovereignty depends on the organized aggression against the enemies of true Christians—all nonwhites and all non-Protestants. Similarly, the theology of hate eschews all forms of rapture doctrines. Rapture doctrines are Jewish fables that lead to apathy. As Richard Butler, former leader of the Aryan Nations, states (2003):

> WE BELIEVE in the preservation of our Race, individually and collectively, as a people as demanded and directed by Yahweh. We believe our Racial Nation has a right and is under obligation to preserve itself and its members.

> WE BELIEVE that there is a day of reckoning. The usurper will be thrown out by the terrible might of Yahweh's people as they return to their roots and their special destiny. We know there is soon to be a day of judgment and a day when Christ's Kingdom (government) will be established on earth, as it is in heaven.

For hate believers, the battle of Armageddon is quickly approaching, and the elect must wake up from their apocalyptic slumber and be ready to drive out the forces of evil. The fundamental obstacle is the dulled consciousness of white Israelites unaware of their racial identity. As stated by the Las Vegas Skinheads (2003):

> They say ignorance is bliss, and in these decadent and evil times our people have become comfortable. Too comfortable in fact, to see the injustices inflicted upon them daily. American whites have become mentally weak and sheep-like, thanks due largely to the opinionated mass media. White youth emulate the culture of alien people, while their culture and the accomplishments of their mighty race have been all but forgotten. So think of skinheads as a sword of truth in a sea of lies. Defenders of a blood that's walked the earth for seven thousand years and risen above all. Consider skinheads the modern day protectors of the race that brought culture, technology, and enlightenment to the face of the earth.

Since embracing violence is a means of preserving the faith, and there is no sympathy for the devil, the coming of the great and terrible of day of the Lord requires aggressively preparing for Christ's return. Members of the Aryan Nations of the KKK, for example, sign a code of conduct stating, "I am an Aryan Warrior. I serve in the movement, which guards my race and our way of life, and I am prepared to give my life in its defense." Many hate organizations are planning for an inevitable militaristic racial battle of spiritual significance.

In order to ensure victory, the elect must strive for self-sufficiency, establishing survival camps and teaching survival skills. The true children of God must be ready by preparing arsenals, learning to make bombs and other devices, stocking up on nonperishable foods for bomb shelters, and practicing war games in clandestine, wooded areas. God, guts, and guns are required—they are the Aryan's sacred call. As Wistrich (1985, 18) states, "God requires gun ownership." Less militaristic hate organizations work to mold public opinion by generating and disseminating propaganda, aggressively recruiting new members, fundraising, learning self-defense and self-discipline, and gathering and evaluating intelligence (National Alliance 2003).

The theology of hate also stresses the importance of spiritual factors as rationales for promoting racism and discrimination. The Aryan elect are to lead the struggle to fight against the violation of God's law, against sin, and against the anti-Christ forces. Jesus is often portrayed as the supreme segregationist—the Aryan warrior who has come to battle Satan's seedline. The theology of hate presumes that Jesus is calling all Aryans to "come out" of Babylon and be separated (Walters 2000). In Matthew 15:24 (NIV), for example, Jesus said, "I was sent only to the lost sheep of the house of Israel."

Hate believers obviously support a theology embracing a militant, nationalistic, racial, and ethnocentrically based protectionism, yet are also sporadically engaged in political mainstreaming—using conventional strategies to gain influence in the political system (Dobratz and Shanks-Meile 1997; Lofton 1985). Although tactics, strategies, and political agendas are often factionalized within hate groups, there are certain issues that tend to link networks of hate believers. These mainstreaming issues center around the promotion of a new "civil rights for whites"—requiring immigration restriction, global isolation, and increased state and local autonomy. The Knights of the Ku Klux Klan and the National Alliance are two large, active hate organizations promoting a "mainstream" political agenda. For example, Thomas Robb, national director for Knights of the Ku Klux Klan, states:

> We envision an America once again guided by Biblical principles and laws. Whose laws better to follow than those of the creator of our universe? Who has a more perfect knowledge of good and evil, or right and wrong, or pain and pleasure than our creator Jesus Christ? Does it not make sense to then heed his advice and the advice of Biblical scholars inspired by God thousands of years ago? . . . The Knights program makes a life long serious commitment [sic] to its potential to bring about a white Christian political and social revolution in the United States perhaps sparking victories for White Christians the whole world over! (Knights of the Ku Klux Klan 2003)

Similarly, the Knights of the Ku Klux Klan advocate:

> Recognition that America was founded as a white nation, and we promote love and appreciation for our unique European (white) culture.

We support the voluntary repatriation of everyone not satisfied with living under White Christian rules of conduct back to the native lands of their people.

Put America first in all foreign matters, and stop all foreign aid immediately. Outlaw the purchase of American property and industry by foreign corporations and investors.

Abolish all discriminatory affirmative action programs.

Put American troops on our border and stop the flood of illegal aliens.

Abolish all anti-gun laws and encourage every adult to own a weapon.

Repeal the federal reserve act, and balance the federal budget.

We support a return to parental authority without the government interference in the raising of our children.

We support state sovereignty resolutions.

We support all U.S. veterans, and advocate a strong defense department to safeguard American citizens. (Knights of the Ku Klux Klan 2003)

Of course, all of these political positions are ordained by God, and reflect an approaching consummation of warfare between the seed-lines.

Finally, this hate theology promotes widespread disdain for "establishment Christianity." According to Gayman (Swain and Nieli 2003, 219), Christianity has extracted biblically mandated ethnic perimeters and boundaries, and transferred all of the unconditional covenants, pledges, and promises made to Israelites to the church. Modern Christianity's goal as a multiracial and international body of believers professing a belief in Jesus Christ is inconsistent with the teachings of the Bible, which identifies the church as an ethnic, racial Israel.

In sum, a skewed theological frame fuels hatred, racial antipathy, and promotes Aryan solidarity. The theology of hate declares that whites are the "chosen ones," and that the white race is genetically and spiritually superior to other races. The theology of hate maintains that Adam was a white man, and the product of a second creation. God's first creation—people of color, particularly Jews—are literally, the children of Satan. Fearing a world conspiracy against whites, and possessing a paranoid fear of the extermination of the white race, hate promoters believe that whites have a special role to play as "elect": driving out the forces of evil in order to protect and uphold Aryan spiritual values.

A Biblical Narrative: Implications for Christians

Hate is never biblically justified. As white civil rights activist Ed King states, "Jesus rejected hatred because he saw that hatred meant death to the mind, death to the spirit, death to communion with his father. . . . When love is negotiated in a way that preserves a place for hatred, hate proves all-consuming" (reprinted in Marsh 1997, 123). Clearly, hate theology is heretical, and contrary to every statement of orthodox Christianity. To neutralize the theology of hate, four biblical principles emerge: the theologies of the family of God, *shalom*, oneness, and racial reconciliation.

First, Christians are to see themselves as members of a divine family headed by God and united by identity and purpose (Eph 2:19; 1 Cor 6:18; Mark 3:31–35; Hos 11). True salvation makes one a part of the family of God, which is composed of believers from every tribe, nation, and culture (1 Cor 12:13–14; Rev 7:9). As Pao suggests, God's people create a "new family" allowing people to relate to one another equally as children of God. In his holy family, there are no "others," only brothers and sisters (Acts 10:34). The diversity of the created was designed to honor the creator. Moreover, as members of God's holy family, we are to love and empower our brothers and sisters (John 10:10; Phil 2). Jesus continually encourages his followers to lift up the fallen, forgive the guilty, encourage maturity in the weak, enable the unable, and eschew dependency (Balswick and Balswick 2000). Empowering involves building others up, expressing interest in the growth of others, and finding ways to encourage all members of God's family to reach their greatest potential (1 Cor 8:1).

Second, God calls all Christians to be about the work of *shalom*. God calls his people to challenge, restore, and transform the culture. *Shalom* is God's pervasive presence of peace, prosperity, wholeness, health, and happiness in society (Sider 1999; Fraser and Campolo 1992). God desires that all people experience *shalom* within our families, neighborhoods, cities, and nations. *Shalom* reigns when God's people humbly fulfill the demands of the law: loving mercy, justice, and faith (Matt 23:23; Mic 6:8). Obviously, *shalom* is required for God's family to maximize its social and moral development, as well as provide material and emotional stability of its members. *Shalom* does not require merely fair procedures, but necessitates new opportunities. Christians are called to work for a social structure that: (1) upholds the dignity and worth of all individuals; (2) promotes policies that empower the poor and the marginalized; (3) resists the centralization, concentration, and inevitable abuse of wealth and power; (4) provides equitable and nondiscriminatory access to economic and political resources; and (5) supports quality education, health care, and public safety (adapted from Sider 1999, 49–98). Believers seeking racial, social, and economic justice are a witness to others, and, ultimately, are honoring God.

Third, the idea of one creator, one creation, and one body affirms a common humanity of all people (Gen 1:26; Ps 148:11–14; Isa 45:22; Mic 4:1–2; see also Hiebert's chapter). Unity is an essential part of the gospel (Eph 2:14–15). Oneness also presumes God created one race, and Jesus came to restore God's original intention of the essential oneness of all humanity (DeYoung et al. 2003; Yancey 2003). This oneness theology supersedes biology, ethnicity, and even culture (Luke 10:25–37; Rom 12). Believers are called out of various ethnic/racial groups and united as one in Christ (Ware 1998, 62). "There is no longer Jew or Greek, there is no longer slave or free, there is no longer male and female; for you are all one in Christ Jesus" (Gal 3:28 NRSV). Oneness, however, does not imply total assimilation into a predominant culture, but offers space for new, shared experiences. God's plan is unity with diversity (Ware 1998, 68).

Finally, Christians have been commanded to the ministry of reconciliation (2 Cor 5:18–21). Christ calls believers to love one another by deliberately attempting to interact with different ethnic groups (Yancey 2003). Scriptural evidence is most clearly explained in the story of the Samaritan woman at the well (John 4:4–42). The Samaritans were a people with mixed ancestry (Tienou) and there was notorious enmity between Jews and Samaritans. Yet Jesus went out of his way to create interethnic interactions. Moreover, the New Testament describes the church comprising people from many different nations and cultures (Matt 28:19; 1 Cor 12:13; Gal 3:28; Rev 5:9). According to Perkins (1986), racial reconciliation requires the following of Christians:

- Admit racial separation exists, and misrepresents what God intends for His people. Confession and forgiveness will help heal the wounds of racism.
- Submit to God and seek to build loving relationships across racial barriers.
- Commit to racial reconciliation. It is the church of Jesus Christ which has been given the ministry of reconciliation.

Implications for Citizens

In addition to the aforementioned biblical responsibilities as people of God, our citizenship also requires responsibilities. Obviously, hate activity will not go away, and may even escalate as the United States becomes increasingly diverse. The most accessible and widely used response to organized hate is based on the Southern Poverty Law Center's publication, *Ten Ways to Stop Hate* (2003). They recommend:

Act: Do something—in the face of hatred, apathy will be interpreted as acceptance.
Unite: Work to create a network of those opposed to hate.
Support the Victims: Let the victims know that we want them, and that they are valued and the community cares for them.
Do Your Homework: Know what organizations are involved, their agenda, and seek help from anti-hate organizations.
Create an Alternative: Do not attend a hate rally. Instead, create alternate events to counter hate.
Speak Up: Take every opportunity to expose and denounce hate.
Lobby Leaders: Persuade community officials to take a stand against hate.
Look Long Range: Create a "bias response team," and hold annual events to celebrate your community's diversity.

Teach Tolerance: Promote programs in schools, homes, and churches which value diversity.
Dig Deeper: Work on all the issues that divide a community.

When Christians embrace complexity and serious reflection, and take their responsibilities as members of the body of Christ and their citizenship seriously, the consuming theology of hate will grow dim. Through acts of grace, love, justice, and unity, God not only declares himself but also arouses, empowers, and asserts a world of love and righteousness.

REFERENCES

Aho, James A. 1990. *The politics of righteousness: Idaho Christian patriotism.* Seattle: University of Washington Press.
Alabama Ku Klux Klan. 2003. http://www.alabamakkk.com. Accessed Dec. 15, 2003.
The Anglo-Saxon-Celtic belief. 1946. *Destiny* (January), 175.
Apple, Angela L., and Beth A. Messner. 2001. Paranoia and paradox: The apocalyptic rhetoric of Christian identity. *Western Journal of Communication* 65(2): 206–27.
Aryan Nations. n.d. Race traitors (flier).
Aryan nations of the KKK. 2003. http://www.aryannationsasknights.com. Accessed Dec. 15, 2003.
Balswick, Jack O., and Judith K. Balswick. 2000. *The family: A Christian perspective on the contemporary home.* 2nd ed. Grand Rapids, MI: Baker.
Barkun, Michael. 1997. *Religion and the racist right.* Rev. ed., Chapel Hill: University of North Carolina Press.
Cannon, A., and W. Cohen. 1999. The church of the almighty white man. *U.S. News and World Report* 127 (July 19): 22–23.
Censored Bible Teachings. nd., na. pamphlet.
Cloud, J., J. Grace, T. Roche, and E. Shannon. 1999. Is hate on the rise? *Time South Pacific* 29:26.
Daniels, Jessie. 1997. *White lies: Race, class, gender, and sexuality in white supremacist discourse.* New York: Routledge.
DeYoung, Curtiss, Michael O. Emerson, George Yancey, and Karen Chai Kim. 2003. *United by faith: The multiracial congregation as an answer to the problem of race.* New York: Oxford University Press.
Dobratz, Betty A., and Stephanie L. Shanks-Meile. 1997. *White power, white pride! The white separatist movement in the United States.* New York: Twayne.
False patriots: The threat of anti-government extremists. 1996. Montgomery, AL: Southern Poverty Law Center.
Fraser, David, and Tony Campolo. 1992. *Sociology through the eyes of faith.* New York: HarperCollins.
Gayman, Dan. 1994. *The two seeds of Genesis 3:15.* Rev. ed. Shell City, MO: Church of Israel.
Gentry Dan. nd. *Death penalty for race mixers (is prescribed in the Bible).* Boring, OR: Christian Patriot Association.
Goff, Kenneth. 1955. *America, Zion of God.* Englewood, CO: Pilgrim Torch.
Goffman, Erving. 1974. *Frame analysis.* Cambridge, MA: Harvard University Press.
Goodrick-Clarke, Nicholas. 2002. *Black sun: Aryan cults, esoteric Nazism and the politics of identity.* New York: New York University Press.

Herrell, V. S. 1996. *The Talmudic Jew identified*, http://www.christianseparatist.org
/briefs.html. Accessed May 28, 2006.

Holthouse, David. 2005. Arizona showdown. *Intelligence Report*, no. 118 (Summer):
page number(s). http://www.splcenter.org/intel/intelreport/article.jsp?aid=557.
Accessed May 29, 2006.

Hunt, Scott A., and Robert D. Benford. 1994. Identity talk in the peace and justice
movement. *Journal of Contemporary Ethnography* 22:488–517.

Johnson, Hank, Enrique Larana, and Joseph Gusfield, ed. 1995. *New social movements*.
Philadelphia: Temple University Press.

Kaplan, Jeffrey. 1997. *Radical religion in America: Millenarian movements from the far
right to the children of Noah*. Syracuse, NY: Syracuse University Press.

Kim, T. K. 2005. Electronic Storm. *Intelligence Report*, no. 118 (Summer). http://www
.splcenter.org/intel/intelreport/article.jsp?aid=551. Accessed May 29, 2006.

Kinder, D., and L. Sanders. 1996. *Divided by color: Racial politics and democratic ideals*.
Chicago: University of Chicago Press.

Kingdom Identity Ministries. 2003. *Kingdom Identity Ministries doctrinal statement of beliefs* http://www.kingidentity.com/doctrine.htm. Accessed May 29, 2006.

Kinsman Redeemer Ministries. 2003. http://www.kinsmanredeemer.com/identity.htm.
Accessed May 29, 2006.

Knights of the Ku Klux Klan. 2003. http://www.kukluxklan.org. Accessed Dec. 15, 2003.

Las Vegas Skinheads. 2003. http://www.lasvegasskinheads.net. Accessed Dec. 15,
2003.

Lofton, John. 1985. *Protest: Studies in collective behavior and social movements:* New
Brunswick, NJ: Transaction.

Marsh, Charles. 1997. *God's long summer: Stories of faith and civil rights*. Princeton, NJ:
Princeton University Press.

National Alliance. 2003. http://www.natvan.com/what-is-na/na3.html. Accessed May
29, 2006.

Perkins, John, ed. 1995. *Restoring at-risk communities*. Grand Rapids, MI: Baker.

Potok, Mark. 2004. The year in hate. *Intelligence Report*, 113 (Spring). http://www
.splcenter.org/intel/intelreport/article.jsp?aid=374. Accessed May 29, 2006.

Ridgeway, M. 1990. *Blood in the face: The Ku Klux Klan, Aryan Nations, Nazi Skinheads,
and the rise of a new white culture*. New York, NY: Thunder's Mouth.

Sharpe, Tanya Telfair. 2000. The Identity Christian movement: Ideology of domestic
terrorism. *Journal of Black Studies* 30(4): 604–23.

Shuler, Clarence. 1998. *Is racial reconciliation really working? Winning the race to unity*.
Chicago: Moody.

Sider, Ron. 1999. *Just generosity: A new vision for overcoming poverty in America*. Grand
Rapids, MI: Baker.

Snow, David A., and Robert D. Benford. 1988. Ideology, frame resonance, and participant mobilization. *International Social Movement Research* 1:197–217.

———. 1992. Master frames and cycles of protest. In *Frontiers in social movement theory*.
ed. A. Morris, and C. McClurg Mueller, 133–73. New Haven, CT: Yale University.

Snow, David A., E. Burke Rochford Jr., Steven Worden, and Robert D. Benford. 1986.
Frame alignment processes, micromobilization, and movement participation.
American Sociological Review 51:464–81.

Southern Poverty Law Center. 2003. *Ten ways to stop hate*. Montgomery, Ala.: Southern
Poverty Law Center. http://www.splcenter.org/teachingtolerance/tt-index.html.

———. 2004. Hate groups, militias on rise as extremists stage comeback. *SPLC Report*. 34(1). Montgomery, AL: Southern Poverty Law Center.

Swain, Carol, and Russ Nieli, ed. 2003. *Contemporary voices of white nationalism in America*. Cambridge: Cambridge University Press.

Swift, Wesley. 2003. http://nidlink.com/naryanvic/jcjew.html. Accessed Dec. 15, 2003.

Walters, Jerome. 2000. *One Aryan nation under God: Exposing the new racial extremists*. Cleveland: Pilgrim.

Ware, Charles. 1998. *Prejudice and the people of God: Reconciliation rooted in redemption and guided by revelation*. Indianapolis, IN: Baptist Bible College of Indianapolis.

White, Jonathan R. 2001. Political eschatology: A theology of anti-government extremism. *American Behavioral Scientist* 44(6): 937–56.

Wistrich, Robert. 1985. *Hitler's apocalypse: Jews and the Nazi legacy*. New York: St. Martin's.

Yancey, George. 2003. *One body one spirit: Principles of successful multiracial churches*. Downers Grove, IL: InterVarsity.

Young, T. J. 1990. Violent hate groups in rural America. *International Journal of Offender and Comparative Criminology* 34(1): 15–21.

Zeskind, Leonard. 1986. *The Christian Identity movement: A theological justification for racist and anti-Semitic violence*. Atlanta: Center for Democratic Renewal and Society for the National Council of Churches of Christ in the U.S.A.

II

Family and Table-Fellowship in the Writings of Luke

David W. Pao

In the modern Western appropriation of the biblical message, the Bible is often examined through the lens of individualism. One searches for ways in which the Bible affects our present lives and future destinies as individuals. The frequent references to community concerns in the Bible remain at the margin as we evaluate the significance of various aspects of the gospel message. It is this individualistic practice of reading that needs to be challenged as we enter into discussions of race and ethnicity. In this chapter, we will show how the identity of the people of God lies at the very center of the theological program of Luke, whose writings provide the context for our understanding of the life of Jesus and the ministry of the apostles. We will focus on the use of two related metaphors that were evoked to address the issue of the identity of God's people: family and table-fellowship. Moving beyond the obsession to consolidate the ethnic boundary of Israel according to blood, these metaphors provide ways to redefine God's people according to the life and ministry of Jesus. This ancient message continues to be relevant as we are called to be faithful to the gospel that has transformed us. As individuals, our identities are no longer defined primarily by blood. As a church, we are called to be an inclusive body that is able to witness to the power of the cross. Issues of race and ethnicity lie, therefore, at the very heart of the gospel message.

Family and Identity Formation

We will begin our examination with the context within which the identity of the ancient personality is constructed. A brief discussion of the significance of family in the ancient world will pave the way for our appreciation of Luke's use of the same metaphor in his own writings.

Family in the Ancient World

The differences between the ancient and modern conceptions of family are well illustrated by the fact that no word in Greek and Latin exactly corresponds to our understanding of "family." This absence reflects the different function of the nuclear family within its ancient social context. In the ancient world, the nuclear family did not exist as an isolated social unit (Osiek 1996, 10–11; Moxnes 1997). The nuclear family is defined by its relationship to the wider web of relationship, and the line between family and the extended kinship group is often blurred. While this should not deter us from examining the function of the family metaphor in the ancient texts, it does remind us of the significance of various levels of social relationships as we approach the issue of identity formation. In a similar way, a person is not an "individual" in the modern sense of the term, and the identity of such an individual can be located only within its wider social context.

To highlight the proper social location of the family in the ancient world, scholars have preferred to use kinship language in describing the role of the family (Eickelman 1989; Kellerhals, Ferreira, and Perrenoud 2002). The family is not determined simply by cohabitation or conjugal relationship; it serves as the context where one's social and political relationships are defined with reference to both diachronic (i.e., blood) concerns as well as synchronic (i.e., contextual) factors. The family, in turn, determines the social and political status of an individual. Gender, class, ethnicity, and ideological affiliations are determined by one's familial context, and these references, in turn, provide definition to one's "relationships of power, protection, submission, honor, and duty" (Meeks 1993, 38). In the ancient world, these relationships make an individual. The ancient persons are therefore often described as "collectivist persons" (Malina 2001, 46) who are substantially conditioned by their relationship with the external world.

This understanding of family opens up ways for the development of fictive-kinship. In the Roman imperial system, the emperor functioned as the head of the universal household, and one's position was determined by one's relationship with members of this household (Lassen 1997). Beyond the imposition of the imperial system, elective associations that shared common social concerns or political goals could be found throughout the Mediterranean world. In the case of philosophical schools, one finds fictive-kinship determined primarily by one's ideological affinity. Familial language was used in these contexts when the identity of the person was being reshaped.

For our discussion, the significance of family language in Judaism demands further attention. In the Judaism of the first century AD, the issue of ethnicity was at the very center of its identity. This particular emphasis can be understood as the result of the experience of Israel during the Second Temple (i.e., intertestamental) period. In the defining moment in Israel's history when

God called Abraham, Abraham's descendants were to serve as a blessing to all the nations: "all peoples on earth will be blessed through you" (Gen 12:3 NIV here and elsewhere unless otherwise noted). With the disintegration of God's people as a result of the conquests of the Assyrians and the Babylonians in 722 BC and 586 BC, Israel began to define herself primarily in terms of her separation from the Gentiles. This was the product of an understanding of the cause of the exile as a result of Israel's mingling with the foreigners and their gods. Equally significant is the continuing experience of Israel under the various foreign oppressive powers. When the Romans took control over the land of Israel in 63 BC, the category "Gentiles" came to be understood as the enemies of God and of his people. The hope for the future was no longer the inclusion of all nations in God's kingdom but the destruction of those around her (Pao 2000, 245–48; cf. Donaldson 1997).

The family in the Judaism of the first century AD was, therefore, concerned with the continuation of the covenantal purity of the people. The act of circumcision became a prominent symbol for such an emphasis. When the temple was understood to be at least partly the instrument through which the Romans controlled the land, the family became the temple where God's promises awaited their ultimate fulfillment (cf. Elliott 1991; Wilcox 1996, 526). In this sense, everyday living became cultic acts through which God could be honored. This was a natural development from the extensive use of household language in the description of the relationship between God and Israel. As God's "first-born son" (Exod 4:22) and "daughter" (Lam 2:13), Israel pledged allegiance to her "father" (Isa 63:16; Jer 3:4) and "mother" (Num 11:12; Isa 49:14–17). The absence of organized missionary movement in Second Temple Judaism can thus be partially explained by this focus on the preservation of God's people (McKnight 1991). For those who were willing to embrace the God of Israel, they had to leave their own family, ancestors, homeland, and household deities as they joined the family of the one true God (e.g., Philo *Spec. Leg.* 1.51–53; 4.178; *Migr.*; cf. Barton 1997).

Redefinition of Family of God in Luke-Acts

When we come to the New Testament, we witness a sustained effort to move away from the ethnic boundaries that were constructed in the delineation of the members of the household of God. In this section, we will begin by examining two passages in the prologue of the Gospel of Luke (Luke 1–2) through which the ethnic basis of God's family is challenged. To illustrate the significance of these two passages, other passages throughout Luke-Acts will also be noted.

Luke's prologue serves as a theological introduction to his writings. In this prologue, one finds significant themes that dominate the rest of Luke's program. It is in this prologue that one encounters the beginning of the redefinition of God's household. Immediately after the birth of Jesus was promised to Jesus' mother, Luke draws out the significance of this event in Elizabeth's address to Mary:

> [42b]Blesssed are you among women and blessed is the child you will bear. [43]But why am I so favored, that the mother of my Lord should come to me? [44]As soon as the sound of your greeting reached my ears, the baby in my womb leaped for joy. [45]Blessed is she who has believed that what the Lord has said to her will be accomplished! (Luke 1:42b–45)

The first part of the speech is flooded with household language. Mary is considered to be the blessed one because of her ability to bear this child. She is the "mother" of the Lord, and she belongs to a long list of matriarchs who experienced God's grace through the bearing of a child who became significant players in God's drama of salvation. As a mother, the highest honor lies in giving birth to one who will, in turn, bring honor to the family (Esler 2000, 152). Frequently missed, however, is the appearance of the second word of blessing that points in a different direction. While the first blessing was pronounced on Mary's role as a mother and the honor bestowed upon her as one bearing the child of God (v. 42b), the second blessing focuses on Mary as a believer and as one obedient to the word of God (v. 45). A significant qualification of the first word of blessing can be detected here when Elizabeth moves from the focus on the physical relationship to the spiritual affinity with "the Lord."

This reading is confirmed by two passages in the body of Luke's Gospel. In 8:19–21, one finds "Jesus' mother and brothers" coming to see him (v. 19). When Jesus became aware of their presence, he said: "My mother and brothers are those who hear God's word and put it into practice" (v. 21). The status of being Jesus' physical relatives is superseded by the status of one who is willing to believe and obey his words. What is implicit in Luke 2 is made explicit here: the family of Jesus is not primarily defined by blood but by one's willingness to follow him. The contrast between the two words of blessing in Luke 2 is highlighted by Jesus' own saying.

For an explicit commentary on Elizabeth's speech in Luke 2, however, one has to point to Luke 11:27–28:

> [27]As Jesus was saying these things, a woman in the crowd called out, "Blessed is the mother who gave you birth and nursed you."
> [28]He replied, "Blessed rather are those who hear the word of God and obey it."

This passage parallels the concern found in Luke 8:19–21, but the form can be traced back to Elizabeth's speech in Luke 2. As in the speech of Elizabeth, this passage also contains two words of blessings. While the second word of blessing in Elizabeth's speech simply followed the first, the contrast is explicitly noted in Luke 11: the status of being Jesus' mother cannot be compared with the unique status of those who "hear" and "obey" the word of God. To complete the thought developed in Luke 2 and 8, this passage defines the family of God according to one's obedience to God and his Messiah. An implicit critique of the contemporary Jewish emphasis on the ethnic basis of God's people cannot be missed. The story of Jesus in Luke's Gospel can therefore be understood as a story of the formation of a new people of God, one who is able to relate to God in a new way.

Returning to the prologue of Luke, one finds yet another passage where the household language is used. In the story of Jesus in the temple at the age of twelve, one finds Jesus' parents anxiously searching for him after they realized that he did not follow them on their journey home. The first words of Jesus appear when his parents questioned him:

> [48]When his parents saw him, they were astonished. His mother said
> to him, "Son, why have you treated us like this? Your father and I
> have been anxiously searching for you."
> [49]"Why were you searching for me?" he asked. "Didn't you know I
> had to be in my Father's house?" (Luke 2:48–49)

In the question posed by Mary, one finds the intriguing phrase, "Your father and I." In referring to herself and Joseph, various other formulations could have been used. Instead, the words "your father and I" were used with the apparent intention to highlight the prominence of the "father" motif here in this context (de Jonge 1977–78). The word *father* reappears in the verse that follows in Jesus' reply (v. 49). In this reply, the word *father* is no longer referring to Jesus' earthly father but his heavenly father. The word *house* is not in the text, and the exact reference behind the phrase has long been the subject of debate. The solution seems to lie in the recognition that the ambiguity is intentional as Jesus points to both his father's "matters" and, more specifically, his Father's "house" (Weinert 1983). What is clear in the text is the contrast between the two "fathers," the earthly and the heavenly. As Jesus began his earthly ministry, he made it clear that the gospel of the kingdom that he was to proclaim was one that would draw one near to the heavenly Father. The gospel is not one that would reaffirm the barrier between Jews and Gentiles, it is one that focuses on the creation of a family where God is the Father of all. This choice between the two fathers is all the more significant when one recognizes that the father-son relationship is "the dominant kinship relationship" in ancient Near Eastern societies (Moxnes 1997, 34).

The father-son language can be found throughout Luke's writings (Mowery 1990). God is the Father of Jesus (Luke 9:26; 10:21–22; 22:29; 22:42; 23:34, 46; 24:49; Acts 1:4, 7), and Jesus is expected to do the will of his Father (Luke 22:42). With Jesus, the disciples are also called to address God as Father. As disciples, not only are we called to imitate our Father (Luke 6:36) and to focus on his kingdom (Luke 11:2), we will also receive the Holy Spirit that our Father has promised us (11:13; Acts 2:33). Ultimately, our Father's kingdom will become our kingdom (Luke 12:32). With God as our Father, those who believe and obey the word of God are to relate to one another as "brothers and sisters" (Luke 6:41–42; 17:3–4; 22:32; Acts 2:29; 6:3; etc.). Jews are to relate to Gentiles as brothers (15:23, 36) with an emphasis on equality (cf. Schäfer 1989). This is possible only with the recognition of the common Father we have in heaven.

With Luke's emphasis on the family of God through the work of Jesus Christ, one also finds extensive discussion of one's relationship with Abraham, the patriarch of Israel. The explicit challenge to the physical connection with Abraham first appears in the preaching of John the Baptist: "And do not begin to say to yourselves, 'We have Abraham as our father.' For I tell you that out of these stones God can raise up children for Abraham" (Luke 3:8). Physical descent alone can no longer serve as the basis of the community of God's people (Siker 1991, 108–10). Those who repent can now be considered as the sons of Abraham (e.g., Luke 19:9). The fact that Abraham was chosen precisely for the blessings of the nations is explicitly noted in Acts 3:25 with the quotation from Gen 22:18: "Through your offspring all peoples on earth will be blessed." The transformation of God's people is best captured in the speech of James as he describes the conversion of the Gentiles using election language of the Old Testament: "Simon has described to us how God at first showed his concern by taking from the Gentiles a people for himself" (Acts 15:14; cf. Dupont 1985). The use of the term *people* (*laos*) is striking when the physical descendants of Abraham are replaced by those who worship in the name of God's own Messiah. One can only agree with DeSilva (2000, 204) when he notes that in Acts 15 one finds "a decisive turning point in the construction of the 'family of God' and 'family of Abraham.'"

The core identity of a believer can no longer be derived primarily from one's ethnic affiliation. We belong in the family of God, and this forms the center upon which all our relationships should find their anchor.

Table-Fellowship and Inclusion

Through the use of kinship language, the community of God's people finds a way to speak to the dawn of the new era when God will become the Father of all who believe and obey his word. The outworking of such a vision can be found in both discourse and narrative form in relationship to an act that is itself performed primarily in the household context. In this section, we will focus on Jesus' participation in table-fellowship and his parables where the ideal banquet is portrayed. The emphasis on table-fellowship will further contribute to our understanding of the inclusiveness of the new family of God. It is through this metaphoric act of table-fellowship that a new level of intimacy among members of God's household is envisioned.

Banquets and Meals in the Ancient World

While parents and children constituted the core of an ancient household, the act of eating was the primary activity in which all members of the household participated. The mother was often defined by her role as a nurturer; the father by his authority as the one who presides over the household meals. In this sense, then, meals can be understood as a sort of kinship language where the identity of the community was made clear. The social function of the meal is best captured in the incisive words of Douglas (1971, 61): "If food is treated as a code, the message it encodes will be found in the pattern of social relations being expressed. The message is about the different degrees of hierarchy, inclusion and exclusion, boundaries and transactions across the boundaries." As such, the significance of the meals lay beyond the mere act of consumption: "Each meal is a structured social event which structures others in its own image" (Douglas 1971, 69). As a social act, the act of eating together was a powerful symbol for those who either chose to or were invited to participate in the same table. Recent anthropological studies have confirmed that "the action of eating together" was indeed "one of the most powerful operators of the social process" (Bloch 1999, 133). It could also be considered as a way to symbolize the act of "playing the same game" (cf. Barth 1998, 15).

In the wider Greco-Roman world, banquet and symposium provided the context for the development of fictive-kinship groups (Smith 2003, 13–130). In the act of sharing a meal, members of the group celebrated their common identity and goals. One finds banquets organized by groups sharing the same social class, philosophical beliefs, and cultic practices. On a literary level, the ideology of the group was also often expressed in the symposium genre. The prevalence of the meal-motif can also be found in works of various other genres.

Closer to the world of Luke, Jewish meals also played an important role in consolidating group identity and in serving as a context where the community's past and future merged. The significance of the Jews/Gentiles distinction as noted above found its manifestation in Jewish meal practices. The numerous feasts of the Jewish calendars were celebrated over the table where the history of Israel was remembered. More important, dietary restrictions and peculiar table practice became important when they served as identity markers that separated those who were outside from those who belonged to God's people (cf. Cohen 1999, 53–55). The biblical story that depicts Daniel as one who "resolved not to defile himself with the royal food and wine" (Dan 1:8) became the paradigmatic example for those living among the Gentiles.

In this context table-fellowship became important for the shaping of the sectarian mentality of opposition and exclusivity. In the Qumran community, for example, the priestly cultic laws are transferred to the community rituals, among which the partaking of food is of special concern. The emphasis on purity is reflected in the detailed regulations concerning meals. Cohen (1987, 131) has rightly noted that "the sectarian community is a place of purity that not only rivals the temple but also supplants it." Meals became the primary means through which the solidarity of the true people of God was expressed.

The defining moment in the history of Israel is today remembered in the annual celebration of the Passover feast. In the expectation of God's final act of deliverance, the meal metaphor is again evoked. In Isaiah 25:6 one finds the beginning of a long tradition where the ultimate victory of God and his people is symbolized by the celebration of the eschatological or messianic banquet. In the remembrance of the exodus event and in the anticipation of

God's final act on behalf of his own people, Israel finds its identity as God's elected ones.

Inclusive Banquets in Luke-Acts

The Second Temple Jewish concern of the identity of God's people with the expectation of the eschatological banquet provides the proper context for our understanding of the banquet motif in Luke's writings.

In Luke's Gospel, the story of the feeding of the five thousand in the "wilderness" (Luke 9:12) parallels the feeding stories of the Old Testament, especially the provision of food during Israel's sojourn in the "wilderness" (Green 1997, 363). The "bread" evokes the manna tradition, while "fish" may reflect Second Temple Jewish understanding of quails "from the sea" (Num 11:31) as flying fish (Bovon 1993, 28). The seating in "groups of about fifty each" (Luke 9:14) and the presence of leftovers (Luke 9:17) also recall Israel's exodus traditions (Exod 16:32–33; 18:21). Such parallels point to the reenactment of the foundation story of Israel where God's people became one community under God as they entered the promised land. If this story reflects the ecclesiological significance of the gospel meal-scenes, other stories and discourse in meal settings provide further definition of the community of God's people.

In the various accounts of Jesus' dining with his companions, one consistent theme emerges: Jesus is in the practice of sharing the table with the outcasts. In Luke 7, one finds Jesus' "eating and drinking" interpreted as his being "a friend of tax collectors and 'sinners' " (v. 34; cf. 5:27–32; 19:7). The expression "tax collectors" refers to those who work for the Roman overlords, and "sinners" are those who were considered impure and therefore not to be included in the worshiping community (Neale 1991). Similarly, in Luke 15:2, the Pharisees and the teachers of the law characterize Jesus as one who does not maintain purity of the table: "This man welcomes sinners and eats with them." Connected to this accusation is one that points to Jesus' lack of concern for the dietary laws: "But the Pharisee, noticing that Jesus did not first wash before the meal, was surprised" (Luke 11:38). This failure to understand Jesus' mission prompted Jesus to issue the six woes against the Pharisees (Luke 11:39–52).

Beyond this characterization from those who opposed him, Jesus has also provided us with a picture as to what the banquet of the kingdom will look like. The most extensive discussion can be found in Luke 14, a chapter that contains several sections all related to the banquet motif. Significantly, these speeches were presented when Jesus was dining with the Pharisees. Some have pointed to the Greco-Roman symposium genre as providing the framework for these various sections in the context of a meal (Smith 2003, 253–59), while others see an inherent critique of the pagan banquet practices (Braun 1995; Osiek and Balch 1997, 206). What all can agree on is the significance of the theme of reversal in this chapter. This theme of reversal highlights the new conceptions of the community of God's people with the arrival of the messianic era.

The first parable (Luke 14:8–11) focuses on how one should not assume the position as the head of the household when participating in the banquet. The parable concludes with the introduction of the reversal motif: "For everyone who exalts himself will be humbled, and he who humbles himself will be exalted" (v. 11). In its context, this statement is directed against Jewish leadership who assumed that they would be the ones to determine who can participate in God's messianic banquet. This reversal opens up the way for the inclusion of those who are "humbled."

This theme is explicitly noted in the second parable (14:12–14) where Jesus mentioned how one's banquet should include "the poor, the crippled, the lame, [and] the blind" (14:13). To redefine the identity of God's people is to redefine the common practices of hosting a banquet.

The theme of reversal in the first parable and the one of inclusion in the second find their climax in the third (14:16–24) when Jesus commented on "the feast in the kingdom of God" (v. 15). When the invited guests failed to respond to the call, the head of the household invited the outcasts to participate: "bring in the poor, the crippled, the blind and the lame" (v. 21). This invitation is accompanied by the exclusion of those who were first invited: "I tell you, not one of those men who were invited will get a taste of my banquet" (v. 24). This parable points to the redrawing of the boundaries of God's people when the messianic age becomes a reality (cf. Snodgrass 1998). Those who assume that they belong will be excluded, and those who were excluded will be included when they respond to the call (cf. 15:22–32).

Significantly, these three banquet parables find their conclusion in a passage that again evokes the family metaphor. The urgency and priority of the call of the Messiah is dramatically noted: "If anyone comes to me and does not hate his father and mother, his wife and children, his brothers and sisters—yes, even his own life—he cannot be my disciple" (14:26). This family of God is constructed around the christocentric call to bear the cross: "And anyone who does not carry his cross and follow me cannot be my disciple" (v. 27).

This vision of God's eschatological family and banquet is played out in the history of the early church as recorded in the second volume of the writings of Luke. In Acts 10, the inclusion of the Gentiles in the family of God is expressed through a vision where foods that were deemed unclean are sanctified by God (vv. 9–16). The redefinition of purity forces Peter to draw this conclusion: "I now realize how true it is that God does not show favoritism but accepts men from every nation who fear him and do what is right" (vv. 34–35). This incidence resurfaces in the significant discussion of the Jerusalem Church in Acts 15 where issues of grace, law, and ethnicity are discussed. Basing his words on the divine invitation to participate in table-fellowship with the Gentiles, Peter concludes with this striking statement addressed to a people who had long emphasized their distinctive status as God's elected people: "He made no distinction between us and them, for he purified their hearts by faith" (15:9). It is precisely in this context that one finds the articulation of the power of God's grace: "We believe it is through the grace of our Lord Jesus that we are saved, just as they were" (15:11).

This section will not be complete without a reference to the one meal that becomes the basis of all Christian table-fellowship. In Luke 22, the Last Supper recalls the Passover meal of Israel (v. 7) and anticipates the banquet of the King-dom (v. 16). For our concerns, the Last Supper serves also as a "ritual of sepa-ration" (Brumberg-Kraus 1999, 181) as the unique identity of the community is formed. Through this ritual, the family of God is to be distinguished from other families who claim also to be of the divine. The creation of this family is well illustrated in the concluding words of Jesus:

> [29]And I confer on you a kingdom, just as my Father conferred one on
> me, [30]so that you may eat and drink at my table in my kingdom and
> sit on thrones, judging the twelve tribes of Israel. (Luke 22:29–30)

In these verses, one finds the reference to God as Father, the reference to the messianic kingdom with the eschatological banquet, and the fulfillment of the Israel by flesh in the Israel established on the work of Christ on the cross. With-out the cross-event that follows, neither the Christian family nor the Christian table-fellowship would be possible.

Race, Ethnicity, and the Family of God

The preceding discussion has shown how the ecclesiological concern for the inclusiveness of the community of God's people lies at the very center of the gospel message. To talk about such concerns as merely "the implications" of the gospel message betrays the power of the cross. In the ancient mentality, for an individual to be "saved" (or "born-again") was to challenge the web of rela-tionships in which he or she was defined. To claim to be a Christian is, there-fore, unavoidably a polemic claim in which one has to relativize the primary field of reference through which one's identity is derived.

Modern Christians are not only tempted to see the practice of religion as a personal and private matter, we are also tempted to reuse biblical symbols to support our own agendas. As Clapp (1993; cf. Loughlin 1996) has reminded us, our focus on "family values" has turned Christianity on its head. Instead of seeing the historical and the contemporary church as our "family," we consider our nuclear family as the primary locus in which our Christian faith can be ex-pressed. In doing so, the prophetic voice of the church is subsumed under our desire to create a "church" that will address our needs and fulfill our desires.

In the New Testament, ethics is practiced in the context of the household, and building up the Christian household is as important as developing per-sonal virtues. Within this household, the Christian vision finds its concrete ex-pression. Outsiders can easily identify Christians as members of the same family (Hellerman 2001), and insiders address one another as such. Within this family, the focus on commitments became meaningful. Resisting the model of "vol-untary associations" as were prevalent in Greco-Roman times, early Christians considered themselves accountable to one another as members of the same household.

The emphasis on the primacy of one's Christian identity and the commit-ment that follows such an identity-claim does not, however, automatically translate into a detailed program that can be applied to every single local congregation when confronting issues of race and ethnicity. Nevertheless, the preceding discussion does suggest ways that we can proceed. First, the living out of the vision of inclusion is part of the missionary program of the church. While the church is called to personal evangelism, the emphasis on the effectiveness of forms of ministries within one generation, class, gender, and race should not be used as an excuse for not attempting to live out the manifestation of God's kingdom on earth. Instead of simply serving as agents that fulfill the needs of individuals, local churches should also become the place where the power of the cross can be experienced. It is this power that, in turn, can inform us of a broader vision of the church as it anticipates the full manifestation of the salvation of God. Although one cannot point to one abstract model for the local churches in their various contexts, Luke's vision does force us to see the outworking of God's family as part of the mission of individual congregations.

Second, local churches can reflect the power of God precisely because they draw people from diverse socioeconomic and ethnic locations. The affirmation of the prominence of our identity as members of God's household does not eliminate our connections with our own respective contexts. As ethnic persons, we are invited to celebrate the richness of God's people. The ultimate agent in the act of inclusion is God himself, and not the majority party that attempts to include the minority by assimilating them into the dominant culture. It is only with the recognition of all believers as contextualized individuals that a true family of God can be envisioned.

Finally, our discussion of table-fellowship as an intimate act of sharing forces us to move beyond tokens of inclusion that are prevalent in our culture. If worship is to be considered as a prime example of such intimate acts in the celebration of our faith in God, it is in this act that inclusion should be practiced. The ways local churches struggle to deal with the expected pain and conflicts in this intimate act of sharing should, in turn, testify to the power of the cross in spite of human weaknesses.

Our knowledge of the numerous obstacles to the practice of Luke's vision should not deter us from recognizing the role of the church as powerful witness in the multi-cultural world of the twenty-first century. The family of God will one day participate in the "wedding supper of the Lamb" (Rev 19:9) and "a great multitude that no one could count, from every nation, tribe, people and language" will glorify God (Rev 7:9). The responsibility of the church is to live out this vision in this present age by the power of the blood of the lamb that "had been slain" (Rev 5:6).

REFERENCES

Barth, Fredrik. 1998. Introduction. In *Ethnic groups and boundaries: The social organization of culture difference*, ed. F. Barth. Prospect Heights, IL: Waveland.
Barton, Stephen C. 1997. The relativisation of family ties in the Jewish and Graeco-Roman traditions. In *Constructing early Christian families: Family as social reality and metaphor*, ed. H. Moxnes, 81–100. London/New York: Routledge.
Bloch, Maurice. 1999. Commensality and poisoning. *Social Research* 66:133–49.

Bovon, François. 1993. The role of the Scriptures in the composition of the gospel accounts: The temptations of Jesus (Lk 4:1–13 par.) and the multiplication of the loaves (Lk 9:10–17 par.). In *Luke and Acts*, ed. Gerald O'Collins and Filberto Marconi, trans. Matthew J. O'Connell, 26–31. New York/Mahwah, NJ: Paulist.

Braun, Willi. 1995. *Feasting and social rhetoric in Luke 14. Society for New Testament Studies Monograph Series* 85. Cambridge: Cambridge University Press.

Brumberg-Kraus, Jonathan. 1999. "Not by bread alone . . .": The ritualization of food and table talk in the Passover Seder and in the Last Supper. *Semeia* 86:165–91.

Clapp, Rodney. 1993. *Families at the crossroads: Beyond traditional and modern options.* Downers Grove, IL: InterVarsity.

Cohen, Shaye J. D. 1987. *From the Maccabees to the Mishnah.* LEC 7. Philadelphia: Westminster.

———. 1999. *The beginnings of Jewishness: Boundaries, varieties, uncertainties.* Berkeley and Los Angeles: University of California Press.

De Jonge, Henk J. 1977–78. Sonship, wisdom, infancy: Lk 2, 41–51a. *New Testament Studies* 24:317–54.

DeSilva, David A. 2000. *Honor, patronage, kinship and purity: Unlocking New Testament culture.* Downers Grove, IL: InterVarsity.

Donaldson, Terence. 1997. *Paul and the Gentiles: Remapping the apostle's convictional world.* Minneapolis: Fortress.

Douglas, Mary. 1971. Deciphering a meal. In *Myth, symbol, and culture*, ed. Clifford Geertz, 61–81. New York: Norton.

Dupont, Jacques. 1985. Un peuple d'entre les nations (Actes 15.14). *New Testament Studies* 31:321–35.

Eickelman, Dale F. 1989. *The Middle East: An anthropological approach.* 2nd ed. Englewood Cliffs, NJ: Prentice-Hall.

Elliott, John H. 1991. Temple versus household in Luke-Acts: A contrast in social institutions. In *The social world of Luke-Acts: Models for interpretation*, ed. Jerome H. Neyrey, 211–40. Peabody, MA: Hendrickson.

Esler, Philip. 2002. "Keeping it in the family": Culture, kinship and identity in 1 Thessalonians and Galatians. In *Families and family relations as represented in early Judaisms and early Christianities*, ed. Jan Willem van Henten and Athalya Brenner, 145–84. Studies in Theology and Religion 2. Leiden: Deo.

Green, Joel B. 1997. *The Gospel of Luke.* NICNT. Grand Rapids, MI: Eerdmans.

Hellerman, Joseph H. 2001. *The ancient church as family.* Minneapolis: Fortress.

Kellerhals, Jean, Cristina Ferreira, and David Perrenoud. 2002. Kinship cultures and identity transmissions. *Current Sociology* 50:213–28.

Lassen, Eva Marie. 1997. The Roman family: Ideal and metaphor. In *Constructing early Christian families: Family as social reality and metaphor*, ed. H. Moxnes, 103–20. London/New York: Routledge.

Loughlin, Gerard. 1996. The want of family in postmodernity. In *The family in theological perspective*, ed. S. C. Barton, 307–27. Edinburgh: T & T Clark.

Malina, Bruce J. 2001. *The social gospel of Jesus: The kingdom of God in Mediterranean perspective.* Minneapolis: Fortress.

McKnight, Scot. 1991. *A light among the Gentiles.* Minneapolis: Fortress.

Meeks, Wayne A. 1993. *The origins of Christian morality.* New Haven, CT: Yale University Press.

Mowery, Robert L. 1990. God the father in Luke-Acts. In *New Views on Luke and Acts*, ed. Earl Richard, 124–32. Collegeville, MN: Liturgical.

Moxnes, Halvor. 1997. What is family? Problems in constructing early Christian families. In *Constructing early Christian families: Family as social reality and metaphor*, ed. H. Moxnes, 13–41. London/New York: Routledge.

Neale, D. A. 1991. *None but the sinners: Religious categories in the Gospel of Luke*. JSNTSup 58. Sheffield: JSOT.

Osiek, Carolyn. 1996. The family in early Christianity: "Family Values" revisited. *Catholic Biblical Quarterly* 58:1–24.

Osiek, Carolyn, and David L. Balch. 1997. *Families in the New Testament world: Households and house churches*. Louisville: Westminster John Knox.

Pao, David. 2000. *Acts and the Isaianic New Exodus*. WUNT 2.130. Tübingen: Mohr Siebeck.

Schäfer, Klaus. 1989. *Gemeinde als 'Bruderschaft': Ein Beitrag zum Kirchenverständnis des Paulus*. Bern: Peter Lang.

Siker, Jeffrey S. 1991. *Disinheriting the Jews: Abraham in early Christian controversy*. Louisville: Westminster John Knox.

Smith, Dennis E. 2003. *From symposium to Eucharist: The banquet in the early Christian world*. Minneapolis: Fortress.

Snodgrass, Klyne. 1998. Common life with Jesus: The parable of the banquet in Luke 14:16–24. In *Common life in the early church: Essays honoring Graydon F. Snyder*, ed. Julian V. Hills et al., 186–201. Harrisburg, PA: Trinity Press International.

Weinert, Francis D. 1983. The multiple meanings of Luke 2:49 and their significance. *Biblical Theology Bulletin* 13:19–22.

Wilcox, Max. 1996. The Jewish family in the first two centuries c.e. In *Religion in the ancient world: New themes and approaches*, ed. M. Dillon, 523–32. Amsterdam: Adolf M. Hakkert.

12

Church as a Lifestyle: Distinctive or Typical?

Vincent Bacote

What immediately comes to mind if you are asked to define *church*? The doctrine of the church (ecclesiology) has been a weakness in evangelicalism. Any attempt to arrive at an explicitly evangelical ecclesiology is destined to be an arduous challenge due to the number of streams that comprise the evangelical tradition. This difficulty requires Christians to press on toward greater understanding. As part of this book, revisiting ecclesiology means asking how a deeper understanding of the church can shape Christian identity and practice in a distinctive way, especially in regard to matters of race and ethnicity. My aim is to engage the vision of the church as a distinctive people, a position presented by Clapp (1996) and other current scholarship. The recognition of the church as being central to our identity and behavior in the world should yield a perspective and social practice that opposes and critiques a racialized society.

A Typical People?

In *Divided By Faith* (2000), Michael Emerson and Christian Smith argue that American religion, including white evangelicalism, "likely does more to perpetuate (a) racialized society than to reduce it" (170). American factors such as consumerism, voluntarism, and individualism contribute to the considerable inertia that remains in the United States toward problems of race and ethnicity. One result of the preceding factors on ecclesiology is that the identity of the church (implicitly if not explicitly) is that of an atomistic conglomerate; the church is nothing more or less than a group of individuals who voluntarily come together because of a commonly held salvation attained in an individualistic fashion (an emphasis on a personal relationship with Jesus). Emerson and Smith found that the factors mentioned above make it difficult for white evangelicals to conceive of the race problem at a corporate or structural level. Rather, race problems can be resolved through means such as interpersonal relationships. United with an atomistic conception of the church, there is little impulse to view the church as a corporate entity or community whose identity supersedes and even constitutes primarily the identity of the individual members. Practically speaking then, such atomistic conglomerates play little if any role in shaping the identity of church members, and fail to place demands on them. One way this may work out is that individual identity is primary and corporate identity is peripheral and embraced when convenient. For example, belonging to a particular group of people is embraced when there is cause for celebration (as when someone says "our country has a distinguished heritage") and rejected when the group identity has negative consequences (as when someone says "I didn't own any slaves, so why blame me?"). The end result is that on race matters, evangelical churches tend to remain segregated. The churches are homogenous enclaves where everyone has voluntarily chosen to worship with "similar" people.

Emerson and Smith's work leads to the conclusion that in spite of any rhetoric of faith that suggests that the evangelical church is a community whose primary identity transcends race and ethnicity, the reality is the opposite. This does not mean that there are no efforts made to address matters of race and ethnicity, but that the ecclesiology of evangelicalism (diffuse as it is) tends to be insufficient in countering this problem. It also means that if one examines the evangelical church on this issue and asks "Who are these people?" the answer is "Typically, they're not much different from everyone else." I hasten to add that this is not a "white" problem exclusively. In minority church communities generally, and African American churches particularly, there are many voices that call for maintaining the integrity of the church by remaining distinct and either resisting or de-emphasizing an ecclesiology that would lead to blended congregations. Admittedly, there are good reasons for this (see the chapter by Priest and Priest for an example), and desires to emphasize cultural distinctiveness and survival (against cultural dilution and assimilation) are not inherently bad. From the standpoint of ecclesiology, however, the identity of the church rises above racial and ethnic allegiances and appropriately affirms them when the church acquires a gospel-based perspective on humanity. For some, this latter point could be interpreted to mean that every church needs to appear a certain way (like a mixed congregation) in order to demonstrably rise above the status quo. Such an interpretation misses the point. Whether a church is mostly ethnically homogenous or ethnically diverse in appearance is not the major point, and it is not mandatory for a church to reflect the globe in order to be distinctive (and it is impossible in some geographic areas that are homogenous). The crux is whether the congregations, regardless of their racial/ethnic composition, have been shaped in their identities by the church to the extent that the members live in a way that contradicts the typical approach to matters of race and ethnicity. In terms of the place of race and ethnicity specifically, my contention is that a deep understanding of "church" ought to obliterate explicit and subtle racial/ethnic idolatry, not by destroying rich human differences, but by rendering them less prominent in identity construction and maintenance. How do we move toward the idea of the church as such a distinctive people?

The Church as Distinctive

God has always intended to have a people set apart to himself, a distinctive covenant community. From the call of Abraham in Genesis 12 through the entire New Testament, it is clear that the "people of God" (Israel, and later the church) should have an identity and way of life that radically contrasts with the surrounding world in several ways. How are the people of God distinct when contending with race and ethnicity?

Clapp's book is a helpful starting point for thinking of the church as a unique, distinctive group of people. His book is subtitled "*The church as culture in a post-Christian society.*" In the midst of the pluralistic ethos of postmodernity (and in a post-Constantinian era, where there is no state sponsorship of the church), Clapp presents the view that "the radical option is nothing more or less than for the church to be a way of life" (1996, 32). By the term *radical*, Clapp is referring to his preferred stance for the church as opposed to strategies of retrenchment (an approach that maintains the status quo that privatizes the faith) and relinquishment (capitulation to the surrounding culture). Clapp's radical approach draws on the view of culture defined as that which "lends significance to human experience by selecting from and organizing it. It refers broadly to the forms through which people make sense of their lives, rather than more narrowly to the opera or art museums. . . . Culture encompasses the everyday and the esoteric, the mundane and the elevated, the ridiculous and sublime. Neither high nor low, culture is all pervasive" (74). With this definition at hand, Clapp welcomes the culture wars, which "can be welcomed on the count that they help return us to a place where we can conceive of Christianity as a way of life, as a specific manner of being and doing in the world. And they make it possible for Christians, like those who inhabit other ways of life, to move more easily and directly into the public, the social, the political and the economic realms—and to do so *specifically as Christians*" (75). With Christianity understood as a way of life, in the midst of the culture wars it becomes possible "for the church not merely to be relevant to culture, but to *be* a culture, a "cultivating process that produces people in a particular way"; not merely to contribute to politics from the sidelines but to *do* politics of a peculiar kind—a kind that once turned the world upside down." The church understood as a culture, Christianity conceived as a way of life, yields an ecclesial identity of the church as a distinctive people.

Dykstra and Bass share a similar insight when they write about Christian practices. In "A Theological Understanding of Christian Practices" (2001), Dykstra and Bass consider Christianity as constitutive of a way of life. In that light, they define Christian practices as "*things Christian people do together over time to address fundamental human needs in response to and in the light of God's active presence for the life of the world*" (18). Christian practices are the result of the relationship of beliefs, virtues, and skills with behaviors, relationships, and symbols. When these come together in a coherent fashion, a distinctive way of living emerges. The practices themselves are "constituent elements in a way of life that becomes incarnate when human beings live in light of and in response to God's gift of life abundant" (21). While *Practicing Theology* identifies twelve specific practices, the important insight for this essay is that Christians, the people who comprise the church, are distinguished from others by virtue of a way of life reflected in the "constituent elements" made incarnate as they live from day to day. (It is important to note that the expression of distinctly Christian practices will vary in differing contexts, but they will be elements of life that are similar as they pose challenges to non-Christian ways of living.) Specifically, in terms of the issues of race and ethnicity, Dykstra and Bass's view suggests that the church can and should be a group of people whose conduct includes elements like those in Dykstra and Bass's work (and others) that subvert the typical practice of our society. Difficult practices such as hospitality (an openness and welcome to strangers and the provision of food and protection), for example, ought to reveal that the church is a culture that contradicts the egocentric tendencies left unchecked by an individualism that easily ignores racial/ethnic concerns external to personal relationships.

One key element in this approach is that a focus on practices resists the bifurcation between theology and ethics, between belief and action. A frustration of many minorities in the evangelical world is that all of the Bible-based thinking and preaching often fails to result in any distinctively different practice toward nonwhites. In spite of the typical presentation of a "biblical" view of the church in which all humans who respond to Christ are brothers and sisters, numerous minorities in the evangelical world, whether at Christian colleges or within Christian organizations, have experiences that reveal that Christian identity (for white evangelicals) is primary until it reaches the color line, after which racial and ethnic allegiances rise to the top. In such situations, minorities are perplexed that they are treated as someone other than a fellow member of the Christian family, and they wonder how white evangelicals can be committed to the truth of the Bible yet live in a way that contradicts it. Speaking concretely, as a teacher at a prominent evangelical institution, I have had several minority students express the frustration that their white peers are unconscious of the manner in which they assume that "white" is "normal," and that Christian behavior is (for many) no different from middle-class suburban behavior. Students who do not fit the "normal" mode often suffer as a result of being "abnormal" in appearance or customs and many feel unwelcome by their Christian brothers and sisters. The minority students are aware of a breach between belief and action, but their peers are often oblivious. To move toward a remedy, an ecclesiology that emphasizes the vital link between belief and practice is important for the formation of Christians whose lives are marked by conduct distinguished in its contradiction to the typical status quo in society. To return to the practice of hospitality mentioned above, what difference might it make in evangelical institutions if minorities experienced a dignifying welcome and embrace as their typical experience? If minorities routinely experienced the affirmation of their (in some cases) unique contribution to college life or institutional leadership, non-Christians (and many older, minority evangelicals) would be stunned by the strong bond of belief and practice.

What ought to be the result of the church's distinct way of life? Christian practice in this view reveals the identity of the church, or to put it differently, the church's public performance, broadly considered, tells and retells the narrative that constitutes the church's self-understanding. Considered from this perspective, evangelicals should ask "What narratives are revealed by the evangelical church's 'typical' approach to race and ethnicity? What political, economic, and social practices are laid bare?" In terms of the concerns of this essay and this volume, the answer to these questions seems depressing and daunting because "typical" means an individualistic, voluntarist approach where race issues are critical only when related to interpersonal relationships. The implication is that when someone says, "I don't have any problems with people different from me," they and their church are not compelled in any way to address the ongoing problem. Yet, this answer need not be final for evangelical ecclesiology. Rather, the pursuit of an ecclesiology that focuses on distinctive Christian practices can present an opportunity to begin shifting the tide toward a distinct social existence.

Distinct in Identity and Worship

Corporate and Catholic Identity

What are some specific ways in which the church is distinct? For the purposes of this essay, two aspects are primary: identity and worship. As stated above, modern individualism is a significant factor in the church's inability to conceive of an identity that rises above race and ethnicity. Making corporate identity more central is a vital aspect in addressing this challenge. Both Clapp and Volf offer us helpful insights that point us toward corporate identity. Clapp considers the modern understanding of the individual, critically summarizing the post-Enlightenment individual as follows:

> The individual was invented by a succession of Enlightenment
> thinkers and became, in its most extreme but perhaps also its most
> widespread interpretations, a view of the self as "a single atomic iso-
> late, bounded by the skin, its chief value residing precisely in some
> core of individuality, of difference." Thus it remains popular—almost
> second nature—to think we get at our "true self" by peeling away so-
> cial ties like the skin of an onion. The "real me" is not my member-
> ship in the worldwide church, my shared kin with the Clapps around
> the country, nor my connection—with three million other people—to
> the geography and culture of Chicago. The "real me" is my unique,
> individual core self. The individual values itself most for what is

supposedly different and unconnected about it. . . . Can we really believe that we are not, to the core, who we are because of our kin, our
occupations, our political and social situations, our faith or philosophical associations, our friendships? And if our "true self" is whatever stands apart from those around us and is altogether unique
about us, most of us are in trouble." (Clapp 1996, 91)

Clapp goes on to suggest that in pre-Enlightenment cultures, when people
used terms like *I* and *mine*, they thought of these terms as being loaded with
plurality. More narrowly, first-century persons, including the Jews and first
Christians, thought of themselves in terms of corporate personality. Drawing on New Testament scholar Charles Talbert, Clapp concludes that the
Pauline language of the church as a "body" means (in Talbert's words) "that
individual Christians in their corporeal existence are the various body parts
of the corporate personality of Christ through which the life of Christ is expressed" (92). The result of this conception for the church as a distinct people is that:

> the church no longer must support a view of the self as individuated
> and able to determine the good apart from all "accidental" ties of
> history or community. We can reaffirm that just as there can be no
> individual Americans apart from the nation America, so can there be
> no Christians apart from the church. . . . We can be like the early fol-
> lowers of Christ the Way, who trained fresh imaginations and became
> a new humanity by devoting themselves "to the apostles' teaching
> and fellowship, to the breaking of bread and prayers" (Acts 2:42) . . .
> we can regard and the embrace the church as a way of life. (93)

In *Exclusion and Embrace* (1996), Volf argues that Christians should have
distance from their own culture ("culture" in the sense of ethnicity or nationality) because of their primary allegiance to God. The result of such distance is
that there is space to receive the other, the different person. Particularly helpful
for this essay is the use of the idea of *catholic personality* to speak of ways that
we can be open to others. The "catholic personality is a personality enriched by
otherness, a personality which is what it is only because multiple others have
been reflected in it in a particular way" (51). It follows that such a personality
needs a *catholic community*. Isolation from other churches in other cultures is
not an option, and in an interesting way, Volf inverts the idea of the local
church as part of the universal church:

> Every local church is a catholic community because, in a profound
> sense, all other churches are a part of that church, all of them shape
> its identity. As all churches together form a world-wide ecumenical
> community, so each church in a given culture is a catholic commu-
> nity. Each church must therefore say, "I am not only I; all other
> churches, rooted in diverse cultures, belong to me too." Each needs
> all to be properly itself. (51)

The catholic identity and community call attention to the fact that Christian ec-clesial identity is far more complex than the atomistic, rugged individual.

Corporate personality and catholic personality reveal that Western individ-ualism has produced a myopic vision. Christians whose self-perception is pri-marily individualistic fail to recognize that they are more than people who responded to a gospel invitation, uttered a sinner's prayer, and then associated with a local fellowship. They have become open to others and are a part of the communion of saints throughout the ages. As a part of this communion, they are not just constituted by their personal history and local context, but now share a rich identity drawn from every age and culture where Christians live and have lived. Sadly, most of us do not think of our ecclesial identity this way. To move forward, corporate identity, a necessary element in countering the sta-tus quo on race and ethnicity, must be learned in the church. The church must cultivate people who see themselves as a very dense "we" when they say "I." How do we achieve this?

Arriving at corporate identity requires a commitment from churches to do more than have introductory new members' classes that give a brief overview of salvation and church membership. Since "membership" can be easily perceived as similar to joining a club, fraternity, or other voluntary association, it is a diffi-cult but necessary task to teach Christians that belonging to the church means belonging to another people. Ephesians 2:19 is instructive here, as Paul empha-sizes that Christians are God's one people while also using terms such as *citizen* and *household*. Terms such as these only serve as slogans if the Christians are not taught that *church* means an identity that stands above and relativizes the priority of other identity-forming characteristics (such as race, ethnicity, class, region, gender, etc.). If "Christian church" becomes the central aspect of our identity, a significant step has been taken toward grinding new lenses of perception that subvert the status quo. Imagine: What would it be like for Christians to regard race and ethnicity as an important but more peripheral part of their identity?

The typical approach to race and ethnicity will go unchallenged without a catechesis (teaching) that profoundly shifts Christians' understanding of them-selves in relationship to the church and world. Perhaps the most important point of emphasis here is that the church should understand that part of its mission is a reshaping of identity. While the cultivation of an ecclesial corpo-rate identity is not the sole task in addressing the struggle with race and eth-nicity, it is vital. If we can institute this in our instruction when people join the church, then it becomes increasingly possible to address Volf's concern about Christians who are so tied to their selves and cultures that they "echo its reign-ing opinions and mimic its practices" (54). Instead, churches can produce Christians with a conscious corporate and catholic personality who can incar-nate a way of life that is useful salt in a decaying world.

The Role of Worship

Worship is the second significant aspect. In the liturgy (the process and ele-ments of worship, with *worship* understood as our response to God in ways that range from confession to adoration) the church comes together and publicly confesses and reinforces its identity. Rather than having a conception of worship as a privatized escape from the world (a comfortable, sentimental time in the sanctuary), Clapp argues that it is a time when the church corporately indicates that following Christ is a way of life. A key objective in worship is to help Christians learn to see through "common sense." It is where Christians learn "to see the world as it really is: the wonderful, if now rebellious, creation of the God of Israel" (96). As Dawn states, worship conveys "the framework of faith in which everything is to be understood" (1999, 339). The acquisition of this vision is not natural or an automatic result of conversion. Christians must be inducted and immersed into the culture of the church. How does this happen? "Hearing the story of God preached, through the exercise of praise, Christians learn and rehearse what it means to be Christians. Liturgy is the primary responsibility of the church because without worship there can be no people capable of seeing and witnessing to the God of Israel. Just as capitalistic Americans could never become such exquisite consumers apart from the rites of advertising and credit cards, so Christians can never achieve the skills and vision necessary to be the church without attention to baptism and Eucharist" (Clapp 1996, 99).

Clapp argues that baptism, preaching, and Eucharist are vital to the Christian cultural formation. Baptism is the public rite of initiation into the church. Clapp argues that it is a form of resocialization and enculturation into the standards of the kingdom of God rather than the world. In particular, the familial metaphors in the New Testament speak of baptism in a manner analogous to admission into a family. Clapp—making particular reference to Romans 6; 8:15–17; and Galatians 3:26–4:6—notes that Paul reminds believers that "they have a new identity because they have been baptized into Christ and adopted as sisters and brothers. When children are adopted they take on new parents, new siblings, new names, new inheritances—in short, a new culture" (Clapp 1996, 100). In this new culture God is the new parent, Christians are the new siblings and the new inheritance is the freedom and the resources of the community. As Dykstra and Bass state, baptism "incorporates the baptized person into a social and historical Body that spans centuries and cultures" (Dykstra and Bass 2001, 30). Not only are the baptized persons initiated into a new local community, they are brought into the communion of saints present and past. They are brought into an amazing extended family. Their new culture is the church. Understood this way, baptism is a political act that threatens the surrounding culture because Christians have publicly declared an allegiance to a God other than the biological family or the state. While noting that we live in an era different from the first centuries of the church or the Reformation (when Anabaptist baptism was a blasphemous act), Clapp suggests that baptism can still be a form of subversive political action, particularly when the church is seen as alternative culture. In such a view, "when we recognize that 'the people of God do not go to church; they are the church,' baptism can quickly, easily and *accurately* be seen as an act of civil disobedience" (Clapp 1996, 101–2).

This view of baptism raises the important question of the perception of baptism in evangelicalism. While the debates surrounding infant versus adult baptism (in all their complexity) continue, one wonders if the average baptized Christian sees the great significance of this initiatory rite. Whether one views baptism as a response to the gospel and public declaration of faith or as entry into the covenant community and sign and seal of God's promises (to name two of the perspectives on adult and infant baptism, respectively), is it the understanding of the church that those who pass through the baptismal waters are becoming part of a unique family that has a way of life that subverts the status quo? When adults or teens are baptized and when those baptized as infants "confirm" their baptism, do they have any awareness that baptism "ritually sketches the contours of a whole new life"? (Dykstra and Bass 2001, 31). In those churches where voluntary association and consumerism factor heavily into the "choice" of membership, is there any communication and reception of the view that to be a Christian means to take on a way of life, to become a participant in another culture? If so, does this understanding mean that baptism is more than a reflection of a private, personal response to Christ? I fear that most people, even those with some prebaptismal instruction, really do not know what baptism symbolizes, that it is the public identification with another regime and way of life. Certainly, people may know that it means that they have "decided to follow Jesus," but are they following Jesus as someone other than simply a source of eternal life? As stated above in the section on corporate identity, we need to recover some kind of catechesis so that Christians know that they are entering another world that operates differently from that which is "typical." Linking it to the discussion of corporate and catholic identity, baptism (or confirmation) is the public adoption of another identity, one that relativizes all other characteristics. Given the legacy of race and ethnicity in evangelicalism, a central aspect of baptismal catechesis should focus on baptism's expression of an alternative view of race matters. Perhaps even the liturgy should include some statement to the effect that the new life and allegiance in baptism speak against norms of a racialized society.

While baptism is the adoption into a new culture, Clapp argues that preaching gives us a new language and grammar. "The preacher is the one who tells us the story of Christ and relates our lives to it. The preacher, the Christ-storyteller, has the crucial task of helping us articulate our lives—our weal and woe—theologically, in relation to God" (Clapp 1996, 103). The preacher performs this task not only from the pulpit but also in the role of spiritual director. In either case, church leaders have the task of teaching Christians the language and grammar of the faith. This is an increasingly difficult task, and the subject of countless debates about relevance in preaching.

In the current era, with the debates over the return to traditional forms of worship or seeker-sensitive services, the issue of the theological language and grammar taught in the church is extremely pertinent. From pulpits and various contexts of spiritual direction (such as small groups), what language are people taught? What content, what conception is conveyed when the categories of creation, sin, and redemption are used to enculturate the people of God? How does the church understand itself with the language and grammar passed down from contemporary church leadership? Does the quest for either pristine tradition or sleek relevance make the language of the church unduly archaic or overly accommodated to popular trends? What language *needs* to be taught in order for the church to understand itself as a culture that subverts the typical? What language can be taught in catechesis that helps people to think of themselves with a corporate identity and catholic personality that recognizes their vital relationship to others? Some attempted answers follow in the penultimate section of the essay.

Eucharist is the third aspect of worship and the one that should affect our practice of eating. Eating is a social activity that links persons together in webs of mutuality and reciprocity. It "symbolizes relationships and attitudes: we eat to celebrate birthdays and holidays, we gather and serve meals to mourning family and friends at a funeral. Eating mediates social status and power" (Clapp 1996, 107). Clapp notes that an anthropologist could learn a lot about the church simply by observing its eucharistic practice. The answer to the question "Who eats with whom?" reveals, for good or ill, the culture of the church. In cultivating the church as a peculiar people, Clapp suggests the Eucharist has at least four culture-forming and sustaining functions:

1. The Eucharist discloses and forms us to be a people who are based on the common good of Christ's lordship.
2. The Eucharist discloses and forms us to be a people who are radically egalitarian.
3. The Eucharist discloses and forms us to be a people who have the resources to face conflict and admit failure.
4. The Eucharist discloses us and forms us to be a people who are nonviolent. (Clapp 1996, 108–11)

The common meal of the church should cultivate an egalitarian people under Christ who confess their faults, reconcile across deep differences, and presume against violence (one need not be a thoroughgoing pacifist to consent to the fourth point).

As with baptism, the success of the Eucharist as culturally formative is dependent upon the seriousness applied to it in the church. If it is a hollow ritual, whether taken daily, weekly, monthly, or quarterly, it will be a practice that has little significance. Whether one views the bread and cup as conveying grace (sacramental) or as a potent symbol (ordinances), considerable gravity must attend this rite so that it regains its political significance. A eucharistic practice that cultivates an egalitarian community requires the same intentional catechesis as baptism if it is to really make a difference. Otherwise, Eucharist will be a ritual devoid of its fullest meaning and implications.

The church as a distinct people is a community whose worship conveys the real world through divine illumination. Baptism, preaching, spiritual direction, and Eucharist are core cultural activities of the church. "In the liturgy, day to day and week to week, we 'do the world as God means it be done.' This means that in worship we vigorously enflesh a restored and recreated world—a world returned to its genuine normality through holy abnormality—in a civic and cultural form, a public, powerful, visible, political form that challenges and stands in contrast to all other cultures. Worship is not simply world-changing. It is, indeed, world-making" (Clapp 113).

Clapp, Dykstra and Bass, Dawn, and Volf help buttress the view that the church has a distinctive self-understanding (corporate and catholic personality as opposed to individualism) and public practice that yield a distinct way of life. I, along with them, am aware of the challenges to the church as a culture in our era. As Clapp's final chapter reveals, there is hope about the difficult path ahead. Reflecting on this as a long process, he says,

> Church as a way of life is incremental obedience, passion subdued but sustained over years. It is discipleship for the long haul, over a road that is inevitably bumpy and includes detours, switchbacks and delays. It is the persistent if not perfect unlearning of the world system's established separation of the practical and theoretical, the profane and sacred, the political and the spiritual, the theological and the sociological. Church is a way of life lived not with the expectation that Christians can, through managerial arts or sudden heroism, make the world right. It is instead a way of life lived in the confidence that God has, in the kingdom of Christ, begun to set the world right—and that someday Christ will bring his kingdom to fulfillment. . . . In the meantime, Christians are about surviving and alleviating the worst effects of a world bent on self-destruction, about reminding that world of its true nature as fallen and redeemed creature, about demonstrating to some real degree that there is and can be communal solidarity on God's good earth. (1996, 199–200)

The vision of distinctiveness and the recognition of the long, sustained process involved, raise questions for the evangelical world. What current catechesis is present among evangelical churches, and, at present, how is corporate identity formed in the church? What catechetical revision will be required to cultivate a deep conception of corporate personality and corporate responsibility in the church? How can baptism and Eucharist regain their culture-forming power? What worlds are made through the various approaches to worship in the evangelical world? Is a world made that cultivates a people so distinct and radical that their life together serves as an alternative vision to the status quo on race and ethnicity? In light of this essay's main concern, does the broad palette of evangelical teaching and worship push against Emerson and Smith's conclusion that evangelicalism "likely does more to perpetuate (a) racialized society than to reduce it" (2000, 170)? Thus far, the answer to this question seems to be "no." Nevertheless, a negative answer does not mean a surrender to frustration and futility. Maybe the call to distinctiveness is a helpful catalyst in the effort to arrive at an ecclesiology that cultivates a countercultural church that reflects the vision of God's kingdom.

Implications for Christians, Congregations, and Related Institutions

Thus far, several questions have been raised asking how the church in identity and practice can be different from the status quo. I have begun to suggest the development of a catechesis that cultivates a corporate identity and church culture that is clearly distinct from our racialized society. One way to address the concerns of this book and essay in a fashion specifically helpful in matters of race and ethnicity is to articulate the way that certain biblical themes/doctrines are perceived in light of the church as a distinctive people and to highlight two specific Christian practices that comprise the church as a culture, a way of life. Consider these steps toward a catechesis that cultivates a distinctive Christian vision.

Creation and Theological Anthropology

The reality of a fallen creation often serves as reason for pessimism. Within the church or without, fallenness provides the rationale for frustration and futility in attempts to improve the relationships of people who are different from one another, whether through ethnicity, gender, class, or race. While fallenness makes conflict understandable, it need not be the final word on God's created people. In light of redemption, the church as a distinctive people can harness the creation narrative pre- and post-Fall and affirm with God that the creation is excellent (Gen 1:31). The Fall did not rescind God's conclusion about the creation. Though distorted, the creation still belongs to God. The human race created in the divine image, in all of its diversity today, should still celebrate the great pronouncement that the people God has made are "very good." The church as a distinctive people should reflect in language and practice (toward one another and the world outside) that humans of all sizes, shapes, and shades are worthy of respect and honor by virtue of being God's creation. The redeemed community, by virtue of the new, divinely illuminated vision it gains at conversion, should cultivate a doctrine of creation that affirms the significance of all people.

Christology

The people who comprise the church are those who have responded to the gospel of Jesus Christ, God's ultimate Word. Catechesis should convey that Christ is far more than the guarantor of a future eternal destiny. In contrast, the response to Jesus should be to live under his Lordship in a distinctive way that reflects an allegiance to him in every area of life. To take Philippians 2 as an example, Christians with a distinctive vision will model their lives after Christ by seeking the path of humility and service to others. Christ, who is the Lord, exemplified humility and service in his incarnation and death, and was exalted as a result. The church's aim should be to seek the good of the other, whether they are "other" by virtue of appearance or even if they are an enemy, and to anticipate God's response to lives of service. In the church, it is vital for Christians to seek the good of others, particularly those who are different from us in race and ethnicity. The church reveals itself as a distinctive community when the followers of Christ exemplify practices that contradict allegiances of ethnicity, class, and nation, and serve the other.

Pentecost

The miracle of tongues in Acts 2 is often considered when the topic is spiritual gifts. A distinct and fully Christian vision extends beyond this and arrives at a conception of a diverse community. Acts 2 brings together God's people from dispersion, and they experience a foretaste of the final restoration when they all hear the gospel in their own language when the Spirit comes. We can also see a reversal of Babel, where humans came together to elevate themselves and were confounded and dispersed because God gave them different languages. Here, the people of different languages come together and all hear the same wondrous message about God and respond with repentance and conversion. It is significant that they did not all become able to understand one language, but that the unity is in the message that all heard and then took back to their regions and countries. If there had been only one language, an implication may have been that they all needed to conform and lose the valuable aspects of their diversity. From the standpoint of the distinctive vision, the church cultivates people who affirm diversity (not uncritically) and translate the culture of the church into forms that appropriately affirm the distinctiveness of differing ethnic groups. The church that cultivates a culture does not call for an assimilation to whiteness, or American values, or other regional virtues. It will call for transformation, but that does not mean that the goal is a bland sameness.

Eschatology

Everyone likes to know the end of the story. Eschatological books, particularly of the dispensational flavor, are now best sellers. The popular focus on eschatology is on issues such as the rapture and the final judgment. These are very significant, yet a distinctive vision leads us beyond these matters to ask what kind of eschatology does our community reveal? As Newbigen asked, "What kind of churchmanship will enable us so to preach the gospel that men and women are called to be disciples in the fullest sense—men and women and children whose personal and corporate life is a sign, instrument, and foretaste of God's kingly rule over all creation and all nations?" (Newbigen 1986, 133). Eschatology from this perspective can help enculturate the belief and practice that the church in the present is a reflection, though imperfect, of God's kingdom. In that kingdom there will be people from every tribe, tongue, and nation (Rev 7:9–17) worshiping God together. The church as a culture should proclaim and practice the social life of the coming kingdom, contradicting the social forces that reinforce a racialized society.

Two significant practices that make the church distinct are hospitality and, more briefly, forgiveness.

Hospitality

As mentioned above, hospitality is a Christian practice that welcomes, serves, protects, and feeds "others." Christine Pohl argues that hospitality "is a way of life fundamental to Christian identity" (1999, x). It was so fundamental to the early church that the embrace of strangers was one of the marks that distinguished Christians from others in society. In the challenging terrain of a racialized society, hospitality as a practice means that Christians should be willing to give respect and dignity to those who are different from us. A result of this respect is that the ones offering hospitality recognize that they are not above the "others" whom they welcome. Within the life of the church, hospitality creates a context for interethnic/racial interaction. Marriage is a good example where the church can exemplify this practice. A thoroughgoing practice of hospitality in the church would provide a welcome to spouses of different ethnicities without requiring them to become culturally different in order to be married. And, if a Christian identity is the central identity, any deep-seated reservations or suspicions of different ethnic groups ought to be set aside. Hospitality practiced in this way would be quite distinctive.

Forgiveness

Forgiveness is a vital practice because it is an absolute necessity if there is to be genuine healing and transformation regarding race and ethnicity. The church comprises a community of the forgiven. God has forgiven us and does not hold our sin against us. A genuine practice of forgiveness in the church would model a commitment to limitless forgiveness (as Jesus commands in Matt 18:22). If the church is to be distinct it will require a willingness to forgive the numerous misunderstandings that will doubtless occur in working toward life as a Christian community that reflects a culture contrary to a racialized society. The ability to forgive and the attendant refusal to hold on to offenses are vital elements in the various kinds of relationships in the church, and essential if there is to be reconciliation across racial and ethnic boundaries. The deep power of grace and redemption is concretely modeled when forgiveness is willfully sought and willingly offered. This practice must be central to churches that squarely face the problems raised in this volume.

The doctrines of creation, theological anthropology, Christology, Pentecost, and eschatology, and the practices of hospitality and forgiveness serve as examples of the effects of a distinctive vision. The recovery or development of these and other doctrines and practices in this distinct way helps to provide ways of perceiving and acting that could begin to alter the social practice of the racialized church that Emerson and Smith discovered.

Conclusion

What does *church* mean? The church conceived as a distinctive people provides a way of thinking about the church that can counter modern individualism and consumerism, though the process will take much time. If the identity and practice of the church can be reconceived along the lines suggested, it may be possible to see some subversion of the racial status quo in evangelical churches. Central to my proposal is the development of catechesis that cultivates a view of church as a way of life. I am aware that many evangelical churches do not have a significant catechesis, yet I am not deterred by the current state of "crisis." Just as challenging a racialized society is a process, so is developing and implementing a catechetical program for evangelical churches as I propose. A catechesis that cultivates corporate identity, meaningful worship, and more deeply and broadly conceived doctrines and practices may produce a church that is truly distinctive. The result, then, will be a people and culture far from typical.

REFERENCES

Clapp, Rodney. 1996. *A peculiar people*. Downers Grove, Ill.: InterVarsity.
Dawn, Marva. 1999. *A royal "waste" of time: The splendor of worshiping God and being Church for the world*. Grand Rapids, MI: Eerdmans.
Dykstra, Craig, and Dorothy Bass. 2001. A theological understanding of Christian practices. In *Practicing theology*, ed. Miroslav Volf and Dorothy Bass, 13–32. Grand Rapids, MI: Eerdmans.
Emerson, Michael, and Christian Smith. 2000. *Divided by faith: Evangelical religion and the problem of race in America*. Oxford: Oxford University Press.
Newbigen, Lesslie. 1986. *Foolishness to the Greeks: The gospel and western culture*. Grand Rapids, MI: Eerdmans.
Pohl, Christine D. 1999. *Making room: Recovering hospitality as a Christian tradition*. Grand Rapids, MI: Eerdmans.
Volf, Miroslav. 1996. *Exclusion and embrace: A theological exploration of identity, otherness, and reconciliation*. Nashville, TN: Abingdon.

13

The Samaritans: A Biblical-Theological Mirror for Understanding Racial, Ethnic, and Religious Identity?

Tite Tiénou

"As we all know, Samaritans are of mixed-blood origins. Since their ancestry is both Jewish and non-Jewish, Samaritans are half caste or racial half-breeds." This statement, made by a student submitting his research on the Samaritans to his peers and myself as the professor, provided the initial impetus for my interest in probing the nature of Samaritan ethnicity and identity. As I heard the student's statement, I was not as sure as he was about what we "all know." I remember telling him that he needed to provide convincing biblical evidence for his description of the Samaritans. Soon after this event I decided to examine all the biblical passages on the Samaritans in order to see how the Bible itself describes the nature of the boundary between Jews and Samaritans. The closer scrutiny of biblical texts led me to make two observations: first, the Bible shows that hostility marked the relationships between Samaritans and Jews; second, the Bible gives no evidence that this hostility was based on biological criteria of race such as skin color, hair texture, or nose shape. Also, "purity of blood" (or the lack of it) does not seem to be a factor in Jewish antipathy toward the Samaritans. In light of these observations, I wonder why it is easy and commonplace for people like this student to be certain that "the Jews bore permanent enmity towards Samaritans, whom they considered to be a mixture of races and religions" (Maldonado 1994, 53).

There is, indeed, a long history of enmity between Samaritans and Jews. As we will see in this chapter, this enmity may have been expressed in the form of Jewish prejudice toward Samaritans during the first century, at the time of Jesus. The way Jesus dealt with this

Jewish prejudice (in Luke 10, the parable of the "good" Samaritan, and in John 4, the encounter with the Samaritan woman) has helped numerous Christians challenge the ethnic and racial prejudice of their own times and has been a source of much Christian preaching and teaching on racial reconciliation. It is not the intent of this chapter to argue against such use of these passages. Rather, my purpose is to strengthen their right usage by examining the pitfalls of reading back into biblical texts notions and ideologies that may be ours but are absent from the texts themselves. That is the reason we must ask, How can contemporary authors and commentators be so sure that Samaritans were "considered to be mixture of races" by Jews when "for most of human history . . . the observable biological differences associated with race were not used as ethnic markers?" (Pitchford 1992, 1615). So, unless we can show conclusively that race was a key factor in Jewish-Samaritan conflicts, it is unwise to read racial differentiation back into biblical texts even if it "seems strange to us today . . . that the biological variations among human groups were not given significant social meaning" (Smedley 1999, 693).

It is undeniable that hostility existed between Jews and Samaritans. But how are we to understand the nature of the difference between them if, in the hostile relationships between Jews and Samaritans, as in the Bible in general, "race did not matter" (Goldenberg 2003, 196)? Yet, given the long history of hostility between Jews and Samaritans, an examination of Samaritan identity can be useful for Christian understanding of "race" and ethnicity. This understanding may provide the basis for how Christians should deal with ethnic conflicts today. Hopler, for example, has nicely used the story of the Samaritan woman in John 4 as a basis for lessons in cross-cultural and cross-ethnic communication of the Christian faith (1981, 22–25).

In light of the preceding, I intend, in this chapter, to set forth a case for discarding racial terminology and race categories in descriptions of Samaritans. I will do so by first arguing that portraying the Samaritans in racial categories imposes on the biblical materials the problematic notion of race and is an example of the "assumption that the way things are now is the way things were in the past" (Goldenberg 2003, 7). I will propose, second, that ethnicity is the appropriate analytical tool for understanding the identity of the Samaritans because "ethnicity is about social classifications emerging within relationships . . . in which people distinguish themselves from others" (Fenton 1999, 6; italics in original).

Racial Classification Inappropriately Applied to the Samaritans

In the Bible the words *Jews* and *Gentiles* are used for broad distinctions in the human family. In Jewish self-understanding, the Gentiles are people who are not Jews. In this sense, it is more accurate to speak of Israel and the nations even though many present-day translations of the Bible still retain the vocabulary Jews and Gentiles (Lagrand 1999, 29–31). This biblical classification of humankind into two broad categories does not usually or necessarily refer to specific races or

ethnic groups. In the New Testament, especially, the term *the nations* is "a desig-
nation of the big collective of non-Israelites, . . . with little or no attention paid to
the ethnic component of this mass" (Dahl 1974, 57) because, in "biblical
thought . . . the concept of peoplehood . . . is familial and natural without being
racial or biologistic" (Levenson 2002, 160; italics in the original).

The biblical distinction between Israel and the nations does not negate the
fact that the nations are composed of many specific peoples as is evident in the
lists of Genesis 10 (table of nations) and Acts 2. What about the Samaritans? Do
they belong to the category "the nations" or do they fit within Israel? The Samaritans, it seems, belong to a special category because, as one author writes, they
"occupied a curious middle position between Jews and Gentiles" (Köstenberger
2002, 45). That is, Samaritans are neither Jews nor Gentiles. Jews certainly perceived Samaritans to be different from themselves. We see a glimpse of Jewish
attitudes toward Samaritans in the following parenthetical statement recorded in
John 4:9 (NIV): "For Jews do not associate with Samaritans" or, in another possible translation, "For Jews do not use dishes Samaritans have used." James Lagrand has observed that "Jesus and his disciples probably would not have called
persons from the province of Samaria Ιουδαῖοι [Jews], but it seems clear that
they would have considered them Israelites (1999, 141; italics in the original).
Samaria and Judah seem to be relatives. Of Jerusalem (capital of Judah) it is said:
"Your older sister was Samaria, who lived to the north of you with her daughters"
(Ezek 16:46). So Samaritans are not Jews; they are also not Gentiles. The fact that
Samaritans were Israelites without being Jews sheds light on their ambiguous
status and is the basis for the disputes about genealogy (see John 4:12).

It is not surprising, then, that mutual suspicion was normal given the ambiguous status of the Samaritans (neither full Jews nor full Gentiles). Samaritans did not like Jews and Jews did not like Samaritans. What were the reasons
for the Jews' antipathy toward Samaritans? Could it be that Jews "felt Samaritans were semi-pagan, semi-civilized half-breeds. They would make themselves
religiously unclean if they had anything to do with these people" (Hopler 1981,
23)? Or did Jews think that "although the Samaritans had descended from Jacob
according to the flesh, yet, as they were altogether degenerated and estranged
from true godliness, this boasting would have been ridiculous (Calvin 1949,
150–51)? How did Jews and Samaritans really perceive and describe themselves?
How did they perceive each other and what did one group think of the other's
perception and description? The answers to these questions can help determine
the nature of the boundary separating Jews and Samaritans.

People who refer to Samaritans as "racial half-breeds" or people with
"mixed blood" give the impression that race was the important factor of division between Samaritans and Jews. These people may think they are just re-
stating the views of Jews. Consider, for example, the following description of
Samaritans in *The Dictionary: Finding Meaning in God's Words*:

> They were a "mixed race" with foreign blood and false worship. The
> Jewish historian Josephus indicates that the Samaritans were also
> opportunists. When the Jews enjoyed prosperity, the Samaritans

were quick to acknowledge their blood relationship. But when the Jews suffered hard times, the Samaritans disowned any such kinship, declaring they were descendants of Assyrian immigrants. (Tasker 2001, 333)

Josephus is known for his hostility toward the Samaritans. He depicts them as transplanted foreigners in his *Antiquities of the Jews* (Book 6, Book 11, and Book 13, in Josephus 1960, 211–12, 229, and 269). This is not surprising since "in Jewish non-canonical writings there are few references to Samaritans, all disparaging" (Caldwell 2003, 634). Josephus's disparagement of the Samaritans is expressed in the way he disputes and ridicules their claim to be descendants of Joseph. For him this illustrates the Samaritans' pretension of kinship with the Jews, which he finds unacceptable (see *Antiquities of the Jews*, Book 9, chapter 14, in Josephus 1960, 211–12). Disparaging references to Samaritans are not, however, limited to Josephus and "Jewish non-canonical writings." The canonical writings, the Old and New Testaments, do not generally present a positive image of Samaritans. For example, 2 Kings 17, perhaps the most important Old Testament text relative to the Samaritans, describes their religious practices as corrupt and inconsistent: "They worshiped the Lord but they also worshiped their own gods in accordance with the customs of the nations from which they had been brought" (v. 33). When God's displeasure with Jerusalem is expressed in these words "Samaria did not commit half the sins you did. You have done more detestable things that they" (Ezek 16:51), it is understood that the sinfulness of Samaria is a fact. It is therefore likely that "by the time of Christ, for a Jew to call someone a Samaritan was an insult" (Caldwell 2003, 634). We see evidence of this in the Gospel according to John (8:48) where the Jews ask Jesus if he is not a Samaritan in a way that does not appear complimentary.

There is, moreover, at least one New Testament reference to a Samaritan as a foreigner (Luke 17:18). In this passage Jesus expresses his astonishment that the Samaritan, "this foreigner," is the only cleansed leper (of the ten healed) who returns to thank him. But here it is clear that Jesus is not castigating the Samaritan for his foreignness. Rather, he points out the Samaritan's gratitude, in contrast to the unthankful attitude of the nine lepers (presumably Jews) who were also healed. Jesus' commendation of this Samaritan for his gratitude is consistent with his positive portrayal of another Samaritan whose kindness and mercy exceeded that of a priest and a Levite (Luke 10). The way Jesus presents the Samaritans as more righteous than Jews is reminiscent of a similar contrast between Samaria and Jerusalem in Ezekiel 16. The positive portrayal of Samaritans in Luke 10 and 17 does not, however, change the overall negative Jewish attitudes toward Samaritans.

One may accept the idea that, generally, Jews considered Samaritans to be foreigners. It is even possible that "on the whole, Samaritans were considered to be irremediably impure" (Köstenberger 2002, 45). These facts alone do not provide a sufficient basis for identifying the Samaritans as a "mixed race," "half breeds," or people with "mixed blood." Moreover, the vocabulary of race, with race as understood by present-day audiences, uses an idea that is absent from either canonical or noncanonical writings.

For most audiences today, the word *race* conveys the idea of physical biologically based human groupings. This idea of race could not have been what Jews and their writers had in mind when they described the Samaritans. We know this because the notion of race as biology grew out of a particular context and history as Meneses and Paris demonstrate in their chapters in this book. They show that this idea of race is erroneous. In this they join many others who call for abandoning the use of the term *race* because it "suffers from its history of mistaken science" (Fenton 1999, 68; see also Thomas 2003; and Unander 2000). While I agree with Pitchford that "the biological meaning of race, and racial categorization, is unclear" (1992, 1617), I do not want to suggest that the idea of race has been abandoned. Race is part of everyday vocabulary as well as many official documents around the world. Moreover, we know that race "does have tremendous social significance" (Pitchford 1992, 1617) and that "the social convention of classifying people on the basis of their bodily markings will typically have profound, enduring, and all too real consequences" (Loury 2002, 23; italics in the original). These are the reasons some sociologists and anthropologists continue to use the term *race* and study it in contemporary societies. Contemporary sociological studies of race are generally studies of race as socially constructed. That is, sociologists attempt to understand the fact that "racial distinctions are meaningful because we attach meaning to them" (Pitchford 1992, 1617). In the case of the Samaritans, however, commentators and preachers seem to be using race with the meaning of "biologically separate, exclusive, and distinct populations" (Smedley 1999, 696). This idea of race is precisely what is absent from the Bible where "classification of humanity certainly occurred, but it was of a religious nature, polytheists (idolaters) as opposed to monotheists, or gentiles as opposed to Jews" (Goldenberg 2003, 185). Using the vocabulary of race in portrayals of the Samaritans is therefore inappropriate for two major reasons: our notions of race are absent from the writings describing the Samaritans; and "the term 'race' has a pseudoscientific pedigree linking it to flawed and harmful theories of biology that are extremely problematic in general, and particularly so for an analysis of assimilation and shifts in identity" (Thomas 2003, 9).

For Christians, especially those who want to be guided by the Bible, the depiction of Samaritans in racial categories distorts the biblical texts in that it imposes on them ideologies of race that these Scriptures never intended to teach—that Samaritans and Jews belong to two separate races. Consider this statement made by Morris in his commentary on the fourth chapter of John: "a woman from Samaria (v. 7) means a member of the race that inhabited the general area" (1971, 256).

It would seem, then, that the vocabulary of race, caste, mixture, or impurity, in reference to the Samaritans, is secure in Christian language. This vocabulary appears to be justifiable in light of the biblical texts where Samaritans are mentioned specifically. For this reason, an examination of the nature of Samaritan ethnicity must deal with the question of origins because "the origin

and early history of the Samaritan sect are problematic in almost every aspect"
(Anderson and Giles 2002, 9). The statement made by Anderson and Giles regarding Samaritan origins may surprise readers familiar with the account of
the resettlement of Samaria by the king of Assyria (2 Kings 17:24–40). Nevertheless, according to Broadie: "Samaritanism and Judaism spring from a common matrix in the Israelite religion. . . . what point did the two groups separate?
There are two conflicting answers to this question. One answer is Samaritan
and the other is Judaist" (1981, 1).

The "Judaist" recounting of the separation between Samaritans and Jews
is, of course, the one known to Christians and readers of the Bible. Two texts in
the Old Testament deal with Samaria and Samaritans (1 Kings 16 and 2 Kings
17). According to 1 Kings 16 Samaria was founded in the context of political
strife and rebellion in Israel, the northern kingdom. Omri, the victorious leader
of one of the two rebellious factions against Zimri, "built a city on the hill, calling it Samaria, after Shemer, the name of the former owner of the hill" (1 Kings
16:24). Omri, who was succeeded by Ahab, apparently made Samaria his capital for "he reigned twelve years, six of them in Tirzah" (1 Kings 16:23) and was
buried in Samaria (1 Kings 16:28).

The story of the founding of Samaria does not have a direct bearing on ethnicity. It may, however, shed light on the religious aspect of Samaritan identity
and on the subsequent conflicts between Jews and Samaritans. Jeroboam,
Nadab, Baasha, and Zimri, all kings of the northern kingdom (Israel) before
Omri, and Ahab who followed him in Samaria, all "did evil in the eyes of the
Lord" and led their people into sin. Ahab, in particular, established Baal worship in Samaria "and did more to provoke the Lord, the God of Israel, to anger
than did all the kings of Israel before him" (1 Kings 16:33). It should be noted
that the record links his marriage to Jezebel, the Sidonian, and his worship of
Baal (1 Kings 16:31). The false worship and idolatry practiced by Ahab were
more than personal religious preferences. He and the other evil-doing kings of
the northern kingdom, as leaders, set examples for the people to follow. So,
even before the settlement of foreigners in Samaria by the Assyrian authorities, the religion of the land could be characterized as unfaithfulness to the
covenant established by the God of Israel. Idolatry (or unfaithfulness to God's
covenant) is the link between 1 Kings 16 and the other specific mention of
Samaria in the Old Testament (2 Kings 17).

The seventeenth chapter of 2 Kings is usually taken as the beginning of
Samaritan history. In this text we learn that the Israelites were removed from
their homeland because they "persisted in all the sins of Jeroboam" (v. 22). The
land was then resettled with "people from Babylon, Cuthah, Avva, Hamath and
Sepharvaim" (v. 24). In spite of this plurality of peoples brought into Samaria
and the likelihood that some Israelites were still residing there, Josephus calls
all Samaritans Cutheans (*Antiquities of the Jews*, Book 9, chapter 14, in Josephus 1960 211–12). This narrowing of the identity of the Samaritans accentu-
ates their foreignness and paints them "with the brush of illegitimacy of both
blood and religion" (Sloyan 1983, 9); that is, Samaritans are illegitimate in terms
of their ancestry and their religion is also illegitimate.

The Samaritans do not, of course, accept the idea that they are illegitimate and that their religion is false. In fact, "the Samaritans reserve for themselves the name Israel, allow the name Samerim only as an equivalent to the Hebrew Shomerim, those who observe (the Law)" (Caldwell 2003, 633). Justin Martyr seems to agree with the Samaritan viewpoint for he writes in his *Apology* (1:53): "All other nations the Prophetic Spirit calls Gentiles, whereas the Jewish and the Samaritan people are called Israel and the House of Jacob" (1948, 90). It is remarkable, in this respect, that the woman at the well, the only Samaritan who is given a significant voice in either the Old or the New Testament, clearly articulates the Samaritan perspective. She points out the common ancestry between Samaritans and Jews (by referring to "our father Jacob" [John 4:12]) while acknowledging the difference between them: "Our fathers worshiped on this mountain, but you Jews, claim that the place we must worship is in Jerusalem" (John 4:20). This statement of the woman makes it clear that the key difference between Samaritans and Jews is not ancestry. The difference is religion and religion marks the boundary, for as Lagrand points out, during the time of Jesus Samaritans were considered to be among off-center sects such as the scribes, the Pharisees, and the Essenes (1999, 142).

In spite of the foregoing, it is not uncommon to find writings depicting the Samaritans as "half-caste" or "half breeds." Some of these writings give the impression that the corruption of Samaritan religion is the result of racial impurity or mixing. One clear example of this is found in the following statement from Tasker in his *Gospel According to St. John: An Introduction and Commentary*: "The Samaritans were a half-caste people who owed their origin to the mingling of the remnant left behind when Samaria fell in 722 B.C. with the foreigners imported by the Assyrian conquerors. Their worship in consequence became contaminated by idolatry" (1983, 79 reprint; italics in the original). Race is still seen as a factor for making a distinction between Jews and Samaritans even when religion is recognized as an important aspect of the hostility between the two groups. A case in point is Morris (1971, 256) who, after a careful review of the history of hostility between Jews and Samaritans in which he emphasized the religious factors, nonetheless tells us that "Samaritan" refers to "race" in John 4. In this case the Samaritans are "racialized" without any reason.

What is the basis for the racialization of the Samaritans? One may look for it in the weight of the evidence found in 2 Kings 17 and in a theory of Jewish and Israelite identity predicated on racial purity. While 2 Kings 17 does state that the Israelites were removed from the northern kingdom and that their territory was repopulated with foreigners, one must not conclude that the entire population was deported. Rather, it is likely that the deportation targeted prominent people: heads of families, community leaders, priests and other religious officials (Thomson 1919, 15–24). Deportation, then as now, was partial, not total. So, the foreigners brought into the northern kingdom by the Assyrian monarch found a remnant Israelite population just as the returned exiles of the southern kingdom found a remnant Jewish population in Judah. One can therefore nuance one's understanding of 2 Kings 17 without agreeing with

Hjelm (2000) in her rejection of the thrust of that passage as historically misleading. In all probability, Samaritans "included (1) the foreign colonists who were introduced by Sargon in 722 (II Kings xvii.24), and at a later time by Esarhaddon and Assurbanipal (Ezra iv.2,10), (2) the remnant of Israelites who were not carried away after the fall of Samaria, but who under the pressure of foreign immigration had fallen into idolatrous practices, though they still nominally worshipped Jehovah (Ezra iv.7)" (Ottley 1915, 230).

The total deportation thesis does, however, fit nicely with the theory of Jewish identity based on racial purity. Jeremias articulates the theory of Jewish racial purity when he asserts that "the division of the people into social classes was entirely ruled by the principle of maintaining racial purity" (1969, 270). He elaborates further by stating that "only those families who had preserved the divinely ordained purity of the race, which Ezra restored through his reform, belonged to the true Israel" (1969, 297). This is puzzling in light of Jeremias's own contention that "pagans" could be received into the Jewish community because "the fact that they belonged to the religious community weighed more heavily than their ancestry" (1969, 270). If religious conversion changes one's identity, then the identity itself cannot be, strictly speaking, a racial one.

Even if Jews at the time of Jesus could have notions of purity of ancestry similar to some contemporary ideas of racial purity, one can see mixing throughout Israel's history. If the people of Judah are considered descendants of Judah, one of Jacob's twelve sons, one can point out the fact that their ancestry is part Canaanite for Judah married Tamar, the daughter of Shua the Canaanite (Gen 38: 1–5). And Ruth, the Moabite, seems to be counted as a member of God's covenant people (Ruth 2:11–12). So foreignness and ancestry could not prevent one from being a member of the household of Israel. Lagrand contends that "if . . . the absolute prohibition were defined in terms of national origin and 'blood lines' David himself would be posthumously 'excluded from Israel'" (1999, 174). The consequence of this mixing is that by the first century of this era, "only a minority of . . . Jews could genuinely trace their genealogy to one of the twelve tribes of Israel" (Hillyer 1978, 872). We can see from the preceding that the nature of the difference between Samaritans and Jews is complex and cannot be easily described in terms of purity of ancestry.

Samaritans as an Ethnic Group

It is an undeniable fact that in the long history of mutual hostility between the two groups, both sides came to the conclusion they were really two peoples, two ethnic groups in our contemporary speech. We have here a case of the birth of ethnicity over time and by a mechanism of boundary creation and maintenance (Barth 1998, 35, 36). The question is, What is the boundary between Jews and Samaritans? Thus far I have argued that race, especially in the modern usage of it, should not be treated as a boundary marker because it cannot adequately address the issue of identity for either Jews or Samaritans.

There is not a "Samaritan race." Consequently, "Samaritans" cannot be "half breeds" because they do not descend from two authenticated "pure breeds"! Who, then, were/are the Samaritans? What is their ethnicity? These questions call for an examination of the nature of Samaritan identity. This identity can be understood only in contrast to Jewish identity because in their history "Samaritans self-defined by their ability to keep a tradition, a religion, and a holy text, have stubbornly refused to disappear" (Anderson and Giles 2002, 145) in contrast to those (the Jews) who did not keep the tradition.

As we seek to understand the nature of "Samaritan" identity, we must do so in the broader context of Jewish identity, religion, and theology. What does it mean to be a Jew? Hamilton has attempted to provide an answer to this question in his article "Who Was a Jew? Jewish Ethnicity during the Achaemenid Period." A few sentences of his opening statement are worth reproducing here:

> The question of Jewish identity is one of the most interesting and provocative 'ethnic' problems of the past three millennia. . . . For the historian interested in the nature of ethnicity, Jewishness presents a rare opportunity to study the phenomenon over a very long time span and in various environments. . . . The nature of Jewishness varied from time to time and place to place. . . . The ethnic label 'Jew' does not lend itself to an essentialist definition, but is seen as 'a series of nesting dichotomizations of inclusiveness and exclusiveness. (1995, 102)

Even in the English language one can see changes in the dictionary definitions of *Jew*. For example, the 1933 edition of *The Shorter Oxford English Dictionary* has the following entry for *Jew*:

> I. A person of Hebrew race; an Israelite. (Orig. A Hebrew of the kingdom of Judah; later, any Israelite who adhered to the worship of Jehovah as conducted at Jerusalem) (Tasker 1967, 1063)

In the 1989, second edition of *The Oxford English Dictionary*, the entry for *Jew* reads:

> I. A person of Hebrew descent; one whose religion is Judaism; an Israelite. Orig. a Hebrew of the kingdom of Judah, as opposed to those of the ten tribes of Israel; later, any Israelite who adhered to the worship of Jehovah as conducted at Jerusalem. (Tasker 1989, 228)

Note that in 1989 the vocabulary of race disappears in the definition of *Jew* and the weaker or softer "descent" is introduced. Also, "the kingdom of Judah" is contrasted to "the ten tribes of Israel." One aspect remains unchanged: adherence to the worship of God with Jerusalem as the center.

Since religion seems to be the constant in various definitions of Jewishness, it is not surprising that for Hamilton (1995) religion is at the core of Jewish ethnicity. This suggestion is in substantial agreement with the conclusions reached by Sparks in *Ethnicity and Identity in Ancient Israel*. According to him, "the most common markers of ethnic identity—language and phenotypical appearance—played no vital role in Israelite ethnicity" (1998, 328); instead "religious identity center[ing] in the person of Yahweh" was the determining factor (330). Circumcision, the Torah, and the temple were central markers of Jewish identity.

In light of the above, faithfulness to God's covenant or the lack of it was the main point of contention between Samaritans and Jews. A Samaritan might not be able to identify a Jew by sight, but a short conversation about religion, about such matters as where one should worship, could soon elucidate who is what. Religion is the boundary!

Jewish identity cannot be essentially religious while Samaritan identity is racial. Expressions such as "half breed" and "mixed blood" are contemporary readers' racialized readings and interpretations. "Samaritan" identity is not racial but is religious. This religious identity can be used as an ethnic marker. The Samaritans can therefore be called an ethnic group.

An examination of the hostility and conflicts between Jews and Samaritans, and each group's use of history, ancestry, and religious practices does, indeed, point out some lessons for us today. One of them is that we can expect proper ethical behavior from people and groups we despise, as in the parable Jesus told in Luke 10:29–37. Most Bibles entitle this "The Parable of the Good Samaritan." A notable exception is *The Original African Heritage Study Bible* in which the title is: "The Lawyer's Question: The Samaritan of Extraordinary Mercy." More important, this Bible warns in a note: One should avoid calling this passage 'the good Samaritan' as if most of them were not good. African Americans have known the subtle humiliation in being dubbed 'a good Negro.' . . . The Samaritan that Jesus sets forth in this parable is a man of unusual spirituality who has the true understanding of God's mercy to others. . . . In fact, Jesus makes the Samaritan a teacher of the disciples (Felder 1993, 1499). The characterization of Samaritans as "half-breeds" or "mixed race," with all the baggage that this vocabulary brings with it, can blunt the force of the lesson Jesus intended to teach. In the parable, the priest and Levite are not just cruel and heartless, they are also godless in that they have not acted according to Micah 6:8; they failed "to act justly and to love mercy." By contrast, the Samaritan's "extraordinary mercy" puts him in the ranks of those who are pleasing to God. In this parable, Jesus' intended lesson seems to echo the Lord's indictment of Jerusalem found in Ezekiel 16: "Samaria did not commit half the sins you did. You have done more detestable things than they" (v. 51). Can we afford not to learn this lesson in a society fragmented along ethnic lines?

In this chapter I have argued that biblical scholars, writing in an age dominated by the idea of race, wrongly read later racial meanings back into biblical texts without such meanings. Though they may have done so unwittingly, the way they read the Bible nevertheless illustrates "how strongly the perspective of one's own time and place shapes one's view of another time and place" (Goldenberg 2003, 200).

One of the most pernicious ideas in the world today is that of race. Its scientific validity is contested (see Unander 2000). It is not a concept deriving from the Bible itself. But if Bible scholars like Jeremias, writing in the heyday of racial ideologies, read their own racial ideologies into the text, giving the impression that race is "divinely ordained," they teach believers to link race to their most sacred authority: the Bible. That is, the biblical apparatus of commentaries is now contaminated with outmoded racial ideas. The result is that Christians and their institutions become some of the key transmitters of the idea that race is simply a natural God-ordained part of our world. Christians are among the few people today who continue to employ a discourse of "racial half-breed," which they do without any biblical authority. The very vocabulary continues to teach listeners to understand the world in racial terms. In a world where people marry others of all different ethnic backgrounds, we cannot afford to have pastors and Bible scholars who fail to understand or address these matters sensitively, both pastorally and in the biblical and theological supports that they provide for others.

REFERENCES

Anderson, Robert T., and Terry Giles. 2002. *The keepers: An introduction to the history and culture of the Samaritans.* Peabody, MA: Hendrickson.
Barth, Fredrik. 1998 reissue. *Ethnic groups and boundaries.* Prospect Heights, IL: Waveland. (Orig. pub. 1969.)
Broadie, Alexander. 1981. *A Samaritan philosophy.* Leiden: Brill.
Calvin, John. 1949. *Commentary on the gospel according to John,* vol. 1, trans.William Pringle. Grand Rapids, MI.: Eerdmans.
Caldwell, T. A. 2003. Samaritans. In *New Catholic encyclopedia,* 2nd ed., 12, ed. Bernard L. Marthaler et al., 633–34 Detroit: Thomson/Gale.
Dahl, Nils A. 1974. Nations in the New Testament. In *New Testament Christianity for Africa and the world,* ed. Mark E. Glasswell and E. Fasholé-Luke. London: SPCK.
Felder, Cain Hope, ed. 1993. *The original African heritage study Bible.* Nashville: Winston.
Fenton, Steve. 1999. *Ethnicity: Racism, class and culture.* London: Rowman and Littlefield.
Goldenberg, David M. 2003. *The curse of Ham: Race and slavery in early Judasim, Christianity and Islam.* Princeton, NJ: Princeton University Press.
Hamilton, Mark W. 1995. Who was a Jew? Jewish ethnicity during the Achaemenid Period. *Restoration Quarterly* 37(2): 102–17.
Hillyer, Norman. 1978. Tribe. In *The new international dictionary of New Testament theology,* ed. Colin Brown. Exeter: Paternoster.
Hjelm, Ingrid. 2000. *The Samaritans and early Judaism: A literary analysis.* Sheffield: Sheffield Academic Press.
Hopler, Thom. 1981. When cultures collide: A surprising look at John 4. *HIS* (May): 22–25.
Jeremias, Joachim. 1969. *Jerusalem at the time of Jesus.* London: SCM.
Josephus, Flavius. 1960. *Complete works,* trans. William Whiston. Grand Rapids, MI: Kregel.
Justin Martyr. 1948. *Writings of Justin Martyr,* ed. and trans. Thomas B. Falls. New York: Christian Heritage.
Köstenberger, Andreas J. 2002. John. In *Zondervan illustrated Bible backgrounds commentary,* ed. Clinton E. Arnold, Grand Rapids, MI: Zondervan.

Lagrand, James, 1999. *The earliest Christian mission to "all nations" in the light of Matthew's gospel.* Grand Rapids, MI: Eerdmans.

Levenson, John D. 2002. The universal dimension of biblical particularism. In *Ethnicity and the Bible,* ed. Mark G. Brett, 143–69. Boston and Leiden: Brill.

Loury, Glenn C. 2002. *The anatomy of racial inequality.* Cambridge, MA: Harvard University Press.

Maldonado, Jorge. 1994. *Even in the best of families: The family of Jesus and other biblical families like ours.* Geneva: WCCC.

Morris, Leon. 1971. *The Gospel according to John.* Grand Rapids, MI: Eerdmans.

Ottley, R. L. 1915. *A short history of the Hebrews to the Roman period.* New York: Macmillan; Cambridge: The University Press.

Pitchford, Susan R. 1992. Race. In *Encyclopedia of sociology,* vol. 3, ed. Edgar F. Borgatta and Marie L. Borgatta, 1615–19. New York and Toronto: Maxwell MacMillan.

Sloyan, Gerad S. 1983. The Samaritans in the New Testament. *Horizons* 10(1): 7–21.

Smedley, Audrey. 1999. "Race" and the construction of human identity. *American Anthropologist* 100(3): 690–702.

Sparks, Kenton L. 1998. *Ethnicity and identity in ancient Israel.* Winona Lake, IN: Eisenbrauns.

Tasker, R. V. G. 1960. *The Gospel according to St. John: An introduction and commentary.* Leicester, England: InterVarsity; Grand Rapids, MI: Eerdmans.

———. 1967. *The shorter Oxford English dictionary.* Oxford: Clarendon.

———. 1989. *The Oxford English dictionary,* 2nd ed., vol. 8. Oxford: Clarendon/Oxford University Press.

———. 2001. *The dictionary: Finding meaning in God's words.* Nashville: Thomas Nelson.

Thomas, Hugh M. 2003. *The English and the Normans: Ethnic hostility, assimilation and identity 1066–c. 1220.* New York: Oxford University Press.

Thomson, J. E. H. 1919. *The Samaritans: Their testimony to the religion of Israel.* Edinburgh and London: Oliver and Boyd.

Unander, Dave. 2000. *Shattering the myth of race.* Valley Forge, PA: Judson.

14

The Bible and the Communion of Saints: A Churchly Plural Reading of Scripture

S. Steve Kang

God's gracious heart for people from every nation, tribe, and tongue is unmistakably portrayed throughout Scripture. From Genesis to Revelation, Scripture is replete with glimpses of God sovereignly gathering his people to himself (Conde-Frazier, Kang, Parrett 2004). Particularly through the incarnation, death, and resurrection of Jesus Christ, our Triune God has inaugurated the kingdom of God on earth, and the church—the people of God—is to testify to God's gracious heart for the world. In this sense, the church has been commissioned to dwell in the presence of the Triune God, whose gracious election invites *all* God's people to be continually formed by the living Word of God, especially through the written Word of God.

This chapter discusses how the whole people of God should faithfully engage Scripture in view of God's kingdom, particularly in light of the historic and global church. From an American church perspective, it asserts that a responsible reading of Scripture and faithful obedience to God must be construed in the context of the holy catholic church and the communion of saints—spanning *all time* and *all space*—for all those who have and continue to be formed by the God of Scripture. The chapter begins with a discussion on how the prevailing modernistic reading of Scripture in the American church has led to fragmentation in the formation of the whole people of God, impeding the progress of faithful reading and obedience to Scripture in multicultural contexts in which the American church finds itself. Second, a modest proposal offers a more encompassing reading of Scripture, in light of the enormousness of the scope and meaning of Scripture and God's vision for all his kingdom's people. Third, a sampling is displayed of rich "voices from the margin" in the modern American church—invaluable partners—in line with the plural reading proposed here. Last, in the way of praxis, a biblical vision of God's kingdom, which must guide the very fabric of the churchly plural reading of Scripture, is briefly discussed.

Perils of the Modernistic Reading of Scripture

Quest for an Elusive Objectivity: Sucking the Life Out of God's People?

Traditionally, the mainstream American church has been rather confident about its ability to objectively decipher the universals of the Christian faith. Such a tendency can be traced back to the Enlightenment, particularly to a rationalistic approach to theological inquiry and biblical interpretation (Marsden 1980). For example, the popular theological and hermeneutical methods shaping contemporary evangelicalism have been profoundly influenced by positivistic and mechanistic scientism, exclusively utilizing logical procedures and scientific method (Noll 1994). The American church has often neglected to consider theology as a systematic interpretive reflection on the content *and* practice of faith taking place in the church, that is, proclamation, sacraments, prayer, confession, and praise. Moreover, the task of theology has, by and large, been construed as deciphering the truths of "the ancient biblical text to the contemporary affirmation of doctrine" and labeling the truths as "self-evident"—to which any rational being, regardless if one is a Christian or not, should agree (Grenz and Franke 2001, 13).

In the process, the American church has experienced at least three major areas of unfortunate bifurcation (Kang 2003a). First, in the public realm, especially in academia, the gap between faith and learning has aptly forced faith to become a private matter that must not enter into public discourse. Coupled with such a phenomenon, the locus of theology and scriptural interpretation has shifted from the church to a select, academic Western elite where (post-) positivism rules. Second, the gap between theology and spirituality continues to widen; theology is largely understood as a cognitive endeavor, whereas spirituality is seen as an affective endeavor or a set of religiously desirable behaviors. The incessant pursuit of objectivity has, by and large, demythologized the mystery of the Christian faith, rendering various ways of sanctified knowing other than reason—i.e., senses, intuition, and imagination—as hindrances to the task of theologizing. Accordingly, many salient issues concerning the life of the church and the world have been precluded as legitimate topics of theological discourse. Third, an ever-widening gap has been in motion between the Text, the written Word of God, and the multiplicity of contexts in which God's people live in the world. The academy's theological undertaking that has largely ignored the interpreter's sociohistorical embeddedness is a major culprit of this ever-widening gap, which inevitably influences one's approach to Scripture, rendering truths of Scripture acontextual (Lints 1993). Corollary to the acontextual interpretation of Scripture is the ahistorical approach. Here, the modern interpreter confidently deciphers the intended meaning of Scripture directly and precisely, without interacting with the rich tradition of scriptural interpretation by the historic church under the guidance of the Holy Spirit (Grenz and Franke 2001). It is no wonder God's people feel increasingly helpless; Scripture no longer seems relevant for the complex challenges of an ever-changing world.

As a result, the formation of God's people in the American church has been characterized by fragmented, impotent attempts to fulfill the church's mandate to be the witness of God's kingdom on earth (Wells 1993). No wonder God's people live in the cycle of either keeping the status quo or accommodating the ever-morphing fads of society, instead of realizing the Triune God's vision of his kingdom, where all God's people—from every nation, tribe, and tongue—boldly testify, in unison, to the transforming power of God's love, here and now.

Perils of Privileging a Single Interpretive Framework: A Case of Historical-Grammatical Reading

Recognizing the interpretive gap between the time and place when Scripture texts were written and the modern-day reader, many biblical scholars, employing historical-grammatical exegesis (by theologically conservative scholars) or historical-critical exegesis (by theologically liberal scholars) have endeavored to build bridges by examining the texts "from a distance." Conservative scholars have sought to critically examine the texts by employing scientific methodology in a value-neutral and disinterested manner, deciphering, without prejudice, what the text meant, when the text was written by the human author for the original hearer (Barton 1998; Osborne 1991).

These scholars approach the task of interpretation as if they are able to transport themselves into the biblical times with modern scientific assumptions and approaches to master the Word of God, abandoning Karl Barth's solemn reminder, "The text must always be master, not we" (Barth 1991, 93). Here, biblical scholars have failed to see that the apostle Paul's first-century church is the very church to which exegetes now belong and must serve. Unfortunately, many academic exegetes simply interpret Scripture independent of and outside the historic and global church. For example, Christian Old Testament scholars often privilege Judaism's exegesis of the "Hebrew Bible" to be somehow more "literal" or prior, in comparison with the church's christological-spiritual exegesis of the Old Testament. However, both Judaism and the church have their own defining way of reading Torah: God's law for Israel and Jesus Christ as the Torah, respectively (Jenson 1997).

Seen in this manner, the problem with the historical-grammatical exegesis is not a methodology itself but historicist assumptions, which inevitably reduce the text to its historical-grammatical sense (McCormack 1995). Such exegesis ultimately denies, whether consciously or subconsciously, Scripture as a gracious unfolding of the life of the Triune God. It also denies the work of the Spirit, who graciously continues to enlighten and illumine the breadth and depth of God's people's communion with one another in the kingdom of the Triune God here and now. Commenting on Barth's theological exegesis, Bruce McCormack writes:

> Years of "impartial" exegesis had taught Barth that "impartiality" was
> no guarantee of objectivity. "Impartiality" was just a lack of critical
> self-awareness. . . . The results of such "impartiality" had been subjec-
> tivism, and it was precisely for the sake of a more genuine objectivity
> that Barth now sought to be partial. Every exegete operates with some
> kind of dogmatic interest. The question is . . . which is most likely to
> produce a faithful understanding of the sacred texts of the Church?
> Barth was aware of the dangers which surrounded his choice and . . .
> sought to build into his hermeneutic certain safeguards which would
> stem the flow of an unchecked subjectivism. (McCormack 1991, 338)

Barth's revolt against the reigning biblical scholarship reminds the church of
the critical importance of reading Scripture in light of her dogmas—the path in
which the Spirit has guided and continues to guide the church.

However the gap may be bridged in the course of the church's interpretation of Scripture, one crucial element of the exegesis must be underscored. The
church needs to realize that, in the life of the Triune God, there is fundamentally no historical difference theologically, if not socially, politically, and so forth
(Jenson 1997), between the church in which the apostles John and Paul wrote,
or in which Irenaeus shaped the canon, or in which Luther declared *sola scrip-
tura*, or in which the (post)modern Christian now reads Scripture. Past and
present, in the life of the Triune God, "do not need to be bridged before understanding can begin, since they are always already mediated by the continuity of
the community's language and discourse" (Jenson 1997, 280).

Of course, there are definite historical distances between Isaiah and Paul
and between them and a modern exegete, and the task of historical critique is
to display such differences. Moreover, Scripture is not a theologically homogeneous unit, nor does it demand the church's unanimous diachronic consensus.
In its faithful interpretation of Scripture, the church reminds itself that the historical distances exist only within the story of Scripture's community; "they
make the historical *compass* of the one community whose book this is" (Jenson
1997, 281).

Given these facts, a question remains: Can the Church, should the Church,
read its Scriptures with any other guiding assumption than that in Jesus Christ,
God has himself appeared in human history? We must not be too quick to
answer. The question is not a purely theoretical one, to be decided dispassion-
ately. It is a question thatreaches to the very heart of the Christian faith (McCormack 1991, 338).

In Search of a Churchly Plural Reading of Scripture

Scripture is the Word of God and continues to become the Word of God to all
God's people, through the witness of the Holy Spirit, as the church reads Scripture in the course of activities specific to the church, that is, preaching, liturgy,
catechetics, endurance of suffering, and works of charity (Jenson 1997, 277). If

the church is to consist of God's people from every nation, tribe, and tongue—as God intends—it is essential that the authentic churchly reading of Scripture must result in a plural reading of Scripture. However, such a plural reading by no means privileges a radical perspectival reading or some arbitrary reader-response reading of Scripture. Instead, what such a plural reading advocates is the acknowledgment of the enormousness and precarious nature of interpretive tasks of Scripture that the church must approach and appropriate with humility.

A More Churchly Plural Reading of Scripture: Voices from Modern Protestantism Calling for a Brand of Plural Reading of Scripture

In recent years, a number of notable voices within the American church have explicitly or implicitly called for a brand of plural reading of Scripture that is faithful to the gospel of Jesus Christ, presenting the possibility for a churchly reading of Scripture for the whole people of God. Noll asserts that the particularity of the work of "Christ opens us to the particulars of all human cultures, situations, moments, and instances" (1998, 8). He contends that "because God revealed Himself most clearly in a particular set of circumstances, every other particular set of cultural circumstances takes on a fresh potential importance. . . . The implications for Christian scholarship from the fact of the particularity of redemption are mind-boggling. This divinely-infused particularity establishes the universality of truth more vigorously than ever did the advocates of the Enlightenment, but it also affirms the perspectival character of truth more radically than any of the post-modernists" (1998, 8).

Vanhoozer zeroes in on how such divinely infused particularity must influence our reading of the Bible when he asks, "How then can we affirm the priesthood of all believers without falling prey to interpretive relativism?" (1999, 27). He asserts that Scripture should be construed to be overdetermined in its meaning. "There is a single meaning in the text, but it is so rich that we may need the insights of a variety of individual and cultural perspectives fully to do it justice. To speak of overdetermined interpretation is, thus, to attest to the abundance of meaning, to a richer hermeneutic realism. The single correct meaning may only come to light through multicultural interpretation" (1999, 27).

He then proceeds: "The Holy Spirit leads the Church, in all its cultural and racial variety, into a deeper appreciation of the one true interpretation of the Scriptures. This should not surprise us, for the event of Jesus Christ itself takes all four gospels together to articulate it. This is a 'Pentecostal plurality,' as it were, which believes that the objective textual meaning is best approximated by a diversity of reading contexts and communities" (1999, 29).

Hall (1998) concurs that learning to read Scripture through the eyes of Christians from a different time and place will readily reveal the distorting effect of one's own cultural, historical, linguistic, philosophical, and theological lens. Moreover, the best exegesis has taken place within the community of the church throughout the centuries. Hall maintains: "The Bibles have been given to the church, are read, preached, heard, and comprehended within the community of the church, and are safely interpreted only by those whose character is continually being formed by prayer, worship, meditation, self-examination, confession and other means by which Christ's grace is communicated to his body. . . . This holistic, communal approach is surely a methodology that warrants a close investigation in our highly individualistic, specialized, segmented world" (42).

Plural Reading of Scripture: Realizing the Apostles' Creed

As God's people, declaring the glorious life of the Triune God, we affirm our belief in the holy catholic church and the communion of saints. "Catholic" simply means "universal," not only in its wide geographical extent but also in the common character shared in the crucified and resurrected Jesus Christ in his eternal relations within the Triune God. Toward that end, understanding the dimensions of time and space in catholicity and the communion of the saints becomes crucial for all God's people, in order to engage in plural reading that characterizes the churchly reading of Scripture.

The Temporal Dimension of the Communion of Saints

What is time? There was a "time" when there was no time, that is, pretemporal eternity (McCormack 2000). God created time, and there will come a time when time ceases to be, that is, once the eternal kingdom of God ushers in fully. From a Trinitarian perspective, eternity should be construed as nothing less than the infinity of the life that the Father, the Son, and the Holy Spirit share with one another (Kang 2003b). In the eternal life of the Triune God, all the saints of the past, present, and even the future have already begun to enjoy true communion with one another.

Then, what does it mean for God's people to "believe in the holy catholic church and the communion of saints" here and now, especially in terms of reading Scripture with the eternal kingdom in view? In approaching Scripture, the whole people of God should read Scripture in view of the unfolding drama of the Triune God's election of his people in Jesus Christ. This is where the whole people of God are to invoke the Holy Spirit to absorb them into the biblical reality. Entry into the biblical reality entails communion not only with the saints of the present but also, mysteriously, with the saints of the past, ranging from biblical characters such as Abraham, Mary, and Paul to saints of the church such as Augustine, Teresa of Avila, and Jonathan Edwards. The saints of the past are brothers and sisters living and communing with us, afforded by the work of Jesus Christ, through whom we have communion with the Triune God and all his people. Yes, these saints have been dead for a long time, and yet they are more alive than ever! Moreover, these saints from church history, while on this earth, have triumphantly struggled to live out their lives in the scriptural reality; they too are more alive than we are in the eternal kingdom now.

From such a perspective, the community of all God's people can trace the faithfulness of the Triune God in his gracious dealings with his people, and dwell and linger deeply in the life of God. God's people are then ushered into a more full realization of the community that God has in store for them through rich communion with the communities that nurtured and profited from the church of saints, through their lives and work in a particular time and space.

The Spatial Dimension of the Communion of Saints

The confession of one catholic church acknowledges a commitment to commune not only with the saints of one local body who share similar socioeconomic backgrounds—that is, those in upper-middle class, suburban Anglo America—but also with the diverse saints of every permutation and from every background within the global body. The Triune God, in his sovereign will, has been bringing people to himself from all around the globe and has brought many of his people to the United States. Despite a slow response, God has been graciously assembling such a community throughout the world. In such a multifaceted context of the church, churchly plural reading of Scripture forces God's people, especially in the United States, to examine deep-seated values and presuppositions that derive from modern Enlightenment thought and Western triumphalism (Sanneh 2003).

Exemplary Partners in Churchly Plural Reading of Scripture in America

Until recently, Western theology and scriptural interpretation have dominated the discipline with their normative truth claims and universalizing applications. More specifically, in Western theology, God's relationship with the privileged Western white male has been construed as if it represented God's relationship with all humanity. In turn, this kind of triumphant theology has coercively, and thus unilaterally, defined and rendered the raison d'être for the subjugation of the nature and vocation of the remainder of God's people.

However, increasing numbers of "voices from the margin," especially from ethnic minorities within the United States, have offered a critique of and corrective to this widely held notion in the disciplines of theology and scriptural interpretation. These Christian scholars begin with an articulation of the experiences of their faith communities; this is their point of departure for understanding the God-human relationship depicted in Scripture and experienced in the world. These "contextualized" theologians and biblical scholars also, in turn, critically reflect on their experiences in light of Christian traditions. In the process, they articulate distinctly Christian yet perspectival strands of Scripture reading that must be integral partners in a churchly plural reading of Scripture. The telos of a churchly plural reading of Scripture is to humbly seek the overdetermined nature of God's Word in the pages of Scripture, and, thus, to obediently testify to the graciousness of the Triune God.

Womanist Reading of Scripture and the Exercise of Corporate Christian Human Agency

Those engaged in womanist theology/ethics approach scriptural reading from an oppressed black female's perspective. Naming the oppression the "colonization" of the black female mind and culture, womanist theological ethicists point to two sources that largely shaped their experience: white oppression and African American denominational churches (Grant 1989; Williams 1993; Mitchem 2002). In one sphere of their lives, African American women were reminded by whites, in every facet of their existence, of their place as colored people—as biologically, socially, and culturally inferior people (Haynes 2002). Thus, their vocation was defined for them: to serve white people, both male and female, young and old, at all costs. In another sphere, African American denominational churches, while providing emotional support and space for faith expressions, suppressed and contributed to render invisible African American women's thought and culture, through their patriarchally biased liturgy and leadership.

Womanist theology/ethics exposes the racism, sexism, and classism of American society and the church, and reveals how the systematic oppression of African American women throughout history has affected and continues to affect the livelihood of these women (Canon 1995). Those engaged in such theology are keenly aware of the role society has played in the construction of the selfhood of African American women and of symbolic African American women (those who have had and continue to have life experiences similar to those of African American women, namely, the black family, the homeless, the destitute, and the young people lost in the drug and gang culture in America) (Sanders 2000).

They contend how skin-color consciousness and the value placed on color have birthed a pathological pattern in American culture. Delores Williams calls it "white racial narcissism"—a method by which the devaluation and abuse of black people have been gradually cemented into America's national consciousness. In the process, African American women, both actual and symbolic, have been socialized as the ultimate nobodies. Black consciousness is consequently created by a social context that differs from that of white people. As a result, black theologians and white theologians have different mental grids, and these different mental grids determine the sources and the method each theologian uses in the construction of theological statements.

For example, Williams contends that, for African American women, the story of the non-Hebrew female slave Hagar is a salient paradigm through which the God-human relationship must be understood. Williams contends that God's response to Hagar's plight was not a triumphant liberation from her oppressors. Instead, God participated in her survival, which gave ultimate purpose to her life, a sense of communal fellowship, and personal worth. The wilderness experience continues, and God is there for both actual and symbolic African American women.

Williams's reading of Scripture assumes that readers often view their own lives through the lenses of those who depict their livelihood in Scripture. Seen in this light, African American Christian women are able to identify with the plight and survival of biblical figures who were marginalized as a result of their race, class, and gender, while privileged white Christians identify with those whose lives were marked by triumph and victory.

According to womanists, African American women have never thought of themselves as individuals whose goal is to attain their own freedom. Instead, they see themselves as moral agents who exist for the common good of the community. In the process, they have sought to create a rich legacy and vision, *shalom*, for their community, realizing the enormous power of shaping the lives of its people, young and old, male and female, against powerful societal oppression. In that light, African American women read Scripture communally to set one another free and to mend wronged relationships in Jesus Christ, who liberates all God's people from all bondage. Thus, they approach scriptural reading as an essential part of their God-given kingdom vocation to free the church—both the oppressed and the oppressors—from sexism, classism, and racism that have been and continue to be the fabric of society and of the church.

Hispanic Scriptural Reading and the Recovery of the Peoplehood of God

As a contextualized theology, Hispanic theology also seeks to interpret Scripture in the context of their sociocultural experience. Gonzalez (1990) criticizes the not so innocent history of the United States when he points out the deepseated racial superiority and evil intentions and deeds of Anglo Americans in regard to those who are different from them. He contends that, in U.S. history as well as in church history, the traditional Christian doctrines and scriptural readings have often been used in oppressive ways. Gonzalez argues that all God's people, as people of the Book, must read Scripture plurally as they eradicate the sins of society and the church.

As a Mexican American, Elizondo (2002) traces the history of the Americas from the perspective of oppressed Mexican Americans. He calls Mexican Americans *mestizaje*, the mixed people, the new race, who were created as the result of two colonization encounters, between Indios and Spanish Catholics, then later between their descendants and Protestant Americans. Elizondo exposes the confluence of a multiplicity of historical factors that brought about racism, which in turn led to rationalization, legitimization, institutionalization, and perpetuation of the violence of racism. He contends that, in the name of God, both Catholicism and Protestantism have played a major role in this immoral atrocity.

Consequently, as biologically and culturally mixed people, and as neither Mexicans nor Americans, Mexican Americans have internalized shame, guilt, and an inferiority complex as a doubly marginalized people. In the process, they have come to believe that to be free is to become like Anglo Americans in every way. With such a reality in mind, Elizondo claims that Jesus of Scripture was a *mestizo* in every way and that by identifying fully with Jesus, the *mestizo*, Mexican Americans can reconstruct their peoplehood and live out God's purpose in the world—namely, promoting intermixing and celebrating it, as fiesta, in every way.

Realizing the profound impact of mainstream American society on the lives of Hispanic Americans, both Elizondo and Gonzalez challenge the church to ponder how the American West was won (while Mexicans and Indians lost) and how the American church was actively involved in the expansion of the American dream. They believe that all God's people exist to retell the whole history of the church and interrogate the western triumphalism endorsed by the Eurocentric reading of Scripture, for the purpose of reconciling with one another in the name of Jesus Christ and boldly living out the *shalom* among all saints for the world.

A Native American Challenge to the America-the-Chosen-Nation Motif

European Christians who first arrived in New England (and South Africa) sometimes framed their lives in terms of the exodus account, in which they identified themselves with "the children of Israel," the land they traveled to as "the promised land," and the people who already lived on and owned the land as "the Canaanites." That is, such hermeneutical appropriations of the biblical text contributed to European justifications for conquest and domination. Not surprisingly, when Euro-Americans presented Christianity to Native Americans, it was often not experienced as "gospel" good news. Indeed, it is the hermeneutic framing themselves as Canaanites that has sometimes been the starting point for Native American reading of the Bible—a reading of the Bible from the perspective of the Canaanites.

Warrior (1995), a member of the Osage Nation of American Indians, reads the exodus from the perspective of the Canaanites. From such a viewpoint, he proceeds to discern the unique parallels between the humiliated people of the biblical times and his own people in the history of America. He believes that the exodus motif is an inappropriate way for Native Americans to think about liberation.

The covenant to Israel had two parts: deliverance and conquest. But that deliverance was conditional. The Almighty God who delivered the Israelites promised to be with them as long as they lived up to the terms of the covenant: "Do not mistreat an alien or oppress him, for you were aliens in Egypt. Do not take advantage of a widow or an orphan. If you do and they cry out to me, I will certainly hear their cry. My anger will be aroused, and I will kill you with the sword; your wives will become widows and your children fatherless" (Exod

22:21–24). Warrior contends that the liberationist picture of Yahweh is not complete—the parts of the story that describe Yahweh's command to ruthlessly annihilate the indigenous population are particularly ignored. In a sense, Yahweh the Deliverer became Yahweh the Conqueror.

Reflect on the book of Joshua. After ten chapters of stories about Israel's successes and failures to obey Yahweh's commands, an account of the conquest is given: "So Joshua took the entire land, just as the LORD had directed Moses, and he gave it as an inheritance to Israel according to their tribal divisions. Then the land had rest from war" (Josh 11:23). However, it is important to note that the Israelites had only divided up the land at this particular point. They were far from actually conquering all the lands (see Josh 13:1–7).

The second chapter of the book of Judges also qualifies the Joshua 11:1–5 account of a completed conquest, for it stated: "The angel of the LORD went up from Gilgal to Bokim and said, 'I brought you up out of Egypt and led you into the land that I swore to give to your forefathers. I said, 'I will never break my covenant with you, and you shall not make a covenant with the people of this land, but you shall break down their altars. Yet you have disobeyed me. Why have you done this? Now therefore I tell you that I will not drive them (the indigenous people) out before you; they will be thorns in your sides and their gods will be a snare to you.' When the angel of the LORD had spoken these things to all the Israelites, the people wept aloud, and they called that place Bokim. There they offered sacrifices to the LORD" (vv. 1–5). Therefore, on one reading, the Canaanites have status only as the people who were removed from the land by Yahweh in order to bring the chosen people in, after the land was safely in the hands of Israel.

Warrior claims that the Canaanites, not the Israelites, should be at the center of theological reflection and political action. This is because: (a) they are the last remaining ignored voice in the text; and (b) because it will cause Euro-Americans to read the entire Bible, not just the parts that inspire and justify themselves. American Christians need to be more aware of the way that ideas, such as those portrayed in the conquest narratives, have made their way into Euro-Americans' consciousness, ideology, and historical relationship with Native Americans (Woodley 2001). At one level, it is such a historical hermeneutic (first developed by European Christians) that makes conversion to Christianity for Native Americans particularly problematic. As Warrior (1995) reflects: "If indeed the Canaanites were integral to Israel's early history, the Exodus narratives reflect a situation in which indigenous people put their hope in a god from outside, were liberated from their oppressors, and then saw their story of oppression revised out of the new nation's history of salvation. They were assimilated into another people's identity and the history of their ancestors came to be regarded as suspect and a danger to the safety of Israel. In short, they were betrayed" (293–94). Clearly, when Native Americans encounter the Bible, they bring a different perspective to the reading of the text—a reading that all Christians, both Native American and Euro-American must struggle with.

Korean American Theology and the Concept of Marginal Community

Reflecting on his plight as an immigrant in America, Lee (1993) appropriates the story of Abraham as the story of a pilgrim through which Asian American immigrant Christians should not only articulate their identity and vocation but also interpret Scripture. He contends that Asian American Christians are God's pilgrims called to be on a sacred journey and must possess visions of a symbolic "homeland," not only for themselves but also for all God's people.

Lee believes that a bicultural existence for Asian Americans has thrust them into the spiritual wilderness. They have left the security of home in pursuit of the sovereign God's promise. He asks, "Why did God bring us into this American wilderness of marginality?" and "To what kind of future is God leading us?" Moreover, Lee maintains that all Christians are called to be marginalized people who seek God's will and obey it, as God's instruments in the world in order to accomplish his will.

Park (1993) construes the victims of sin as people oppressed by those who sin against them. Utilizing the Korean concept of *han*—resigned hope, helplessness, and resentful bitterness as the result of an extended period of time of external oppression and exploitation—Pak reinterprets traditional doctrines of sin and salvation in the broader context of interrelationships between God, human beings, and the world. In discussing some of the major roots of *han* in the world—detrimental effects of a capitalist global economy, patriarchy, racial and cultural discrimination—Park maintains that collective sin generates a great deal of personal *han* as well as collective *han*. In this scheme, Park argues that when victims are oppressed and not fully restored, God's heart is wounded as a cosufferer with those who are marginalized.

Lee (1995) utilizes the notion of marginality—the possibility of "in-betweenness," "in-bothness," and "in-beyondness"—in describing the plight of Asian Americans. For him, the ultimate purpose of liberation from the margin is not to occupy the center by toppling the power that has dominated the margin. Instead, those on the margin should form creative and dynamic cores in order to overcome the effects of marginality and to harmonize the margin and the center in their coexistence.

In conceptualizing the predicament of the Asian American church, these Asian American theologians assert that the church should be God's community-in-process toward becoming the image of Jesus Christ, rather than merely a socially constructed institution that is characterized as victims and victimizers. In their schemes, they call for a brand of multiple churchly reading of Scripture that enables all marginalized Christians to see themselves as God's people who are in the process of moving from the margins of society to the center of God's kingdom. They are called to invite those Christians in the center of the existing church to forsake their privileged churchly and societal positions and to journey toward the center of God's kingdom.

A Biblical Vision toward the Churchly Plural Reading of Scripture: God of All Creation and God of All Culture

Now, in the way of praxis, this section examines a panoramic view of God's vision for the eternal kingdom in which all God's people are already a part. While the church may readily acknowledge that God is God of all creation, it often recedes from acknowledging the same God is God of all culture. Perhaps this is due to the ready witness of the full consequences of original sin, as manifested in culture.

Pentecostal Plurality

Communion with the Triune God became reality when the Father and the Son sent the Holy Spirit on the day of Pentecost to effectuate the work of Jesus Christ by initiating the gathering of God's people as the holy catholic church. On the day of Pentecost, when the disciples were all together in one place, the promised Holy Spirit came down from heaven in power. On that day, by sending God the Holy Spirit, the Triune God graciously and powerfully demonstrated his plan to claim his own in Jesus Christ. Just as Jesus Christ became the second Adam, the head of God's people, able to reverse the power of sin over his people, Pentecost became the Holy Spirit's full reversal of humanity's sedentary disobedience and its enduring consequences at the Tower of Babel.

Commenting on the Tower of Babel incident, John Chrysostom, the fourth-century bishop of Antioch says its "purpose was that, just as similarity of language allowed their living together, so difference in language might cause dispersal among them" (Chrysostom 2001, 169). Jerome says, "Indeed, when the tower was being built up against God, those who were building it were disbanded for their own welfare. The conspiracy was evil. The dispersion was of *true benefit* even to those who were dispersed" (Jerome 2001, 169). Despite their disobedience, God forcibly yet graciously dispersed them throughout the world so that they could fulfill his creation and cultural mandate through which the whole people of God were to glorify God by all God provided for them. At Pentecost, the Triune God graciously began to redeem all culture and his people who have been formed by their own culture. Again, his desire is not to obliterate the sociocultural embededdness, but to glorify himself through the redemption of culture.

It is a Pentecostal plurality through which God the Holy Spirit sanctifies cultures and redeems his people. Scott (2000) and Neill (1970) argue that on the day of Pentecost Jews of the Diaspora traveled to Jerusalem from regions that coincided with the Table of the Nations in Genesis 10, suggesting that, indeed, the coming of the Holy Spirit on the day of Pentecost was to further advance the Triune God's enduring plan for his people. Corresponding to the Tower of Babel incident, increasing numbers of Christians began to settle in Jerusalem instead of expanding their witness from Jerusalem to all Judea and

Samaria and to the ends of the earth. However, after Stephen's death great persecution broke out "against the church at Jerusalem, and all except the apostles were scattered throughout Judea and Samaria" (Acts 8:1). The Triune God, in his sovereign will, dispersed his people throughout the world in order that they might live as God's global community—embodying Christ's body and claiming God's people throughout the world.

The Global Community of All God's People

In order to form that global community of all God's people who are shaped by the Holy Scripture, the Holy Spirit has gathered and continues gathering his people from every nation, tribe, and language, the latter being the most crucial precursor to culture. God has enabled and will continue to enable his people to realize his kingdom on earth, which defies human imagination. The community of God's people is from myriad peoples, languages, and cultures across the world, gathered together through the redeeming and transforming work of the Holy Spirit (Hays 2003). In this community, Scripture functions as the chief constitution through which the prior sociocultural multiplicity of all God's people—infinite variations of the confluence of sociocultural constructs, such as race, ethnicity, class, gender, and others that construct various people groups in the world—is not obliterated, but redeemed and transformed by the sovereign and gracious work of the Holy Spirit. In that light, the church must be diligent in seeking the vastness of the original meaning of Scripture by acknowledging, interrogating, and utilizing varying sociocultural constructs that the Triune God has gracious endowed to the whole people of God.

The church is the one and only sociocultural institution that Jesus Christ established for the community of all God's people; here we are called to enter, dwell, and linger in the life of the Triune God. Yet, the church is not merely a voluntary gathering of like-minded people with similar interests, as in a homogeneous unit. The church is the earthly embodiment of the risen Christ, the community of all God's people in Jesus Christ in time and space that draws near to the Triune God through a churchly plural reading of and obedience to Scripture. Consequently, in one's participation in the church, the whole people of God, the Holy Spirit declares the individual who is elected by God and grants her identity as a partaker in the life of God. Likewise, it is the Holy Spirit who graciously endows various socioculturally constructed groups of God's people with vocations through which they live out God's vision for his kingdom on this earth together. In the process, the community of all God's people must function as mutually formative participants, continually invoking the Holy Spirit's transforming work through a churchly plural reading of Scripture, in order for their community to be drawn near to the life of the Triune God. To rectify the surge toward individualized and privatized faith, the community of God's people must submit to the Triune God's loving intention to attest Jesus Christ to the whole world and to summon his people to faith in Jesus Christ.

The Vision for God's Eternal Kingdom: An Essential
to the Churchly Plural Reading of Scripture

For the church to realize its communion with the Triune God, it needs to recognize how the church has privileged human reason and cognition as the exclusive mode of engaging the spiritual task of theology and scriptural reading.
Moreover, the church needs to recover the rightful place of holy imagination
and intuition (aided by reason, of course) in order to envision her presence in
the Triune God and her communion with all God's people. Imagining how the
church will commune with the Triune God upon Christ's second return, Jenson contends, "In the Kingdom the difference between hearing and seeing will
be transcended, so that while we now live by hearing and *not* by sight, the hearing of the redeemed will be itself a seeing. The redeemed will not cease to be
created by the address of God" (1999, 345).

Perhaps the clearest picture of such a global community of God's people can
be gained in the study of the book of Revelation 20–22. In it, the common de-
marcations of human beings, such as gender, age groups, and marital status are
not mentioned, with the notable exception of the multitudinous nationalities of
the saints, distinctly shaped by the God of all creation and God of all culture. In
Revelation 21:24, 26, and 27 describing the eternal kingdom, John declares: "The
nations will walk by its light, and the kings of the earth will bring their glory into
it. . . . People will bring into it the glory and the honor of the nations. Nothing impure will ever enter it, nor will anyone who does what is shameful or deceitful,
but only those whose names are written in the Lamb's book of life." Again, Revelation 22:3–5 reads: "But the throne of God and of the Lamb will be in it, and his
servants will worship him; they will see his face, and his name will be on their
foreheads. And there will be no more night; they need no light of lamp or sun,
for the Lord God will be their light, and they will reign forever and ever."

The book of Revelation was written so that the original readers would be
able to envision the new covenant, new temple, new Israel, new Jerusalem, and
new creation. These first-century Christians faced many trials that sorely
tempted them to compromise. It is in this crucible that John penned Revelation, in order to "exhort God's people to remain faithful" and to live boldly as
God's people in time and space, for we are grafted into the life of the Triune
God (Beale 1999).

As the community of all God's people enters the Triune God's presence
through the work of the Holy Spirit, the illuminator of the Triune God's life, all
God's people can confidently invoke the Holy Spirit to empower them to live
for him. God is seen continually at work to gather all his people in Jesus Christ
under his rule—from the Garden of Eden in the first chapters of Genesis to the
glorious eternal kingdom of God in Revelation. However, Scripture does not
simply end "with Eden restored, but with the glorious realized vision of God
with his covenant people in thrilling communion and a perfect, recreated environment. . . . This is the overall trajectory of biblical theology" (Desmond and
Rosner 2000, 687). The idea of the community of the whole people of God

communing with the Triune God should stand at the heart of biblical theology, and the holy depiction of the multifaceted community of all God's people reflecting God's glory should constitute the heartbeat of the churchly plural reading of Scripture.

Such a churchly practice should not be motivated by some sort of gnostic desire to escape from its call to be the faithful witness of the Triune God in the world. It is just the opposite; the church is to realize itself as the earthly manifestation of the risen Christ and to proclaim the risen Christ to the world. The church is called to live in that vision of the inaugurated kingdom through which we humbly seek to love one another as Christ commands us. The love of God does not function as a commodity in a zero-sum society, but grows in a marvelous synergy. The sacrificial love of God does not diminish as it flows through us, but it multiplies in individuals and in the community of God, here and now and forever more. The God who revealed himself through Jesus Christ and Scripture invites us to approach him with full confidence, especially as the pluralistic, hermeneutical scriptural community that obeys God's Word—loving God completely, loving ourselves accurately, and loving others compassionately and humbly. This is the crux of being absorbed in Scripture—entering, dwelling, and lingering in the biblical reality—and being in the life of the Triune God.

As gathered kingdom citizens in the world, the church's multifaceted communities, which are God's instruments of genuine freedom and peace, must come together locally and globally to deliver one another from the encumbrances and bondages that have historically hindered the church from becoming the earthly witness of God's eternal kingdom. In the end, the road to societal reconstruction is possible only when kingdom citizens gather together and authentically live out the kingdom life in the world. In that we pray, "Your kingdom come, your will be done on earth as it is in heaven."

REFERENCES

Barth, K. 1991. *Homiletics*. Louisville, KY: Westminster John Knox. (Orig. pub. 1966.)
Barton, B. 1998. Historical-critical approaches. In *The Cambridge companion to biblical interpretation*, ed. J. Barton, 5–15. Cambridge: Cambridge University Press.
Beale, G. 1999. *The book of Revelation: The new international Greek testament commentary*. Grand Rapids, MI: Eerdmans.
Chrysostom, J. 2001. Homilies on Genesis 30.13. FC 82:229. In *Genesis 1–11: Ancient Christian commentary on scripture*, ed. A. Louth, 168–69. Downers Grove, IL: InterVarsity.
Canon, K. 1995. *Katie's canon*. New York: Continuum.
Conde-Frazier, E., S. Kang, and G. Parrett. 2004. *A many colored kingdom: Multicultural insights for spiritual formation*. Grand Rapids, MI: Baker.
Desmond, A., and B. Rosner, ed. 2000. *New dictionary of biblical theology*. Downers Grove, IL: InterVarsity.
Elizondo, V. 2002. *Galilean journey: The Mexican-American promise*. Rev. ed. Maryknoll, NY: Orbis.
Gonzalez, J. 1990. *Mañana: Christian theology from a Hispanic perspective*. Nashville: Abingdon.
Grant, J. 1989. *White women's Christ and black women's Jesus*. Atlanta: Scholars Press.

Grenz, S., and J. Franke. 2001. *Beyond foundationalism: Shaping theology in a postmodern context.* Louisville: Westminster John Knox.

Hall, C. 1998. *Reading scripture with the church fathers.* Downers Grove, IL: InterVarsity.

Haynes, S. 2002. *Noah's curse: The biblical justification of American slavery.* Oxford: Oxford University Press.

Hays, J. 2003. *From every people and nation: A biblical theology of race.* Downers Grove, IL: InterVarity.

Jenson, R. 1997. *Systematic theology: The triune God,* vol. 1 and 2. New York: Oxford University Press.

Jerome, 2001. Homilies 21 FC 48:170. In *Genesis 1–11: Ancient Christian commentary on scripture,* ed. A. Louth, 169. Downers Grove, IL: InterVarsity.

Kang, S. S. 2003a. The church, spiritual formation, and the kingdom of God. *Ex Auditu* 18, 137–51.

———. 2003b. *Being in God's time: A case for a more communal and historical account of the Church's formation.* Unpublished manuscript, Wheaton College, Wheaton, IL

Lee, J. Y. 1995. *Marginality: The key to multicultural theology.* Minneapolis: Fortress.

Lee, S. H. 1993. Asian-American theology: Call to be pilgrims. In *Korean American Ministry* (expanded English ed.), ed. S. H. Lee and J. Moore. Louisville: General Assembly Council—Presbyterian Church [U.S.A.].

Lints, R. 1993. *The fabric of theology: A prolegomenon to evangelical theology.* Grand Rapids, MI: Eerdmans.

Marsden, G. 1980. *Fundamentalism and American culture: The shaping of twentieth-century evangelicalism, 1870–1925.* New York: Oxford University Press.

McCormack, B. 1991. Historical criticism and dogmatic interest in Karl Barth's theological exegesis of the New Testament. In *Biblical hermeneutics in historical perspective,* ed. M. Burrows, and P. Rorem. Grand Rapids, MI: Eerdmans.

———. 1995. *Karl Barth's critically realistic dialectical theology.* Oxford: Oxford University Press.

———. 2000. Grace and being: The role of God's gracious election in Karl Barth's theological ontology. In *The Cambridge companion to Karl Barth,* ed. J. Webster. Cambridge: Cambridge University Press.

Mitchem, S. 2002. *Introducing womanist theology.* Maryknoll, NY: Orbis.

Neill, S. 1970. *Call to mission.* Philadelphia: Fortress.

Noll, M. 1994. *The scandal of the evangelical mind.* Grand Rapids, MI: Eerdmans.

———. 1998. *The Christ of the academic road.* Paper presented at the Institute for the Study of American Evangelicals Conference, Wheaton, IL.

Osborne, G. 1991. *The hermeneutical spiral.* Downers Grove, IL: InterVarsity.

Park, A. 1993. *The wounded heart of God.* Nashville: Abingdon.

Sanders, C. 2000. African Americans, the Bible, and spiritual formation. In *African Americans and the Bible,* ed. V. Wimbush, 588–602. New York: Continuum.

Sanneh, Lamin. 2003. *Whose religion is Christianity?: The gospel beyond the West.* Grand Rapids, MI: Eerdmans.

Scott, J. M. 2000. Acts 2:9–11 as an anticipation of the mission to the nations. In *Mission of the Early Church to Jews and Gentiles,* ed. J. Adna and H. Kvalbein, 87–123. Tubingen: Mohr Siebeck.

Vanhoozer, K. 1999. "But that's your interpretation": Realism, reading, and reformation. *Modern Reformation* (July/August): 21–27.

Warrior, R. A. 1995. A Native American perspective: Canaanites, cowboys, and Indians. In *Voices from the margin: Interpreting the Bible in the third world,* ed. R. Sugirtharagjah, 287–295. Maryknoll, NY: Orbis.

Wells, D. 1993. *No place for truth: Or whatever happened to evangelical theology?* Grand Rapids, MI: Eerdmans.
Williams, D. 1993. *Sisters in the wilderness.* Maryknoll, NY: Orbis.
Woodley, R. 2001. *Living in color: Embracing God's passion for diversity.* Grand Rapids, MI: Chosen Books.

PART IV

Engaging Racial and Ethnic Realities in Congregational Settings

15

New Immigrant Filipinos Bring Changes to Their Parish

Kersten Bayt Priest

On a warm Saturday evening in September cars fill the parking lot and tree-lined streets around a large Catholic church. Filipino families have prepared for weeks to share their ethnic style of worship and celebration with the rest of the congregation. The parish has changed a great deal since its founding in the late 1950s when English-speaking European Americans—the children and grandchildren of Chicago's "old immigrants"—founded the church, opened a school, and named it for a European saint. In 2002, when I first visited the parish, both neighborhood and church were filled with people from across the globe and the parochial school's principal could proudly report over sixty heritages represented among his students. At the altar hung a bright banner: "How wonderful it is, how pleasant, for God's people to live together in harmony" (Psalm 133:1 English Bible). In the center of the banner, brown, black, red, white, and yellow hands formed a circle. The loving Christian message resonated for me because I had recently participated in a failed church merger undertaken to achieve racial unity (see chapter by Bayt-Priest and Priest). Furthermore, as the child of immigrants, I understood some of the anxiety new Americans face. Thus, when I was asked to do fieldwork at St. Ansgar, a church that has extended a warm welcome to new immigrants and seemingly achieved a workable harmony, I was ready to look, listen, and learn!

Scholars of American religion recognize that the United States has a long history of racialization that extends into church life and needs rectifying (cf. Emerson and Smith 2000; De Young et al. 2003). In addition to slavery and the extermination of African and Native peoples, discrimination in America has included long-standing laws of immigration and citizenship that consistently privileged Europeans such as my own relatives. Only recently were such race-based laws revised (1965)—as evidenced in America's changing citizenry. Renewed fears about nonwhite, non-Christian immigrants since the events of September 11, 2001, can obscure the fact that research shows the majority of new immigrants identify as Christian (Warner forthcoming). As newcomers, these new Americans have unique social concerns, including concerns related to working and coping with life in a racialized society. Creating community and addressing these unique social concerns within preexisting nonimmigrant congregations is often difficult. Thus separate immigrant congregations are often formed as places where values of the ethnic home culture can be nurtured and sustained (Williams 1988). Recognizing the concerns of new immigrants, it is instructive to examine a case such as St. Ansgar Parish—particularly for Christians hoping to model the biblical vision of people from every tribe and nation gathered together building a workable unity amid diversity on this side of heaven.

Method and Research Question

The members and leaders of St. Ansgar generously agreed to participate in Loyola's McNamara Center research, opening their community for use as a case study.[1] As the key field researcher at this site, my method involved attending services and church gatherings, hearing stories, writing extensive field notes, and conducting formal and informal interviews of leaders and, particularly, new immigrant members. I also attended suburban community events and researched archival materials. Later, when people knew me, I took photos and videotaped events at their invitation.

Worshipers at St. Ansgar Parish self-consciously celebrate distinct ethnic worship, meaningful to various immigrant subcommunities, with the slogan: "Together in Harmony, we can build a beautiful city." These new ways of worship are the result of ongoing interaction in church life between members—white and nonwhite—over several decades. "Harmony" did not happen overnight. I will focus specifically on how Filipinas and Filipinos who comprise the single largest group (40 percent) slowly moved from peripheral parish involvement into worship leadership, and emerged—within one generation—as a valued distinctive ethnic subgroup in the Catholic church, both locally in Chicago and in its national and worldwide presence. To begin, we will situate St. Ansgar Filipinos within the larger Filipino American immigration story.

Filipino Americans

Numbering approximately two million in the United States, Filipino Americans rank a close second to America's largest Asian immigrant group—Chinese Americans. Filipinos emigrated in four waves beginning in 1903 with the *Pensionados*—one hundred young men specially selected by the Philippine government to attend American universities and return as leaders. A second and much larger wave of immigrants came and stayed to fill labor shortages on Hawaii sugar plantations and California farms. The third wave came through recruitment of Filipino men to the U.S. military. And the fourth wave, by far the largest, comprised skilled workers and professionals who came after the Immigration Act of 1965 was passed. Today many young Filipinas have arrived to join their Latina counterparts as in-home childcare workers (Parreñas 2002, 39–54). Although Filipinos are the fastest growing Asian immigrant group, their diaspora experience and communities are under-researched, with a few notable exceptions (Almirol 1985; Bonus 2000; Espiritu 1995; 2003; Okamura 1988a; 1988b; Posadas 1999; Root 1997; San Juan 1998). Even less information is available on Filipino religion (San Buenaventura 1996; 2002; Strobel 1996). Most Filipino immigrants identify as Catholics—a result of Spanish colonization over centuries. It could be assumed, given the silence in the literature, that Filipinos assimilated into neighborhood Catholic parishes as nondistinct new immigrants. However, as we will observe, when invited and given an opportunity at St. Ansgar, Filipino ethnic worship emerged into *public* Catholic religious space—as a "practical accomplishment"—due to changing contextual factors in the church, both locally and internationally. To understand the changes for St. Ansgar Filipinos we will first review the parish's history; second, examine historic Catholic policy in Chicago and the Vatican; and finally, analyze specific changes in local congregational life.

St. Ansgar Parish: History

Saint Ansgar Roman Catholic Church was founded in the late 1950s, comprising suburbanites moving out of Chicago to raise their young families. Parish founders were of German, Irish, Polish, and Italian heritage. Pictures in the commemoration book (1960) reveal men's and women's groups posed in fashionable suits, ties, and dresses along with photos of children's Scout troops. Their township was 99.5 percent white at the time (1960 census report) but demographic shifts soon took place for primarily two reasons: 1) the town passed a fair housing ordinance in 1968—one of the first in the nation; and 2) federal law reversed racially biased immigration quotas in 1965. By 1980 11.2 percent of the town was nonwhite with 1,291 persons identifying as Filipino. In 2000 there were 3,372 Filipino residents. Saint Ansgar drew recent Catholic émigrés to its mainstream, Euro-classical masses. Many Filipinos were glad to pay the tuition for Catholic school as a safety measure for their children in a suburb where some neighbors expressed their racism by throwing bricks through immigrant Filipino windows. Difference—specifically non-European ethnicity—was *not* an asset in the township. Ruefully, a Filipina explained her thoughts in those early years: "I thought—If they [just] get to know me, they would know what I'm like and won't do these sorts of things." An important strategy was to emphasize alternative statuses. Their efforts were facilitated by the group's ability to speak English (because of English-based Philippine education), their workplace skills as doctors, dentists, nurses, and teachers and, importantly, their neighborhood church participation made possible because of Filipino Catholic heritage.

Saint Ansgar's Thirty-fifth Commemorative Anniversary Book indicates the impact Filipinos had on their parish. Filipinos were listed among the largest donors to the church, and were featured on three luminescent gold pages: first, a Filipino couple and their children were pictured; second, a list of twenty Filipino families were listed by name; and third, a Filipina doctor was recognized—with dual addresses given for an office in the Philippines *and* in the United States. Each Filipino donor gave eloquent thanks to God, the clergy, the parish—and importantly—its founding members.

Filipinos with global networks had entered the church and were making their presence felt with large families and finances. All the indicators of American Catholic congregational participation and professional status were emphasized, including children's attendance in Catholic school, making large donations to the church, obtaining membership in the church's classical worship choir, and wearing formal American clothes. Furthermore, individuals I interviewed could list their multiple civic involvements, from being ballot judges to volunteering in public school and for corporate-sponsored charity. Publicly marked Filipino ethnic identity—such as wearing distinctively Filipino clothes or participating in church with specifically Filipino worship—was absent until the 1990s.

St. Ansgar Filipinos: Private Ethnic Community

Like immigrants in Hawaii and California (cf. Okamura 1998; Almirol 1985; Espiritu 2003), St. Ansgar Filipinos organized a formal Filipino social network linked to their existing neighborhood Catholic church. Twenty families were founders. The priest, through whom they initially tried to organize as a Catholic Filipino group, resisted extending them tax-exempt status. However, they got it on their own. The "Filipino Families of (township name)" met, and continue to meet, every other week in homes to share devotional worship in Tagalog and English for their three resident saints—San Lorenzo, Our Lady of Fatima, and Santo Niño—as well as socialize and plan for various events. Four times a year they hold social dinner dances (ballroom dancing) in the spacious banquet room of the church, solidifying social networks and raising funds to donate back to an increasingly appreciative parish. At first, ethnic music or food was done solely for special private occasions—to celebrate weddings, graduations, and so on for Filipinos either within their group or around the Chicago area. Apparently, parishioners would hear the Filipinos singing in the downstairs banquet hall and eventually said: "You know, you guys [are] always singing in the basement, singing in other places, why don't you sing at St. Ansgar?" At the local level, curiosity on the part of various Euro-American members was the beginning of new interactions and worship in the public space of the parish.

However anti-ethnic approaches and attitudes of pastoral leadership, Chicago's archdiocese, and Rome were slower to change.

European-American Style Catholicism

Chicago's Catholic Church was led for decades by an English-speaking Irish archdiocese, wielding its sometimes-ineffectual power over multiple ethnic parishes and associations. It was not uncommon for several Catholic churches to be on a single city block—each using a different European language (Kantowicz 1995, 2001). Racial privileging of European immigrants during industrialization had brought a great deal of diversity during the Great Migration of 1880–1920, but it was diversity among whites. Two world wars, greater restrictions on immigration, and the promotion of American-style Catholicism by a cardinal intent on assimilative patriotism discouraged ethnic elaboration or identification. During the 1960s, assimilative political agendas across the United States were challenged, coinciding with several important events: the lifting of immigration bans; initiatives for civil rights; and Rome's Vatican II resolutions that recognized the religious place of non-European worshipers in a new way as also belonging to God. The first Filipino saint was canonized in 1987: the martyr San Lorenzo de Ruiz. New global relations—political, economic, and religious—were the historical context for St. Ansgar church to move beyond worship forms in the classical European tradition and consider new ones. Despite the broad changes, the practical accomplishment of new ways to fellowship and worship was a negotiated process, between old and new immigrant subcommunities; white and nonwhite Catholics.

Changes in the Local Church: Filipino Catholic Involvement

The first public presentation of ethnic Filipino worship music by Catholic members at St. Ansgar took place, according to the memories of Filipino leaders, in 1988 or 1989. This was during the tenure of the priest who resisted the formation of a Filipino association. Although he was resistant to ethnic organization, he warmly invited Filipino families to bring their children to stay in the service during mass. For young mothers this was an appreciated gesture. Some Filipino leaders skeptically observed to me that probably the priest's goal was to get Filipino families to enroll their children in the Catholic school to bolster its dropping numbers. The priest even instituted a parallel leadership organization apart from those already established in the church called: "The twelve disciples." He invited Filipinos to participate as lay leaders in this way. Some served as children's Scout assistants too. Several joined the classical church choir. But community involvement in the larger public arena was still organized around mainstream Euro-American church life.

Reminiscing about the changes in public worship, a Filipina leader explained the interactive negotiation in the following way:

Father—started that, you know—was welcoming everybody. But he
was kind of like (having) the English club. You know these are a lot of
German people, in the church. So he didn't like them to say, you
know, things, you know. So, uh, we couldn't even have a mass in the
church. And I remember when we first started—we only sang *one*
Tagalog song. One! And because they thought it's kind of like, you
know, polka style they liked it . . . very much. And they said, Oh we
like to do another one. . . . —I used to shake [demonstrating with
physical shaking how scared/nervous she was] (laughing) O my God,
I was scared! . . . so when they heard it, then they liked it. And then
everything was in English. That one piece. And then, you know, so
each time they would ask us.

Over the years Filipino members have experienced a gradual acceptance into
the public space of sanctuary worship. Perhaps because of the predominantly
German heritage of the congregation, the polka-like aesthetics rang a cultural
chord and many liked it. Song by song, first in translated English and eventually Tagalog—always with the priest's express permission—Filipinos were invited to share their style of worship. It is important to recognize the trepidation
of the Filipinos within the process as indicative of the unequal power relationship between themselves (Filipino community) and the Catholic leadership
and older Euro-American members. In fact, even today there are older non-
Filipino members within the church who are resentful of the changes and have
expressed personal dislike of Filipino members.

In addition to the concern over public participation within an unequal
arena of power, there was another concern: how Filipinos should present themselves. In an interview, one Filipino individual explained the predicament:
"And then they were asking, they were *expecting* us to do a, you know, *presenta-*
tion . . . [saying] "I can *hardly* wait for tonight" and I said: 'O my God, they really expect us to sing and have a *show!*'" Worry over non-Filipinos' assessments
regarding the show of ethnicity in a multicultural event is not surprising given
that performances assume an audience and audiences have the power to ap-
prove or disapprove. What had been private in-group ethnic affairs were changing into churchwide extravaganzas featuring the Filipinos as the "other" for the
anticipating gaze of on-looking non-Filipinos. Ethnic masses paradoxically allowed for greater participation in the public religious sphere at the same time
that the church was marking greater difference through categorization—that of
ethnic Filipinos on display, reminiscent of what Said articulates in his book,
Orientalism (1994). According to Said, "orientalising" of non-Europeans takes
place when a minority's cultural productions are reduced to "exotic" represen-
tations for "outsiders"—historically by Europeans who have held more power.
However, the "exotic" representation by Filipinos at St. Ansgar has been a more
complex reality—a joint project—between vigorous Filipino participants *and*
non-Filipino Catholics. According to immigrant members I interviewed, the arrival of a new priest committed to inclusion was a key factor for greater involvement and positive change.

Local Changes: New Pastoral Vision and Ethnic Ministries

Father Kujic, a Polish priest in his fifties, arrived eight years ago with a wholehearted commitment to diversity in a multicultural approach. His office is decorated in exquisite Asian art and he takes lessons from a Chinese artist. Although raised in the city of Chicago (known for its racial segregation) and trained at nearby Mundelein Seminary, Father Kujic can recall being exposed to people of different races and cultures by his parents. He has also traveled extensively and dialogues with leaders of different faiths. Father Kujic related how he approached St. Ansgar's parishioners: "I told the people, my one wish was to have a potluck when I arrived, nothing else, so that everyone could bring the food that is special to them." He reasoned that this would be a good way for everyone to appreciate the diversity within the parish—just as "many notes together make a harmony." To achieve his vision of harmony, the priest chose nineteen individuals to be part of a new "Faith and Culture Commission." The group includes representatives from Mexico, Puerto Rico, Sri Lanka, Philippines, Cuba, India, Poland, Lebanon, Taiwan, Bosnia, Japan, as well as representatives of older German, Italian, Irish, and African American diaspora communities. However, compared with their counterparts, Filipinos organize far more annual ethnic worship events in the church.

The banner that stands at the front of the church throughout the year is the permanent motto of Father Kujic and the other priests for their congregation. With multicolored hands radiating in a symbolic circle, it reminds members: "Together in Harmony, We can build a beautiful city." When a particular ethnic worship service is conducted, it is done in recognition that this is one way among many. Any particular ethnicity is a symbol within a larger symbol—that of multicultural pluralism—a scriptural ideal and a way worldwide Catholicism is making peace with its multiethnic membership. In keeping with worldwide Catholic mandates to welcome immigrants into the church, Chicago's archdiocese has hired individuals to head ethnic affairs for ethnic groups in the Chicago area. The Asian Ministries administrator explained Filipino Catholic experience thus: "Some people acculturate and are not that interested in highlighting their 'Filipino' identity. Many times these are people who have a lot of bad memories, were poor, or just want to go on with life. Then there are people who really want to 'keep their identity'—it's important."

Clearly social class has a bearing on one's experience of ethnicity. Not all immigrants have the same socioeconomic status vis-à-vis one another within their ethnic group or even across ethnic groups. For example, St. Ansgar's Filipino ethnic worship leaders are precisely those individuals who have discretionary funds to travel and often bring back important items for the religious community (i.e., traditional cloth, music scores, audiotapes, devotional items). For them, status accrues as a result of their international travels. Yet, they were also very generous and seemed glad to do their work as religious devotion. Recruitment for volunteers was informal and conducted through the Filipino Family Association. Even if someone volunteered at the last minute, he or she

was included in dancing, flower decorating, sewing worship costumes, cook-
ing, cleaning up, and so forth.

However, class tensions do occur within the parish—between immigrant
groups of differing economic status. All oppressions are necessarily entangled
and race scholars theorize these multiple oppressions are "intersected" within
"matrices of domination" (Crenshaw 1991; Collins 2000) such that "oppression cannot be reduced to one fundamental type"—for example, race or gender
or poverty. Rather, if one is poor *and* from a historically stigmatized racial
group, then poverty is experienced even more painfully as an interlocked oppression *with* race. The matrices of domination are those places in which the
combination is painfully reinforced for an individual/group. Religion, and,
more specifically, the congregation, is potentially another context where injustice is experienced in face-to-face exchanges. For example, when I asked an undocumented immigrant member if she had experienced racism in the United
States she could only recall two instances and both had occurred in the parish.
The most disturbing to her was when a high-status immigrant nurse—*not* of
her minority group—had called to insist she pick up her daughter from the
Catholic school. The nurse implied that because the girl had visited their home
country during the summer (a poor nation) she must be treated for lice. The
memory brought tears because of the shame associated with her class/ethnic
identity in conflation with "dirtiness." When taken to a doctor, the daughter did
not, in fact, have lice.

Diversity among New Immigrants

Latinos are a highly stratified immigrant group in the parish just as they are in
the United States. Both high-status families (i.e., Cubans) and low-status families (i.e., undocumented Mexicans) are members. The celebration for Our Lady
of Guadalupe (the Latino mass) was a smaller event and the post-mass dinner
was done without tablecloths or the carefully practiced dances and musical
events done at Filipino masses. Spanish speakers clustered, chatted, and ate at
tables by nationality. The most congenial expressions of friendship were exhib-
ited between high-status Latinos and their Filipino Catholic friends who came
as guests to this particular celebration, thus underscoring class-based ties over
ethnic bonds.

The senior priest at St. Ansgar did not address class differences in the year I
attended. He emphasized repeatedly that diversity (i.e., ethnicity) should be celebrated as harmonious Catholic multiculturalism. His approach mirrors that of
the U.S. Conference of Catholic Bishops as articulated in their pastoral statement
entitled "Welcoming the Stranger among Us: Unity in Diversity." Within the
document the pope's 2000 Mass for the world's immigrants in Rome is given
full explication and the ramifications are made explicit: "Knowledge of cultures
cannot just come from books, but must come from the concrete efforts of individuals to get to know their neighbors, in all their diversity" (U.S. Conference of
Catholic Bishops 2000, 3). The official Catholic multicultural approach promotes

a notion that all groups can come together side by side in an egalitarian mode of interaction in relation to common social, economic, and political practices. "Cooperation in pursuit of the common good" is unproblematized at St. Ansgar and it is assumed that everyone would agree as to what that "common good" is. Presently, the "common good" of the Vatican promotes "respect for the good of each cultural tradition and community" in such a way that religious/symbolic ethnicity reinforces the centralized historic church—within the public space of the parish sanctuary. And on one level this is perceived and experienced by minorities themselves as good. For example, one member said that although her most intimate religious fellowship is with a small Catholic Bible study of Chinese women from across the metro area, she greatly appreciates Father Kujic and St. Ansgar because she can walk to church and be in a congregation where one sees, in her words, many other "black-haired and brown-eyed people." Diversity for her meant not being the minority nonwhite member.

Filipino leaders are well aware that the archdiocese wants ethnic minorities to bring their ethnic worship out of the private domain of home worship and into the public sanctuary, and support the initiative. But the effect is varied for each church member/subcommunity in the multiracial/multiethnic congregation. Even for St. Ansgar's Filipinos, multiculturalism is a mixed blessing. Prior to public involvement they were peripheral to the majority Euro-Americans whose only ethnic celebration was a German/Polish Bratfest (sausage barbeque) to raise funds from the neighborhood for their church. Now Filipinos are the largest single contingent in the church (40 percent) but are only one ethnic group among many that are comprised in the council of the "Faith and Culture Commission." As multicultural leaders, their ethno-religious symbols have different meanings when moved from private practice into the public gaze, and this carries a different responsibility, one of performance. Such self-conscious Filipino-ness can be a burden and a form of categorization that exoticizes them through worship that is observed as "other." However, on the other hand, for many first-generation professionals who remember vigorous religious participation with relatives and community in the Philippines before coming to the United States, the larger public platform has created new possibilities. They take their new voluntary roles quite seriously and invest much time, money, creativity, and even international travel to commission the carving of statues of saints, and the purchasing of cloth, devotional items, and Tagalog music scores and audiotapes. Worship, in the Catholic Filipino tradition, has also afforded the opportunity to self-define in elaborate symbolic form who their community is—for non-Filipino onlookers as well as for themselves and their children.

The "Upside" of Multiculturalism: New Ethnic Communities

Several worthy goals are accomplished at St. Ansgar through multicultural worship. The priest at St. Ansgar delivers homilies for each ethnic mass with care to research and explain the ethnic meanings for all members present. He also frames each specific celebration within larger multicultural frames so that everyone feels welcome. Simultaneously, Filipinos use their various ethnic feasts to express an ever richer version of themselves in relation to their homelands—both Philippine and United States. For them an important benefit of expressive ethnic worship is that children get more involved, which is a concern for many devout Filipinos (as well as other minorities). Home-based devotionals have seen the youth stop coming, but the public rituals provide a creative project to bring teens and young professionals back into church as collaborators and appreciative observers of their parents and the youth who perform. Thus ethnic dance and music done after the mass and during the feasting time in the parish banquet hall is an important way for ethnic and religious symbols to be negotiated and shared between generations (cf. Cha in this volume). Those who do not dance set up audio equipment, operate video cameras, roll audiotape, beat drums, clack the *tinikling* poles or help make and collect artifacts. Constructing a beautiful and exotic identity within an American context in counterpoint to societal racializing (i.e., reducing a person's identity to a simple category such as "Asian" or "nonwhite") is viewed as a worthwhile endeavor. Several young people have begun to match funds with their parents to return to the Philippines, research its history and culture, buy books on Tagalog for beginners, and even purchase Filipino artifacts on eBay.

Enculturating children to their Filipino identity takes time and effort. While parents use their time in one another's homes after devotionals to practice songs, teens—boys and girls alike—take the extra time after school and on weekends, under a Filipina choreographer's tutelage, to master complex dances. Young people are thus included and highly affirmed through the thunderous applause that hundreds, both Filipino and non-Filipino, give them when they publicly perform in the social hall after mass. Their ethnic worship wins approval not only for themselves but for the whole Filipino Catholic membership.

Ethnic worship symbols do mark communal boundaries at St. Ansgar but also allow for the creation of new meaning relevant to all worshipers: first-generation parents, second-generation children, and non-Filipinos. For example, when I attended the Feast of San Lorenzo, the final event of the evening was five teenage Filipino-American boys standing in a semi-circle, checking their pitch, and singing a song in tight a cappella harmony. The master of ceremonies explained prior to their performance that this particular song was originally an English version Celine Dion/Whitney Houston duet in commemoration of September 11, which he had translated in "as poetic a form as possible" to "bring hope." The young men's harmonious Tagalog won loud applause and I overheard an older Filipino say in amazement: "And they don't even know how to speak Tagalog!" Shared values found voice through American/Tagalog music made by two generations of diaspora Filipino Catholics in multicultural worship performance. For the translator, he had made a poem, marking his bicultural and bilingual proficiency. For the teens, the song was further opportunity to align with Filipino identity while simultaneously mastering music for an appreciative multicultural church audience in an ethnic feast. For Filipino adults, the song was reassurance that their youth could appreciate their identity as Filipinos in technical execution of words they did not know. For one singer, the song was bittersweet, given the recent tragic death of his father. For all individuals who considered themselves "American," the tie to September 11's tragedy was an expression of solidarity and a call for unity— regardless of ethnic differences within the large banquet audience. And for the priest, his parish was living out harmony.

Multiculturalism, Ethnic Boundaries, and Race

At St. Ansgar, Filipinos are not the only minority group. But their numbers, socioeconomic position, and affinity with the archdiocese have propelled them to central leadership. Today they no longer fear giving offense when they sing translated worship songs. Adults do choreographed dances that represent various areas of the Philippines and its cultures. During performances, the master of ceremonies explains the meanings of the performances for onlookers. The rural lifestyle of the Philippines and its agricultural seasons are important themes. For adults, all the musical and material images of the Philippines— rural, colonial, and contemporary—vividly evoke childhood memories. Chicago's suburbs are a world away from those places, but music and movement in worship and celebration can bring all those memories back as aesthetic reinvention within a multicultural feast.

In the Feast of San Lorenzo, the Filipino choir vigorously sang a Tagalog anthem that, as translated in the bulletin, exults: "Teach us to offer our lives completely to God and our mother country. . . . Since we are of the same race and flesh, one country of origin, Pearl of the Orient . . ." Catholic multicultural initiatives have allowed Filipinos to elaborate new worship forms and identities—drawing new ethnic boundaries in public space, boundaries that potentially racialize and divide. The parish priest may speak of multicultural meanings in the martyrdom that included not only San Lorenzo but several others including Spaniard and Frenchman. However, Filipinos sing of their saint who makes the nation proud and unites their race. San Lorenzo was actually of Chinese and Filipino descent and Filipinos are quick to point this out. Further complicating the matter, Filipinos traditionally use figures of saints that are white in appearance, and include devotional pamphlets specially ordered and carried from the Philippines. The European features of the saint are a by-product of colonial Catholicism that missionized the Philippines by using European practices and images. By stark contrast, the painting chosen by Father Kujic to depict San Lorenzo on the bulletin depicted a famous Filipino painting of the saint with dark skin and hands clasped together in fervent prayer. Taken together, the constructedness of race is actually quite complex— at multiple levels—across distinct historic, geographic, and political periods in various local contexts: Spanish Filipino colonization, St. Ansgar Filipino members' devotional practices, and the priest's multicultural artistic sensibilities (cf. Omi and Winant 1994). Race, at a more mundane level, could be taken to mean "shared pride in ethnic/national/religious identity." But what about those for whom race/ethnicity may reference other histories—such as black Americans?

The handful of black families at St. Ansgar have gone to great effort (with the generous funding of one African American woman) to host a special Black Madonna mass. Afterward, a Dixieland ensemble played while church members enjoyed a banquet of soul food complete with fried chicken and biscuits. In reminiscing, Father Kujic was especially pleased that his choice of cloth matched the Afrocentric pattern and colors that a black member had bought to decorate the Madonna. The choir from St. Sabina, a politically engaged black church in south Chicago, provided the Afrocentric worship aesthetic during mass, at high volume with rhythms and harmonies unique to southern Afro-Christian spiritual traditions. Unfortunately, the black ethnic mass has discontinued because, as Father Kujic implied, it was too costly for the few vested members. However, a black member *did* volunteer to recruit parish members for a Catholic-sponsored racial reconciliation weekend retreat for the larger metro region. It is important to recognize that a reconciliation meeting between Christians assumes that unity requires more than celebrating difference.

The African immigration experience in America, if their disenfranchisement through slavery could be called such, racialized the peoples from many different African ethnic groups by labeling them with a new identity (Negro) created through dehumanizing socioeconomic relations. Slave/free slave churches became the primary social institution for racially excluded blacks and as such, the church was a safe haven in an otherwise hostile society. This unique experience marked the dawn of a powerful ethnoreligious history expressed in aesthetic symbols constitutive of black community. Saint Sabina, a predominantly black Catholic church in south Chicago, has embraced a monoethnic religious model for its predominantly black membership. Architecture and interior built by early European immigrants has been redecorated with vibrant African designs and colors as well as tall, permanent, dark woodcarvings of African figures with upraised arms. By contrast, St. Ansgar's expressions of difference are brought into the public domain only during ethnic mass as special figures—one of many multicultural devotional objects that must share the public space for only one weekend of the year. The Black Madonna, the dark-skinned Our Lady of Charity of Cuba and Mexico's Our Lady of Guadalupe are impermanent. Permanent alcoves and platforms are reserved for the European figures of Christ, the Virgin, and other biblical saints including the parish's European name saint. The European-featured Santo Niño picture also hangs year-round.

Put broadly, ethnic multiculturalism promotes a symbolic unity that runs the risk of assuming that if a public space is filled with diverse symbols, their coexistence is evidence of equality. In contrast, a racial/ethnic religious model often assumes inequality in social relations, the assumption being that coexistence does not rule out the presence of differential power within those relations. The multicultural approach is in line with the official stance of U.S. bishops and archdioceses. A justice approach would address inequality and often use public worship space to agitate against symbolic unity that ignores power. Priests who serve parishes that are predominantly Latino or black often lean toward the racial/ethnic religious model. For example, Chicago's Latino parishes have been known to take more vocal political stances on issues of justice (i.e., protests against the Citizenship and Immigration Services, formerly the INS) that are outside the status quo ideology of harmony and incorporation in side-by-side unity. Local Latinos who have united outside the church for ethnic religious activities have been cajoled to bring their rituals back into the official sanctuary—under the authority of central Catholic order. It is an ongoing negotiation that will continue.

In the spring of 2002, Chicago Filipino representatives from twenty-two churches met for the first time to discuss issues pertinent to their religious communities. A Filipino priest from California facilitated. A Filipina representative from St. Ansgar came away feeling that her church was a leader in archdiocese multicultural initiatives and was concerned that regardless of whatever changed, the church should remain inclusive—particularly the language—so that everyone could participate. Her daughter is in a biracial/biethnic marriage and she is sensitive to the fact that heightened ethnicity could exclude in the very act of building ethnic cohesion (cf. Cornell and Hartmann 1998). Precisely because Filipinos see their faith as primarily ethnic fellowship and worship and *not* racial/ethnic protest, their approach is understood as nonresistant, inclusive, and moderate, which is compatible with the multicultural approach of Catholic hierarchies. Therefore, they are invited to lead in integrative efforts.

Conclusion to the Case Study

To achieve harmony among its diverse members—many of whom are highly mobile immigrants—Catholic leadership is promoting spiritual formation that celebrates diversity in multicultural public worship. The impetus for change was launched by the pope himself. For non-Europeans, historically pushed to the periphery, this has meant that their cultural worship traditions have gained international, national, and local respect. Of course, *how that change is actually achieved* is contingent on the particularities of given parishes. This case study examines how a predominantly Euro-American Catholic parish changed over the years into a multiethnic church that is a model of a multiracial church united by faith. It is instructive that harmony was achieved not merely because individuals of many races attended the same parish thus making it multiracial. Rather, several factors led to positive change at St. Ansgar. First, Filipinos, in particular, brought valuable resources, both social and financial, to the congregation. Second, several Euro-American members, especially Father Kujic, showed genuine interest and affirmation, which opened public space for new immigrants (and others) to participate and lead. Third, even though interpersonal negotiations were often awkward, and doing ethnic worship in public has sometimes received unkind evaluation (i.e., angry letters to Father Kujic), the church has continued to opt for "welcoming the stranger." New immigrants have been embraced into a new church home. Fourth, for first- and second-generation Filipino Catholics, as well as non-Filipinos, doing and teaching ethnic worship has become the way to distinguish themselves and create valued community, done through rituals and symbols that carry multiple meanings, not the least of which is a sense of remembered and imagined sacred beauty to identify with (Anderson 1983; Williams 1988). Even European Americans have rethought how their own heritage can enhance worship for the greater parish. Finally, harmony at St. Ansgar has meant that ethnic worship is done in public events to underscore their unity in diversity, which also happens to bring together individuals from across historic racial divides.

Implications for Christians, Congregations, and Related Institutions

LEADERSHIP. Denominations, seminaries, and leadership boards should recognize that thoughtfully produced mandates can facilitate change in a globalizing world that desperately needs morally persuasive answers to issues of race and ethnicity. Pastoral theologies must speak wisdom for this age. For example, the Chicago region's Mundelein Seminary (the largest U.S. Catholic seminary) now requires seminarians to learn a pastoral language—Spanish, Polish, etc.—before they graduate. Students must be able to conduct mass and preach in the language. Individual leaders can foster a lifestyle of welcoming by learning different cultural styles of worship, food, art, and music. When a spiritual leader appreciates the cultural differences of others, a strong signal of worthiness is expressed. The apostle Peter was challenged on just such an issue when, in a vision, God commanded that Peter eat food he considered "unclean" while he resided in a foreigner's house (Acts 8). Of course, teaching congregations that are not used to experiencing difference is a challenge and requires careful preparation to explain the meaning—just as Father Kujic did for his whole parish when an ethnic ritual was introduced.

MULTICULTURALISM OR JUSTICE? Institutions must make efforts to balance the joyful celebration of multicultural affirmation with issues of justice. We continue to live in a world where some people are not accorded the same value because of racialization. Even today many people of color do not get equal treatment in hiring or housing. Because history is continually changing, the idea of whom we consider to be most needy shifts. To assume race is all about black and white people ignores how recent immigration is creating new hierarchies of dominance and powerlessness. God's people should be aware of how they can be involved to make this right. To celebrate cultural worship traditions is good. To recognize the whole experience of people—including their economic position—is imperative. The Scripture asks: "What does the LORD require of you?" The answer: "To do justice, to love kindness and to walk humbly with our God" (Mic 6:8).

BE AWARE! Finally, to unite by faith does not provide the definitive answer to the problem of race because physical proximity—being comembers of a multiracial/ethnic congregation—does not necessarily mean racial hierarchies and stereotypes are eradicated. In fact, as we have seen, new and highly complex ethno/racial categorizations—both self-assigned and assigned by others—can emerge. People can assume that because someone is of a minority group (or the majority group) that he or she must be of a certain type. For example, folk knowledge says if someone is Asian American, then that person must be smart, successful, and enterprising. However, the truth about people is more complex. Filipinos who immigrated in the 1960s and 1970s, and had English competency, have done quite well as new Americans. On the other hand, recent Filipina immigrants arriving as domestic workers are not doing very well. Furthermore, in any one ethnic group there can be a good bit of difference between the generations (see Cha's example for Koreans). Well-intentioned people must combine their Christian concern with knowledge. Taking a class, reading good books, watching TV documentaries, and most important, getting to know people cross-racially/cross-culturally are important ways to avoid stereotyping people. Now is the time to bravely take steps, welcome others into our lives, and demonstrate that dividing walls can indeed be broken down so that we may indeed live in harmony.

NOTE

1. This research was conducted under the aegis of the RICSC project (Religion, Immigration and Civil Society, Chicago) at Loyola's McNamara Center and was funded by Pew Foundation's Gateway Cities Project. Many thanks to those who have read, listened, and given input on multiple renderings of this paper: Fred Kniss, Kathleen Adams, Judith Wittner, Stephen Warner, Raymond Williams, Michael Emerson, Bob Priest, Peter Kevisto, Brian Howell, Traci, Katrina, Kristin, Diana, and Tim. Thanks to my research assistants: Paul Priest and Shelly Priest. Special thanks to the leadership and members of St. Ansgar Church who warmly welcomed me. All names have been changed to pseudonyms to protect the privacy of the church and those interviewed.

REFERENCES

Almirol, Edwin B. 1985. *Ethnic identity and social negotiation: A study of a Filipino community in California.* New York: AMS.

Anderson, Benedict. 1983. *Imagined communities: Reflections on the origin and spread of nationalism.* London: Publisher: Verso.

Bonus, Rick. 2000. *Locating Filipino Americans: Ethnicity and the cultural politics of space.* philadelphia: Temple University Press.

Collins, Patricia Hill. 2000. *Black feminist thought: Knowledge, consciousness and the politics of empowerment.* 2nd ed. New York: Routledge.

Cornell, Stephen, and Douglas Hartmann. 1998. *Ethnicity and race: Making identities in a changing world.* Thousand Oaks, CA: Pine Forge.

Crenshaw, Kimberle Williams. 1991. Mapping the margins: Intersectionality, identity politics, and violence against women of color, *Stanford Law Review* 43(6): 1241–99.

De Young, Curtiss Paul, Michael O. Emerson, George Yancey, and Karen Chai Kim. 2003. *United by faith: The multiracial congregation as an answer to the problem of race.* Oxford: Oxford University Press.

Emerson, Michael, and Christian Smith. 2000. *Divided by faith.* Oxford: Oxford University Press.

Espiritu, Yen Le. 1995. *Filipino American lives.* Philadelphia: Temple University Press.

———. 2003. *Home bound: Filipino lives across cultures, communities, and countries* Berkeley and Los Angeles: University of California Press.

Kantowicz, Edward R. 1995. The ethnic church. In *Ethnic Chicago: A multicultural portrait,* ed Melvin G. Holli and Peter d'A. Jones. Grand Rapids, MI: Eerdmans.

Okamura, Jonathan Y. 1988a. Filipino hometown associations in Hawai'i. In *Asians in America: Asian American family life and community,* ed. Franklin Ng. New York: Garland.

———. 1988b. Beyond adaptationism: Immigrant Filipino ethnicity in Hawai'i. In *Asians in America: Asian American family life and community,* ed. Franklin Ng. New York: Garland.

———. 1998. *Imagining the Filipino American diaspora: Transnational relations, identities, and communities.* New York: Garland.

Omi, Michael, and Howard Winant. 1994. *Racial formation in the United States: From the 1960s to the 1990s.* 2nd ed. New York: Routledge.

Parreñas, Rhacel Salazar. 2002. The care crisis in the Philippines: Children and transnational families in the new global economy. In *Global woman: Nannies, maids, and sex workers in the new economy,* ed. Barbara Ehrenreich and Arlie Russell Hochschild, 39–54. New York: Henry Holt.

Posadas, Barbara M. 1999. *The Filipino Americans.* Westport, CT: Greenwood.

Root, Maria P. P. 1997. *Filipino Americans: Transformation and identity.* Thousand Oaks, CA: Sage.

Said, Edward. 1994. *Orientalism.* 2nd ed. New York: Vintage.

San Buenaventura, Steffi. 1996. Filipina spirituality and immigration from mutual aid to religion, *Amerasia Journal* 22 (Spring): 1–30.

———. 2002. Filipino religion at home and abroad: Historical roots and immigrant transformation. In *Religions in Asian America: Building faith communities,* ed. Pyong Gap Min and Jung Ha Kim, 143–84. Walnut Creek, CA: Alta Mira.

San Juan, E. 1998. *From exile to diaspora: Versions of the Filipino experience in the United States.* Boulder, CO: Westview.

Strobel, Ley Mendoza. 1996. "Born again Filipino": Filipino American identity and panethnicity, *Amerasia* 22:2.

U.S. Conference of Catholic Bishops. 2000. *Welcoming the stranger among us: Unity in diversity.* Washington, DC: United States Conference of Bishops.

Warner, R. Stephen. Forthcoming. The De-Europeanization of American Christianity. In *A nation of religions: Pluralism in the American public square,* ed. Stephen Prothero. Chapel Hill: University of North Carolina Press.

Williams, Raymond Brady. 1998. *Religions of immigrants from India and Pakistan: New threads in the American tapestry.* Cambridge: Cambridge University Press.

16

Constructing New Intergenerational Ties, Cultures, and Identities among Korean American Christians: A Congregational Case Study

Peter T. Cha

The Immigration Act of 1965 dramatically altered the racial, ethnic, and religious landscape of the United States. Abolishing existing immigration policies that exclusively favored European immigrants, the new immigration law opened the door to millions of non-European immigrants. Between 1985 and 1995 alone, more than four million immigrants—about 85 percent of the total number of immigrants who came to the United States during that period—came from Latin America, Asia, and the Caribbean Islands (Chiswick and Sullivan 1995, 216–17). The growing presence and unique cultural contributions of these immigrants and of their American-born children are profoundly reshaping American culture and society, expediting the formation of multicultural America.

   Post-1965 immigration has also affected the American Christian community significantly, a phenomenon that has remained relatively unnoticed and obscured. Challenging the commonly held view that recent immigrants are largely affiliated with world religions other than Christianity, Stephen Warner recently reported that most—at least two thirds—of post-1965 immigrants identify themselves as Christians (Warner 2004, 21). However, this does not mean that the Christian beliefs and practices of these immigrants are identical with those that are embraced by mainstream American Christians; their religious views and experiences are, in fact, reshaping the profile of American Christianity. Warner thus summarized, "The new immigrants represent not the de-Christianization of American society but the de-Europeanization of American Christianity" (Warner 2004, 20).

Given these trends, the particular experiences of these immigrants and of their faith communities, in short, cannot be overlooked when one aims to understand how race, ethnicity, culture, and Christian faith intersect in contemporary American life. This chapter will focus on the experiences of one such immigrant Christian community, a Korean American congregation. Particularly, the study will examine how this congregation employs various cultural and theological resources to meet the unique and particular challenges its members encounter and how this process, in turn, reflects, as well as contributes to, the larger project of the construction of a Korean American subculture and of its members' ethnic identities.

The Challenge of Generational and Cultural Conflicts

One of the most difficult and painful challenges facing many of today's immigrant communities is generational and cultural conflicts between first-generation immigrants—those who were born and reared overseas—and their American-born second-generation children. Given that the majority of current immigrants came after the Immigration Act of 1965, the first wave of second-generation children is entering adulthood. Influenced by American culture and its social values, these young adults are asserting their opinions, claiming their rights, and even challenging their parents' traditional value systems and perspectives. Many immigrant parents, meanwhile, are hurt and alarmed by their children's behavior, causing some to react by digging deeper into their traditional mode of thinking and practice. As a result, the generational and cultural gulf between the two generations widens while the tension escalates.

As a post-1965 immigrant community, the Korean American community also suffers from the acute pain of generational conflicts (Pai, Pemberton, and Worley 1987, 14–23; Hertig 2001, 15–41). In many ways, the Confucian-based Korean culture both strengthens as well as undermines the generational tie in the Korean immigrant family. On the one hand, its strong emphases on "filial piety"—the children's duty to obey and submit to their parents—and on the primacy of family encourage both generations to fortify and value their family ties, particularly the parent-child relationship. On the other hand, however, its unswerving support for hierarchical relational order promotes a parent-child relationship that emphasizes the unconditional obedience and submission of the child, an aspect that alienates and repels many second-generation children (Pai, Pemberton, and Worley 1987, 14–23; Pai and Pemberton 1992, 114–27). Consequently, while both parties might value the importance of family bonds and unity, they nonetheless disagree on what these family ties should look like.

Many frustrated and embattled Korean immigrants and their children turn to their ethnic churches for guidance and direction. However, many immigrant churches are unable to respond to this challenge effectively since they are also embroiled in similar intergenerational conflicts. In many ways, the relationship between the two generations is even more volatile and contentious in the Korean immigrant church. A pastor summed up the hardships second-generation members face in the following way: "Cultural and language barriers that exist between first- and second-generation Koreans work against their [second-generation members'] assuming wider roles in the church. . . . Rarely will their gifts be utilized in making important decisions for the [Korean immigrant] church. Even though some of them . . . have important professional positions in the workplace, in the eyes of the first-generation leadership, they are still children. . . . Therefore, any pastor or church leader interested in keeping second-generation Koreans in the [immigrant] church must face the hard fact: *There is not enough incentive for them to stay in a church that is dominated by the Korean-speaking members*" (Song 1997, 28; italics his).

Discouraged by their current experiences and bleak future prospects, frustrated second-generation leaders and members are deserting their immigrant churches in large numbers to form their own, independent congregations (Lee 1996, 51–52; Ly 2000, C1).

Given these experiences and the current direction of second-generation Korean American ministries, some researchers who study the Korean American church are openly wondering about the future of the church, especially if second-generation young people continue their "silent exodus" (Kim and Kim 1995, 8–9; Song 1997, 24–29). There are, however, some notable exceptions. A few Korean American congregations are forging intentional partnerships between the two generations, overcoming a number of significant cultural barriers and obstacles, including the challenge of generational conflicts.

The Research Setting

Lakeshore Presbyterian Church (LPC), located in a suburb of Chicago, is a twenty-five-year-old Presbyterian Church (USA) congregation. It is home to two vibrant congregations: the Korean-speaking congregation (KC) and the English-speaking congregation (EC). While the KC planted the EC more than ten years ago, the dramatic growth of the EC took place during the past seven years under the leadership of a young Korean American pastor named Caleb, going from thirty members to three hundred. Up to 90 percent of the EC members are second-generation Korean American young adults in their twenties and thirties; they are, on the whole, well-educated young professionals who are beginning their careers.

Between the fall of 1999 and the summer of 2000, I studied the LPC using the research methods of a congregational study and in-depth ethnographic interviews. The congregational study involved (1) extensive participant observation in various gatherings of both the KC and EC, (2) many informal conversations and formal interviews with the pastors and selected lay leaders of both congregations, and (3) a careful examination of church documents in both

Korean and English. In addition, I also employed in-depth interviews that involved twenty-six respondents, all of whom were second-generation Korean Americans. These interviews provided rich details of how these young adults experience their surrounding cultures and societies as well as their church.

One of the reasons that I was drawn to the LPC was the desire to know why this particular Korean immigrant congregation is attracting hundreds of Americanized, young professionals when others are losing their young people. While it is true that the LPC EC offers many strong ministry programs and resources that appeal to second-generation young people, most respondents made it clear that they chose to participate in this particular congregation because of its ties to the KC, not in spite of it. Why, then, do many second-generation members find the EC-KC relationship very attractive? How does the LPC's intergenerational experience affect the EC and its members?

The LPC as a Place of Intergenerational Healing

As another Sunday worship service begins, Pastor Caleb officially welcomes everyone as he does every Sunday. Today, however, he extends a warm welcome to a group of special guests, senior members and leaders from the KC. Toward the end of the worship service, the pastor invites the group to the front and comments: I know many EC pastors serving in Korean immigrant churches that are frustrated because of ongoing conflicts with the first-generation leadership. One of the blessings I have enjoyed in serving at the LPC is that we experienced absolutely no major conflict with the KC and its leadership. They have been absolutely supportive of our ministry. We are their pride and joy . . . and we need to continue to honor them with an attitude of respect and honor.

In response, the senior pastor of the KC, Reverend Kim, greets the EC with a brief message in English, "We are very proud of you. You are our joy and hope!" Then the group sang a Korean hymn as an expression of blessing to this young congregation. When the group finished its song, the second-generation congregation responded with prolonged, loud applause. It was clearly a moving moment for the KC delegates as well as for the EC. After the worship service, one lay leader who recently came from another immigrant church in the area explained: This is why I come to this church, because the first-generation leaders and members affirm us and bless us . . . not trying to control us. Because they relate to us this way, we want to honor them and respect them. For many of us who grew up experiencing much pain and tension in our relationships with our parents and first-generation church leaders, coming to this church has been a very healing experience.

Constructing the Narrative of an Intergenerational Partnership

Such a heart-warming intergenerational experience does not emerge spontaneously or effortlessly. One of the significant ways that the EC constructs and legitimizes its intergenerational partnership is by developing and effectively employing a compelling narrative that extols the virtue and benefits of this project. Adopting the image of a parent-child relationship, Pastor Caleb explained: We see them [the KC leaders and members] as parents that provided everything for us. They provided security for the EC when we were starting off, when we were still weak financially. I think they also provided a sense of emotional security. And now they are cheerleaders for us. So we want to give them the opportunity to see their dream come to fruition through us. It is a source of inspiration.

In another version of the narrative, the pastor adds a theological dimension to the story when he commented: I think that we can learn a lot from God's creation and his biological principles and how God wants to see his people multiply through the family tree. Our church is like a family. I can definitely see how they [KC members] gave birth to our congregation and provided a lot of nurturing and nourishment in our early days. Now we are maturing and they are aging, so it is our desire that we would be there for them as they were for us.

This narrative, often told by Pastor Caleb during his sermons as well as in settings such as the New Membership Class, is effective because it is particularly tailored for an intended audience. By employing the image of family relationships, images that are very familiar as well as significant to Korean Americans, this narrative presents the KC-EC relationship as natural and normal, especially in the Korean American context. Moreover, by granting it a moral and theological grounding, Pastor Caleb makes sure that the narrative is prescriptive as well as descriptive. In a compelling way, the pastor calls the young congregation to be there for the KC because only that course of action would satisfy the ethical norms revealed in God's created order.

The most compelling and attractive component of the narrative, however, at least to its second-generation young-adult audience, is the part that highlights the reversing roles of the parent and child as the former ages and the latter matures. In Pastor Caleb's narrative, the "children" do not play the inferior or passive role that is emphasized in the traditional Korean culture. Instead, Pastor Caleb narrates a story in which the parents are now "cheerleaders"— they are no longer the main players—while their grown-up children begin to serve as the providers and caregivers, the role formerly played by the parents.

A Generational Transition: An Institutional Adaptation

In many ways, these changing roles in the narrative accurately describe the current experiences and relationships of the KC and the EC. Although the EC functioned like a department of the KC in its early years, heavily dependent on the KC, as the EC's size grew dramatically and as the KC membership plateaued, the two congregations' relationship evolved: the EC became increasingly autonomous. Reverend Kim began to publicly acknowledge Pastor Caleb as his "equal" and began to challenge the EC to see themselves as the future leaders of the LPC. In response, playing their part in the narrative, the EC has taken up a more visible leadership role in the LPC, including taking a leading role in the $10 million building project that the two congregations are jointly pursuing.

Many EC members are clearly appreciative of and are drawn to the LPC's unfolding narrative of an intergenerational partnership and transition of power. The efficacy of this narrative, evidenced by the growing number of members who support the EC-KC partnership, cannot be attributed simply to its persuasive construction or to its being told repeatedly by a popular pastor. Rather, as indicated above, this narrative is compelling and credible to them because it is backed up by the actions of the first-generation leadership. Some members noted that other immigrant churches in the area, hoping to hold onto their second-generation young people, promise a similar scenario in which the generous support of the first-generation congregation and the eventual full autonomy of the second-generation congregation are explicitly pledged. However, too often, such promises fail to become reality. To its second-generation members, then, the LPC's narrative is appealing because it is neither an empty promise of the first-generation leadership nor a mere wishful tale of the second-generation leadership. Rather, the narrative's unique appeal is that it is a living story that is being coauthored by the leaders of both generations, as they cooperatively and dialogically chart out their common course facing a common future.

Reinterpreting the Doctrine of "Filial Piety": The Core of the Narrative

Perhaps the most significant aspect of the LPC EC's intergenerational narrative is a reinterpretation of the Confucian teaching of filial piety, a teaching that emphasizes the children's duty to obey their parents. Many studies have observed that the practice of filial piety is highly valued and repeatedly taught not only in Korean American homes but also in Korean immigrant churches (Park 1996, 78–80; Vaux and Vaux 1996, 80–87). However, as first-generation parents and elders sought to socialize the next generation with the Confucian doctrine of filial piety, the second-generation young people's response to this traditional teaching has been largely negative. Many young adult respondents of this study also confessed that they struggled with their parents' hierarchical way of relating to them over a wide range of issues. Given the tensions associated with the teaching of filial piety, then, the second-generation Korean American congregation faces a particular challenge that the first-generation counterpart does not: how should it approach a value orientation that is very central to its ethnic traditional culture and yet is shunned by most of its own members?

According to a recent study (Chong 1998), some second-generation congregations seem to strongly emphasize this traditional virtue just as their parents' congregations have done. In addition to giving frequent and special attention to it, these congregations also continue to define filial piety in a traditional fashion:

it is taught as one's unquestioning obedience to parents. Furthermore, some of these congregations provide one of the strongest forms of legitimation to their teaching of the Confucian virtue by equating one's obedience to parents with one's obedience to Christ (Chong 1998, 276–77).

The LPC EC, in contrast, takes a decisively different approach in interpreting and practicing filial piety. While continuing to emphasize its significance, the EC does not accept the traditional understanding of filial piety but reinterprets and contextualizes it to the EC's own particular context. Rather than equating it with full obedience to parents, the congregation interprets this Confucian teaching in a much wider and dynamic way, keeping some elements of the traditional component of the norm while adding a new range of meaning to this ancient teaching. The congregation's reinterpretation and reformulation of this key Confucian norm involves the following three steps or components.

To begin with, the EC does not teach and promote filial piety as a Confucian ideal but as a biblical norm. Filial piety is emphasized at the EC because it is one of the Ten Commandments in the Bible, not because it is a cherished Confucian norm. As such, it is presented not as a culturally defined and sanctioned ethical teaching that is relevant only to Korean American or other Asian American members. Lest some of the EC members regard this teaching as a cultural value that can be dismissed as outdated and irrelevant, Pastor Caleb declared in his Mother's Day sermon: "On this Mother's Day, I want to remind you that it's God's will that we honor our parents. We need to know that God is very serious about this command because we find that this command is included as one of the Ten Commandments and is quoted seven other times in the Bible. 'Honor your father and mother' is the only verse in the whole Bible that has been quoted seven other times. When God wants to emphasize something, he usually repeats it twice in the Bible. But, when it comes to our responsibility to honor our parents, God repeated it eight times."

By grounding this teaching of honoring parents in the Bible, the word of God, the EC legitimizes the importance of this teaching as well as its universal application. Furthermore, in formulating and presenting filial piety as a biblical norm, Pastor Caleb reinterprets and, to an extent, transforms it as well. Rather than teaching its members to give complete obedience to parents, some of whom are non-Christians, the pastor exhorts its members to "honor" one's parents. Again, in his Mother's Day sermon, Pastor Caleb defined "honoring" in the following way: "The word 'honor' in original Hebrew means 'to weigh someone down with value and worth.' In other words, honoring someone means 'to place so much value and worth on someone to the point of that person saying,' 'Wow, I'm overwhelmed with all this honor you're giving me.'" It is clear that such a picture of honoring parents, one that challenges children to appreciate and respect their parents, is quite different from obeying one's parents without questioning. By replacing "obedience" with "honoring," the EC has not only Christianized filial piety but also de-ethnicized it to a degree, making it more palatable to Americanized second-generation young adults.

The second significant component of the EC's reinterpretation of filial piety involves its recognition of the changing nature of the parent-child relationship and its effort to find those ways of honoring parents that are appropriate for children who are young adults or adults. In his sermon, Pastor Caleb observed: "There will come a time when the father will become the son, and the son will be the father to his own father, and when the mother will become the daughter, and the daughter becomes the mother. When this time comes, we need to be there for them, as they have been for us." Given these changes—even reversals—in the parent-child roles, Pastor Caleb argues that one's way of honoring parents should also change and evolve. In the same sermon, he made the following points: "As children, we honor our parents by obeying them. As young adults, we honor our parents by appreciating them. Finally, as adults, we honor our parents by affirming and taking care of them." This interpretive scheme explains and justifies why "obedience," an expression of honoring parents that is appropriate for young children, needs to be replaced by "appreciation" and "affirmation" of parents as the primary expressions of filial piety. Again, Pastor Caleb elaborates this point in his sermon: "As our parents get older, their self-esteem and confidence wear out. Their affirming friends start to die off, and they no longer feel useful in the marketplace. Their grown children are busy with their lives and many live lonely lives. Our parents have a great deal of need, a desperate need to know that they are still important and worthy of our respect and love." The picture of a parent that emerges from the sermon is not the "godlike" parent of the Confucian world who exercises unlimited power in his dealings with his children. Rather, it is a picture of aging parents who struggle with loneliness and diminishing self-esteem, feeling helpless in a foreign land. In such a setting, the filial child is not a powerless, submissive pawn, waiting to carry out the wishes and commands of one's parents. Rather, she is an agent who is able to encourage, nurture, and provide for her parents. Such a picture of filial devotion is not particularly Korean. Caring for a person in need with compassion and benevolence is as much Christian as it is Confucian.

Finally, the EC and its members' understanding of honoring parents is also mediated through the particular experience of their ongoing relationship with the KC and its members. If Pastor Caleb's preaching and teaching on this topic provides a theological and ethical framework for this "value orientation," their intergenerational experience at the church provides a concrete and meaningful way to practice and rehearse it. As the EC and its leaders show their respect to and care for the aging KC, it not only serves as a role model to its members but also offers them an opportunity to participate in the practice of filial piety, with their peers, in a corporate setting.

Furthermore, the KC-EC's intergenerational relationship and partnership serve to validate the reinterpreted and transformed version of filial piety that the EC promotes in its teaching. As discussed above, one of the unique strengths of the KC-EC relationship is that it is not based on the traditional model of age-based hierarchicalism. Rather, as the EC and its leaders seek to honor their elders, the KC and its leaders have been intentional in affirming and empowering the younger generation. This ethos of reciprocity and mutuality not only makes the practice of honoring and respecting elders easier for second-generation young people but also reveals the potential transformative power of the reinterpreted form of filial piety. That is, the LPC's intergenerational experience demonstrates that the act of honoring elders and parents does not have to contribute to or reinforce the hierarchical nature of the intergenerational relationship that is assumed in the Korean American context. Instead, the EC's version of filial piety depends on as well as contributes to the formation of a new form of intergenerational relationship at the LPC, a relationship that is liberating and transformative for both generations.

Intergenerational Ties and the Construction of a New Subculture

Many sociologists and historians have long recognized the especially close tie that exists between religion and the maintenance of ethnicity in immigrant communities of the United States (Herberg 1960; Smith 1978; Williams 1988; Warner 1998). During the past century, the Korean immigrant church has also played a particularly significant role in the maintenance of Korean culture and ethnic identity (Takaki 1989, 278–93; Hurh and Kim 1990, 30–31; Min 1992, 1383–84). The church has not only affirmed and reinforced the traditional culture of first-generation immigrants but also took seriously the task of transmitting its ethnic culture to the next generation, offering Korean language classes and other cultural activities for American-born children.

In the past, those studies that have focused on the phenomenon of cultural transmission in Asian American communities have viewed it as largely unidirectional (Bacon 1996; Zhou and Bankston 1998; Kim, Moon, and Song 1998). The "Knower" (first-generation parents, teachers, and pastors) provides the "not-yet-Knower" (second-generation children, students, and church members) prepackaged cultural content. When done effectively, it is assumed, cultural socialization will convince second-generation young children to accept and internalize these cultural norms and traditional values. However, what is not clear is what will happen when these second-generation young people are no longer children but are young adults who assert their own sense of identity as the "Knower."

The formation of an intergenerational relationship in the LPC illustrates that the EC and its members are not passive recipients who dutifully embrace the cultural values and norms their parents and the KC members hand to them. Instead, their own appropriation and application of filial piety demonstrates that the EC and its members are engaged in the project of constructing a new culture that is both complex and reflexive, a project that is being shaped by—as well as shaping—a number of converging factors that make the EC and its members' experiences unique. Rather than simply embracing their parents' traditional cultural value orientation of filial piety, or the mainstream American approach to relating to one's parents, the EC and its members identify and appropriate certain aspects of both cultures that appeal to them and reconstruct a new, bicultural value orientation that serves them better. Furthermore, given the EC's spiritual orientation, the congregation's theological framework functions as a hermeneutical grid through which various cultural elements are further evaluated, filtered, reinterpreted, and even transformed. Consequently, the new subculture emerging in the LPC EC is a second-generation version of a Korean American subculture with a clear Christian orientation. The unique formation and nature of its subculture, in many ways, will continue to distinguish the EC from not only first-generation immigrant congregations but also from predominantly white churches, forging a unique congregational identity and its own niche in the American religious landscape.

Intergenerational Ties and the Construction of Its Members' Identity

In addition to the shaping of the congregational culture and identity, the EC's formation of particular intergenerational ties also contributes to the formation of its members' individual identities. Many of the members, during the interview, identified a number of benefits they receive from the LPC's intergenerational experience. A number of them, as mentioned earlier, noted that their experience in the LPC brought them healing and hope, hope of not only being reconciled with their elders but also of being recognized as adults by them. Such affirmation and recognition by their parents' generation, in turn, seems to have a profound impact on their own self-identity. Studies that have explored identity formation among Asian Americans have indeed noted that these individuals tend to form their understanding of who they are in a relational context (Yeh and Huang 1996; Sue, Mak, and Sue 1998, 313–16). Particularly, there are indications that their parents continue to play a significant role in these young adults' self-understanding (Uba 1994, 28–31; Bacon 1996, 242).

Unfortunately, however, many of the EC members do not receive much affirmation or respectful treatment from their parents. Although these young adults are well-educated, competent professionals, many of them struggle to obtain a comparable identity and status in their own homes. For these frustrated young adults, then, the LPC EC becomes an alternative multigenerational family in which they can realize and experience their identities as capable Korean American adults. One woman respondent, comparing her experiences at home and at the LPC, made the following observation:

> Even though my sister and I take responsibility for a lot of the administrative duties in the house, we are the ones who take care of problems when they arise with the outside world. I would probably guess that my sister, who is married and has two kids, feels like I do that she is still a little kid in my parents' eyes. I don't ever see that changing. I think it is always going to be that way. Part of the reason that I like the LPC so much is that there is a transition from us being the kids of the church to being the adults of the church.

At the LPC EC, then, second-generation young adults are able to experience something that is very significant and yet is often elusive—being ushered into adulthood with the blessings and affirmation of their first-generation elders. Because such an experience is not commonly found in other Korean American settings, the LPC therefore becomes a family that is even more meaningful and critical to second-generation adults.

Furthermore, the LPC's intergenerational relationship also plays a critical role in the construction of another important type of identity among its members: their ethnic identity. According to Fredrik Barth, a major cultural "value orientation" such as filial piety plays a critical role in the construction of ethnic boundaries, and therefore of ethnic identities, by offering individuals a particular way of looking at themselves and the surrounding world (Barth 1969, 14). Indeed, a recent study (Chong 1998) identified the traditional Confucian value of "filial piety" as one of the most significant Korean values second-generation young people used to define their ethnic boundaries and meanings. One of the respondents who participated in the study observed: "It's very important for me to cherish my Korean culture. I think Koreans in general have a better value system than Americans, like having respect for parents. American kids "dis" their parents and I think that kind of thing is at the root of a lot of problems in this society" (Chong 1998, 270).

Given that the LPC EC has substantially reinterpreted this Confucian norm, what impact, if any, does this congregation's "value orientation" of honoring parents have on its members' ethnic identity? While acknowledging the practice of honoring parents or respecting elders as an important Korean cultural value, the EC members are also aware that their version of filial piety is quite different from the traditional form. As one EC member noted, the EC members practice filial piety "more the American way." Their Americanized Confucian norm, in turn, seems to shape how second-generation members think about what it means to be Korean Americans. One member reflected: "We don't speak Korean fluently but we are Korean Americans because of what we share with each other. . . . When we talk about our struggles with our own parents and how our American friends don't understand why we must respect and honor our parents and their wishes, we reinforce the idea that we are not Americans, even if we were born here, and that we are not Koreans like our parents are." As with their own second-generation subculture, members of the EC are in the process of constructing their own Korean American ethnic identity that reflects their bicultural realities; and their understanding and practice of filial piety plays an important role in the formation and maintenance of this identity.

A study (Waters 1990) of third- and fourth-generation descendents of European immigrants noted that these individuals construct their own ethnic identities without belonging to a community, making their ethnic identity project very individualistic and "optional" in nature. The EC's second-generation Korean American members, however, seem to take a different pathway in constructing their ethnic identity. As visible minorities whose identities are often based on involuntary racial ascription by others, their ethnic identity is not optional. Their ethnic identity formation, often contested and even negated by outsiders, thus requires their participation in a community of individuals who share not only common experiences but also a common culture that informs who they are and what they are. In this sociocultural context, the LPC EC thus plays a critical role in the lives of its members; it provides a unique setting in which its members can participate in and benefit from the construction of such a subculture and identity.

Implications for Christians, Congregations, and Related Institutions

One of the fundamental missions of the church is to contextualize the universal message of the gospel into the particular context in which each church is situated. This is especially true for those congregations that serve specific ethnic communities. Whether they are historic black churches, Messianic synagogues, or post-1965 immigrant congregations, their very existence and survival are deeply tied to their ability to competently exegete not only the text of the Bible but also the context of their members' culture and lived experiences.

The case study of the LPC demonstrates the significance and strategic value of the congregation's ability to analyze and engage its Korean culture. Why are well-educated and acculturated second-generation Korean American young adults drawn to an ethnic immigrant congregation? At LPC, they find a spiritual community that understands the issues that are very critical to them. At their church, these young adults do not have to explain why they continue to struggle with their parents, why they cannot simply declare independence from their parents as their Caucasian peers do. In their congregation, they also find rich spiritual and cultural resources that allow them to address a particular set of life challenges. Many, in fact, began their journey of faith through the ministry of the LPC because the good news proclaimed there spoke to their hopes and fears, to their lived experiences.

Unfortunately, as noted earlier, most Korean American churches have not enjoyed similar success in addressing the challenges of generational and cultural conflicts. A critical lesson that the LPC's experience offers is that a culture with which congregations must learn to engage is not static and fixed; it continually changes and evolves. An ethnic congregation that rigidly holds onto its traditional ethnic culture risks the possibility of being obsolete. Over time, culture changes as groups of individuals seek to make sense of the rapidly changing world in which they live. In such a world, as the LPC has done, a congregation must learn to interact reflexively with its members and their changing cultural context, willing to reinterpret and even modify certain cultural values and norms using biblical guidelines. In short, in order to do their ministry of contextualization with effectiveness, ethnic congregations need to vigilantly engage with its ethnic culture that continually changes, constantly dialoguing with it rather than seeking to preserve it in one form.

The study of the LPC's experiences also demonstrates the vital and significant role ethnic churches play in today's multicultural world. Currently, there is a growing movement within the American evangelical community to promote a multiracial congregation model as a response to the problem of race in America (Emerson et al. 2003; Yancey 2003). This emerging model rightly critiques the homogeneous church model that has attracted many followers with the appealing promise of church growth while tacitly approving, among other things, the segregation of churches along racial lines (Emerson and Smith 2000, 153–68). It would be, however, equally alarming if the pendulum were to swing in the other direction too extremely, categorically dismissing all homogeneous congregations as ones that are sustained by racist or ethnocentric impulses or are trapped in an outmoded model of ministry. In today's multicultural world, the Christian community needs to recognize the value of diversity as well as of unity, of ethnic congregations as well as of multicultural ones.

How should a multicultural congregation, then, seek to minister to second-generation Korean Americans or any other ethnic minority members? Minimally, the congregation must seek to grow in its ability to identify with one another not only at a spiritual level but also on a cultural level, for as the LPC's example illustrates, both are necessary and intertwined. Particularly, those who belong to the dominant culture must seek to understand the culturally specific challenges their brothers and sisters from other backgrounds face and to find ways to minister to them in ways that are both biblical and culturally sensitive. This, in turn, means that those who serve in multicultural settings need to be in continual conversation with those who serve in different ethnic Christian communities, learning from their experiences as well as employing some of the resources developed in those communities. Kersten Bayt Priest and Bob Priest's article of the failed merger between the white and black congregations illustrates how critical this component is in multiracial congregations.

This study also highlights another way through which ethnic congregations can help multicultural congregations to be truly multicultural, not simply "assimilated" congregations with one dominant culture (Emerson et al. 2003, 165–67). As mentioned above, the LPC EC has been involved in an elaborate project of constructing a new subculture that is particularly meaningful to its members. This new subculture, in turn, provided the EC members with a set of reinterpreted symbols and meaning to understand who they are and to constructively address some of the life challenges they faced individually and collectively. One of the functions ethnic congregations serve, then, is to help their members to deepen their understanding of their ethnic cultures and identities, to learn how to express their faith commitment using their own distinctive cultural symbols and signs. When and if God leads them to multiracial congregations, these individuals are prepared to contribute to a multicultural congregational life, bringing unique voices and gifts to the table.

Finally, another significant lesson this case study offers is that in order to be effective in today's fragmented society, Christian communities need more than comprehensive cultural knowledge or a new paradigm of ministry. How should a congregation respond to competing cultures within its community? How can a congregation avoid culture wars or identity politics that can be so divisive and destructive to the life of the Christian community? As the LPC experience illustrates, a key to the successful bridging of the generational and cultural divide lies in the practicing of the biblical values of mutual submission and servanthood. In his epistle to the church in Philippi, as the apostle Paul pleaded for unity in the church (2:1–11), he offered the following words of concrete advice: "Do nothing out of selfish ambition or vain conceit, but in humility consider others better than yourselves. Each of you should look not only to your own interests, but also to the interests of others. Your attitude should be the same as that of Christ Jesus: Who, being in very nature God, did not consider equality with God something to be grasped, but made himself nothing, taking the very nature of a servant, being made in human likeness" (Phil 2:3–7).

In the LPC experience, the first-generation leadership did not insist upon exercising the power that their culture granted them. Rather, they chose to make room for their young people, inviting them to grow into leadership roles. The second-generation young people, in turn, responded with an attitude of honoring their elders, thus setting up an ongoing cycle of mutuality and reciprocity between the two groups. The experience of the LPC demonstrates how God's people should address the issue of power and control as they serve in bicultural or multicultural congregational settings. For, in the end, whether they are ethnic congregations working out generational conflicts or multicultural congregations living in the tension of unity in diversity, what will set them apart from other institutions in the world is not so much their successful cultural negotiation but their expression of love for one another. As that familiar old gospel song reminds of us, "They will know we are Christians by our love, by our love."

REFERENCES

Bacon, Jean. 1996. *Life lines: Community, family and assimilation among Asian Indian immigrants.* New York: Oxford University Press.

Barth, Fredrik. 1969. *Ethnic groups and boundaries.* Boston: Little, Brown.

Chiswick, Barry, and Teresa Sullivan. 1995. The new immigrants. In *State of the union: America in the 1990s, vol. 2, Social Trends,* ed. Reynolds Farley, 211–70. New York: Russell Sage Foundation.

Chong, Kelly. 1998. What it means to be Christian: The role of religion in the construction of ethnic identity and boundary among second-generation Korean Americans. *Sociology of Religion* 58:259–86.

Emerson, Michael, and Christian Smith. 2000. *Divided by faith: Evangelical religion and the problem of race in America.* New York: Oxford University Press.

Emerson, Michael, Curtiss DeYoung, George Yancey, Karen Chai Kim. 2003. *United by faith: The multiracial congregation as an answer to the problem of race.* New York: Oxford University Press.

Herberg, Will. 1960. *Protestant, Catholic, Jew: An essay in American religious sociology.* 2nd ed. Garden City, NY: Doubleday.

Hertig, Young Lee. 2001. *Cultural tug of war: The Korean immigrant family and church in transition.* Nashville: Abingdon.

Hurh, Won Moo, and Kwang Chung Kim. 1990. Religious participation of Korean immigrants in the U.S. *Journal of the Scientific Study of Religion* 29:19–34.

Kim, Kwang Chung, and Shin Kim. 1995. Korean immigrant churches in the United States. In *Yearbook of American and Canadian churches, 1995*, ed. Kenneth B. Bedell, 6–9. Nashville: Abingdon.

Kim, Kwang Chung, Ailee Moon, and Young In Song. 1998. Young Korean Americans' learning of being ethnic Christians: Their experience at the church of their parents. Unpublished paper.

Lee, Helen. 1996. Silent exodus. *Christianity Today* (August 12): 51–52.

Ly, Phuong. 2000. "It's our church": Young Korean Americans seek spiritual freedom. *The Washington Post*. February 20.

Min, Pyoung Gap. 1992. The structure and social function of Korean immigrant churches in the U.S. *International Migration Review* 26:1370–94.

Pai, Young, and Deloras Pemberton. 1992. *Handbook for Korean-American families: Improving communication*. Nashville: Cokesbury.

Pai, Young, Deloras Pemberton, and John Worley. 1987. *Findings on Korean-American early adolescents*. Kansas City: University of Missouri—Kansas City, School of Education.

Park, Andrew S. 1996. *Racial conflict and healing: An Asian-American theological perspective*. Maryknoll, NY: Orbis.

Smith, Timothy. 1978. Religion and ethnicity in America. *American Historical Review* 83:1155–85.

Song, Minho. 1997. Constructing a local theology for a second-generation Korean ministry. *Urban Missions* 15 (2): 23–34.

Sue, David, Winnie Mak, and Derald Sue. 1998. Ethnic identity. In *Handbook of Asian American psychology*, ed. Lee C. Lee and Nolan W. S. Zane, 289–323. Thousand Oaks, CA: Sage.

Takaki, Ronald. 1989. *Strangers from a different shore: A history of Asian Americans*. Boston: Little, Brown.

Uba, Laura. 1994. *Asian Americans: Personality patterns, identity, and mental health*. New York: Guilford.

Vaux, Kenneth, and Sara Vaux. 1996. *Dying well*. Nashville: Abingdon.

Warner, R. Stephen. 1998. Introduction: Immigration and religious communities in the United States. In *Gatherings in diaspora: Religious communities and the new immigration*, ed. R. Stephen Warner and Judith G. Wittner, 3–34. Philadelphia: Temple University Press.

———. 2004. Coming to America: Immigrants and the faith they bring. *Christian Century* (February 10): 20–23.

Waters, Mary. 1990. *Ethnic options: Choosing identities in America*. Berkeley and Los Angeles: University of California Press.

Williams, Raymond. 1988. *Religions of immigrants from India and Pakistan: New threads in the American tapestry*. Cambridge: Cambridge University Press.

Yancey, George. 2003. *One body, one spirit: Principles of successful multiracial churches*. Downers Grove, IL: InterVarsity.

Yeh, Christine, and Karen Huang. 1996. The collectivistic nature of ethnic identity development among Asian-American college students. *Adolescence* 31 (123): 645–61.

Zhou, Min, and Carl Bankston III. 1998. *Growing up American: How Vietnamese children adapt to life in the United States*. New York: Russell Sage Foundation.

17

Divergent Worship Practices in the Sunday Morning Hour: Analysis of an "Interracial" Church Merger Attempt

Kersten Bayt Priest and Robert J. Priest

Late in the summer of 1995, against the backdrop of a public debate over church burnings, racial hate crimes, and the Confederate flag flying over the South Carolina state capitol, and shortly after the Southern Baptist Convention publicly apologized for its historic racism, two South Carolina pastors persuaded their congregations that "desegregating the eleven o'clock Sunday morning hour" would demonstrate to a wider world that "unity in Christ" dissolves racial boundaries. This chapter focuses on the attempted merger of these two small congregations.[1]

Fellowship Church (all names in this paper are pseudonyms) was an independent Baptist congregation (forty-two adults plus children) comprising primarily African Americans. Community Church was a Southern Baptist Church (fifty-four adults plus children) primarily made up of European Americans. These congregations had much in common: physical proximity, comparable middle-class socioeconomic levels, families in the same school district, pastors with professional training from the same institution, a biracial family in each congregation, and both were meeting in transitional spaces. Leaders from both congregations met together during the fall. In December each congregation hosted the other for Sunday worship. A decision was finalized to worship together for two months, at the end of which each congregation would vote on whether to permanently merge. Fully merged choir rehearsals, Sunday school, worship services and other events began in January and continued for eight Sundays. A final vote was taken.

Our family began attending Fellowship Church with the intention of joining, just weeks before the idea of a merger was announced by the pastor. With his approval, Kersten commenced gathering data through ethnographic fieldwork: for four months prior to merger, two months during the trial merger, and an additional four months afterward as Fellowship Church dealt with the fallout of what had transpired. As newcomers to the church we held no leadership in the church, and saw our role as being supportive observing participants. We attended Sunday services, social gatherings, Bible studies, prayer meetings, congregational business meetings, and public planning and debriefing sessions related to the merger. Kersten accompanied our children to children's choir rehearsals, and filmed the director teaching the children to sway/step. She attended adult choir practices, occasionally substituted on the piano, and sang in the choir. She also acquired audiotapes of services and, with permission, filmed several of the merged services. Field notes were kept recording observations and the results of informal interviews. The research focus was on interaction and worship patterns both prior to and during the merger. While this chapter has been jointly written about an experience we went through together, the formal research on which it is based was primarily conducted by Kersten Bayt Priest (1998).

In recent decades, sociologists and anthropologists have studied congregations, often focusing on belief, organization, or function. This chapter follows the call of Ammerman (1997) and Warner (1997) to redirect congregational studies toward a focus on "interaction" and "practice." As anthropologists our assumption is that *culture*, that is, *learned and shared patterns of interaction, behavior (practice) and judgment,* is part of what makes group life possible. Furthermore, we assume that congregations have cultures, and that many congregational cultural elements are not narrowly scripted by the Bible and will thus vary across social communities, even among biblically focused churches. Given America's historic race-based refusal to allow black Americans full rights of assimilation, separate social institutions (such as churches) became settings in which divergent cultural patterns were nurtured. Fellowship Church quite naturally reflected patterns of interaction and ritual practice widely shared among historic African American churches, while Community Church shared patterns of interaction and ritual practice with many Euro-American congregations. This merger effort, in short, would involve not merely unique cultures of two small communities, but rather two particular instances of congregational culture, each widely shared among larger social communities. How, we wondered, would people respond to other worship practices? How would divergent practices be negotiated in the new arena of a single worship service? How would responses to divergent culturally shaped worship practices influence the larger project of creating "interracial" unity? And what broader lessons might be learned by a careful microanalysis of this single brave effort?

The Creation of Unity through Worship Practices at Fellowship Church

Fellowship Church's worship service depended on distributed expertise, responsibilities, and the participation of all. Brother Elliot was the "sound man." He opened the building, set up and monitored the sound system, taped the service, and made tapes for anyone who requested them. Sister James and Sister Lester were ushers. They welcomed people, handed out bulletins, and organized the collection of the offering. Sister James also taught children's Sunday school, and planned church social events. Sister Higman, church secretary, introduced herself to visitors, acquired personal information from them, and during the service formally welcomed and introduced them by name. She then read a word of meditation and gave announcements, and also taught children's Sunday school. Mother Ames supervised the Sunday schools, prepared communion elements, sang with the Praise Team, and always sat in the front left row with her husband, Deacon Ames. Deacon Ames also sang with the Praise Team. He regularly led in the opening prayer, preceded by brief personal words testifying to God's faithfulness. Together with his adult son and Brother Harris, he helped serve communion, with all wearing white gloves. Brother Harris, a successful businessman and the church treasurer, typically led in responsive reading, sang on the Praise Team, and was a favorite soloist. Brother Jackson sang with the praise team, and taught the adult Sunday school. Sister Kinley sang with the adult Praise Team, planned youth events, taught children's Sunday school, and supervised the children's choir. Pastor Page preceded each service with the men of the church, teenagers and older, gathering in the hallway, holding hands, and praying. He led the call to worship, in singing of hymns, in supervising communion, and the ministry of the Word. He was often referred to as "the man of God." His musically gifted wife, Sister Page, was pianist and director of the Praise Team. The Praise Team led in special numbers. Sister Harris, whose brother is a nationally famous musician, was the lead singer, often prefacing a song with personal testifying.

Worship at Fellowship was coconstructed. Multiple participants, through testimony, prayer, song, and sermon built a unified worship experience. Unity was constructed through various aligning activities. In music people "tuned" to one another, aligning through pitch, texture of voice, volume, and notably through rhythm—rhythm maintained through a *szforzando* vocal technique with a percussive "hitting" of notes and breaking off of breaths in the middle of phrases for heightened emotional emphasis (cf. Wilson 1996, 75, Spencer 1990, 136), as well as through clapping and swaying or stepping. In the practice of "stepping" or "swaying" (see Yarger 1996; Myers 1991), Fellowship members matched their body motion to the music and motion of others. During children's choir practices, the director explicitly taught the children to "step" together from right to left, guiding them with her upright forearms as a visual metronome.

DIRECTOR   All right, everyone look at me

GESTURE →   (arms raised from elbows in upright parallel position)

DIRECTOR   Do it **this** way.

GESTURE →   (tilting her parallel arms to the left and back to center)

DIRECTOR   Chi::::: moo::::: chi::::: mani

GESTURE →   (moving body and arms in rhythm to the beat)

CHILDREN   Chi:::: moo:::: chi:::: mani

BODIES →   (moving in a mirrored match to the director's arms, they step from right to left to right on the beat of the sung music)

On Sunday, children began each song watching the director for the cue to begin their first step together. Congregational members aligned their bodies to those of the children, swaying in their seats to the rhythm of the stepping children. When the song was done, the congregation further ratified and aligned with the children's "stepping":

ADULTS   Amen! Amen! (clapping)

PASTOR   Thank you so very very much. Youth Praise Team? Good job. (chuckles)

ADULTS   (chuckling softly)

PASTOR   Singin' and **steppin'** simultaneously?

ADULTS   (more chuckling)

PASTOR   That's pretty cool. (chuckles)

ADULTS   (loud chuckles)

PASTOR   It's all **right!**

Unity was constructed not merely through the aligning activities of bodies moving unitedly but also through interactive activities. When an individual led in public prayer, or in a testimony, or even the sermon, congregational members frequently responded, "Yes," "Amen." These responses signaled agreement, affirmation, and heartfelt response. No sermon or solo ever stood alone, unaccompanied by congregational response. A truly moving service was co-constructed by leaders *together with* members in the pews.

The service involved a base pattern, within which personal and improvisational responses were desired. The service began with formal old English, gradually transitioning to usage of vernacular. It began with somber music—slow syncopated hymns. Slowly it built in energy and volume, shifting from somber to joyful and ecstatic. As the Praise Worship Team ended with a deeply moving song, Sister Allen was standing and testifying.

TABLE 17.1. Conversation Analysis Notation System

Bold	Indicates especially loud volume relative to surrounding talk.
::::	Colons indicate prolongation of immediately prior sound.
( )	Empty parentheses indicate transcriber's inability to hear what was said.
~	Indicates rapid speech.
/ /	Indicates point where current speaker's talk is overlapped by another's talk.
[	Indicates point where new speaker breaks in.
→	Indicates action of speaker concurrent with talk.

SISTER ALLEN	Glory glory glori::: Thank you Jesus Hallellu::ia my God
PASTOR	Amen.
SISTER ALLEN	O::h glory to Go:d
PASTOR	Amen.
SISTER ALLEN	wo:rthy
PASTOR	Amen.
MEMBER	( )
SISTER ALLEN	Thank you Thank you Thank~you~Father~for **soul** salvation tha ( ) Oh Hallelujia ( ) / / ( ) 　　　　　　　　　　[
PASTOR	**I:::** invite you please to open your Bibles. . . .
SISTER ALLEN	→(sitting down, nodding and opening her Bible) ( ) Thank you, thank you

Sister Allen is Mother Ames's younger sister, a regular visitor at Fellowship Church. Sister Higman and Mother Ames would also often stand during worshipful moments—eyes shut, hands held high. Sister Allen's testifying was in a more expressive mode than normal for this congregation. However, it exemplified an ideal that was valued—though practiced in more restrained forms. On this particular Sunday Pastor Page transitioned into a sermon on worship from a biblical text where King David danced exuberantly before the Lord while his wife criticized such public display as undignified:

PASTOR	and many of us don't expand our physical expression of worship because we're not willin to be **u:ndi:gni:fied.**
MEMBERS	**Amen.**
PASTOR	Because we want to be maintainin a certain → (straightened back, tilted head and lifted eyebrows) bit of **dignity** in the house of **Go:**d now!
MEMBERS	Mhm.
PASTOR	**you** know we don't wanna we don't wanna ah look **bad**
MEMBERS	**Yeah. Mhm.**
SISTER ALLEN	**I know.**
PASTOR	We don't want people to **ta:**lk about us,
SISTER ALLEN	**That's right.**
PASTOR	That kind of thing uh but if you want to expand your physi~now that's and that's **to**tally up to **you** now

SISTER ALLEN	**Right.**
PASTOR	if you if you want to expand your physical expression of worship, a prerequisite for that is humbleness and meekness.
SISTER ALLEN	**That's right. Amen.**
PASTOR	and abasin' yourself in your own sight.
SISTER ALLEN	**That's right.**
PASTOR	Amen?
MEMBERS	**Amen.**

Ideal worship involved a total community in synchronized movement, interactive affirmations, and—as the service built in energy and spirit—individual expanded expressions of a few members.

Organizing the Merger

In the weeks preceding merger Pastor Page preached repeatedly about the unity of brothers and sisters in Christ, black and white. He acknowledged the two churches had different traditions, but suggested tradition was not sacred, and explicitly preached against an ethnic Christ. The one issue, Pastor Page said, that needed to be addressed if there was to be a merger, was the leadership structure. Fellowship had a church board comprising founding members, male and female. Pastor Page said there had been no effort to organize this structure in accord with biblical teaching. Community Church, on the other hand (unlike most Southern Baptist Churches), had male "elders" explicitly selected against criteria given in the Bible. Community Church entered merger discussions with this issue as their only stated concern. Pastor Page believed Community Church had followed a more biblical pattern, and was supported by key leaders Deacon Ames and Brother Harris. No one publicly voiced objections.

Pastor Page warned his congregation that "little things" could interfere with this merger—that people needed to be flexible, and above all "have their heart right." Leaders from both congregations led in fasting and prayer. Pastor Page, who also worked another job, felt his gifts lay in preaching, not administration—and announced that Pastor Smith, or "Chip" as he was known to his congregation, would handle administrative matters. Since the Community Church music leader held a paid position, and had a formal degree in church music, he would coordinate the music ministry, but work in close consultation with Sister Page. Pastor Smith suggested meeting in Community facilities during the merger period, since they were larger, but Fellowship members protested—and it was agreed to meet at each place alternate weeks. In a crucial planning meeting Pastor Smith provided elaborate handouts diagramming all responsibilities and structures of his church, and then asked Pastor Page to explain his church. Pastor Page replied briefly, "We don't do it that way," but indicated that if everyone working in a given area just got together with their counterparts it could all be worked out. Pastor Smith enthused, "All that's left is for you to join us."

Losses of Position

During the trial merger Pastor Page maintained a prominent position with Pastor Smith in leading the services, teaching the combined adult Sunday school, and preaching. Community had no counterpart to the children's choir, but a number of their young people joined the group that Sister Kinley continued to lead, and learned to "step" with the others. The children's choir sang twice in merged services. But while Pastor Page and Sister Kinley retained key positions during the trial merger, others did not. Sister James and Sister Lester no longer organized ushers. The adult Sunday school was used to address key issues during this period—with the pastors, the lead elder from Community, and the music director doing the teaching. Brother Jackson, who normally taught, did not teach. Since the sound system from Community was clearly more expensive and sophisticated, this was the sound system employed, set up, and operated by a person from Community. Just before the first service, Brother Elliot wandered aimlessly through the halls. Within weeks the former "sound man" ceased attending, and submitted his keys to Pastor Page. Mother Ames deferred to Community leadership for supervising Sunday school. It was decided that Community's Sunday school curriculum for children would be followed, and consequently Fellowship's Sunday school teachers became de facto assistants to Community's teachers. Community had no concept or tradition of a church "mother," and corresponding patterns of deference and respect were therefore lacking. Since Pastor Smith was the primary administrator, planning the services and the bulletin, others were unwittingly excluded. Sister Higman no longer had her allotted slot to make announcements and welcome visitors. Deacon Ames no longer opened with brief testimony and prayer. In Community's schema, deacons were not leaders, elders were. And while Deacon Ames was an older, revered, and godly man, the new teaching stressed that elders should be "apt to teach"—which Deacon Ames did not feel gifted to do. Elders from Community were young and seminary trained. As the weeks progressed, Deacon Ames and Mother Ames seated themselves gradually toward the back of the church. In the first merged choir practice, a majority were from Fellowship Church, but Bill, the Community music director, planned and directed the practice. With only ten minutes left, Sister Page asked why he had not "given her the floor," since she was director at her church. While Bill apologized, and she later directed portions of practices, it was always within the framework of his plan for the service. Her own members were uncomfortable with her direct confrontation of Bill, did not back her up, and soon she relinquished most of the planning to Bill. A few weeks later she signed up for a night class at a community college that precluded further participation in the choir.

Shifts in Practice

The merger period introduced new practices. As Mother Ames prepared the communion elements, with white gloves laid out, Pastor Page quietly told her to remove the gloves, "They don't do it that way." During a moving solo by a visiting black musician the first Sunday, Mother Ames stood in worship. No one joined her. While Community members sometimes raised hands in worship, individuals did not stand. Nor did people move together in unison. When the children's choir sang and stepped—only a few swayed with them. "Amens" and "yeses" diminished. In one sermon prior to merger, members responded verbally 138 times. In a sermon preached during merger there were 34 verbal responses. Pastor Smith quoted directly from Greek and Hebrew as he exposited biblical texts, and encouraged people to take notes during his sermons. The King James Version was not used, as it had been at Fellowship. Dress was less formal. Full body hugs were common. Honorifics such as "mother," "deacon," "sister," "brother," or even "pastor" were not used by Community members. Their pastor was simply "Chip." First names were the order of the day—quite a change for members used to referring to their pastor as "the man of God." Community members introduced themselves in terms of what they do. "I'm Don and I'm a lawyer," one elder introduced himself. They asked visitors or strangers "And what do you do?" Fellowship members were more likely to ask where one is from, and whom one knows.

The words of praise songs (only occasionally hymns) were projected on the wall. Bill's voice, amplified by a head microphone, modeled an aesthetic from the classical Euro-Western tradition—a sweet unsyncopated and unbroken melodic line with minimal crescendo or decrescendo. He did not move rhythmically or express facial emotion while singing. In contrast to the Fellowship tradition where music began with slow and somber hymns and built steadily in volume and intensity to a deeply moving, uplifting, and physically involved worship, Bill began the service with "peppy" music to wake people up and then moved toward slower, softer, "more reverential" music prior to the sermon—often ending with a song sung a capella. Bill led the merged choir in *sotto voce* warm-ups, expected everyone to conform exactly to notated musical scores, and worked hard to get everyone to sing in unison. Apart from one Sunday when Sister Page led, the choir did not step or sway to the music. Repetition and rhythm were limited. There was no lead singer providing an improvisational counterpoint to the steady rhythm of the choir—no vocal "chasing" of the soloist in counterpart chorus creative of multitextured sound and heightened volume.

Assessments and Judgments

Different practices, of course, reflected different ideals—and conflicting ideals resulted in various forms of assessment and judgment. There was a clear pattern at Fellowship of leadership being based on giftedness, experience, and age, while at Community it rested on formal credentials, professional training, and technical expertise. Elders and pastor at Community were young and seminary trained. They foregrounded their credentials, and discursively displayed their authoritative relation to the biblical text through their mastery of Greek and Hebrew. Bill's musical authority also rested on formal training and technical expertise. He commented that those who are good at math are often skilled in music. Sister Page, on the other hand, had extensive music experience, and was enormously gifted, playing by ear. She, her lead singer, and choir composed improvisations of unusual power and beauty. In their view, one was not musical, however proficient one might be at playing piano, if one could only follow the sheet of music, and could not compose or play by ear. A reference to voice lessons elicited chuckles from Fellowship members, with the lead singer commenting that singing was "either something you've got or you haven't got." Deacon Ames, Mother Ames, Sister Page, and others lost standing in the new situation in part because key decision makers (Bill and Pastor Smith) were from the other church and operated out of different criteria of judgment.

Different worship ideals underpinned judgments. Bill led an adult Sunday school lesson on worship. Drawing from Isaiah 6 he presented worship as the individual silent, face down, before a Holy God. Worship is reverence, and reverence is silent. Bill and Pastor Smith clearly had a model of worship as hushed reverence. Hushed music and hushed voices signaled deep worship. Pastor Page's premerger sermon on worship summarized an alternative view of worship—worship as a community dancing like David before the Lord. Worship involves the body in motion. Worship is loud praise. Emotionally, as presented by Bill and Pastor "Chip," worship humbles proud sinners and *brings them low*. Worship, in the Fellowship frame, takes the suffering, afflicted, stigmatized, and downtrodden and gives them hope and joy; it *lifts them up*. Prior to merger, Brother Harris introduced a worship song: "It's *always good* to be in *God's* presence and whenever we're **in** His presence (.) You know (.) We should get a *real good feelin'* about ourselves." This was a typical refrain at Fellowship, but diametrically opposed to the Community worship paradigm. The following are some of the contrasts in the two paradigms:

TABLE 17.2. Worship Style Comparison

Fellowship Worship Style	Community Worship Style
Communal: interactive community	Dyadic: God and the individual self
Began with slow, somber hymns	Began with upbeat, peppy music
Moved toward high volume, loud praise	Moved toward quiet reverence
Improvisational	Scripted
Syncopated rhythm	Standard rhythm
Synchronized stepping	Minimal and unsynchronized movement
Textured "gravelly" voice	Modulated "sweet" voice
Percussive use of voice	Unbroken melodic line
Emotionally lifts one up	Emotionally humbles, brings one low

Fellowship members wondered if people were really worshiping, with their "arms at their sides." Sister Page commented that worshipers seemed to be "on automatic pilot." When the structure of the service moved toward "quiet reverence," Fellowship members felt it had lost life, joy, and energy. On the other hand, more expressive and elaborated forms of worship appeared to trigger negative assessments from Community members. In a choir practice being led by Sister Page, Pastor Smith, passing through, joked, "Break out the tents!" which she understood as criticism. When it was suggested that Brother Jackson accompany the choir on drums, Pastor Smith agreed but with the caution to "hold it down." In a public meeting assessing the merger effort, Pastor Smith verbally affirmed the idea that different people worship in different ways, but he cautioned, "Worship must never be performance!" Fellowship musicians replied defensively that their music was "ministry not performance"! Pastor Page's brother-in-law stressed, "Many people enjoy a plethora of musical styles." The lead soloist said, "I grew up singing for white folks. I felt like I had to explain why I sang as a black girl the way I did—but if God has gifted someone shouldn't she praise God in that way?" Pastor Smith agreed to allow more space for special numbers, but also warned that the words must be doctrinally sound, and said any proposal for special music should be approved through him. This was the way it had always been done at Community, but introduced a control Fellowship members were not used to. Brother Jackson—an occasional soloist, commented half humorously/ half resentfully afterward, "It's not as though we're going to sing, "Hold that Mule!" Brother Jackson was referencing a story told by gospel singer Shirley Caesar about "Shoutin' John," who, despite resistance from his dead but dignified church, insisted on dancing and shouting his praise to God. When a church delegation visited to warn him to stop, they found him plowing with a mule. Upon discovering their intent, Shoutin' John sang out, "Hold that Mule!" and proceeded to "shout" all the reasons he had for dancing and praising God.

Months later, one Fellowship member commented: "If we had worshiped the way we would have liked, they would have thought we were going off the walls." On the Community paradigm, elaborated embodied expression suggested "performance"—that is, pride and self-centeredness. On the Fellowship paradigm, elaborated embodied expression implied a Godward focus, and helped move others to such a Godward focus, while pride and self-consciousness, as exemplified in the conduct of David's wife Michal, resulted in a socially conscious quietness, stiffness, and dignity that was incompatible with true heart worship of God. On their model, Community members behaved too much like David's wife Michal.

Fellowship Responses to the Merger Effort

One by one, Fellowship members began to drop out of choir, with comments like, "I just can't sing that white music." Sister Kinley chose to resist the exclusion of a valued worship tradition and, in celebration of Black History Month, led her youth choir in a special presentation of three songs (one in Swahili) and a scripted recital of the life stories of black missionaries. Responses were clearly ambivalent, at best. Pastor Page relinquished administrative control to Pastor Smith, and seemed to expect that accommodation was a necessary part of merger. His efforts to align with Community leadership and practice moved him out of alignment with Fellowship leadership and practice. When he accepted the church keys back from Brother Elliot without protest or expression of concern, and seemingly accepted other exclusions without protest, he laid the foundations for strong bitterness in his own congregation. In the last weeks of trial merger, Fellowship members' attendance dropped. After the trial merger, Community voted unanimously, with one abstention, for merger. Believing the merger effort had gone well, Community members were shocked when a deeply divided Fellowship voted two to one against the merger.

Analysis

In his essay "Religion, Boundaries, and Bridges," Warner (1997) argues that if we wish to understand religious boundaries and bridges we must focus not on belief but on embodied ritual. He argues that while differences of belief build boundaries, ritual has the capacity to build bridges and transcend differences of belief. He points to the "emotional power of doing things together" (224), which produces solidarity, often even in the absence of ideological consensus (225), and explores the bonding power of music (226ff.), the emotional bonding produced by shared "rhythmic muscular movement" (231), and the power of any synchronized repetitive action to produce "solidarities" (231–32). Warner's description of how ritual produces solidarity nicely describes Fellowship Church prior to the merger.

Warner does not merely argue that ritual creates unity within the context of a specific ethnic group, but that ritual has the power to unite people across ethnic and ideological divides. This is doubtless true in many settings. For example, he describes attending a Korean Presbyterian service where he could not understand a word, but by his participation in the common liturgy (a liturgy familiar from his own Presbyterian upbringing), he was able to be included. Bodily actions were able to "bridge linguistic and other cultural boundaries" (1997, 224). The situation Warner describes is one where Koreans had learned an exact set of ritual and musical practices from American Presbyterian missionaries, thus creating a situation where the one thing they obviously had in common was ritual. But what happens when two distinct groups with two distinct sets of valued ritual practices attempt to bridge boundaries?

In our case study, the two churches did not differ significantly in religious belief. But they did differ in historically shaped worship practices. When one aligns one's body with others in ritual, or "tunes" to another to coproduce music mutually assessed as "beautiful," one builds solidarity. But when one expects others to align, to harmonize, and they do not, this produces profound disalignment.

Warner argues that ritual practices are learned, and therefore can be taught. This is true, but should be balanced with other considerations that emerge from our study. Much of culture is "out-of-awareness," and for that reason is unlikely to receive pedagogical attention. Furthermore, while it is certainly true that ritual practices are learned, they are learned in the context of a specific community and history, and come accompanied and undergirded by symbolic associations and deeply felt aesthetic and moral judgments. A specific worship pattern is originally learned, not as one possible pattern, but as the right pattern. If, in one community, worship participation and align- ment require specific embodied responses, and nonparticipation or disalign- ment is marked by a motionless body, then any invitation to conform to a congregation of motionless bodies is experienced as an invitation to stop wor- shiping deeply and meaningfully. It might seem that an invitation to call the pastor by his nickname "Chip" rather than by "Pastor Smith" involves but a minor linguistic shift, easy for anyone to learn. But, in fact, Fellowship members were uncomfortable with such a shift—a switch that would violate deep sensibilities about how one should refer to a pastor. Even if people can understand the practices of others, and desire to embrace them, some practices are difficult for fully formed adults to learn. For Kersten, even the simple act of learning to step/sway in alignment with fellow choir members was a chal- lenge. However our three-year-old, as can be viewed on film, quickly learned to step in alignment with others.

Again, Warner's stress on the unifying power of ritual fails to address the racial and social-class hierarchies within which ritual practices emerge. African American worship practices reflect a specific racial history and are grounded in shared memories both of oppression and of a God who uplifts, strengthens, and delivers. As the worship service evokes this shared memory (through a transition to use of vernacular and of embodied and emotionally elaborated expression, etc.), members reencounter the God who saves, uplifts, strengthens, and delivers. For many white Christians, who of course do not share this history, the use of "vernacular" rather than "standard English," and the use of highly embodied and emotionally elaborated worship practices have other associations, such as with lower social class. That is, at the very point in the service where many African Americans were most deeply encountering a God who saves, uplifts, and strengthens, white members were uncomfortable with what was felt to be lower-class linguistic practice, emotional expressivity, and embodied behavior. Since class itself is dependent on linguistic, emo- tional, and embodied displays and alignments, white members who affirm and align with such practices intuitively feel themselves to be jeopardizing their own class position. From the standpoint of many African American worshipers in a mixed congregation, it is precisely at the point where normally they would be moving toward the heart of the worship experience that they most experi- ence the "peculiar sensation" of "double-consciousness" that Du Bois (1903, 2) wrote of, of "looking at one's self through the eyes of others, of measuring one's soul by the tape" of critical white onlookers.

Finally, Warner's suggestion that shared ritual practices can bridge ethnic divides, and that such practices can be learned, fails to address the crucial question of "Whose ritual practices?" Scholars of ethnicity (Barth 1969; Jenkins 1994) argue that ethnic boundaries emerge from interactive settings where there is competition over resources. Such resources, as Jenkins (1994) stresses, can be symbolic. A church merger potentially creates a *zone of interaction that is an arena of competition over symbolic values and symbolic space.* Instead of providing a "safe space" for valued expressions of worship that received intervalidation by others, the merged church, for many Fellowship members, became a setting where space was denied them and their practices, or where valued practices received ambiguous or negative assessments. When one expects mutual affirmation within the framework of shared aesthetic values, and receives instead judgment and criticism, solidarity evaporates. While Fellowship was a suburban church whose membership was comparable educationally and economically to Community's, status issues nonetheless took on racial overtones. When personal interactions highlight and link personal identity with secular occupations ("I'm Don. I'm a lawyer.") and seemingly wish to similarly categorize others ("And what do you do?"), such interactions introduce into the church the very status considerations of the larger society that historically excluded and subordinated based on race. And when it is white church members highlighting such considerations in a cross-racial interaction, in a manner uncharacteristic of appropriate interaction in the "intimate culture" of Fellowship congregational life—and when white members, following a "first-name rule," fail to use expected honorifics—it is not surprising that many black members infer evidence of racism. When the very "racial" hierarchy, subordination, exclusion, and stigma experienced in the wider society are replicated within an "interracial" church, church ceases to be a place of safety, a place of affirmation, a place of uplift. Indeed, such an interactive setting frequently produces ethnic boundaries, a marked sense of self versus other, and a tendency to essentialize self and other "racially." That a majority of Fellowship members would vote to withdraw from such a new zone of interaction should not surprise.

Implications for Christians, Churches, and Related Institutions

Bill Taylor was an African American seminary student and member of Fellowship during this period. Several years after these events, a white church in a changing neighborhood invited Rev. Taylor to become its pastor and help them become multiracial. Deeply convinced that churches need to lead the way in racial reconciliation, Rev. Taylor accepted the call. But, mindful of what he had learned through painful experience, his acceptance was contingent on several explicit conditions for the current church leaders. For example, they were free to call him "Pastor" or "Reverend" or "Rev," but must commit never to call him by his first name, something which he explained would be decoded as signaling disrespect among the African American community they wished to reach.

Reverend Taylor also explained that worship practices were a critical component of any effort to create a multiracial church, and thus secured an agreement that within a year a worship leader would be added to the staff, a worship leader he himself would recruit and select. While the drama of this new story is only now being played out, this leader is attempting to incorporate painful lessons learned from the events recounted in this chapter. What are some of these lessons for those who wish to constructively engage racial realities?

1. Culture matters. Although blacks and whites have long lived in the United States, and thus share culture at many levels, because an ideology of race historically created radically different experiences for blacks and whites in America, the "race divide" came to partially coincide with enduring and divergent cultural patterns, especially in church cultures. People are cultural beings. Churches are cultural institutions. Even worship takes culturally contingent forms. Shared culture enables effective communication and underpins alignments and solidarities. A lack of shared culture naturally leads to misunderstandings and ethnocentric judgments.

2. Good intentions, pure hearts, and spiritual disciplines are not enough. To the extent that cultural differences are involved, sanctification is not what is at stake. One must not treat complex cultural and structural dynamics in purely moralistic and spiritual terms. Rather, one must acquire adequate social, historical, and cultural understandings as important preconditions underpinning any church-based initiative to bring African Americans and Euro-Americans together.

3. Cultural flexibility, a willingness to learn and participate in other practices, and willingness to signal strong appreciation and affirmation of others and their practices are critical to racial reconciliation. Any insistence on united worship, if accompanied by cultural rigidity and ethnocentric judgment on either side, will result in conflict, hurt, dominance, exclusion, or social withdrawal. The race problem in America is not merely a unity problem, but is a problem of racialized hierarchy, where African Americans have been stigmatized, subordinated, and excluded. When ethnocentric members of dominant racial groups encounter cultural difference, their very ethnocentrism results in judgmentalism that helps replicate the stigma, subordination, and exclusion of a racialized society. If such individuals also have status anxieties related to social class, they may be exceptionally poor at aligning with stigmatized social others, and exceptionally prone to ethnocentric judgment and social withdrawal. Calls by white Americans for racial unity in congregational settings will be one-sided and even counterproductive if not matched by cultural sensitivity, respect, and a willingness to learn other practices and align with them, and if not matched by an equally deep concern that the church address the full range of problems (stigma, subordination, humiliation, pain, grief, exclusion, poverty) associated with race.

4. Worship practices matter. Perhaps the single most important person in any effort designed to bring people together in worship is the worship leader. Worship leaders who have been nurtured in a single cultural tradition, and have deeply internalized the values and ideals of that particular tradition, are poorly prepared to lead such an interracial worship service. Rather, worship leaders must have extensive training in diverse cultural worship traditions, must be able to celebrate the diverse musical aesthetics and embodied traditions of others, and must be able to coach their whole congregation in appreciating and practicing worship in alignment with people of other ethnic or racial groups. The published writings of Hawn (2003a, 2003b) provide excellent resources along these lines.

5. Leadership matters. Leaders in multiracial churches need to have had long and in-depth relationships across racial lines, need to be particularly well prepared at helping people understand and appreciate other cultural practices, need to be particularly attentive to "whose practices" are being included and affirmed, and need to ensure that key decisions are being made with the interests of all ethnic groups adequately in mind.

6. Research and writing matter. We need scholars who take Christianity and the church seriously as a base from which to carry out social engagements. All across America Christians and congregations are experimenting with efforts at racial reconciliation. For example, mergers of black and white congregations have occurred in Minnesota (Clancy 1999), New Jersey (Schaad 1999), Kentucky (Woodfin 1998), Alabama (Burke 1996), Michigan (Chambers 1998), and in Texas, Virginia, and Tennessee (Foster 1997, 2–4). This represents just one kind of experiment, but churches are conducting all kinds of experiments with racial reconciliation (see chapters by Howell and K. Priest). Each of these settings may be thought of as a laboratory, a laboratory where ideas are being tried, and results are available for investigation. It is important that these experiences form the basis of new insights and understandings that can be helpful to others, so that the exact same mistakes not be repeated, and so that new insights need not be discovered from scratch each time. No other value justifies writing about the painful experiences recounted in this chapter except the hope that we would learn from them. It is hoped that at least some readers will themselves catch the vision of using research and writing to help convert experiences into knowledge available for others.

Finally, we do not believe that there is a single path for all congregations to pursue. Every congregation should welcome people of any ethnic group and should help its members be agents of racial reconciliation. But different congregations may have different callings, and may well create particular contextualized worship cultures in pursuit of those callings—worship cultures that, for purely cultural reasons, may be more appealing and helpful to members of some ethnic groups than to others. That is, we do not believe congregations that largely comprise one ethnic group should be assumed to be morally defective.

But while we do not believe ethnically homogeneous congregations are necessarily the result of sinful racism, it is historically true that many churches have maintained separate worship out of sinful racism. This means that the witness of a Christian community comprised primarily of racially homogeneous churches faces major credibility problems. Furthermore, if an ethnically diverse America comprises primarily racially homogeneous congregations, this contributes to the racialization of our society (Emerson and Smith 2000). If Christians, in the intimate culture of congregational life where one deeply encounters others, are socialized to deep sensibilities that are themselves ethnocentrically attuned primarily to the culture of their own group, then when they leave church and go into an ethnically diverse and racialized society, they will be poorly prepared to constructively engage ethnic and racial others. That is, racially homogeneous congregations are a weak base from which to try to address the problems of our racialized society (DeYoung et al. 2002). Therefore, we need increasing numbers of churches that will make the commitments necessary, as outlined above, to become appropriately "multiracial." In the process, such churches will provide a clear witness to the unity found in Christ, while also nurturing intercultural and interracial skills and understandings in a new generation growing up in such churches, a generation that will help lead the way for other Christians, churches, and fellow citizens.

NOTE

1. Funding for this research was provided by the Louisville Institute. Special thanks to Raymond Williams, Michael Emerson, and Nancy Ammerman for reading and providing feedback on earlier versions of this paper.

REFERENCES

Ammerman, Nancy T. 1997. *Congregation and community*. New Brunswick, NJ: Rutgers University Press.
Barth, Fredrik, ed. 1969. *Ethnic groups and boundaries*. Boston: Little, Brown.
Burke, Kip 1996. Black and white together, http://www.strang.com/nm/stories/nm 896n3.htm.
Chambers, Sandra K. 1998. Black, white churches merge to make statement for racial unity, http://www.charismamag.com/issues/cm199/cm1995.htm.
Clancy, Frank 1999. How one small church bridges the racial divide. *USA Weekend* (Sept. 10–12, 1999).
DeYoung, Curtiss Paul, Michael O. Emerson, George Yancey, Karen Chai Kim. 2003. *United by faith: The multiracial congregation as an answer to the problem of race*. Oxford: Oxford University Press.
Du Bois, W. E. B. 1903. *The souls of black folk*. Chicago: A. C. McClurg.
Emerson, Michael O., and Christian Smith. 2000. *Divided by faith: Evangelical religion and the problem of race in America*. Oxford: Oxford University Press.
Foster, Charles R. 1997. *Embracing diversity*. Bethesda, MD: The Alban Institute.

Hawn, C. Michael. 2003a. *Gather into one: Praying and singing globally*. Grand Rapids, MI: Eerdmans.

———. 2003b. *One bread, one body: Exploring cultural diversity in worship*. Bethesda, MD: The Alban Institute.

Jenkins, Richard. 1994. Rethinking ethnicity: Identity, categorization and power. *Journal of Ethnic and Racial Studies* 17:197–223.

Myers, William R. 1991. *Black and white styles of youth ministry: Two congregations in America*. New York: Pilgrim.

Priest, Kersten Bayt. 1998. *Disharmony in the 11 A.M. worship hour: A case study of an abandoned interethnic church merger*. Master's thesis, University of South Carolina.

Schaad, Jacob. 1999. Life among the casinos. *Presbyterians Today* (June 1999): 18–21.

Spencer, Jon Michael. 1990. *Protest and praise: Sacred music of black religion*. Minneapolis: Fortress.

Warner, R. Stephen. 1997. Religion, boundaries, and bridges. *Sociology of Religion* 58(3): 217–38.

Wilson, Olly W. 1996. African music, influence on African-American music. In *Encyclopedia of African-American culture and history*, ed. Jack Salzman, David Lionel Smith, and Cornel West, 1:71–76. New York: Simon & Schuster/MacMillan.

Woodfin, Gorman. 1998. Two colors, one church. *Christian World News*, http://www.cbn.org/newsstand/cwn/980807e.asp.

Yarger, Lisa J. 1996. "That's . . . where stepping came from": Afrocentricity and beliefs about stepping. *North Carolina Folklore Journal* 43(2): 109–19.

18

Power and Reconciliation in an Urban Church: The Case of New City Fellowship

Brian M. Howell

Jenna and William Wallace were the first black couple to join New City Fellowship after its founding in 1991. Although there were several racially mixed couples, white couples who had adopted black children, and white families with significant experience in black communities, people were praying that this church, dedicated to racial reconciliation in the divided city of St. Louis, would attract "stable, middle-class black families." Thus, when Jenna and William arrived, the church was eager to embrace them. Jenna, however, took some convincing. "[William] came home and told me about this church and I was just . . . well, I did not want to go. I mean, I'm looking at this church and I said to him, 'Why do I want to start going to that white church?' I work with white people six days a week, do I have to see them on Sunday too?" Jenna and William laughed as they told me this story, but it was a revealing account. Although the church positioned itself from the beginning as a multiracial church, hired an African American assistant pastor, and put its church offices in an all-black section of the city, Jenna's first thought was that she was being asked to go to a "white church." When I pressed her to describe her first impressions, she went on, "Well, they had this white pastor who preached . . . well, he wasn't exactly like a black preacher, you know? And people just sat, and sang. It was so quiet, Brian! My lord, I thought, I don't think I can be this quiet!" But not only did Jenna eventually join the congregation, within a few years she was on staff.

Now, eight years after this interview, the congregation has grown from an average weekly attendance around two hundred to more than seven hundred. Throughout this growth, the percentage of African Americans in the congregation has remained fairly steady at about 25 percent (approximating St. Louis's demographics in which

30 percent of the city is black), while the church has added significant numbers of Latinos and Africans (mostly Congolese) to the point that they have added Spanish and French ministries (making the overall ratio approximately 65:35, white to nonwhite). This chapter will address some of the specifics of how this multicultural vision has been realized thus far. In particular, I will focus on the question of power. How does a congregation that is often initially perceived as "white" by people of color manage to attract and retain those members? How do they come to feel included and valued as members? When the head pastor and a majority of the leadership are of one ethnic/racial group (particularly when they are from the socially dominant group) how do they avoid the impression that they are still "in control"? In order to answer these questions, the first part of this paper will briefly explore the question of what is meant by "power," especially in the context of a multiracial congregation. Then, the example of New City Fellowship (NCF) will illustrate how power is expressed and experienced by the members in ways that allow for a sense of inclusion and mutuality. In keeping with my understanding of power used here, I focus on issues of religious practice and discourse. These are certainly not the only aspects of power that are important (economic influence and institutional control should not be forgotten), but it is through the more representational features of congregational life that we will see how power relationships and status become reversed and redefined in ways that bring traditionally marginalized people to the center. In the end, while NCF may not be replicable in a formulaic sense, I do believe there are insights from this case that will help inform an understanding and practice of unity throughout the body of Christ.

Power and Faith

Power, like culture, is a slippery word that almost defies definition. Certainly there are obvious manifestations of power: the coercive power of the state to enforce laws or the power of a bully to steal your lunch money. But anthropologists and social theorists have identified other sorts of power as equally, if not even more profoundly, important. Eric Wolf (1999; 1994) has pointed out that in addition to the sorts of power in interpersonal relationships and the use of force (by the state or government) are powers that exist in "settings themselves" that serve to "render some kinds of behavior possible, while making others less possible or impossible" (1994, 219). When Jenna first walked into NCF, she did not see how she could worship in the way she was used to. Certainly no one would physically stop her from running in the church if she so chose, but sitting among all these quiet white people, how could she even move, let alone shout? Could that sort of worship even "mean" the same thing knowing (or believing) that these white people think you've lost your mind?

Part of this aspect of power, then, is encompassed by the behaviors and visible clues in the environment. But these visual clues and behaviors are subsequently reinforced or reinterpreted through language. Numerous theorists, from

Foucault (1984; 1980) to Habermas (1981) have emphasized the importance of language/discourse in shaping individual interpretations of reality and even the ability to think about possibilities or options for their lives (see also Schieffelin, Woolard, and Kroskrity 1998). Certainly, within a congregation, ways of speaking prove to be extremely important for those attempting to determine what is possible and permissible. In Bayt-Priest and Priest's article (this volume), when white leaders referred to the gospel choir's practice as a "performance" instead of "worship," it had the effect of signaling that those forms were not acceptable and shaping the way many perceived what they saw. In the same way, DeYoung et al. (2003, 171) note that in churches attempting to become multiracial, the issue of naming becomes an important symbol for power relations. When the majority in the Fort Bend Chinese Church resisted changing the word *Chinese* to *Community*, it served to reinforce the power of the majority to maintain a sense of ethnic exclusion.

These two aspects of power—practice and language—come together to create a space that is either dominated by a single tradition or open and flexible to multiple groups. This is where the example of NCF becomes particularly helpful. Although the congregation is nested in denominational, doctrinal, and social contexts that seem, historically and symbolically, to be powerfully dominated by a white-majority tradition, by redefining themselves through practices and language, NCF has been able to create a congregation where those who are in the minority numerically feel empowered to participate fully in the life of the congregation.

Spiritual Power in Social Place

Both the social and denominational context of NCF would seem to inhibit the creation of a congregation in which power is thought to be shared across racial lines. St. Louis—the city where, in 1846, Dred Scott sued for his freedom only to be declared property by the U.S. Supreme Court—is still marked by deep racial division. As in many major cities, a conspicuous segregation between most black areas (the so-called inner city) and the obviously wealthier and increasingly distant white suburbs ("the county") has become a major facet of the landscape. Economic, political, and social power has clearly shifted to the white-dominated suburbs in the past fifty years. For that reason, NCF has positioned itself, socially and physically, in a strategic location in one of the more integrated areas of the metro St. Louis area.

The more intriguing aspect of NCF's context, however, is the denominational setting in which it has grown. The Presbyterian Church in America (PCA) was officially created in 1973 when it separated from the Presbyterian Church in the United States (PCUS). The PCA represented a theologically and socially conservative wing of the denomination formerly known as the Presbyterian Church of the Confederate States, having broken with its northern branch over a number of theological disputes, including the biblical support for slavery. Throughout much of its existence, this denomination defended slavery and, later, segregation, through tacit and active support of racist southern laws and practices (see Thompson 1973, 286, 294, 530–51).

While it may not be surprising that a denomination with an embarrassing legacy such as this would now be concerned with encouraging racial reconciliation, it is striking that within many more liberal, historically antiracist denominations, efforts at multiracial and reconciliatory Christianity have failed. That this congregations has, within this context, been reasonably successful amplifies the argument that doctrine, theology, or "worldview" alone is not the critical factor in multiracial congregational health. Instead, as people come together at NCF, it is how public language and practice frame the theology and community life that are the more critical elements.

Religious Practice at New City Fellowship

Classifying the religious activities of churchgoers under the heading "ritual" can have the unfortunate effect of distancing Protestants who tend to equate "ritual" with rote or meaningless action. But speaking anthropologically, there is a clear sense in which various gatherings at NCF do fulfill the classic definition of ritual to "bring the world as lived and the world as imagined, fused under the agency of a single set of symbolic forms" to bear on the individual members (Geertz 1973, 128). The world as imagined at NCF is that of racial/ethnic unity, while the world at large is, obviously, less than unified. Anthropologists studying ritual throughout the world point to the importance of these symbolically rich moments both to reflect ideal social order and reshape that order (see, for example, Robbins 2001; Stromberg 1986). However, in the context of most Protestant, particularly evangelical congregations, the notion of religious practice cannot be confined to actions in sacred space or necessarily clearly distinguished from "ordinary" life. Thus, to understand how the members of NCF come to understand themselves and their congregation, we must focus on religious practice in both "ritual" moments and the more ordinary interactions in which language and practice serve to inform all members' understandings of their faith and themselves.

The best starting illustration (and key "ritual") at NCF is, like most Christian churches, the Sunday morning service. The service may begin anywhere from five to ten minutes after the appointed start time, with the congregation being called together by the worship leaders and band (comprising electric instruments and drums) breaking into an energetic praise chorus or spiritual. For many years (I observed intermittently from 1995 through 2001) leadership in worship/singing consisted of generally three or four people, intentionally comprising some combination of men and women, black and white. As more Latinos and Asians have joined the church, they have tried to diversify the worship team further, but whereas Latinos are not identifiable by "race," and the number of Asians is relatively small, this has not been as consistently followed as a black/white, male/female balance.

The music ranges from contemporary praise choruses, to traditional spirituals and gospel songs with the occasional traditional Presbyterian hymn. As the linguistic diversity of the congregation has increased, so have the languages of the songs. In a service observed in 2003, there were, in addition to songs in English, songs in Spanish, French, and Lingala (an African language spoken by a number of the Congolese families in the church). Sermons are generally delivered by the head pastor—a white man in his late forties—although when he does not preach, the role is usually passed to one of the black leaders (assistant pastor or elder). It is not uncommon for members of the congregation, black and white, to call out during worship, raise hands and clap enthusiastically along with singing, prayer, and preaching. This includes older white members who become most animated (raising their hands, crying, or kneeling) while singing hymns such as "Come Thou Fount of Every Blessing," in addition to white and black members who call out during gospel praise choruses such as "Oh, Freedom!" and "Happy Day."

However, as Jenna observed earlier, the emotional response of these members does not begin to approach what she had experienced in the black church context. Even in 2003, when the percentage of people of color represented was higher than when Jenna first joined, displays of emotion during worship were relatively contained and brief. Although many raised their hands, and most people clapped between songs, each hymn or chorus tended to be sung several times and then simply ended, as opposed to leading into a time of unstructured worship and spontaneous praise as is common in many black congregations. The resulting worship style was neither "black" nor "white" in terms of being entirely reflective of a particular aesthetic tradition.

But in the juxtaposition of these two traditions—black and white—there is, in the minds of many of the people participating, no privileging of one over the other. DeYoung et al. (2003, 168) refer to this as the "creation of a hybrid culture" that is neither one nor the other. At NCF, this hybrid culture has the effect of shifting traditional power relationships away from those who would dominate through a familiarity with "the system" to a more equalizing practice in which no one ethnic/racial group can claim absolute superiority. Each feels symbolically represented without feeling privileged.

In a similar way, the ritual language of NCF brings together motifs and themes that further equalize the membership by symbolically placing different traditions and social location in a common theological frame. For example, in prayers, "testimonies," and other sorts of exhortations during worship, urban themes familiar to African Americans are quite consciously included, but in a way that put the social problems of the so-called inner city on a par with the problems of suburban life. Social ills typically thought to be the most grievous sorts of socially destructive behaviors become "normalized" as generic sin. Reference to the temptations of drugs and drug dealing (often using the more specific "crack"), and gang violence are frequently placed alongside the more "suburban" issues of materialism and judgmentalism as signs of a depraved world. Consider this excerpt from a sermon by the head pastor: "The gospel is for those who suffer in abusive relationships, in gangs, in crack houses, and in lonely neighborhoods in the county. We have to say to the mother of the crack baby, the gangbanger, the Wall Street lawyer, this gospel—this grace—is for you!" The equalizing of experiences—putting the Wall Street lawyer in the same category as the gangbanger, and the lonely suburbanite next to the crack house dweller—serves as a powerful symbol of the equality of those in the congregation, regardless of racial, economic, or social background. This language opens up an inclusive space in which the experiences of various ethnic groups are placed on a common plane as equally valuable or equally depraved.

In addition to the Sunday morning service, the leveling power of language and experience is carried over into other forums. As the church has grown in membership, the leaders have instituted what they call "reconciliation meetings" (using the term taken from Washington and Kehrein's [1993] well-known book on racial reconciliation) in which issues of race are discussed openly in a guided discussion. In one meeting, members were asked to think about what they had, as individuals, "sacrificed" to join NCF as opposed to an all-white or all-black church. After breaking into small, intentionally interracial groups of six to eight persons, the groups reported on their discussion. Black and white members alike reported "sacrificing" a worship environment in which they were comfortable. One black woman echoed the sentiments of Jenna when she said she missed the "high praising" of the black church for what she perceived as the more subdued atmosphere of NCF. Almost immediately following her comment, however, a white man stood to confess that he often found the service too raucous and the music not to his tastes. He lamented, "I miss hearing a pipe organ." Although there were whites who wished the service were more energetic and blacks who were not comfortable with a "traditional" black-style service, it was clear that most felt the mixture of traditions represented a "sacrifice" of the style most comfortable to them.

This discomfort is analogous to the idea of "liminality," introduced by anthropologist Arnold van Gennep (1909) and developed by Victor Turner (1969) as a phase of ritual practice in which individuals or communities go through transformations in which everyday social structure is inverted, displaced, or symbolically destroyed for the purpose of either transforming or reestablishing social identities or norms. In Turner's studies of ritual, he focused on ways in which traditional social relationships were temporarily inverted for the purpose of giving those who normally are socially less powerful an opportunity to exert power. Individuals are thrown into unfamiliar or ambiguous social identities in which the standard rules of authority, prestige, and hierarchy do not apply. Whether in white members trying to sing the gospel songs that seem strange to their idea of "church," black members struggling with the significance of hymns of praise that feel like a dirge, English speakers singing in French, or North and South Americans being lead in Congolese worship dances, members from every group reported feeling constrained in their ability to express worship as they would like. At times one group feels "high" in Turner's sense, while another is "low." This uncomfortable/liminal experience leads to what Turner calls "communitas" in which the members are momentarily released from the hierarchies of social life to experience "relatively undifferentiated" community in which the structure (in this case, racial, ethnic, or linguistic hierarchy) is subverted (Turner 1969, 97). Social power is reversed and decentered, as the normal categories fail to work in defining the tradition, experience, and relations of the members.

Reconciliation meetings themselves often become these rituals of reversal in which members experience the ambiguity and discomfort of liminality. In one early meeting, when the congregation's focus was still primarily on black/white relations, black members were asked to share the ideas they carried from childhood concerning whites. All of the black members present reported that at one time or another they had been explicitly told to distrust white people. While the information itself certainly surprised some of the white members, the meeting as religious practice also contributed to the sense of inadequacy of the whites. The meeting, led by a black elder, was dominated by the black members. Except for a few questions from whites, the meeting was devoted to the idea of black members sharing knowledge that white members "needed to hear." One white member told me later, "When each black person stood up and said that they were told 'Don't trust white people,' it was like a hit to the gut, you know? I mean, we think we're trying to do the right thing, but you realize, man, there's a lot I don't understand." For this person, and other white members, the feeling of being powerless to get this sort of information on their own is like a "hit to the gut" as they learn about the black experience from those who know. At the same time, the racialized nature of the discussion cut across class lines as middle-class and urban-poor black members reported similar encounters with white racism and prejudice, while white members, whether members of the urban poor themselves (of which there were very few at the time) or members of the wealthy professional class (which constituted the majority of white leaders if not members) were collectively "silenced" in the presence of black experience. Whites, by virtue of their whiteness, experienced, at least momentarily, social powerlessness as they listened to the black members tell their stories.

This process works in the reverse as well. For black members, the sense of "needing" the whites occasionally comes in the more obvious terms of financial issues (notably for those members joining through the outreach ministries to the inner-city poor), but also in terms of feeling like the traditional black church is somehow lacking. For one black couple, a well-educated middle-class family, the original impetus to attend NCF was dissatisfaction with the authoritarian form of church government of their Baptist congregation. As the woman became involved, however, she found elements of the practice that she felt had been lacking in her past church life. "I realized that I was really learning. The teaching made me want to keep attending." Like the white member who felt he needed the voice of black members to understand race and reconciliation, this black member came to see her own religious experience as lacking an element that she could get through participating in this quasi-white church. As both black and white (and later Spanish- or French-speaking) members experience themselves as *needing* to hear the voices of the other, power becomes diffused. This is the sense of *communitas* elaborated by Turner, during which people experience an "essential and generic human bond" (1969, 97). If no one group can claim privilege in the life of the congregation—no single group can claim to have all the resources necessary to live a full Christian life—individual members experience themselves as being equally powerful and equally powerless to form a complete community.

A Spirit of Power

It is the powerlessness experienced by all members at various moments that leads to the element of power most central to the Christian, that of spiritual power. The power of God and the gospel is a foundational theological concept for any church. But thinking and talking about the Holy Spirit is very different in various theological traditions, and the denominational background of NCF would seem to pose a barrier in this as well.

The official theological position of the PCA reflects what is known as "five-point Calvinism." As a church within this denomination, NCF also teaches this version of Reformed theology, often understood through the acronym T.U.L.I.P. The letters stand for: "Total depravity," the condition of sinfulness and separation from God into which each person is born and from which no person can extricate himself or herself; "Unconditional election," Calvin's theology of the "elect" as those who are predestined for salvation; "Limited atonement," the atonement of Christ is limited to the elect; "Irresistible grace," which asserts that no one who is one of the elect can resist the grace of God to be saved; "Perseverance of the saints," meaning that anyone who is of the elect will, by definition, continue to live as a Christian in spite of "earthly trials."

Officially the Holy Spirit is understood to operate in each sphere of this theology (e.g., "irresistible grace" is said to be brought by the Holy Spirit), yet the radical Calvinism of the PCA articulates a distinct theology of the Spirit as compared with the Baptist-dominated traditions generally associated with "black Christianity" (see Lincoln and Mamiya 1990). More important, as Weber (1956) argued, theological convictions cannot be separated from cultural, historical, and social settings that may shape and, more significantly, be shaped by them. Indeed, Weber pointed to very much this form of Calvinism in his famous discussion of "The Protestant Ethic and the Spirit of Capitalism," in which he argued that the commitment to predestination historically led to the worldly asceticism and emotional sobriety necessary for capitalist enterprise. Without devolving into caricature, the vast majority of PCA congregations in St. Louis exhibit a cultural and social conformity (white, middle- to upper-middle-class, suburban, and highly educated members practicing traditionalist forms of Protestantism) that seems both a product of their social and religious history and now powerfully sustained by this particular interpretation of Calvinist theology.

Institutionally, the PCA emphasizes a rational, education-centered approach to religious life through its emphasis on education in leadership. Ordination in the denomination requires the completion of a three-year (minimum) master of divinity degree, including the study of Greek and Hebrew. Those advancing to ordination are required to exhibit competency in a wide range of theological issues, including the Westminster Confessions and Catechism, a comprehensive theological treatise originally composed for the Church of England in 1647. The denomination does embrace a doctrine of "parity of the elders," and distinguishes between "ruling" and "teaching" elders, meaning not every elder is required to have formal theological education. However, men named elders within the denomination carry that status to every congregation in which they are involved, and those who do receive theological education are likely to be called as teaching elders. Institutionally, then, eldership is often granted in conjunction with the higher levels of education within the denomination and long-time membership. Thus, while "spiritual power" is theologically the provenance of God only, in practice, education, denominational familiarity, and church authority de facto closely link and limit spiritual/institutional (and by extension, social) leadership to those who are already within the tradition, or willing to undergo considerable education under the auspices of the guardians of that tradition.

The leadership of NCF clearly embraces the doctrines of the PCA, teaching T.U.L.I.P. in the new members' class, and consistently offering a Sunday school class on the Westminster Confession. In accordance with PCA readings of Scripture, eldership and preaching are restricted to men, and members of the leadership regularly participate in the wider PCA community. But, through innovative practice and leadership, NCF has been able to recast this tradition so that power does not remain in the hands of those educated few comfortable with the traditions and vocabulary of the PCA, and nonelders are empowered to exercise spiritual leadership in other forms. Through an emphasis on total depravity and an active discourse of the Holy Spirit, spiritual power, like social power, is understood to flow freely throughout the membership of the congregation.

In Weber's analysis of Calvinism, it was the doctrine of predestination that played the most significant role in shaping community behavior. He argued that the insecurity surrounding the status of one's salvation led to great psychological distress, causing the Calvinist to pour his or her life into a "calling," soberly engaging in the work of this world, to bring comfort to his or her uneasy soul. And while the doctrine of election is officially embraced by NCF, it is not the main theological focus. Instead, it is NCF's emphasis on "total depravity" that proves to be an essential element in the vision of racial unity and an openness of spiritual power. Just as in the Pentecostal revivals sweeping the non-Western world, the language of human sinfulness and the role of the Holy Spirit become a way for people to embrace the idea of spiritual equality and ecclesial empowerment (Robbins 2004, 127; Cox 1995, 123ff.).

The emphasis on total depravity takes the power for moral improvement, salvation, and sanctification out of the hands of individuals (and their education, will, economic stability, or moral fortitude) and places them firmly into the hand of God. Members of every ethnic group are encouraged to consider how, if left to their own devices, they would fall into destructive and debilitating sin. In one meeting, in which several pastors from Mexico were hosted as part of the initial stages of instituting a Spanish-language Latino ministry, members of NCF were asked to introduce themselves with their name, something about their family, and a brief word on "where you would be today if it weren't for the power of the gospel." It was striking to hear white, middle-class men, raised in educationally privileged suburban homes, state without a trace of irony the depths of personal depravity they imagined for themselves were they not Christians. Pastor Harding himself declared that were it not for the power of the gospel in his life, "I would be involved in drugs, pornography, probably divorced. I believe I might not even have lived to see my grandchildren." In graphic terms, then, an emphasis on total depravity takes spiritual power away from attributes like education, personal piety, or familiarity with Christian/Reformed traditions. Spiritual power becomes not just theologically and doctrinally about the actions of God, but experientially the sole provenance of the Holy Spirit.

In the discourse of NCF, repeated references to "God's Spirit," the "Holy Spirit," or "the Work of God" as a present, active force in every facet of the congregation's existence constantly puts the notion of God's accessible power before the congregation. At a retreat in 2001, one speaker emphasized that without "the Spirit of God actively changing our hearts, we would never have real reconciliation, only integration." During the administration of the Lord's Supper, members of the congregation stand along the walls of the sanctuary and are often encouraged to observe the racial diversity as a sign that God is working. As individuals become involved in the activities of the church, they interpret their membership and ability to relate to people of other races as the active work of the Holy Spirit in their lives.

This emphasis on the activity of God's Spirit in the lives of individual believers' acts as the means of solace against the hard truth of utter depravity. Like the traumatized Calvinist of Weber's study, members of NCF follow the sobering teaching of depravity with an affirmation of grace, and, in terms of the success of reconciliation, the activity of the Holy Spirit. With the emphasis on depravity, signs of success—whether in church or life—can only be interpreted as grace and spiritual power. However, the discourse of the Spirit accomplishes more than the more static idea of "grace" (although that term and concept is widely referenced in formal and informal interactions at NCF). The active "hand of God" working in their midst is a source of power available to all, regardless of social background. In fact, drawing again on the theme of liminality and reversal brought up earlier, the discourse of the Spirit at NCF suggests an advantage in accessing spiritual power among those who would typically be classified as most disadvantaged (the poor, racial minorities, and women).

Theologically, the Holy Spirit shows no favoritism at NCF, yet on an experiential level, he does. In white church tradition generally, and in the PCA in particular, demonstrations of emotion have been linked to "the flesh" and a dissolution of the confident grace indwelling the elect saint. Although Calvin has been called the "theologian of the Holy Spirit," contemporary theologians have argued that in the face of Pentecostal emphases on experience and "the Spirit," Reformed Christians have underplayed the Holy Spirit (see Horton 1992). But even these scholars, along with esteemed Reformed theologians such as Kuyper and Barth, seem to give very little credence to emotional experience or display as relevant to the work of the Spirit (cf. Kuyper 1946). As a result, contemporary Presbyterianism has often represented one of the more extreme forms of anti-emotionalism in the Protestant church. The more emotionally charged tradition of Pietism (and its relatives Methodism, Mysticism, Pentecostalism, and Charismatic Christianity) began as a sixteenth-century reaction against the overly rationalistic Reformed theology now represented by the PCA and other conservative Calvinistic denominations (see Poewe and Hexham 1994, 20n). Without a doubt, for Christians like Jenna, for whom emotion is more than merely emotion, freedom to express enthusiasm in worship is very much about the power of the Spirit and how that power is encouraged or discouraged by congregational life.

In the context of NCF, this interpretation of spiritual power and the Holy Spirit is not invoked as a direct challenge or abrogation of the denominational position. Some white members committed to the Reformed theology of NCF saw the encouragement of emotional worship as simply a kind of corrective to, in their terms, the "dry" or "propositional" faith of the traditional churches. But in the discourse and practice of the congregation, emotion clearly serves a more important role toward a reinterpretation of spiritual power.

Many, if not most, of the African American denominations exhibit a theology of emotion in their practice and doctrine. Many scholars of black Christianity emphasize the critical importance of emotionalism in conversion and subsequent experiences of the Spirit in the life of black Christians (Grindal 1982; Williams 1982; Sernett 1975). Black members of NCF reported that emotional expressions during services are the natural response to the recognition of grace in the face of their own sin, and very much an act of the Holy Spirit. But white members are brought to a new understanding by not only witnessing the emotion of their black brothers and sisters but also by being given a way to view this emotion as an expression of grace. During one service in which several black members were especially exuberant, Pastor Harding admonished white members unaccustomed to such displays to interpret the expression in the context of black experience. "I know some of you will turn this over in your minds and talk about it later. . . . Is it real? What is it all about? . . . But let me tell you, I know what some of these women have been through and they have something to shout about!" White members who have also begun to express themselves in more emotional and physical ways report that they are also interpreting their actions as the natural expression of grace and their awareness of their own plight. As one white member said, "I didn't grow up with shouting or even clapping in church. It was just, you know, quiet . . . like this [holds hands in lap while sitting bolt upright]. But seeing how some of my black sisters and brothers can shout or sing . . . well, it just made me feel like I was missing something." Emotion is both a personal and communal reminder of grace and the activity of the Spirit in the presence of utter depravity and the common ground of salvation. As Grindal suggests, these emotional experiences remind each believer of the conversion experience and the presence of God; it "reinforces in the people's minds their own existence as a successful spiritual community" (1982, 92).

In this way the role of the Holy Spirit at NCF is a democratizing force for spiritual power. Power becomes diffused throughout the congregation if not, in fact, even concentrated in the hands of those who would seem to be more powerless in this "white church." African American women, who are most likely to express the vibrant emotions of "black" worship, become the visible embodiment of spiritual power. Although NCF does not encourage (nor have I ever observed) "spiritual gifts" (i.e., speaking in tongues, prophecy, being "slain"), invoking a theology of the Holy Spirit transforms emotional experiences from mere "emotionalism" into genuine (i.e., biblically and theologically justifiable) encounters with and signs of God. Those who find themselves able to engage in such public emotion are then validated, affirmed, and empowered as people exhibiting the Spirit.

Implications and Applications

Lest it appear that NCF is a utopia of racial harmony, this congregation, like all congregations, has gone through periods of stress, disunity, and tension just like any other congregation. Several efforts to start church plants, satellite congregations, or daughter churches have suffered as a result of accusations that the parent church refused to use its resources to support the new churches. As the church moved from a black-white model of reconciliation to a more multiethnic vision, there were black members who felt pushed out or neglected. Moreover, it could certainly be argued that the discourse of spiritual power and even the moments of reversal present in congregational life do not only fail to challenge the racial worldview of the wider U.S. society, but, in certain respects, solidify it and encourage people to strongly identify themselves by racial categories (cf. Paris, this volume).

But in contrast to many examples, such as Bayt-Priest and Priest or McGlathery and Griffin (both this volume), the notable difference in how multiculturalist efforts have gone forward at NCF seems to as least partly reflect an awareness of white members that power and control (and a lack of access to it) is often at the heart of racial tension and division. Though I would not argue that all of the efforts noted here have been intentional, by attending to the symbolic aspects of control, and highlighting the spiritual equality of the body in practice and discourse, members of NCF are thinking differently and, in many ways, experiencing the transforming of their minds on matters of race, "normality," and the centrality of reconciliation to the gospel (Paris, this volume).

For Christians thinking through the practical considerations of how the example of NCF might inform their own church life or Christian walk, I would reemphasize several issues: first, because Christian religious life is driven by theological commitments, discussions of race must also be framed by those commitments. It should be clear to all Christians that social justice, responsibility to others' well being, and authentic community are at the heart of the gospel. Whether in the story of the Good Samaritan (Luke 10:25–37) or Peter's vision of Gentile salvation (Acts 10), the gospel clearly turns on the notion that reconciliation to God and loving human community are mutually inclusive and must work to erase social barriers between people (see Allen 1992, 97–101). What is notable in the case of NCF is not simply that it was able to fashion a compelling account of the need for addressing racial, economic, and political issues in the context of its religious life, but that these accounts always flowed, in discourse and practice, directly from their most basic theological commitments. That these theological commitments have not, historically, been those most associated with social and racial justice makes the point all the more poignant. Any theological tradition rooted in the life and person of Jesus Christ has, at its core, the same story of spiritual and human reconciliation. Articulating the consequences of that gospel for our lives in a racialized and often unjust society is the first step toward breaking down the structures and discourses of power that prop up privilege for some and disempower others.

Second, the church has the potential to become a countercultural community in which "normal" relations of social and cultural power can be inverted, subverted, and deconstructed through practical and symbolic means. The kind of hybrid congregation represented by NCF is, in terms of most people's church experience, a misfit. Although I think it is still quite possible to argue that cultural forms derived from traditional PCA (white) practice remain predominant and could (or should) be further de-emphasized at NCF, the overall practice and discourse of the church constantly reminds anyone who might come in that this is not your grandmother's Presbyterian church. Everyone had to be prepared to consistently engage the feelings of discomfort, awkwardness, and unfamiliarity inherent in the practices of NCF. This is, often, most unsettling for white members who have grown used to the idea that the PCA or Reformed Christianity generally, is, or should be, connected to familiar cultural forms. But for NCF, the uncomfortable and unsettling aspects of the religious practice and ritual life are not signs of a problem, but indications that the vision of a multicultural church is alive and well.

As important as discourse, language, practice, and ritual are, however, there are many issues in racialized America that remain thorny for any group, but particularly so for churches. Economic inequality, structural racism in the legal system, unjust immigration laws, and educational discrimination do not affect every person of color in the same way, but are never incidental to anyone thinking about race relations in the United States. Congregational life is affected by these realities and must address them as well through practical, symbolic, and political means. At NCF, some aspects of inequality remain despite the efforts of church members and leaders. The "session" (elder board) is overwhelmingly composed of upper-middle-class, highly educated, white men. Likewise, although some of the black and Latino leaders have either attended or begun to attend the denomination's national seminary (which happens to be in

St. Louis), economic, linguistic, and cultural barriers have made that transition difficult, to say the least. These are real issues that NCF must continue to work through if it is to continue to attract people like Jenna, who see white people six days a week and don't much feel like seeing them on Sunday too.

But Jenna would have been the first to say that she felt powerful at New City Fellowship. Jenna continued to work at NCF until April 11, 2002, when, at age fifty-two, she suddenly went home to be with the Lord. At her funeral, white, black, Latino, and Asian NCF members lined up at the microphone to testify to her presence and power as a leader in their church. They testified to ways she indicated that she knew that her experiences were valued and that she, as much as anyone else, could attest to the power of God in her life. Though she said she still found white people confusing, right up to the end, she, and other members of color, clearly believed that they had the power of God on their side too.

REFERENCES

Allen, Henry Lee. 1992. The sociology of prejudice: Problems and solutions. *Faculty Dialogue* (18): 91–111.
Cox, Harvey. 1995. *Fire from heaven: The rise of Pentecostal spirituality and the reshaping of religion in the twenty-first Century.* Reading, Mass.: Addison-Wesley.
DeYoung, Curtiss Paul, Michael Emerson, George Yancey, and Karen Chai Kim. 2003. *United by faith: The multiracial congregation as an answer to the problem of race.* London and New York: Oxford University Press.
Foucault, Michel. 1980. *Knowledge/power: Selected interviews and other writings 1972–1977,* ed. C. Gordon. New York: Pantheon.
———. 1984. Truth and power. In *The Foucault reader,* ed P. Rabinow. New York: Pantheon.
Geertz, Clifford. 1973. *The interpretation of cultures.* New York: Basic.
Gennep, Arnold van. 1909. *The rites of passage.* Translated by M. B. a. G. L. C. Vizedom. London: Routledge & Kegan Paul.
Grindal, Bruce T. 1982. The religious interpretation of experience in a rural black community. In *Holding on to the land and the Lord: Kinship, ritual, land tenure and social policy in the rural South,* ed. C. Stack and R. L. Hall. Athens: University of Georgia Press.
Habermas, Jurgen. 1981. Modernity versus postmodernity. *New German Critique* 22:3–14.
Horton, Michael S. 1992. Wanted: Apathetic Lutherans and Calvinists (no experience required). *Modern Reformation* 1:4–7.
Kuyper, Abraham. 1946. *The work of the Holy Spirit.* Trans. H. De Vries. Grand Rapids, Mich.: Eerdmans. (Orig. pub., 1900.)
Lincoln, Eric C., and Lawrence H. Mamiya. 1990. *The black church in the African-American experience.* Durham, N.C.: Duke University Press.
Poewe, Karla, and Irving Hexham. 1994. Charismatic churches in South Africa: A critique of criticisms and problems of bias. In *Charismatic Christianity as a global culture,* ed. K. Poewe. Columbia: University of South Carolina.
Robbins, Joel. 2001. Ritual communication and linguistic ideology: A reading and partial reformulation of Rappaport's theory of ritual. *Current Anthropology* 42(5): 591–614.

————. 2004. *Becoming sinners: Christianity and moral torment in a Papua New Guinean society*. Berkeley and Los Angeles: University of California Press.

Schieffelin, Bambi B., Katheryn Ann Woolard, and Paul V. Kroskrity, ed. 1998. *Language ideologies: Practice and theory*. Vol. 16 of *Oxford studies in anthropological linguistics*. London and New York: Oxford University Press.

Sernett, Milton. 1975. *Black Religion and American evangelicalism: White Protestants, plantation missions, and the flowering of Negro Christianity, 1787–1865*. Metuchen, NJ: Scarecrow.

Stromberg, Peter. 1986. *Symbols of community: The cultural system of a Swedish church*. Tucson: University of Arizona Press.

Thompson, Ernest Trice. 1973. *Presbyterians in the South*. 3 vols. Richmond, VA: John Knox.

Turner, Victor. 1969. *The ritual process: Structure and anti-structure*. Hawthore, NY: Aldine de Gruyter.

Washington, Raleigh, and Glen Kehrein. 1993. *Breaking down walls: A model for reconciliation in an age of racial strife*. Chicago: Moody.

Weber, Max. 1956. *The Protestant ethic and the spirit of capitalism*. Trans. T. Parsons. London: MacMillan.

Williams, Charles. 1982. The conversion ritual in a rural black Baptist church. In *Holding on to the land and the Lord: Kinship, ritual, land tenure and social policy in the rural South*, ed. C. Stack and R. L. Hall. Athens: University of Georgia Press.

Wolf, Eric. 1994. Facing power: Old insights, new questions. In *Reassessing cultural anthropology*, ed R. Borofsky. New York: McGraw Hill.

————. 1999. *Envisioning power: Ideologies of dominance and crisis*. Berkeley: University of California Press.

19

An Applied Research Strategy for Christian Organizations

Alvaro L. Nieves

Introduction

For many years I have taught a course titled "Race and Ethnic Relations." Invariably, before the end of the course, students reach a point of frustration with the immensity of the problems they are encountering. Some come to me and say, "The problems are so huge, what can one person do?" Many, for the first time, get a *global* picture of problems and issues of which they had previously been unaware, but are unable to translate this into *local* options and solutions. Before the end of the course they usually begin to see the need to "think globally and act locally." The church or local congregation is one logical place to develop and initiate plans to "act locally."

Church groups (youth and adult) with good intentions often want to help poor people. They work hard to mobilize financial resources and coordinate travel and activities to distant places inside and outside their own country. Scripture suggests an alternative: "When a foreigner resides with you in your land, you shall not do him wrong. The stranger who resides with you shall be to you as the native among you, and you shall love him as yourself; for you were once aliens in the land of Egypt; I am the Lord your God" (Lev 19:33–34 NASB). The world is at our doorstep, but we sometimes fail to realize the opportunities "to act locally" that this provides.

In order to act locally, however, it is necessary to acquire some tools to assess the local context and develop a set of possible options or solutions. An individual, local church, or parachurch organization cannot always afford to hire researchers. It is possible, however, to learn some research approaches that can be applied by an intelligent layperson. There are many different approaches and techniques of investigation. Some of these, such as *ethnographic, participant observer,* and *mailed questionnaires* can be time consuming and expensive and require skills that are not easily acquired. This chapter will introduce some ways in which a concerned congregation can initiate this process. It will focus on the use of data and information from *secondary* sources (i.e., previously collected data). Such data can be obtained more quickly, is less expensive, and often is of superior quality because it has been obtained by experts (such as the U.S. Census Bureau, U.S. Department of Labor, etc.) who specialize in data collection. It is possible to use these techniques to answer a variety of questions or address a number of problems in different situations. Here are some examples:

- A church is interested in expanding or a group perceives a possible need for a church in an area with an unchurched population. What, if any, are the significant racial and ethnic characteristics of this population?
- Not wanting to initiate a completely new church, an existing church realizes the neighborhood is changing and senses a change in needs to which they desire to minister. The changes may be reflected in race, ethnicity, immigrant status, age, family composition, and so forth.
- An existing majority-white congregation has attracted new attendees and some new racial and ethnic minority members. In the past, such persons and families didn't stay long. The church wants a diverse ministry. What can it do?
- A majority-white congregation is approached by a committee from a nearby minority congregation with concerns of possible injustice (racial profiling, housing discrimination, educational issues) in the community. How might the majority church respond, participate, and learn?
- Members of a congregation become aware that there appears to be an increase in the number of people speaking foreign languages in the local grocery store. They bring this to the attention of a Bible study group, Sunday school class, or church board. What is really happening or likely to happen and what are the implications for the church and future ministry?
- A congregation may be considering the possibility of expanding its ministries but is uncertain of the direction to take.

In its approach to research, this chapter is different from much of the predominant literature aimed at research in Christian settings (McIntosh and Rusbuldt 1983; Winegerd 1992; Easum 1996). Many of these authors were writing for the purpose of promoting church growth. The tendency was to focus on the characteristics of the existing congregation, and the needs and limitations that might surface in response to the desire to increase attendance, size, and so forth. The focus of the present chapter, consistent with the text as a whole, is to assist the student or practitioner to begin to ask larger questions about community and justice. It is my sincere belief that the Christian organization that demonstrates its commitment to social justice will find itself increasingly attractive to many it wishes to serve. I see the promotion of justice as a primary tool of evangelism in approaching a skeptical world: "And what does the LORD require of you? To do justice and to love kindness and to walk humbly with your God" (Mic 6:8 NRSV).

Depending on the problems or issues that have been defined or the goals of a proposed study, the source of appropriate data and information will vary. Researchers collect data on individuals across America, but this data can be grouped together (aggregated) in different ways. These different ways can increase our understanding of the similarities and differences of particular groups or categories: young or old, rich or poor, urban or rural, white or nonwhite. In addition, the data may be available in a form that permits analysis of a particular township, city, county, or metropolitan area (see figure 19.1). Congregations, of course, are located within small units like townships; larger units, like cities or counties; and possibly even larger units like metropolitan areas. Although some church leaders may not understand this, there is extensive data available for each of these geographic and political or administrative units. These data can be very helpful for those who seek to "act locally."

Clearly, all of this is an attempt to gain the knowledge necessary to act effectively, to determine needs, and to exercise stewardship in the expenditure of resources for the promotion of justice. In reality we are often impatient to begin, and study and research seem to do little more than delay us. At such times we must, once again, recall the words of Scripture: "It is not good to have zeal without knowledge" (Prov 19:2). Perhaps in this admonition we see the suggestion that, instead of rushing in, we first need to nurture and acquire careful understanding. Research provides one means to accomplish this.

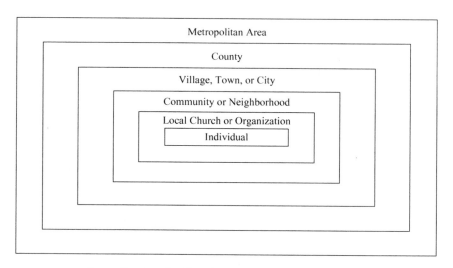

FIGURE 19.1. Expanding Levels of Analysis

An Applied Research Example

Aurora, Illinois, is a city in the far western suburbs of Chicago and has had a fairly large Latino population for many years. Drive around East Aurora and parts of West Aurora and you will see stores, restaurants, businesses, and churches with obvious Spanish names, and signs written in Spanish. Visit the schools, supermarket, and shopping malls and you will see Latinos and hear Spanish being spoken. A church and a parachurch organization with which my wife and I have been involved have been concerned with meeting some of the spiritual and social needs of Latino members of the community. What can we discover fairly easily about the city's Latino population, its characteristics, significance, and possible concerns?

Background Information

Almost any study will begin with the collection of background information (sometimes referred to as a review of the literature[1]). The purpose is to avoid costly mistakes that may have been made elsewhere or in the past. Research in this initial step may be focused on what work has been attempted to address the needs of similar populations elsewhere or in the local area of interest. It will assess the degree to which the programs have been able to alleviate problems or promote change in the desired direction.

The sources of such background information are many and varied. A logical starting point in our modern Information Age is the Internet. The use of one of the many search engines will facilitate an initial appraisal of possible information sources. Some may be general in nature and not particularly linked to the local area of interest. A search on one of the search engines linking terms such as *Hispanic* (*Latino*) and *churches* (or *religion*) might provide a reference to a valuable research summary "Hispanic Churches in American Public Life: Summary of Findings" (Espinosa et al. 2003). Such a source will provide some useful general information aggregated at the national level. Input Aurora, Illinois, to a search engine and you can obtain information from the Aurora, Illinois, detailed profile on population (142,990) including some breakdowns by race (white, non-Hispanic, 52.1%), ethnicity (Hispanic, 32.6%) and gender (72,020 men, 70,970 women). In addition, the number of new houses (1,067) and their average cost ($112,000) is provided.

Using the Internet requires a degree of cautious skepticism since there is a great deal of variation in the quality and accuracy of information available. Discerning the reliability, validity, and appropriateness of particular Internet information and sources may prove tricky. One good strategy is to assess whether the information being viewed would be publicly available if it depended on normal publication. If not, the information may still be useful, but should be approached more cautiously.

Local sources of information may also be available through recent reports developed or commissioned by business, government, social and religious organizations in your area. Agencies and organizations such as United Way, city planning departments, chambers of commerce, and church denominational entities are possible sources of information. Population data about the community of interest are available from the U.S. Census Bureau and information on obtaining and using such data will be illustrated below.

Goals, Needs, and Objectives

In many ways, what I am really concerned with is applying a variety of social science techniques to address organizational or policy-type questions. As suggested by Mayer and Greenwood (1980), the *determination of goals* (8) is the first step in the policymaking process and is tied directly to a *needs assessment* and the *specification of objectives*. Goals are tied to the values of the organization and reflect fairly broad purposes being promoted. The notion of easing social problems in a community, for example, is very broad since it can be addressed at many different levels and within different contexts. In the context of this chapter a broad goal might be expressed as the desire to enhance the role of a local church or organization in the promotion of social justice.

Needs assessment implies the need for research. Research, broadly viewed, is simply a procedure to determine the relevant facts involved in particular social problems contexts. Consistent with the goal of the promotion of social justice stated above, needs assessment might involve the attempt to uncover areas in which injustice or the potential for injustice exists. The question to be considered here may be an attempt to discover the degree to which a particular condition departs from an ideal or the extent or intensity of an observed or perceived problem. For example, is there a perceived need for educational enhancement programs? How might the problem or need be characterized? What are the unique characteristics such as the modal (most frequently occurring) level of education, or English-language proficiency in the target population? What services (GED, ESL, citizenship classes) are presently available? How far away are similar services from the target area of interest? The third step in the process involves the *specification of objectives*. This refers to the "setting of specific targets that can be expressed in operational, usually quantitative terms" (Mayer and Greenwood 1980).

These authors further suggest that this step includes the identification of:

1. the condition to be remedied;
2. a finite population in which the condition exists;
3. a time frame in which change is to occur; and
4. the amount and direction of change sought.

Although it can be treated at a separate stage, identification of possible constraints and limitations may also be included here (Mayer and Greenwood 1980). The assessment of such limitations may be restricted to the organization conducting the assessment. It may also reflect those seen as community characteristics involving issues such as employment, tax base, educational levels, industrial development, and so on. These will often be quite specific to the particular community in which the assessment is being conducted.

Information Gathering and Data Resources

In this modern era we are often inundated with information. This can be both a blessing and a curse. Having access to too much information and data can make the choices on what data to use all the more difficult. Too much data, some of which is unnecessary, can also slow the analysis and delay conclusions and important decisions. The answers lie in defining the question and problem statement well, selecting appropriate existing (secondary) data, and utilizing appropriate techniques for primary data collection.

In the next step, information is sought on the specific population of interest within the local target area. The problem of concern may involve children, women of childbearing age, high school dropouts, the elderly, recent immigrants, and so on. Whatever the category, an effort must be made to investigate and document the characteristics of the relevant population. Demographic characteristics will be important in establishing the nature and extent of the problem or issue. Such characteristics may include but are not limited to the size of the population within a particular geographic area, and the age and gender distribution of the population of interest. Because of our target population, we will also want information about the racial and ethnic composition as well as educational, economic, health, and language usage characteristics of the subpopulation.

U.S. BUREAU OF THE CENSUS. To obtain some of this information, a number of different and additional sources are important and useful. Some of these are available on the Internet. Among them is the site for the U.S. Census Bureau that may be found at www.census.gov. The Census Bureau is the government agency responsible for the decennial (every ten years) population census, which is required by the Constitution of the United States. Some of the more aggregated data and information are available fairly soon after the census is completed. The census makes the more detailed (disaggregated) data available as it is tabulated. This more disaggregated data is what local planners and policymakers are most interested in.[2]

Among documents generated by the U.S. Census Bureau, a number relate to each state's population. These include statistics about different jurisdictions within each state such as metropolitan areas, counties, cities and other places. Information is also available for geographic areas disaggregated below the level of administrative units in what the Bureau refers to as block groups and census tracts. These latter units are at a level that often proves most useful for application at the local level.

The U.S. Census Bureau provides information on population structure that includes the size of a population in a given area, how that population is distributed geographically, and its composition or makeup. It also provides information on what might be referred to as demographic processes such as fertility (births), mortality (deaths), and migration (movement of people in and out of a given area). Additionally, social, economic, and other descriptive information is provided, which can prove very useful.

In addition to the decennial census, other data are provided under the title of *Current Population Survey (CPS)*. These are also available from libraries and through the Internet. The Bureau's Internet site provides access to special reports and news releases that may also prove useful to the researcher. Also available in hard copy and digital form are the *County and City Data Books*, which provide data from the censuses of population, housing, governments, and manufacturing.

In the last ten years, a new breed of analysis software, based on the use of geographic units of analysis, has emerged and is more readily available. This software comes under the heading of GIS or Geographic Information Systems. The strength of GIS lies in its ability to present descriptive statistical data in graphical form that relates to geographic units such as states, counties, municipalities, census tracts, and block groups. Some of these programs[3] can be quite complex and may require assistance beyond the local researcher's ability. Such assistance may be available from universities and county extension agents. Among its other products, the U.S. Census Bureau, in cooperation with other government agencies, has made LandView[4] (now in its fifth generation) a quasi-GIS program (more like an electronic atlas), available. It cannot do all that the more sophisticated GIS programs can do, but it has the advantage of providing a variety of linked data that can be displayed geographically. In addition, it is relatively inexpensive and may also be available for use in libraries that serve as government document repositories.

ADVANTAGES AND DISADVANTAGES OF CENSUS DATA.   There are both advantages and disadvantages to the use of census data. Among the advantages are the relatively low cost of obtaining it (provided the researcher has access to the Internet or local libraries), the great variety of information available, and the variety of media on which it is published (hard copy, Internet, CD, or DVD). Perhaps the principal disadvantage to the local researcher is that local community data can be limited, and is sometimes not particularly current. A second disadvantage is that the volume of data available can quickly become overwhelming. It demands a great deal of discipline to select only the data that are relevant to the problem at hand.

VITAL STATISTICS.   Vital statistics are an additional source of public information that is similar to yet differs from census data. This information is put together from birth record information, death certificates, marriage licenses, divorce decrees, and, sometimes, health records (such as the occurrence of sexually transmitted diseases, gunshot wounds, and other medical conditions that physicians and hospitals must report).

Census and vital statistics data can be used in the local context in a variety of ways. These data can provide information about population growth and decline. They can also indicate whether growth and decline are due to fertility and mortality, or migration. These data can also be useful in examining the nature of households in the community, answering some questions about whether there are more childless couples, single-parent households, multifamily units, and so on. In addition, income information, including poverty-level increases or decreases and possible reasons for this, may also prove useful to the researcher or organization.

ADDITIONAL SOURCES OF INFORMATION Although the U.S. Census Bureau and vital statistics may be the best-known source of community-level statistics, the local researcher should not neglect other possibilities in his or her community. Among these are public libraries, governmental entities (especially city planning, and regional planning commissions), county extension offices (often tied to universities and then with possible research resources of their own), chambers of commerce (in some places there may be more than one—for example, a county chamber, a city chamber, and sometimes an ethnic one such as the Hispanic Chamber of Commerce), United Way, and other community welfare agencies that may also have conducted relevant research. In addition to these fairly obvious sources don't neglect the less obvious such as specific college or university departments (which may also serve as a possible source of researchers or research assistants as well as providing computing resources), financial institutions (banks, loan companies, credit unions) and utility companies (electric, gas, telephone). Police departments, fire departments, hospitals, and civic organizations (including ministerial associations) may also prove to be sources of information or, at the very least, of suggestions on who is doing or has done what research in the interest of the community.

An Example of the Use of Census Data

For this example let's return to Aurora, Illinois. While the more general (national) information gleaned about Latinos and the summary information from the Aurora profile are interesting, we need more specific information on our target area (Aurora, Illinois).

The most readily available source of data is the U.S. Census Bureau. Since the Internet is the speediest way to acquire census data, I will illustrate with this source of data. After logging on and launching whatever Web browser you are familiar with (e.g., Netscape, Microsoft Internet Explorer), type in the URL http://www.census.gov. You will be given a number of follow-on options. On the left side of the page click on "American FactFinder," highlight "About the Data" and click on "Table and Map Formats." In the "Quick Tables" section, click on "Fact Sheet." In the next screen, at the upper right window, labeled "city/town/county or zip," type in "Aurora city," and then select Illinois in the "State" window's pull-down menu and click on "Go." On the next screen the "Census Demographic Profile Highlights" will appear. The first three sections will provide population numbers and percent for Aurora city by gender, age, race, and Hispanic/Latino ethinicity.

TABLE 19.1. Population by Race and Hispanic/Latino for Aurora City and U.S.

General Characteristics	Number	Percent	U.S.
Total population	142,990		
Male	72,020	50.4	49.1%
Female	70,970	49.6	50.9%
Median age (years)	29.3	(×)	35.3
Under 5 years	15,095	10.6	6.8%
18 years and over	97,625	68.3	74.3%
65 years and over	8,940	6.3	12.4%
One race	138,847	97.1	97.6%
White	97,340	68.1	75.1%
Black or African American	15,817	11.1	12.3%
American Indian and Alaska Native	511	0.4	0.9%
Asian	4,370	3.1	3.6%
Native Hawaiian and Other Pacific Islander	47	0.0	0.1%
Some other race	20,762	14.5	5.5
Two or more races	4,143	2.9	2.4%
Hispanic or Latino (of any race)	46,557	32.6	12.5%

Note that in this table there is a total for Aurora, but since Aurora is geographically large and overlaps four different counties, separate population figures are given for the portion of Aurora in each county. This is important since if one were to calculate the percentage of Latinos in Aurora (46,557 /142,990) one would obtain a value of 32.5%. For some additional information click on the "map" link in the next to last column of the table at the line labeled "Hispanic or Latino." This links to a map on which census tracts are shown that are color coded by categories of percent Hispanic. The map legend reveals that percent Hispanic can vary from a low of 4.2% to a high of 85.6%. Clicking on a census tract within the map provides information for that specific census tract. The information includes the tract number, the percent Hispanic and, and the number of persons represented in the tract.

The initial map is at a scale representing a distance of twenty miles across. The user can change this by clicking on the "zoom" selection bars at the top of the map window. The third bar from the right represents a distance of 2.8 miles across. The dark green area represents census tract 8534. Clicking on this census tract provides the information that this tract is 85.6 Hispanic with a population of 7,784 persons. This feature is a relatively easy way to obtain more detailed census tract information. Fortunately, the census provides additional useful information.

Go back to the main section of American FactFinder™ by clicking *main* in the banner at the top of the page. Highlight the "Data Sets" tab at the left side of the screen and click on the "Decennial Census" link that is revealed. Click the first radio button for "Census 2000 Summary File 1 (SF–1)" 100%

data and then on the "Reference Maps" link. The next page will be a map of the United States on which you click the state of interest, Illinois. On this page there are two options. You can click a location on the map of Illinois you know to be close to the place (city, town, village) you are interested in or you may click on "A street address or zip code" at the left on the screen and write in an address or a zip code close to the location of interest. Don't worry about great accuracy since you will be able to move around the map as needed. Figure 2 below is an example of such a map at the street level. The larger numbers (8533, 8534, 8536, 8537, 8541 and 8543) represent census tracts in the central area of Aurora.

Now go back to the "Main" page of American FactFinder™, highlight "data sets," click on "decennial census," select "Census 2000 Summary File 1 (SF1)," and click "Quick Tables." Using the pull-down window that allows the selection of geographic type select "Census Tract," followed by "State, County." Next select one or more geographic areas (i.e., the census tracts) and click "next." Then select one or more tables, for example, DP-1, Profile of General Demographic Characteristics. The quick table produced will provide such information as sex and age, Hispanic or Latino and race, and owner versus renter-occupied housing.

Although we are gaining some insights into the nature of the population by census tract, there is more information that can be useful in planning to serve a particular target area. Going back to the "Main" page of the American FactFinder™, we go to "Data Sets" and select "Decennial Census," click on the radio button for the "Census 2000 SF" and click on "Geographic Comparison Tables." At this point we select a geographic type (county), followed by a state (Illinois), and the geographic area (Kane County). Under the "Table" format, select "census tract," and click on "Next." In the next table we are given a choice of a number of tables. Select GCT–P11 and click on "Show Result." Scrolling down the page we can locate the census tracts that interest us. The results may be seen in table 19.2.

Examining a portion of the resulting table above reveals some interesting characteristics of the population located in the area of interest. For example, it reveals that in three of the census tracts (8533 through 8535) 61, 83, and 73 percent of the population five years and older speak a language other than English at home. In addition, 28, 44, and 38 percent of those age twenty-five years old and older have less than a ninth-grade education.

The high percentage of Hispanics in the area suggests that the language being spoken is likely Spanish and the level of education suggests that there may well be a literacy problem that goes beyond language. The implications of such initial findings are many. It probably means that if you wish to target this area with services, advertising must be undertaken in both English and Spanish. Using radio or television ads will probably necessitate using Spanish language media. Program selection or consideration to promote development in the area should probably include consideration of English classes, possibly GED classes, and perhaps health education programs in Spanish (which might, for example, promote appropriate inoculations of children).

ulation 5 years and ler—Percent who ak a language other n English at home — And speak English less than "very well"	Population enrolled in elementary or high school— Percent in private school	Population 16 to 19 years— Percent not enrolled in school and not a high school graduate	Population 18 to 24 years—Percent enrolled in college or graduate school	Population 25 years and older		
				Percent with less than a 9th grade education	Percent high school graduate or higher	Percent w bachelor's degree or higher
14.4	11.7	15.9	24.6	9.7	80.2	27.7
9.4	15.0	14.7	26.4	6.1	84.2	21.8
6.9	9.9	15.7	18.3	7.1	83.8	25.7
12.9	15.2	14.0	30.6	12.8	65.1	17.2
26.3	10.4	36.7	12.9	17.8	65.5	11.3
36.3	17.7	36.5	10.8	28.2	53.2	8.0
58.4	7.4	43.1	9.2	43.5	31.4	2.0
40.6	7.6	32.3	7.4	37.6	39.6	2.5
48.6	6.1	41.7	8.3	40.0	36.2	3.3
27.0	0.0	40.0	0.0	8.7	55.5	15.8
25.1	14.6	30.8	9.0	9.7	65.7	12.4
4.5	28.9	2.9	65.8	2.9	89.3	43.0
4.2	18.9	9.6	28.6	3.7	90.8	40.2

ple except in P3, P4, H3, and H4. For information on confidentiality protection, sampling
and definitions see http://factfinder.census.gov/home/en/datanotes/expsf3.htm.

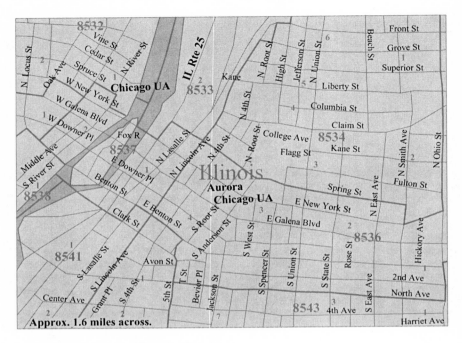

FIGURE 19.2. Census Tracts in Target Area

There is a great deal more data available from the U.S. Census Bureau that can be tied to census tracts or even smaller geographic units called block groups. The main idea here is to suggest that if you wish to develop programs (church, economic, educational, etc.) you need not do so without adequate information. This chapter has suggested a number of ways that data and information can be obtained and utilized, but there are many more. Do not be afraid to explore the census Web site. You will find it increasingly useful as you become more familiar with it.

As just one example, in Aurora, it was this combination of information and data that led the churches and parachurch organization to establish and make available a number of different programs. Several classes for teaching English as a second language (ESL) are ongoing. A computer club provides youngsters with afterschool tutoring in English, math, and social studies (computer games serve as rewards). There is also a summer program, vacation Bible school, midweek feeding and character-building opportunities, and citizenship classes. In addition, occasional programs to provide health, education, and financial affairs tutoring for parents have been developed in cooperation with various community resources (city, county, and community college).

The basis for these was the ability to identify needs through available data. We must be prepared if we are going to be effective. We must also remember that God honors and rewards adequate and effective preparation. Good planning is, after all, part of good stewardship (Luke 14:28).

NOTES

    1. The *review of the literature*, another common idea in research, is simply an examination and acknowledgment of related research. It can help to avoid errors and unnecessary repetition of prior work and can be thought of as *strategic reading*.
    2. Some materials are available in hard copy (bound volumes) from the Superintendent of Documents, U.S. Government Printing Office, Washington, D.C. 20402. These volumes are also available at some public libraries but are more likely to be found at college and university libraries that are designated as repositories or partial repositories for government documents. Since the development of more modern decentralized computing, much information is also available from the U.S. Census Bureau on CD-ROM. In addition, a visit to the Census Bureau's Web site (www.census .gov) provides access to a variety of data and tools including American FactFinder™, which will be introduced later in this chapter.
    3. Among the more sophisticated are *Arc View™*, *Atlas-GIS™*, and *Map-Info™*.
    4. Information about LandView™ can be found at www.census.gov and at www.rtk.net.

REFERENCES

Easum, W. M. 1996. *The complete ministry audit*. Nashville, TN: Abingdon.
Espinosa, Gastón, Virgilio Elizonda, Jesse Miranda. 2003. *Hispanic churches in American public life: Summary of findings*. Nortre Dame, IN: Institute for Latino Studies.
Mayer, R. R. and E. Greenwood. 1980. *The design of social policy research*. Englewood Cliffs, NJ: Prentice Hall.
McIntosh, D. and R. E. Rusbuldt. 1983. *Planning growth in your church*. Valley Forge, PA: Judson.
Winegerd, R. A. 1992. *The dawn research handbook*. Colorado Springs, CO: Dawn Ministries.

Conclusion

Robert J. Priest and Alvaro L. Nieves

While Christians claim "citizenship in heaven" (Phil 3:20 NIV), we live "on this side of heaven" where we find ourselves enmeshed in realities that are anything but heavenly. And yet our prayer, "thy will be done on earth as it is in heaven," commits us to strive for transformed realities even here on earth. Our commitment is double-sided. First we resist conformity to sinful patterns of this world, a resistance that requires analysis and diagnosis of what those patterns are. Second, we strive for transformation and renewal. This again requires a clear vision both of God's ideals and of how, in practical terms, such ideals must be pursued. It is this double-sided commitment that our book articulates.

Do Not Conform to the Pattern of This World (Rom 12:2)

This book begins with Jenell Paris pointing out that Christians are affected by their culture, by the "pattern of this world" (Rom 12:2 NIV), and that they therefore need an active and ongoing process of renewal and transformation. Only through renewal of mind will Christians be able to understand the nature of the transformations that are needed. That is, one task we have set ourselves in this book involves diagnosing and analyzing the nature of racial and ethnic problems in our churches, our society, and our world.

Racial constructs are part of the "pattern of this world" (Rom 12:2) that must be addressed if we are to break free of inappropriate "conformity" to worldly patterns (Paris). Understanding racial constructs involves careful assessment of their scientific merit, or lack of merit (Meneses). Other parts of the assessment involve exploring

324   THIS SIDE OF HEAVEN

the historical processes through which racial categories were constructed and used (Paris, Meneses, Hiebert, Thomas and Sweeney), exploring the variability of racial categories employed in different times and places (Paris, Meneses, Pozzi), and contrasting racial categories with social categories found in the Bible (Tiénou, Pao).

The emergence of the idea that humanity was composed of natural and separate subdivisions (akin to subspecies) and that there are inherent differences in socially relevant abilities and characteristics between these biologically based human types, has no justification in Scripture. In some senses this eighteenth-century construction of race "was one aspect of the secularization of Western society" (Jordan 1968, 217). As "a prototypically 'modern' form of identity" race can be thought of as "the illegitimate child of secular humanism and scientific rationality, dark underbelly of Enlightenment universalism, and ideological grease on the wheels of industrial capital" (Goldschmidt 2004, 14).

And yet Euro-American Christians have clearly, as often as not, "conformed" to such a "pattern of the world" (Rom 12:2); indeed, they have sometimes helped to construct the pattern. Historically, Christians have alternated between resisting such racialized ideologies and helping to construct and sustain the underpinnings of our racialized society (Paris, Hiebert, Thomas and Sweeney). For example, George Whitefield, sometimes thought of as the father of American evangelicalism, encouraged the evangelism of slaves, but also lobbied for the legalization of slavery in Georgia, legalization that then allowed him to own slaves that could labor to support his orphanage (Emerson and Smith 2000, 23–25). This represents an extreme case of a not uncommon pattern of accommodation and even support for black slavery among many Christians prior to the Civil War (Thomas and Sweeney). Whole denominations were birthed—either in opposition to slavery or in support of it (see appendix 1). In the early decades of the twentieth century, mainline Protestant liberals were at the forefront of the eugenics movement, a movement largely rejected by more theologically conservative Christians (Rosen 2004). On the other hand, the civil rights movement of the 1960s was strongly supported by mainline Protestants, with minimal support by evangelicals.

When Christians are "conformed" to the racial pattern of this world, rather than allowing Scripture to correct them, they sometimes subvert the text into ratifying their own prejudices. The *Scofield Reference Bible* (1909, 1917), for example, provided notes to help readers interpret biblical references to Japheth and Ham (Gen 9:25–27) through the lens of Euro-American racial ideologies. An elliptical biblical reference to Japheth being "extended" or "enlarged" (v. 27) is explained as follows: "Government, science, and art, speaking broadly, are and have been Japhetic, so that history is the indisputable record of the exact fulfillment of these declarations." That is, Scofield claimed science and civilization for "the Japhetic races" (Europeans)—which this text purportedly predicted. By contrast, the biblical reference to Canaan's descendants (v. 25)—who of course have nothing to do with Africa or any racial category that an African would fit into—is reframed by Scofield as a prediction about Ham's descendants, which in Scofield's day are understood to be African. Scofield wrote, "A prophetic declaration is made that from Ham will descend an inferior and servile posterity." That is, through a single sentence that summarizes racist opinion about the rightful social place of Africans while seemingly grounding it in the biblical text (although actually changing the referent in the text), Scofield sanctified early twentieth-century racist ideas as biblical and God-given. Someone whose culture already has taught them to believe in the superiority of whites and inferiority of blacks can now open his Bible and find his racial prejudices confirmed as divinely approved truth. This study Bible, both in English and in translation, has sold millions, and has been distributed to pastors around the world. When African pastors search this Scripture for references to their ancestry, it is this note that tells them who they are: "an inferior and servile posterity."

Of course, the *Scofield Reference Bible* simply illustrates a widespread nine-teenth-and early twentieth-century pattern of reading modern racial ideologies back into one's biblical interpretation, something done by scholars as diverse as Harper and Driver (Goldenberg 2003, 22), Jeremias (Tiénou), or Keil and Delitzsch (Hays 2003, 53–54)—scholars who thus codified racial ideologies in the very apparatus used by pastors, theologians, and missionaries to understand the biblical text. A particularly clear example of this is seen in the way scholars treated biblical passages on African Cush (see excellent treatments of this by Goldenberg 2003; Hays 2003; Yamauchi 2004). Tiénou demonstrates in his chapter that a similar process occurred with racialized readings of texts concerning the Samaritans. In any case, many of these older works continue to be printed and reprinted—and the arguments and assumptions that they make are incorporated into more recent commentaries. That is, Scofield, Harper, Driver, Jeremias, or Keil and Delitzsch encoded racial assumptions of their day into their authoritative guides depended on by millions of Christians wishing to understand and teach the Scriptures. This helped to ensure that Christians themselves would be the ongoing "carriers" of such racialized ideologies.

Kang's chapter highlights the idea that Euro-American interpretations of the biblical text will sometimes be ethnocentric and self-serving, such as when New England Puritans and South African Boers identified themselves with "the children of Israel," the land they were going to as "the promised land," and the people already living there as the "Canaanites." Kang points out that when American Indians become part of the hermeneutical community, such interpretations framing them as Canaanites are more likely, immediately, to be recognized as problematic. He calls for a broadening of the hermeneutical community beyond the Euro-American, claiming this will move us toward a more balanced and faithful understanding and proclamation of the biblical text. It is precisely this broadening of the hermeneutical community, and subsequent challenges to and revisions of "received interpretations," that our own book illustrates. Tiénou, for example, helps Euro-Americans to see the problematic racial assumptions and categories embedded in received interpretations of (and homilies on) Samaritans as "racial half-breeds."

As Paris and Meneses demonstrate, the very biological construct of "race"—and the extensive effort to place all people into various racial and color categories—has largely been abandoned by mainstream anthropologists. Yet Christian academics, if they do not become conversant with recent scholarship on these matters, may easily assume and propagate old racial typologies and categories, now discredited. For example, in an otherwise impressive *World Christian Encyclopedia* (Barrett et. al. 2001), every ethnic group around the world is racially categorized under one of five racial headings: Australoid (Archaic White or Proto-Caucasoid), Capoid (Archaic African), Caucasian (Caucasoid), Mongolian (Mongoloid), Negroid (Negro). Furthermore, every group has its skin color listed, under one of twenty possible color combinations: black, brown, grey, red, yellow, white, black/brown, brown/black, brown/tan, grey/black, grey/brown, grey/yellow, red/white, tan/brown, tan/white, white/yellow, yellow/black, yellow/red, yellow/tan, yellow/white. Any one of these colors by themselves (red for American Indians, yellow for Chinese, white for Europeans, black for Africans), in objective terms, distorts what skin color involves. The idea that all twenty of the above gradations of skin color are distinguishable as descriptive of specific groups is pure illusion. It is hard to escape the thought that the authors, in the sheer joy of counting and listing, have incorporated other people's racial categories and lists with little attention to their ideological underpinnings, which Paris reminds us, are a part of the racialized "pattern of this world." And yet when authoritative reference works such as Barrett's et. al. (2001) incorporate such racial ideologies, they accommodate, legitimate, and encourage their readers to become "carriers" of such ideologies.

The arena of popular and "folk" Christian practices and discourses (rather than scholarly ones only) also merits attention. For more than a century, and around the world, evangelical Christians have used the "Wordless Book" to explain the gospel—a book with colored pages, "gold" representing the glories of heaven, "black" representing sin, "red" representing the blood of Christ, "white" representing purity, and "green" representing growth in the Christian life. This book (or strings of colored beads, or colored fingers on a hand) has been widely used in children's ministries, and by cross-cultural missionaries, to explain the gospel. Listeners are taught that their hearts are black, and invited to consider the preferable condition of whiteness. The Wordless Book Song elaborates the imagery: "My heart was black with sin, until the Savior came in. His precious blood, I know, has washed me white as snow." That is, Christians have often articulated a color binary (black versus white) to symbolize the moral binary of good versus evil: black being evil; white, good. The problem, of course, is that Christians have elaborated such symbolism in social contexts where human "racial" identities have sometimes been constructed around the same oppositional color pair: black and white. In social worlds where black and white are ways of identifying people by skin color, and where those who are "black" were historically stigmatized, any invitation to reflect on the benefits of whiteness over blackness (as symbols of good and evil) too easily spills over into and contributes to the stigmatization and subordination of those who are "black."

Contemporary racial identities diverge fundamentally from biblical ones. The peoples of Scripture did not identify themselves as "white" to be contrasted with those who were "black." While Barrett's et al. (2001, 27) encyclopedia categorizes Jews as "Caucasian" with "tan/white" skin, the Bible does not refer to Jews in this way. When color language is applied to skin color in Scripture, we find white being associated with diseased skin, black being neutrally descriptive or sometimes descriptive of diseased unhealthy skin, and "red" (translated "ruddy") being the only color term applied positively to the color of people's skin (see 1 Sam 16:12; 17:42; Song 5:1; Lam 4:7; for a fuller exploration of skin color in biblical and postbiblical times, see Goldenberg 2003). Even here, the color is not used as part of group identity. Our own practice of using black and white as core and contrasting identities for contemporary people has no equivalent in Scripture. Ours is a fundamentally different cultural setting in which to consider the implications of the symbols that we use in our religious discourses.

If the binary opposition contrasting black and white were biblical, that might be one thing. In fact, it is not. Sometimes the Bible does contrast light and darkness, imagery tied not to color but to vision; those in darkness cannot see, while those in the light see and understand. Sometimes the Bible also contrasts red/scarlet and white (Isa 1:18). But nowhere in Scripture does one find the color binary of black versus white as a symbol of evil versus good. Such postbiblical European imagery was not learned from Scripture.

That is, many Euro-American Christians employ a contextually problematic use of color imagery in their religious discourses, doubtless wrongly thinking they are simply being biblical. Given the racial color symbolism of our contemporary world, such usage inadvertently contributes to existing racialized hierarchies and stigmas.

In short, Christians must not dissociate themselves from the evils of our racialized world, assuming that somehow these problems are "the world's" problems, for which the church, with its discursive practices, bears no responsibility. Even if it were true (and it is not) that Christians have been innocent of contributing to the sin, hatred, pain, and suffering associated with our racially and ethnically divided world, the biblical ethical vision of "love for neighbor" would still require that we make such concerns central.

But Be Transformed by the Renewing of Your Mind (Rom 12:2)

When Christian beliefs and discourses are subverted by "the pattern of this world," they contribute to the problems of our racialized world. But when they are appropriately transformed by the biblical text, living in the light of its vision, the outcomes are potentially very different. Christian discourses are potentially profoundly relevant to the world of ethnic and racial ideologies, prejudices, struggles with stigma, resentments, aggressions, boundaries, and hierarchies of wealth, class, and power. Through the doctrine of creation Christians affirm that we have shared origins and shared identity: we are created in the very image of God. In Christian discourses of sin we acquire a vocabulary for speaking of specific moral evils inflicted on those who are vulnerable, but we also acquire a recognition of a common sinfulness from which no person or group is exempt. We acquire self-understandings that require each to direct judgments of sin and failure against the self—and not merely the other. That is, we learn to discover and confess our own sin and failure, and to repent. Through Christian discourses we learn that the cross is both the basis of our own salvation, and the prescriptive model for our own sacrificial engagement with others. When we are reconciled to God, we join a new community—the church—defined by faith in Christ, rather than by genealogy, ethnicity, or race (Gal 3:26–28). Furthermore, we become agents of reconciliation (2 Cor 5:17–20). Members of the new community are reminded that external and worldly hierarchies and boundaries are to be dissolved, and that the critical evidence of membership is "love one for another," and especially love exercised on behalf of those in need. In the Lord's Prayer, this community repeats the refrain, "Thy will be done on earth as it is in heaven," a prayer that commits those who pray to seeking God's will on earth. Finally a future is envisioned in which people of every linguistic and ethnic group gather in unity around the throne of God (Rev 7:9–10).

When read correctly, Scripture calls us to deep and active intentional love commitments. Sometimes, however, Christians have been satisfied with a more limited ethical ideal, one involving mere avoidance of active conscious evil acts. When confronted with the problems of our racialized world, some will imagine that what is at stake is primarily refraining from conscious, willful, and perverse acts. Those who do refrain from these transgressions may comfortably absolve themselves of responsibility for racial problems. In Jesus' story of the Good Samaritan (Luke 10:25–37) there is, of course, the conscious willful evil of thieves who beat up and steal from a traveler. But the judgment in this story is directed, rather, against good and religious people, who would never actively beat up and steal from another, but who fail to exemplify God's ideal of active love toward someone in need. Only the Samaritan in the story exemplifies this ideal. In the context of warning of a coming final judgment, Jesus discusses the economically poor, immigrant strangers, the sick, and the incarcerated and then says in Matthew 25:45, "whatever you did *not* do for one of the least of these, you did *not* do for me." That is, Jesus directs moral judgment against those whose only sin is that of omission.

It is this distinction between sins of commission and sins of omission that Martin Luther King was making in his letter from a Birmingham jail when he questioned which was the greater problem, "hateful words and actions of the bad people" or "the appalling silence of the good people." Hateful words and actions (lynchings, barring a black child from entry into a white school, repeating racial jokes and slurs intended to demean others) are one sort of sin. But white Christian failure to act against lynch mobs, white silence in the presence of racial slurs, and white failures to actively support black Americans as equal members of society—these too, are sins.

At the dawn of the twenty-first century, ethnic diversity is a central part of our world and is accompanied by racial and ethnic ideologies, prejudices, hatreds, boundaries, violence, suffering, and hierarchies of wealth and power. In engaging such realities, this book has not adopted a minimalist ethic calling merely for avoidance of willful conscious racist action. Rather, it is grounded in the view that love of God is exemplified in active love for others. Repeatedly, the Bible says to "love your neighbor as yourself" (Lev 19:18; Matt 19:19; 22:39; Mark 12:31; Luke 10:27; Rom 13:9; Gal 5:14; Jas 2:8). Jesus' insistence on the interethnic dimensions of this love in his story of "the Good Samaritan" simply expresses what Leviticus 19:33–34 (TNIV) had already applied to the immigrant stranger: "When foreigners reside among you in your land, do not mistreat them. The foreigners residing among you must be treated as your native-born. *Love them as yourself*, for you were foreigners in Egypt. I am the Lord your God." Jesus models this behavior, crossing gender and ethnic lines, in his encounter with the Samaritan woman (John 4:4–27).

If racial failures only involved rational conscious choices to commit evil acts, then perhaps a single crisis of repentance would permanently resolve the problem. But our racialized world is grounded in patterns that are not fully understood, with failures often unconscious, habitual, and out of our awareness. Furthermore, the resolution of racial and ethnic problems involves adjusting whole institutionalized patterns sustained by many people. When what is called for is ongoing and continual acts of sacrificial love, then a single point-action individualistic "fix" will not work. While crisis moments of repentance or forgiveness are needed, it is the active and sustained temporal commitments that also need attention.

Biblical mandates, as well as the historical patterns of racial sin in America, and the contemporary challenges of a racially and ethnically diverse nation, require that we direct great energy and effort to the implications and goal of interethnically loving our neighbors, whether they are African, American Indian, Latino, Asian, or European in origin.

Living out such an ethic requires intentionality, the value of which is sometimes not sufficiently appreciated. For more than a century, social scientists analyzed societal patterns using concepts such as "social structure," "culture," "social class," "globalization," "imperialism," "colonialism," or "capitalism." These macrostructures and macroprocesses were often portrayed as beyond human agency. Only more recently have social scientists rediscovered the importance of human actions and intentionality in either the creation, maintenance, or transformation of social and cultural patterns, or all of these. Human consciousness and intentional action are prime movers in social reform.

In the chapter on Columbia Bible College (R. Priest) one can see the larger macro-segregationist structures, but also the significance of individual action. Even the college president had constraints on what he could do, and yet even students could take action, which—fitted together with the actions of others—cumulatively helped bring about change in racialized patterns of life.

Ordinary people, distributed throughout society as mothers and fathers, Sunday school teachers and Cub Scout dads, real estate agents and personnel directors, loan officers and philanthropists, artists and musicians, counselors and journalists, pastors and police, scholars and nurses, each have important arenas in which significant agency is possible.

In this book we encourage readers to conduct their lives with a conscious and sustained intention to bring reconciliation and healing into the very places characterized by racial discord and pain. It is possible for people working together to achieve meaningful change as a result of conscious and prayerful intentionality sustained over time.

Of course, good intentions must be undergirded by "renewed minds" and by appropriate knowledge and understanding. While this book has stressed the important centrality of biblical and theological understandings (Paris, Hiebert, Tiénou, Pao, Bacote, Kang), it has also stressed other sorts of understandings—understandings of history (Paris, Thomas and Sweeney, R. Priest, appendix 1), understandings of cultural dynamics (Jindra, Pozzi, McNeil and Pozzi, Priest and Priest, K. Priest, Howell, Cha), understandings of racial hierarchy and power (Paris, Meneses, McGlathery and Griffin, R. Priest, Howell), knowledge of demographic realities (Nieves), and knowledge of the history, culture, heritage, or even language of specific ethnic communities. America now includes over forty million Latinos. It makes sense that our churches should encourage their young people to take Spanish language study seriously, and deliberately work to develop linguistic competencies that would be helpful in our diverse society. Similarly, churches can also participate in and provide space for ESL classes. It is simply not possible to appropriately engage ethnic others if we do not understand the historical, cultural, and racial realities that condition and constrain our involvement. Only as Christians develop a constructive and sustained relationship with the human sciences (history, anthropology, sociology, economics, political science) while also developing a theologically informed social vision, will we nurture the needed understandings and skills for making a positive difference.

If knowledge and understanding matter, then scholars and teachers have a heavy responsibility (see Jas 3:1). Both our scholarship and teaching must be directed toward acquiring and providing appropriate knowledge and skills. The curriculum and syllabi of seminaries and colleges need to reflect these priorities. The books that we read, and that we assign our students to read, must contribute in this way; books written by authors from a variety of racial or ethnic backgrounds on topics designed to help us acquire relevant understandings are necessary reading. Our schools must represent the ethnic diversity of our society, both in the persons of faculty and students. The curriculum must also reflect and serve a diversity of ethnic and racial backgrounds. African American students should not have to take an American church history course that renders the African American church invisible. International students should not be taught that Euro-American church history is the only church history that matters. Seminary courses on homiletics or worship should not be restricted to Euro-American rhetorical and aesthetic traditions.

If knowledge and understanding matter, then even practical efforts to serve others require that we do the appropriate research that will inform such service (Nieves). As Nieves reminds us from Proverbs 19:2 (NIV), "It is not good to have zeal without knowledge, nor to be hasty and miss the way." Realities are complex, and so we end our book with annotated recommendations for further reading (appendix 2).

Transformed minds should result in transformed practices. As Bacote suggests, we can organize our efforts toward racial reconciliation around the core practices of the church. When diverse people worship the same God, unity is enhanced. But since worship involves embodied practices and musical aesthetics that are culturally variable, it is possible for worship practices to actually divide and alienate (Priest and Priest; McGlathery and Griffin). Done right, such worship practices can help to construct unity in the midst of diversity (K. Priest, Howell). Worship leaders have strategic roles to play (cf. Hawn 2003a, 2003b). Eating and celebrating together are core biblical practices (Pao), that universally are central to the construction of community. Hospitality is a biblically mandated practice, specifically emphasized as the appropriate response to immigrant strangers (Heb 13:2; Rom 12:13). Father Kujic of St. Ansgar provides one impressive illustration of hospitality toward Filipino immigrants (K. Priest). Scripture memory is a venerable Christian practice, which ought to intentionally focus on biblical teaching about our relations with others (passages such as Lev 19:33–34; Amos 5:24; Mic 6:8; Gal; 3:28–29; 2 Cor 5:17–20; Jas 2:1–13; Rev 7:9–10). Giving is a core Christian practice that, when practiced intentionally, has tremendous potential for enabling strategic ministries and initiatives of mercy, justice, and reconciliation. Voluntary service is another practice, such as offering English as a Second Language classes to recent immigrants (Nieves). A relatively recent religious practice for American church youth groups is to go for a week or two during spring break or over the summer to West Virginia, inner-city Chicago, Haiti, or Mexico on a service trip. An astonishing 29 percent of all thirteen- to seventeen-year-olds in America have gone on a religious service or mission trip (Smith and Denton 2005, 53). These trips potentially provide strategic opportunities to help young people learn about cultural, racial, and ethnic realities and to consider the trajectory of their own lives in the context of poverty, stigma, and injustice. In short, Bacote invites us to subject the practices that Christians participate in (baptism, communion, hospitality, celebration, giving, serving, memorizing Scripture, apologizing and confessing, forgiving, etc.) to reflection and scrutiny, to ensure they are each practiced appropriately in relation to the diverse people who make up our communities.

Finally, our intentional efforts must be collaborative and grounded in community (Pao). This book has placed a strong emphasis on congregations, believing that these grassroots institutions are key places where Christian messages are communicated, where Christian practices are encouraged and undertaken, and where community is developed and experienced. Congregations often provide a base for serving the needs of recent immigrants and all who are needy. These needs will vary depending on context. The needs of Korean immigrants and their American-born children in Chicago (Cha) will differ from the needs of Hispanics in Aurora, Illinois (Nieves). And the needs of

Filipinos in a Chicago suburb (K. Priest) will differ from needs of African Americans in St. Louis (Howell). Whether responding to intergenerational challenges of recent immigrants (Cha), to linguistic and economic challenges faced by Hispanic immigrants (Nieves), to racial hate crimes and prejudice (Priest and Priest, Howell), or to any of a wide array of social, economic, and racial challenges, America's 350,000 congregations play potentially strategic roles in nurturing the values, habits, and goals of many millions of people. And so we affirm the strategic role of teachers, worship leaders, preachers, and all other active participants in congregational life—believing that they play a strategic role in reversing the negative effects of our racially divided world. Several of the books listed in appendix 2 also focus on congregational settings as strategic bases from which to engage our racialized world. Both in these books, and in chapters of this book that focus on congregations, one will find discussion of congregationally based strategies that have helped.

Of course, other sorts of religious organizations are also key, such as missionary organizations (McGlathery and Griffin) or colleges (R. Priest). Moving colleges, universities, and seminaries toward greater diversity and reconciliation is not an easy task. When colleges attempt to diversify faculty they discover that the difficulty of recruiting is often tied to overcoming the perceptions and experience of prior exclusion (Lee, Nieves, and Allen 1991). When recruitment occurs, retaining faculty is the next difficult stage. Similarly, the recruitment and retention of minority students to previously majority-white/Anglo institutions can be a daunting task. The task will be a long one. It will require sustained effort over time. It will require collaboration with all appropriate constituencies. It will require that the task be approached with urgency coupled with patience, and ability coupled with humility. A sense of mission must be adopted with a dependence on God's grace and the wisdom that he provides.

And yet colleges and seminaries are particularly strategic settings for nurturing the kinds of understandings, practices, and initiatives that are needed (Lee, Nieves, and Allen 1991). A diverse faculty and student body are absolutely critical if the next generation is to acquire appropriate attitudes, understandings, skills, and relationships for life and ministry in our diverse society.

If Christians of all racial or ethnic identities join together in shared communities with shared faith in Christ, and organize around shared tasks and visions, significant change is possible. This book represents one such initiative, pursued in the context of personal relationships, with sustained effort over time, with the hope and prayer that our efforts will bear fruit. May each of us be intentional and prayerful about the practices, relationships, and initiatives that God calls us to, trusting God to accomplish his ends through us.

REFERENCES

Barrett, David B., George T. Kurian, Todd M. Johnson. 2001. *World Christian encyclopedia: A comparative survey of churches and religions in the modern world*, 2nd ed., vol. 2. Oxford: Oxford University Press.

Emerson, Michael and Christian Smith. 2000. *Divided by faith: Evangelical religion and the problem of race in America*. New York: Oxford University Press.

Goldenberg, David M. 2003. *The curse of Ham: Race and slavery in early Judaism, Christianity, and Islam.* Princeton, NJ: Princeton University Press.

Goldschmidt, Henry. 2004. Introduction: Race, nation, and religion. In *Race, nation, and religion in the Americas,* ed. Henry Goldschmidt and Elizabeth McAlister, 3–31. Oxford: Oxford University Press.

Hawn, C. Michael. 2003a. *Gather into one: Praying and singing globally.* Grand Rapids, MI: Eerdmans.

———. 2003b. *One bread, one body: Exploring cultural diversity in worship.* Bethesda, MD: The Alban Institute.

Hays, J. Daniel. 2003. *From every people and nation: A biblical theology of race.* Downers Grove, IL: InterVarsity.

Jordan, Winthrop D. 1968. *Black over white: American attitudes toward the Negro, 1550–1812.* Chapel Hill: University of North Carolina Press.

Lee, D. John, Alvaro Nieves, and Henry Allen, ed. 1991. *Ethnic-minorities and evangelical Christian colleges.* Lanham, MD: University Press of America.

Rosen, Christine. 2004. *Preaching eugenics: Religious leaders and the American eugenics movement.* New York: Oxford University Press.

Scofield, C. I. 1909. *The Scofield Reference Bible: The Holy Bible Containing the Old and New Testaments.* Oxford: Oxford University Press.

———. 1917. *The Scofield Reference Bible: The Holy Bible Containing the Old and New Testaments.* New and improved edition. Oxford: Oxford University Press.

Smith, Christian, and Melinda Lundquist Denton. 2005. *Soul searching: The religious and spiritual lives of American teenagers.* New York: Oxford University Press.

Yamauchi, Edwin M. 2004. *Africa and the Bible.* Grand Rapids, MI: Baker Academic.

Appendix 1

Timeline: Race and Ethnicity in the United States

1619 Twenty Africans sold as bond servants in Jamestown, Virginia.
1663 Maryland decides that African slaves shall serve for the duration of their lives.
1664 Maryland declares that baptism does not alter slave status.
1713 Great Britain was awarded the contract (*asiento*) to import slaves to Spanish America, with Bristol and Liverpool becoming centers of the slave trade.
1719 Daniel Defoe's *Robinson Crusoe* is published.
1773 Founding of the First African Baptist Church, Savannah, Georgia— the "oldest continuous black congregation in all of North America."[1]
1787 The Constitutional Convention determines that, for the purposes of representation and taxation, slaves will be counted as three-fifths of a man.
1790 The Naturalization Act of 1790 restricts U.S. citizenship to "free whites."
1792 David George leads 1,196 black people to Sierra Leone and founds church in Freetown.
1793 Fugitive Slave Act of 1793, passed by Congress, made it a crime to harbor an escaped slave or interfere with his or her arrest.
1808 The transatlantic slave trade is abolished by Britain and the United States.
1816 The *African Methodist Episcopal Church* is founded in Philadelphia, Pennsylvania.
1816 The American Colonization Society was formed to send free blacks back to Africa. The colony founded for this purpose subsequently became the nation of Liberia (1847).
1821 Lott Carey, an African American, leaves for Africa as a Baptist missionary.
1822 Freedman Denmark Vesey, along with thirty-four others, is convicted and hanged for supposedly planning a massive slave revolt in Charleston.

1830   The Indian Removal Act, disregarding prior Indian treaty guarantees, mandated the removal of Native Americans from east of the Mississippi River to present-day Oklahoma.

1831   Nat Turner, a Baptist slave preacher, leads a slave rebellion where sixty whites are killed. After the insurrection is defeated, Turner is hanged.

1831   Mississippi law declares that it is "unlawful for any slave, free Negro, or mulatto to preach the Gospel."

1832   Alabama law declares that "any person or persons who shall attempt to teach any free person of color or slave to spell, read or write, shall, upon conviction thereof by indictment, be fined in a sum not less than $250, nor more than $500."

1833   In the Abolition of Slavery Act, Britain abolishes slavery, a long-sought goal of the British antislavery movement led by evangelical William Wilberforce.

1835   Cincinnati's Lane Theological Seminary (Presbyterian) fails to satisfy the abolitionist demands of its students, losing these so-called Lane Rebels to the Oberlin Collegiate Institute (later Oberlin College). Oberlin is thus founded as an abolitionist school in the evangelical tradition. Charles G. Finney is recruited as professor of theology. African Americans, both male and female, are admitted.

1836   Texas declares itself independent of Mexico.

1838   "Trail of Tears." The Cherokee are evicted from their land in Georgia, by order of the federal government, and forced to make the long trek to Oklahoma during a harsh winter. This forcible journey leads to extensive suffering and death, and becomes known as the "Trail of Tears."

1839   Africans aboard the Spanish slave ship *Amistad* take command of the ship, and sail into Long Island Sound. In a landmark Supreme Court case, these Africans are granted freedom, and choose to return to Sierra Leone.

1844   When the *American Baptist Foreign Mission Board* refuses to allow slave owners to be missionaries, southern members withdraw, and form the *Southern Baptist Convention*, which later becomes the largest Protestant denomination in America.

1844   The *Methodist Episcopal Church* splits into two conferences because of tensions over slavery. These later merge (1939) and form part of what is now known as *The United Methodist Church*.

1848   The Treaty of Guadalupe Hidalgo, at the end of the U.S.–Mexican War cedes Texas, California, and parts of Arizona, New Mexico, Colorado, Utah, and Nevada—land formerly claimed by Mexico—to the United States. The treaty allows Mexican nationals within this territory a year to choose to become U.S. citizens.

1849   First wave of Chinese immigration to the United States after gold is discovered in California.

1850   The Fugitive Slave Act of 1850 is passed by Congress, requiring the return of escaped slaves.

1852   Harriet Beecher Stowe publishes best seller *Uncle Tom's Cabin*—mobilizing widespread sympathy for the abolitionist cause.

1852   More than twenty thousand Chinese enter California.

1852   Missionary William Speer opens Presbyterian mission for Chinese in San Francisco.

1853   Gadsden Purchase—Additional land is bought from Mexico, securing the final boundaries of the continental United States.

1857   *Dred Scott v John F. A. Sanford.* Supreme Court rules that blacks are not citizens, and thus cannot appeal to rights provided by the Constitution.

1857   "New School" Presbyterians split over the issue of slavery.

1858   California passes a law to bar entry of Chinese and "Mongolians."

1861   "Old School" Presbyterians split over the issue of slavery.

1861   U.S. Civil War begins.

1862   California imposes a $2.50 a month "police tax" on every Chinese.

1863   Emancipation Proclamation, issued by Abraham Lincoln, frees slaves in the Confederate States.

1865   U.S. Civil War ends.

1865   Special Field Order #15. Is issued by General William Tecumseh Sherman, providing forty-acre tracts of captured land along the Atlantic coast, from South Carolina to Florida, for forty thousand former slaves. President Andrew Johnson later reverses this provision.

1865   Central Pacific Railroad Co. recruits Chinese workers for the transcontinental railroad.

1865   The Thirteenth Amendment is ratified, abolishing slavery.

1866   Civil Rights Act is passed by Congress granting citizenship and equal rights to black Americans.

1868   The Fourteenth Amendment is ratified, guaranteeing to all U.S. citizens due process and equal protection under the law.

1870   The Fifteenth Amendment is ratified, guaranteeing black Americans the right to vote.

1872   Civil Rights Act, known as the Anti–Ku Klux Klan Act, makes it a crime to deprive anyone of their rights, privileges, and immunities protected under the U.S. Constitution or other federal law.

1875   Second Civil Rights Act provides for full and equal access to public accommodations, theaters, and other places of public amusement. It imposes criminal penalties for violations.

1877   In the "Compromise of 1877" Rutherford B. Hayes becomes president and federal troops are withdrawn from the South, marking the end of Reconstruction.

1880   Section 69 of California's Civil Code prohibits issuing of licenses for marriages between whites and "Mongolians, Negroes, mulattoes and persons of mixed blood."

1881   Tennessee passes first of its "Jim Crow" laws, segregating the state railroad. Other states follow suit.

1882   Chinese Exclusion Act. Passed by the U.S. Congress, this act suspended immigration of Chinese laborers for ten years, and prohibits the naturalization of Chinese immigrants. This exclusion act was later extended, until its repeal in 1943.

1896   In *Plessy v Ferguson*, the Supreme Court establishes the "separate but equal" doctrine, affirming rights of states to segregate schools and transportation.

1898   Hawaii annexed by the United States. Congress excludes Chinese laborers from Hawaii, and excludes Chinese in Hawaii from coming to the U.S. mainland.

1898   U.S. Supreme Court in *U.S. v. Wong Kim Art* rules that any person born in the United States of Chinese parents is of American nationality by birth.

1898   Treaty of Paris—Spain cedes Puerto Rico, Guam, and the Philippines to the United States as part of the agreement ending the Spanish-American War (ratified by Congress in 1899).

1900   Foraker Act makes Puerto Rico an unincorporated territory of the United States.

1903   Pensionado Act allows Filipino students to study in the United States.

1908   *Berea College v Kentucky.* This U.S. Supreme Court ruling establishes the right of states to force private and religious institutions to be segregated.

1909   NAACP is founded.

1917   Jones Act makes Puerto Ricans citizens of the United States; makes Puerto Ricans eligible for the draft; and allows both houses of the Puerto Rican legislature to be chosen through popular election, although the governor and other top-ranking officials are still appointed by the president of the United States.

1917   Asiatic Barred Zone prevents U.S. immigration from most of Asia.

1922   Cable Act revokes American citizenship of any American woman marrying an alien ineligible for citizenship.

1924   Citizenship Act declares all Native Americans U.S. citizens, entitling Native people the right to vote in national elections.

1924   The Immigration Act of 1924 denies entry to virtually all Asians, except Filipinos.

1924   The U.S. Border Patrol is established.

1931   Cable Act amended. Women who are U.S. citizens can retain citizenship after marriage to aliens ineligible for citizenship.

1942   Executive Order 9066. Interns 110,000 Japanese Americans (mostly U.S. citizens) in ten camps. Ended in 1945.

1942   The Bracero Program brings Mexican farm laborers seasonally to work the fields of the United States. This program continues until 1964.

1946   The Philippines, a United States protectorate, gains its independence.

1948   *Shelley v Kraemer.* U.S. Supreme Court rules that racially restrictive covenants in housing are not legally enforceable.

1954   *Brown v Board of Education of Topeka, Kansas.* U.S. Supreme Court ends "separate but equal" doctrine and rules that school segregation is illegal. This ruling laid the groundwork for a generation of civil rights activity.

1955   Rosa Parks is arrested for refusing to give up her bus seat to a white passenger, which triggers a year-long bus boycott in Montgomery Alabama, until the buses are desegregated.

1960   James Lawson, an African American student at Vanderbilt Divinity School, is expelled by University officials for his role in Nashville's lunch counter sit-in movement (intended to desegregate the city). In protest, the dean and fourteen of sixteen Divinity School faculty resign (or threaten to resign). Lawson is reinstated but does not return to Vanderbilt. Helping to found the Student Nonviolent Coordinating Committee (S.N.C.C.), he goes on to serve for many years as a United Methodist minister.

1961   James Meredith, with the backing of federal troops, becomes the first black student to enroll at the University of Mississippi.

1963   Columbia Bible College becomes the first school of higher education in South Carolina to voluntarily integrate.

1963   The Reverend Martin Luther King Jr. is arrested during antisegregation protests in Birmingham, Alabama, and writes his influential "Letter from a Birmingham Jail," arguing that individuals have a moral duty to disobey unjust laws.

1963   March on Washington, where the Reverend Martin Luther King Jr. delivers his famous "I Have a Dream" speech.

1963   National Black Evangelical Association is founded.
1964   Civil Rights Act of 1964. Bans racial, ethnic, and sex discrimination in business and employment.
1964   Martin Luther King Jr. is awarded the Nobel Peace Prize.
1965   The Immigration Act of 1965 abolishes "national origins" as the basis for allocating immigration quotas to various countries, opening the doors of immigration to people from Asia and Latin America.
1967   In *Loving v Virginia*, the Supreme Court rules that state laws prohibiting interracial marriage were unconstitutional.
1968   The Civil Rights Act of 1968 bans discrimination in the sale and rental of housing.
1968   The assassination of the Reverend Martin Luther King Jr., in Memphis, Tennessee, on April 4, is followed by a week of rioting in cities across the United States.
1978   The Church of Jesus Christ of Latter-day Saints opens church membership and priesthood to black people.
1978   In *Regents of the University of California v Bakke*, the U.S. Supreme Court rules against fixed race quotas in university admissions.
1980   Refugee Act passes and classifies refugees as those who flee a country because of persecution "on account of race, religion, and nationality, or political opinion." This systematized the admission of refugees and classified them as separate from other immigrants.
1983   Bob Jones University loses tax-exempt status because of its rules banning interracial dating and marriage.
1988   President Reagan signs the Civil Liberties Act, authorizing $1.25 billion in reparations payments to Japanese survivors of World War II internment camps.
1995   The Southern Baptist Convention issues formal apology for prior racism and support of slavery.
2000   South Carolina lowers Confederate flag from flying over capitol dome (where it was first placed in 1962).
2000   Bob Jones University removes its ban on interracial dating and marriage.
2000   The United Methodist General Conference apologizes to black churches that left the Methodist Church because of pervasive racial discrimination, and commits to fight for racial justice.

NOTE

1. Andrew Billingsley. (1999). *Mighty like a river: The black church and social reform*. New York: Oxford University Press, 13.

Appendix 2

Resources for Further Reading and Study

Anderson, David. 2004. *Multicultural ministry: Finding your church's unique rhythm.* Grand Rapids, MI: Zondervan. This is an inspirational and practical guide to multicultural ministry by an African American pastor of a large multicultural congregation. The author draws from his rich experience as a pastor, counselor, consultant, and radio talk show host to outline practical steps toward the "dance" of racial reconciliation.

Blount, Brian K., and Leonora Tubbs Tisdale, ed. 2001. *Making room at the table: An invitation to multicultural worship.* Louisville, KY: Westminster John Knox. This collection of essays from professors at Princeton Theological Seminary sets forth biblical and theological foundations for multicultural worship, and calls for worship more inclusive of and relevant to diverse ethnic communities.

Christerson, Brad, Michael O. Emerson, and Korie L. Edwards. 2004. *Against all odds: The struggle of racial integration in religious organizations.* New York: New York University Press. Three sociologists explore the beliefs, practices, and structures that allow integrated religious organizations "to survive and thrive" despite challenges. Based on ethnographies of four congregations, one Bible College, and one campus student group, the book explores what it is like to be part of a multiracial religious organization and provides theoretical analysis of such efforts at racial integration.

Davis, David Brion. 2001. *In the image of God: Religion, moral values, and our heritage of slavery.* New Haven, CT: Yale University Press. This collection of essays, written by this country's leading historian of global slavery, provides an excellent introduction to a wide variety of books dealing with slavery and its abolition, and explores the role of religious ideas in the eventual success of abolitionists. It is especially useful on the international context of American slavery.

DeYoung, Curtiss Paul, Michael O. Emerson, George Yancey, and Karen Chai Kim. 2003. *United by faith: The multiracial congregation as an answer to the problem of race.* Oxford: Oxford University Press. Three sociologists and a theologian review research demonstrating that only 5.5 percent of Christian congregations in America are multiracial and develop the argument that Christian congregations, when possible, should be multiracial. They survey biblical antecedents of multiracial congregations, review the history of such congregations in the United States, consider the various debates about homogeneous versus multiracial congregations, and develop a theological framework for the multiracial congregation. Such multiracial congregations, they claim, are a key answer to the problem of race.

Emerson, Michael O., and Christian Smith. 2000. *Divided by faith: Evangelical religion and the problem of race in America.* New York: Oxford University Press. An enormously influential book, grounded in extensive survey and interview data, which analyzes the role of white evangelicalism in black-white relations. The authors contend that despite recent efforts by white evangelicals to address problems of racial discrimination, the evangelical movement's emphasis on individualism, free will, and personal relationships precludes accurate understandings of racial processes and unwittingly contributes to racialized patterns.

Fields, Bruce. 2001. *Introducing black theology: Three crucial questions for the evangelical church.* Grand Rapids, MI: Baker Academic. An African American theologian provides a brief, accessible introduction to black theology, organized around a response to three questions: What is black theology? What can black theology teach the (white) evangelical church? What is the future of black theology? This is a good introduction to the topic for white evangelical Christians.

Frederick, Marla F. 2003. *Between Sundays: Black women and everyday struggles of faith.* Berkeley and Los Angeles: University of California Press. A forthright and detailed look at how black women choose to live spiritual lives within the painful constraints of race, gender and class in rural North Carolina. The author, a black Christian anthropologist, reveals a world where women of faith change themselves, their families, churches, and community through acts of gratitude, empathy, and "righteous discontent."

Goldenberg, David M. 2003. *The curse of Ham: Race and slavery in early Judaism, Christianity, and Islam.* Princeton, NJ: Princeton University Press. An outstanding work of scholarship, written in an engaging and accessible style, this book traces the history of interpretations of Noah's curse on Ham's son Canaan. It demonstrates that early Jewish sources had neutral to positive associations for Africans, and that it was only over a long history that later racial meanings were illegitimately read back into the text in ways designed to justify racial prejudice of a later era.

Hawn, C. Michael. 2003. *Gather into one: Praying and singing globally.* Grand Rapids, MI: Eerdmans. For churches wishing to embrace recent immigrants from around the world, this book is a must. Michael Hawn, a seminary professor and musicologist, explores the work of five influential church musicians from Argentina, Taiwan, South Africa, Zimbabwe, and Scotland and suggests ways in which congregations can bring Christians together in unity through appropriate usage of diverse expressions in worship. Worship leaders in congregations wishing to be ethnically inclusive will find this book especially helpful.

Hays, J. Daniel. 2003. *From every people and nation: A biblical theology of race.* Downers Grove, IL: InterVarsity. A biblical scholar describes key ethnic groups referred to in the Bible, examines their probable "racial" characteristics (described in terms of modern race categories), and outlines a biblical theology of race. While one might wish the author were more conversant with recent debates on the construct of "race," this is nonetheless an excellent resource. Especially noteworthy is Hayes's extensive treatment of biblical references to Cush.

Jenkins, Philip. 2002. *The next Christendom: The coming of global Christianity.* Oxford: Oxford University Press. A noted historian demonstrates that Christianity's numerical center of gravity is shifting away from an increasingly secular North America and Europe toward Africa, Asia, and Latin America. That is, Christianity is increasingly associated with darker skin, and with poverty rather than wealth. Non-European immigrants frequently bring a vigorous Christianity with them, and, in the process revitalize and change the face of Christianity in North America and Europe.

Jeung, Russell. 2004. *Faithful generations: Race and new Asian American churches.* New Brunswick, NJ: Rutgers University Press. Jeung, a sociologist who is also active in church work, examines Asian American congregations in the San Francisco Bay area, focusing on the ways in which racial identities and religious practices mutually shape the other. A central focus concerns second- and third-generation Asian Americans and the pan-Asian multiethnic churches that they lead.

Marsh, Charles. 2005. *The beloved community: How faith shapes social justice, from the civil rights movement to today.* New York: Basic. A theologian traces the spiritual roots animating the civil rights movement, beginning with Martin Luther King and his Christian vision of a "beloved community," and continuing through more recent faith-based social justice initiatives. He effectively tells the stories of Martin Luther King, Clarence Jordan, Gene Rivers, John Perkins, and various other contemporaries who bear "witness to the Prince of Peace in a violent and suffering world."

Marti, Gerardo. 2005. *A mosaic of believers: Diversity and innovation in a multiethnic church.* Bloomington: Indiana University Press. Marti, a Cuban American sociologist, describes and analyzes Mosaic, one of the largest multiethnic congregations in America (roughly equal parts Asian American, Hispanic, and Euro-American). He suggests that this church, largely comprising single, childless young adults, has grown by providing multiple "havens," arenas of multiethnic companionship and cooperation, which appeal to people in ways that trump ethnic differences.

Okholm, Dennis L., ed. 1997. *The gospel in black and white: Theological resources for racial reconciliation.* Downers Grove, IL: InterVarsity. Essays by African American and Euro-American theologians, biblical scholars, and pastors explore strategic ways in which theological resources ought to shape and inform Christian efforts at racial reconciliation between blacks and whites.

Raboteau, Albert J. 2001. *Canaan Land: A religious history of African Americans.* New York: Oxford University Press. This is an excellent, brief introduction to African American religious history. It is not as comprehensive as Lincoln and Mamiya, but it is just as competent and easier to read.

Volf, Miroslav. 1998. *Exclusion and embrace: A theological exploration of identity, otherness, and reconciliation.* Nashville, TN: Abingdon. A leading theologian insightfully explores the meaning of the Trinity, the incarnation, and the cross for groups of people with historic animosities. This is an outstanding book, with weaknesses. Since the author's conversation partners come from the humanities and not the social science disciplines that empirically investigate ethnic and racial dynamics, there are significant lacunae in the treatment of ethnic conflict or racial conflict or both. The core construct of race remains largely unexamined and the African American experience of race and appropriation of the Christian message in response to racial exclusion is unexplored.

Warner, R. Stephen, and Judith D. Wittner, ed. 1998. *Gatherings in diaspora: Religious communities and the new immigration*. Philadelphia: Temple University Press. This book summarizes research from Warner's "New Ethnic and Immigrant Congregations Project," with twelve scholarly essays, ten of them mini-ethnographies of immigrant congregations in America. These ethnographies explore the ways in which immigrants forge new relations and identities through involvement in religious congregations.

Woodley, Randy. 2004. *Living in color: Embracing God's passion for ethnic diversity*. Downers Grove, IL: InterVarsity. Woodley, a Keetoowah Cherokee, sets forth a biblical, multiethnic vision for the church, and explores the experience of Native American Indians with Euro-American Christianity. He suggests the importance of acknowledging ethnocentrism and painful historical failures, of contextualizing the gospel in ways that respect culture, and of working toward reconciliation and justice.

Yamauchi, Edwin M. 2004. *Africa and the Bible*. Grand Rapids, MI: Baker Academic. A noted scholar reviews biblical texts that make reference to Africa or Africans, situates these texts archaeologically and historically, critiques historical usages of such texts in justifying racial attitudes and practices, and evaluates various Afrocentric reconstructions of such texts. The author is irenic, and is particularly strong on the historical and archaeological detail.

Yancey, George A. 2003. *One body, one spirit: Principles of successful multiracial churches*. Downers Grove, IL: InterVarsity. An African American sociologist reviews what he learned through a major Lilly-funded research project on multiracial churches, identifying several distinct types of multiracial churches, and suggesting specific insights and implications for leadership, worship, interpersonal and intercultural skills, and more. Recommended for seminarians, pastors, and others with leadership roles in congregations.

Scripture Index

General Index

LaVergne, TN USA
24 March 2011
221489LV00001B/8/P